Manhood and American Political Culture in the Cold War

Manhood and American Political Culture in the Cold War

K.A. Cuordileone

ROUTLEDGE

NEW YORK AND LONDON

Published in 2005 by
Routledge
Taylor & Francis Group
270 Madison Avenue
New York, NY 10016

Published in Great Britain by
Routledge
Taylor & Francis Group
2 Park Square
Milton Park, Abingdon
Oxon OX14 4RN

Printed in the United States of America on acid-free paper
10 9 8 7 6 5 4 3 2 1

International Standard Book Number-10: 0-415-92599-1 (Hardcover) 0-415-92600-9 (Softcover)
International Standard Book Number-13: 978-0-415-92599-0 (Hardcover) 978-0-415-92600-3 (Softcover)
Library of Congress Card Number 2004020769

Library of Congress Cataloging-in-Publication Data

Cuordileone, K. A.
    Manhood and American political culture in the cold war / K. A. Cuordileone.
       p. cm.
    Includes bibliographical references and index.
    ISBN 0-415-92599-1 (Hb : alk. paper) — ISBN 0-415-92600-9 (Pb : alk. paper)
    1. United States—Politics and government—1945-1989. 2. Political culture—United States—History—20th century. 3. Liberalism—United States—History—20th century. 4. Masculinity—Political aspects—United States—History—20th century. 5. Sex role—Political aspects—United States—History—20th century. I. Title.

E743.C86 2005
306.2'0973'09045--dc22   2004020769

Taylor & Francis Group
is the Academic Division of T&F Informa plc.

Visit the Taylor & Francis Web site at
http://www.taylorandfrancis.com

and the Routledge Web site at
http://www.routledge-ny.com

Contents

Prologue

In a 1955 essay on the rise of the "radical right" as a force in American political life, Harvard sociologist Daniel Bell noted the "polarization of images" to which the political discourse of his time had succumbed. "In these strange times," he wrote, "new polar terms have been introduced into political discourse, but surely none so strange as the division into 'hard' and 'soft.'" As Bell explained, "Presumably one is 'soft' if one insists that the danger from domestic Communists is small," while one is "'hard'" if one holds that "no distinction can be made between international and domestic Communism." Objecting to the dubious assumptions underlying such stark dichotomies, Bell stressed that liberals—so often accused by the radical right of being "soft" on Communism—had long championed anti-Communist politics; indeed, the "liberal" press scorned by the right actually took conservative positions on economic issues and supported Eisenhower. "Yet, traditional conservative issues no longer count in dividing 'liberals' from 'anti-Communists,'" he complained. "An amorphous, ideological issue rather than an interest-group issue has become a major dividing line in the political community." In the irrational, symbol-driven politics of his time, it seemed to Bell that "the only issue is whether one is 'hard' or 'soft.'"[1]

Bell was speaking to a striking feature of early cold war political culture: the reduction of political identities and issues to dualistic images that tended to supersede a policy-oriented politics and obscure the degree to which a broader political consensus was in fact emerging. The hard/soft dualism that struck Bell as irrational was hardly inconsequential in the political culture of the 1950s. The accusation of softness was the primary weapon with which Joe McCarthy and his allies clubbed their political enemies, who were not so much Communists but eastern establishment liberals and internationalists. The dualistic, "ideologizing" rhetoric that Bell and other scholars ultimately attributed to the McCarthyites' "status anxieties" had entered political discourse long before the radical right made its mark on partisan politics in the early fifties, charging liberals with "softness." Images of "hard" anti-Communist liberals set against dangerously "soft," "Doughface" progressives permeates Arthur Schlesinger Jr.'s 1949 classic manifesto of cold war liberalism, *The Vital Center*, a seminal book whose language, in the words of Garry Wills, "set up the desired contrasts for a decade."[2]

If Bell didn't appreciate the extent to which cold war liberals had indulged in (and perhaps even initiated) the polarizing rhetoric he lamented, neither did he recognize what made that rhetoric so "strange" and symbolically resonant. The hard/soft language surely registers the heightened cold war tensions inspired by that "amorphous ideological issue"—Communism—against, which America stood in stark opposition. But the dualistic imagery was also the reflex of a political culture that, in the name of combating an implacable, expansionist Communist enemy, put a new premium on hard masculine toughness and rendered anything less than that soft, timid, feminine, and as such a real or potential threat to the security of the nation. The power of the hard/soft dualism in cold war political discourse lay here, in the gendered, symbolic baggage that gave such imagery its meaning. In the overheated political climate of the time, that discourse grew shrill on both sides of the partisan divide. The hard/soft imagery that pervaded cold war discourse speaks not only to the pressures of the cold war but also to the apprehensions and idiosyncrasies of the culture from which it was born, and its resonance in the political arena—as well as the entire obsession with "hard" virility that emerged in political life—is intelligible only within the context of the multiple anxieties and uncertainties of the era, a context this study seeks to illuminate.

In the broadest sense, this book is about American political culture in the early cold war years, the milieu within which political images, identities, and figures were defined, shaped, reinvented, and circulated in the shadow of an unparalleled global struggle that set the Communist world against the free world. It examines the rhetoric with which models of the "liberal," the "Communist," the "progressive," the "conformist," the "rebel," the "national security risk," and the totalitarian "mass man" were defined in the years between 1949 and 1963, and the underlying social, political and global tensions that shaped cold war rhetoric. The period spanning the 1940s and 1950s was then, as now, sometimes called an "age of anxiety," as though disquiet and fear defined the very essence of life, thanks to modernity and its terrible consequences—two devastating world wars, the horrors of totalitarianism, the arms race, and the possibility of global nuclear holocaust. Of course, the phrase "age of anxiety" has become something of a historical cliché, applied to so many moments in history that it has become a standard (and perhaps rather empty) designator of social tensions in any given historical time and place. But in one sense the phrase is an apt designation for American life in the 1940s and 1950s because it captures the concerns of Bell's contemporaries, who often used the "age of anxiety" phrase to highlight the psychological malaise that marked the era in which they lived. The term "anxiety" was not simply or primarily a signifier of generalized worries about atomic bombs or Communist conquest. Its persistent reappearance in postwar cultural and intellectual discourse speaks to a new, acute sense of the fragility of the modern self, a concern examined in this book as it was expressed in a myriad of cold war era venues, from popular and academic psychology, film, and fiction, to political commentary, social criticism, and theology.

In a related yet more specific sense, this book aims to understand what Bell, pioneer of the symbolist approach to the study of American politics, had no real category for analyzing: the heightened preoccupation with—and anxiety about—manhood that often surfaced in the partisan political arena, and the hard/soft rhetoric that expressed it. Throughout the book, we see how concerns about masculinity, sexuality, and the self—widely articulated by experts, writers, and social critics—found their way into politics and shaped political discourse and especially cold war liberalism in ways not fully appreciated by historians.

Manhood and American Political Culture in the Cold War is essentially an historical synthesis that crosses freely through a wide interdisciplinary terrain. It pursues several interrelated themes—masculinity, sexuality, and the self—as they appeared in a variety of political and cultural discourses. Selective in its pursuit of these themes, the book is not intended to be a comprehensive treatment of either the culture or politics of the cold war era; nor does it unearth new sources of information (archival or otherwise) that are not widely available. My interest here is in public discourse—the ways in which political identities were shaped, given meaning and deployed in American political culture by influential social commentators, intellectuals, politicians, and statesmen. I have drawn upon a multitude of rich, published primary and secondary sources and built upon strands of old and new scholarship in diverse fields to illustrate the contours of cold war political culture. I might have written a more circumscribed study, perhaps focusing on some obscure or unexamined effusions of the anti-Communist imagination. I chose instead to present a rather sweeping synthesis, in part because this seemed to offer a much more compelling and interesting portrait of cold war manhood than any more limited study I could conceive. While I think there is great value in historical synthesis, I opted for the big picture primarily because I was struck by the extraordinary connections between seemingly disconnected cultural currents and political events, and I wanted to write about them without constraint and for a broad audience. Some of the figures, themes, and historical events treated here will be familiar to readers and scholars of American history; others may not. But I hope this book will provoke readers to look at them in a new light and with an eye attuned to the political implications of manhood and sexuality in cold war America, and the cultural trends and obsessions that shaped political rhetoric. Recent scholarship by Robert Dean has enriched our understanding of the relationship between masculinity, foreign policy, and the internal machinery of the national security apparatus during the cold war.[3] My book, long in the making, will hopefully contribute to the growing literature on the gendered politics of the cold war, particularly in its exploration of political imagery and the cultural tensions that it reflected. Among those tensions is the "crisis of masculinity" declared by male writers and social critics in the 1950s. That "crisis" had its distant origins in late nineteenth-century fears of the feminization of American society. In the 1940s and 1950s, the expression of such anxieties grew and morphed as they collided with global conflicts and social changes and took new forms unique to the cold war years.

The fear and loathing of the red menace that emerged in the early cold war years and inspired a colossal overreaction to the presence of Communists in American life was ultimately rooted in a profound and longstanding revulsion for Communism, and it is not my intention here to trivialize anti-Communism by reducing its every expression to some sort of diffuse anxiety, sexual or otherwise. The growing animus against Communism, however excessive and phobic it became in its various manifestations, was spurred by deeply disturbing external events—the Moscow trials, the Gulag terror, the Kremlin's imposition of a steely grip over Eastern Europe, the Soviet explosion of an atomic bomb, the victory of Mao's red army in China—all of which raised the image of a repressive, monolithic Communism spreading throughout the world. It was a series of internal developments, though, that intensified and made immediate to the American public the possibility of subversion at home—the House Un-American Activities Committee (HUAC) hearings, Truman's Federal Employee Loyalty Program, the Smith Act trials, perceived blunders and security lapses by the State Department, and the Alger Hiss case. These developments predated Joseph McCarthy's rise to notoriety and nourished the overwrought political climate that allowed the unprincipled Wisconsin senator and his allies to exploit the issue of Communist subversion for partisan and personal ends.[4]

McCarthy's political influence is explicable only within the atmosphere of angst and paranoia that already existed before he made his dramatic debut in early 1950 in Wheeling, West Virginia, insisting that Communists had infiltrated the State Department and were responsible for America's powerlessness in the world in the face of Communist expansion. McCarthy and his allies capitalized on extant fears of Communist infiltration in American life and the festering frustrations that had resulted from America's seeming inability to *do* anything to roll back Communism in Eastern Europe and elsewhere in the world it could not be "contained." McCarthy's charges, first made just weeks after Hiss's conviction, shifted politics further to the right and into the realm of the fantastic, placing Democrats and those who worked under their administrations at the center of an "immense" conspiracy. While the Republican Party gave McCarthy free reign, the senator and his allies in Congress and the federal government raised the level of suspicion and paranoia to new heights, putting the Truman administration on the defensive and encouraging a more intensive inquisition to root out "treasonous" reds like Hiss from the federal government. That inquisition resulted not only in a hunt for Communists and their sympathizers within government, but also in the purge of hundreds of homosexuals (real or imagined) from the State Department which they had allegedly infiltrated under successive "soft" Democratic administrations. The right-wing's charge that Democrats had engaged in "twenty years of treason," disingenuous as it was in its implication of both the Roosevelt and Truman administrations in the crime of high treason—and, thanks to the accompanying charges of homosexual infiltration of the State Department, sexually charged—exploited fears of an unrestrained sexuality in American life and at the same time helped to create them.

The rise of the cold war had lasting implications for the future of American liberalism. By the late 1940s a new political "realism" swept through the liberal intelligentsia as leading liberal thinkers and activists—some of them former Marxists and radicals—articulated their own "tough-minded" anti-Communism, and held any position short of an unequivocal rejection of Communism to be hopelessly soft and sentimental. Repudiating the politics of the Popular Front in the 1930s, which had briefly seen a loose alliance of progressive liberals and Communists formed as a united front against fascism, many postwar liberals now moved toward the "vital center" of American politics, midway between the ideological extremes of left and right. The liberal left splintered as anti-Communist liberals founded the Americans for Democratic Action (ADA) in 1948 and thereby distinguished themselves from the politics of the Progressive Party and its standard bearer Henry Wallace, the former member of the Roosevelt administration widely regarded as "soft" on the Soviet Union. Harry Truman, too, demonstrated his own brand of hard-hitting anti-Communism, taking a "get tough" stance with the Soviets, declaring the doctrine of global Communist containment, and introducing the Federal Employee Loyalty Program to eliminate those deemed "security risks" in the federal government. Generally speaking, anti-

Communists in the Democratic Party and the ADA accepted the necessity of "reasonable" domestic security measures, but chafed at the excesses and partisanship of HUAC and, as the primary victims of its wrath, deplored the McCarthyite crusade when it arose in the early fifties.[5]

The lesson of that traumatic encounter with the far right in the early 1950s, and Adlai Stevenson's two crushing defeats in successive presidential elections, was clear by the end of the decade to the most ambitious of liberals: never again could Democrats afford to appear soft. The point is not entirely new, of course; it has been made in passing. Yet to be fully appreciated, though, is the reconstitution of liberal identity that altered the historical direction of American liberalism in the cold war years and eventually brought John F. Kennedy to the White House in 1960.

In the early years of the cold war, Communism—regarded as the mirror opposite of everything for which America stood—was feared, despised, and policed with an intensity that was unique to the United States. At the federal, state, and local levels, governmental institutions mobilized their forces to root out Communists from American life, and they could often rely on the private sector to police itself, as was the case with the Hollywood studios. Locked in a struggle with a foreign enemy that brutally repressed human freedom and dignity within its domain, many Americans accepted without question the necessity of suspending traditional constitutional rights and safeguards in the war against Communism at home. Thus did America begin to resemble its enemy in the name of combating it. If most Americans were untroubled by such a paradox, it was in part because they assumed that those Communist party members who insisted on their constitutional rights under the First and Fifth Amendments, in order to pursue their goal of bringing down the very system that so generously gave them those rights, hardly deserved constitutional protections. In this view, the rights guaranteed by the Constitution were sacred liberties that Communists otherwise held in contempt, regarding them as mere bourgeois tools that served to mask and legitimize economic inequality in a capitalist society. For Americans less tutored in Communist doctrine, it was simply taken as axiomatic that such an invisible and extraordinarily wicked enemy could only be vanquished by extraordinary, extra-constitutional measures.

Communism inspired an animus in American society that was largely absent in democratic, capitalist nations in Europe with their longstanding welfare states and established Socialist and Communist parties. The fear and hatred of Communism has a long history in American life; its ideological roots go back to the nineteenth century, while the repression of Communists and other left-wing radicals in the late 1940s and the 1950s was foreshadowed by the red scare of 1919–1920. The United States was unique not just in its intolerance and persecution of Communists but in its obsessive demonization of them, hence the endless excesses and absurdities emanating from cold war culture: the abandonment of plans to make a Hollywood film about Robin Hood since the theme—taking from the rich to give to the poor—smacked of an endorsement of Communist principles; the brief changing of the name of the Cincinnati Reds to the "Redlegs" lest any confusion exist between the Communist "reds" and the patriots of professional baseball; the New York State Supreme Court Justice who declared that if a woman could be proven to be a Communist sympathizer (or a Henry Wallace supporter), she should not be entitled to custody of her children; the pelting of singer and actor Paul Robeson with stones in Peekskill, New York; the myth that the fluoridation of the water system was a Communist plot; Reverend Billy Graham's sermons pronouncing Communism "Satan's religion."[6] As anti-Communism manifested itself in multiple areas of cultural life—films, books, novels, religious sermons, television, advertisements, magazines, newspapers, government propaganda, sports, pulp fiction, comic books—the multi-tentacled Communist conspiracy to infiltrate American society was dramatized for a mass audience. Intractable, stealthy, monolithic, godless, and mind-controlling, Communism appeared positively diabolical.

So reviled was Communism that the protagonist of Mickey Spillane's bestselling 1951 thriller *One Lonely Night* could take delight in committing gruesome murders in the name of combating the red menace. Outwitting the Communist plan to steal America's secrets, detective Mike Hammer enjoys seeming moral impunity when he brags out of the corner of his mouth: "I shot them in cold blood and enjoyed every minute of it. I pumped slugs in the nastiest bunch of bastards you ever saw. . . . They were Commies . . . red sons-of-bitches. . . . Pretty soon what's left of Russia and the slime that breeds there won't be worth mentioning and I'm glad because I had a part in the killing. . . . God, but it was fun! . . . They never thought there were people like me in this country. They figured us all to be soft as horse manure and just as stupid." If Hammer, the hero in numerous Spillane bestsellers, had a weakness, it was for sexy and frequently malevolent women. But in the end he could typically outsmart an evil-doing seductress and even mete out a humiliating, sadistic punishment. In *One Lonely Night*, when a mink-clad Communist sexpot makes the mistake of betraying Hammer, he strips her naked and whips her with his belt, marveling at the "gorgeous woman who had been touched by the hand of the devil." In Hammer's world, violence was the only defense against Commies and criminals. As historian Stephen Whitfield has suggested, Hammer's ruthless carnage in *One Lonely Night* is presented as "redemptive and even sacrificial."[7]

Spillane's Mike Hammer may be a convenient, wildly inflated symbol of the anti-Communist machismo of the time. Yet the grievances and fixations that Hammer displays do reveal something about right-wing anti-Communism in the unusually tense years of the early 1950s, when McCarthy was on his rampage and Spillane published so many of his bestsellers, including *My Gun Is Quick* (1950), *The Big Kill* (1951), and *Kiss Me Deadly* (1952). As the antithesis of American male softness, Hammer is a stand-up World War II veteran, private investigator, and lone avenger whose vigilante ethos and contempt for things effete—intellectuals, professionals, homosexuals, and the "pansy" bureaucracy that tied the hands of the police and thus hampered the enforcement of law and order—made him a real m*an's man* in a soft, morally bankrupt world. In *One Lonely Night*, Hammer erupts, "if you want a democracy you have to fight for it. Why not now, before it's too late? That's the trouble, we're getting soft. They push us all around the block and we let them get away with it!" Hammer could always successfully combat low-life criminals, bullying mobsters and commie vermin wherever the official establishment—corrupt, feckless, and effeminate—had failed. Historian Kenneth Davis thought Mike Hammer a mirror of the McCarthyite psyche of America, "the ultimate cold warrior, an *Übermensch* for frightened Americans who had heard tales of baby-eating Stalinists."[8]

Hammer, like McCarthy and his brethren, was a self-made superpatriot whose methods could be presented as justifiable and even heroic, given the timidity of the state and its failure to protect America from fifth columnists. And like the McCarthyites, Hammer had another ax to grind: indeed his real object of loathing may have been less the Communist or the criminal and more the flaccid, corrupt, vaguely "liberal" establishment that permitted lawlessness and social disorder, allowed Communists, criminals, and sex perverts to run amok, and encouraged the moral laxity that weakened and emasculated America. In such a world, unconventional, extralegal means were necessary to save the nation from enemies who played dirty and were unconstrained by democratic niceties. When Senator John Bricker, Republican from Ohio, told McCarthy, "Joe, you're a dirty SOB . . . but there are times when you've got to have an SOB around, and this is one of them," there was more than a touch of Mike Hammer in the logic and the swagger.[9]

Against an internal foe—the American Communist Party—which at the onset of the HUAC hearings was (by any standard) tiny in membership, long disgraced by its unapologetic Stalinism, and hideously unattractive to the vast majority of Americans, the red-hunters stood armed with the weapons to halt Communist influence in wide areas of American society, from Hollywood studios to New York City public schools. Real cases of espionage there were, and Soviet agents could (and occasionally did) infiltrate the federal government.[10] Still, if the vast majority of Communist party members in the United States were largely powerless in social *influence*, capable of asserting their militancy in a few labor unions and social movements at best, what made them, and their "fellow-traveling" left-wing allies, appear so threatening in the schools, universities, mass media, and the arts and entertainment industry?

The spy cases had rendered Communists invisible enemies, outwardly "normal" people who could secretly bore from within. To a degree not experienced by previous enemies of America, Communists were often attributed with extraordinary powers to penetrate the psyche. As masters of mind control, they often appeared in popular imagery as almost superhuman, their ideology hypnotic, their propaganda something like a revolutionary narcotic, intoxicating recruits who could then imagine themselves selfless saviors of the poor and downtrodden. In these narratives, the ease with which Communists could lure well-intentioned souls into the party, indoctrinate people to join their ranks, corrupt and brainwash children in the schools, relay subliminal Communist messages to the American public in film and other mediums, or collectively mobilize the masses by skillfully exploiting their insecurities and even their sexual desires, suggests that in the countersubversive imagination, Communism was somehow darkly appealing—at once loathsome and seductive. The fascination with a murky Communist underground and covert control of the psyche found its expression not just on the right-wing fringes of American political culture but also, in more sophisticated form, in the liberal centrist discourse of the time. That fascination and the fantasies about Communism that it inspired speak not just to fears of Communist perfidy but also, as I will suggest, to anxieties about sexuality and the softened self that were the acute concerns of postwar American culture.

While indicative of the historical distinctiveness of the United States, the zealous forms and odd permutations that anti-Communism took in the early cold war years had a cultural basis rooted in the social, economic, political, and demographic changes that had been accelerated by World War II and continued to alter the American landscape through the 1950s. Rarely in American history had so *much* change occurred in so short a span of time; the degree of transformation in the fabric of American life between 1945 and 1960 was immense and arguably second only to the Civil War era. Emerging from World War II relatively unscathed and prosperous, the United States was rather suddenly thrust into the position of a global superpower, and isolationism uttered its last gasps as the nation became entangled in international affairs and bound to military alliances unthinkable at the beginning of the century. For the first time in American history, the maintenance of national security became an ongoing function of the state, and the nation became permanently militarized. Possession of the atomic bomb, the subsequent loss of an atomic monopoly, and the possibility of imminent nuclear war brought previously unknown fears and uncertainties that would hover over the nation in ebbing and flowing degrees of intensity for much of the remaining century.[11]

At the same time Americans confronted new global uncertainties, they experienced extraordinary upheaval at home. The Second World War brought a significant, if temporary, redistribution of income in American society and a major geographic, social, and occupational dislocation of Americans, unloosing people from their hometowns and local neighborhoods, their families, their jobs, and lifestyles. While Americans in the armed services went abroad to serve the war effort, so many at home, including millions of women and minorities, were whisked into the wartime workforce, relocating to cities like Los Angeles or Denver to work in more lucrative defense and defense-related industries. Moreover, the progeny of so many turn-of-the-century immigrant groups—Italians, Poles, Russians, Jews, Hungarians, and other eastern and southern European Ellis Island–era arrivals—now shared the common experience of fighting a war, a good war, in the name of America and *as* Americans. After the war, when so many of these first-generation born Americans moved en masse to suburbia and shared similar lifestyles in similar communities, the ethnic differences that had previously separated recently immigrated Europeans from old-stock Protestant Americans eroded, and the older WASP designation began to lose some of its significance as a clear and definitive racial category. While the "white" middle class enlarged its ranks and became more culturally homogenous, the experience of the war, the baby boom and suburbanization helped to reinforce a sense of generational commonality among white middle-class Americans. Returning veterans were able to take advantage of the GI Bill's generous offer of low-interest home loans and educational opportunities, which along with the thriving postwar economy helped elevate many of them to a standard of living well above that of their parents or grandparents. Just a decade before, American capitalism had been on the defensive. By mid-century it seemed capable of not just delivering on its promise of the American dream but extinguishing economic inequality and social conflict altogether.[12]

The Second World War also exposed—and magnified like never before—the problem of race in America. African American veterans had served in racially segregated military units abroad, where they fought against a dictatorial, racist regime *for* America but not *as* Americans, at least not as full-fledged American citizens with the same rights and privileges accorded to white citizens. Proud black veterans returned home and expected respect, but the incongruities between their military service in defense of democracy in the world and the stubborn reality of racial segregation at home had become all too glaring—thoroughly unacceptable to African Americans and something of an embarrassment to Washington. As the postwar United States became the self-proclaimed leader of the free world, all the unrelenting talk of American commitment to global democracy and freedom began to sound like so much cant. When A. Phillip Randolph threatened Truman with a massive march on Washington in 1948, an American president yielded, for the very first time and for complex reasons, to African American demands on an issue of major importance—the desegregation of the United States military.[13]

Higher-paying wartime job opportunities also gave many African Americans a taste of something more, and as the booming postwar economy gave a lift (albeit a deeply uneven one) to all classes of Americans, a larger and more solid black middle class was now poised to provide the leadership for a mass civil rights movement. Southern whites would be compelled, eventually by the Supreme Court and the presence of the first federal occupation troops in the South since Reconstruction, to undo over half a century of *de jure* segregation and an older, deeply embedded racial caste system. The turmoil and violence that ensued as white Southerners fought to preserve that racial caste system testifies to the depth of change that was beginning to occur in the South by the mid-1950s. Previously unwilling to impose desegregation upon white Southerners, the federal government, faced with domestic upheaval at home and the need to uphold its reputation abroad, would now force the South, with varying degrees of success and failure, to become more like the rest of the nation.

If race was a source of tension in postwar America, so too was gender, even in the absence of any significant, organized women's movement. American women also experienced change in public and private life, though the full impact of that change would not be entirely felt until the 1960s and afterward. The war brought more than six million women into the wartime labor force, offering them new opportunities, however briefly, for higher-paying, higher-status jobs and a newfound sense of financial independence and personal worth. Most women were dismissed from these jobs when the war ended, and an exaggerated ideology of domesticity emerged to remind women of their priorities as wives and mothers. Nonetheless, American women in the 1950s, especially married women, continued their historic march into the paid labor force (albeit mainly into lower paying, traditionally female occupations), helping to shoulder the financial burdens born of the baby boom and the middle-class consumerism of the time. Moreover, if we are to take men's observations (and complaints) seriously, postwar American women expected and demanded more in private life, asserting themselves as "feminists" or as "matriarchs" in the home sphere. Words like these were of course hyperbolic, and they are registers of the anxieties of the time. Yet they also point to postwar women's heightened expectations for individual self-fulfillment, expectations that—insofar as they remained largely unfulfilled by the end of the 1950s—eventually became the wellspring for deep middle-class female discontent and political organizing. In short, postwar women experienced cultural, demographic, and ideological cross-currents that pushed and pulled them in different directions, promising so much and yet constraining them still. These currents ultimately laid the groundwork for the second wave of feminism in the 1960s.[14]

In the postwar years, the United States was fast becoming more urban and suburban, less parochial in outlook, more middle class and consumerist, and, despite all the dutiful church-going of the fifties, noticeably more secular. Organized religion now had to compete for the attention of Americans with an increasingly homogenized popular culture, which, thanks to the revolutionary medium of television, offered up the same steady menu of entertainment, drama, news, and advertising to urban, suburban, and rural Americans alike. By the 1950s Americans traveled in big new cars on big new highways that crisscrossed the American landscape, while jetting across the nation on a commercial airliner, once the privilege of only a select few, was no longer such an anomaly for many upper middle-class Americans. A new youth culture emerged, this one much more conspicuous than those of previous eras, underwritten by a demographic explosion in postwar births and powerful commercial forces that targeted young people and molded the contours of teen culture.[15]

Undiscriminating market forces driven by a thriving economy brought new cultural phenomena to Americans, from the standardized, sanitized fare offered up by McDonalds and Disneyland to the dissonant energies of Chuck Berry, Vladimir Nabokov, Jack Kerouac, Jackson Pollock, and Alfred Kinsey. American society underwent new intellectual scrutiny, as postwar intellectuals, writers, scholars, and filmmakers turned their attention toward the self and the psychological implications of affluence, suburbanization, and mass-produced culture. While the pressures of the cold war surely had the effect of discouraging and constricting political debate and dissent, the cultural marketplace could still unleash a steady stream of fiction, art, music, and social commentary that gave voice to disruptive impulses and prefigured the rebellions of the 1960s.

In the context of these and other unsettling postwar social tensions and transformations, it should not be entirely astonishing that anti-Communism— so emotionally provocative and politically volatile—became entangled with anxieties that ultimately had little to do with Communism. As political winds shifted rightward and Communism appeared increasingly hateful, things that were perceived as hateful could then be imagined as somehow Communist in origin, intent, or effect. If modernism in the art world could be smeared red by arch-conservative anti-Communists, liberal reform movements were even more vulnerable to attack. Thus the burgeoning civil rights movement could be proclaimed by Southern segregationists as the handi-work of Communist agitators. (Communist Party members had in fact championed the causes of African Americans in the 1930s and 1940s at a time when white liberals largely ignored civil rights issues. But to insist, as did Senator James Eastland of Mississippi, that Communists were behind the Supreme Court's 1954 decision declaring segregation in public schools unconstitutional was to move into the realm of the delusional and absurd.) Other social reform issues were tainted red in a guilt-by-association fashion, and not just by fringe reactionaries. Truman's 1948 proposal for national healthcare was denounced by the American Medical Association, which claimed that the plan would bring a "Bolshevik Bureaucracy" to the nation and pointed out that the Communist Party also supported socialized medi-cine. There were few social issues that did not become at some point en-meshed with anti-Communism. Catholic and Protestant clergymen warned that godlessness, materialism, and the erosion of the family morally weak-ened Americans and left the nation vulnerable to Communist infiltration. Child-raising experts established parent education programs that "recog-nized the strategic importance of parents in the preservation of the *free world.*" Even the rising tide of overbearing mothers, rock-n-roll, sexual pro-miscuity, or homosexuality could be seen as weakening Americans to the forces of Communist conquest.[16]

Whatever else anti-Communism most certainly was, once unleashed in the culture it served to redefine America against the wave of social change, operating in some cases as an ideological buffer against discomforting de-velopments and perceived social ills. Racial integration, secularism, afflu-ence, materialism, apathy, youth rebellion, commercialism, conformity, Jewish upward mobility, internationalism, welfare statism, modernism in art, and sexual liberalism were all trends that could be imagined as subver-sive to American order and thus discouraged under the aegis of anti-Communism. Fears of sexual disorder were uniquely powerful inasmuch as they could be much more readily personalized in a way that anxieties about materialism or even the atomic bomb could not.

When viewed from the exclusive vantage point of sexuality, anti-Communism was more than a defense against Communism (or liberal-ism); in its broadest cultural manifestations and most heated imaginings, it was a defense against America itself—its increasing self-indulgence, its god-lessness, its apathy and softness, its lack of boundaries, its creeping sexual permissiveness—which is why it could be so readily wedded to an ideology of family values and sexual containment. Norman Mailer may have over-stated his case when he proclaimed that the "hysteria of the red wave was no preparation to face an enemy but rather a terror of the national self: free-loving, lust-looting, atheistic, implacable."[17] Yet it is hard to escape the conclusion that underlying the excesses and inanities of the anti-Communist imagination—of which the image of the subversive-as-homosexual was the most lurid—was an anxiety about troubling trends *at home* as well as abroad, not least among them sexual disorder. That creeping disorder— whether suggested by the "crisis of American masculinity," by the growing numbers of working women or assertive wives, by Kinsey's evidence of the collective sexual transgressions of the nation, or by the rise of gay and lesbian communities in postwar America—was projected onto an enemy whose quasi-Victorian sexual restraints and rigid material theology made it an altogether unworthy repository for homegrown American anxieties and frustrations.

To suggest that anxieties about sexuality, manhood, and the self surfaced in cold war political rhetoric and intersected with anxieties about Communism and national security is not to argue that the late 1940s and 1950s somehow constitute the historical zenith of sexual anxiety, repression, and rigidity in American history. Fears of a declining manhood and sexual promiscuity were not new in American culture, nor was their appearance in political rhetoric completely novel. Late nineteenth- and early twentieth-century America witnessed a surge of concerns about masculinity, as urbanization, bureaucratization, commercialism, and social reform undermined older sources of masculine identity at the same time female reformers were making their presence felt in the previously all-male public sphere. Moralists and reformers, too, had long fretted about a dangerous sexual laxity in American life, as premarital sex, prostitution, the white slave trade, venereal disease, pornography, loose flapper girls, and sexual "inversion" had seemingly increased with the arrival of modernity. Yet the social problems at issue in the late nineteenth and early twentieth centuries were also qualitatively different in nature and context from those of mid-century America.

It is true that in the late 1940s and the 1950s, conservative ideals that exalted the nuclear family, traditional gender roles, and sexual restraint were promoted after decades of social disruption brought on by depression and war, and they were sanctioned by professional experts, politicians, and religious leaders and expressed in popular culture through magazines, film, television, and advertising. The promotion of these ideals was inseparable from new cold war threats, as the domestic "containment" argument advanced by historian Elaine Tyler May suggests: just as Communism was to be "contained," so too would sexuality be contained within heterosexual marriage and the nuclear family; both served as an emotional refuge from the uncertainties of the atomic age and a bulwark against sexual unorthodoxy. The containment metaphor implies constriction, policing, or repression. Impulses and behaviors falling out of the bounds of traditional sex and gender ideals—female career aspirations, sexual promiscuity, homosexuality—would be monitored, contained, and redirected into "normal" outlets, that is, heterosexual marriage and family life. Sexual conformity could thus triumph in a conformist, politically conservative age.[18]

The image of the era as sexually conservative certainly has validity. Cold war pressures did encourage sexual orthodoxy and restraint in many quarters of American life. But in the translation from foreign policy to cultural life, the "containment" metaphor can be taken too far when presented as a barometer of reality. The rigid sex and gender ideals that have come to define the popular and scholarly conception of American culture in the 1950s were precisely that—ideals—and insofar as they were endorsed on the ideological level, they were artificial and fragile and bore a tenuous relationship to the realities of private and public life. To use an old Marxian metaphor, the superstructure was out of step with the base; the official ideology was out of sync with reality. Sexual "containment" there was, but it was largely unsuccessful.

The popular image of the 1950s as culturally and sexually repressive tends to minimize the profound transformations that were occurring in the realm of sexuality and gender. In the face of such changes, the promotion of an ideology that insisted on the sanctity of the nuclear family, strict gender-role norms, and sexual restraint was largely a rearguard action. Even if the discussion is confined only to the white middle class, the paradoxes and incongruities of the time testify to the artificiality of conservative sexual ideals: while housewifery was exalted in popular culture, and made to seem the natural aspiration of every normal woman, American women continued to enter public life and the paid labor force. At the same time "maturity" was promoted as the hallmark of the well-adjusted male and men were urged to fulfill their responsibilities as breadwinners and fathers, currents of discontent and resistance crept across the cultural landscape, as male writers decried a "decline in masculinity" and the first issue of *Playboy* heralded its trademark celebration of male freedom from marital enslavement. Though husbands and wives in unhappy or unfulfilling marriages more often than not remained married thanks to the pressures of the age, the seeds of a later divorce revolution were sown in so many brittle marriages of the fifties. At the same time the baby boom accompanied exaggerated ideals of family togetherness, a new youth culture emerged and brought a deeper level of generational separation than ever before. While homosexuality was classified by the psychiatric profession as an official pathology and most homosexuals were forced to remain closeted at the workplace or anywhere else they would be subject to discrimination or vilification, gay and lesbian Americans were nonetheless increasingly visible in public life and established thriving and conspicuous urban communities. Though sexual chastity and heterosexual marriage and family life were the reigning values of mid-century America, the Kinsey reports' data on premarital sex, adultery, and homosexuality unleashed an unprecedented public discussion of the sexual habits of Americans, and ultimately suggested that they were hardly chaste or "normal" according to the official sexual norms of the time.

Efforts to contain sexuality existed precisely because there was something larger and more overwhelming to contain. Cultural, economic, and market forces were ushering in a new wave of sexual liberalism, one that collided repeatedly with conservative moral norms and generated a range of responses, from a tension-fraught preoccupation with matters of manhood and sexuality in American life to deep dread of an apparent breakdown in sexual boundaries. Such a breakdown had in fact been occurring at least since the turn of the century, as older moral, religious, and social restraints on individual behavior eroded, especially in the tumultuous roaring 1920s. By mid-century, however, those already weakened restraints were dealt a considerable blow by the dislocations of the war and the accelerated social, economic, and commercial forces of the postwar years. While the sexual revolution so often associated with the rebellious 1960s has its distant origins in the consumer culture of the 1920s, its more immediate catalyst lay in the social fissures, market trends, and ideological contradictions of the 1940s and 1950s. An apparent "epidemic" of male homosexuality, however, added a disquieting new dimension to the mid-century sense of sexual disorder. Testifying to this fact are the obsessions with manhood and homosexuality that found their way into political life and form the subject matter of this book.

Chapter one uses the work of Arthur Schlesinger Jr. to examine the dilemma of modern liberalism and the rhetoric with which its image was reconstituted to meet the challenge of the cold war. Schlesinger's sexually loaded polemics speak less to sexual containment and more to a tense—and uniquely "liberal"—fixation on sexuality, virility, and the dark, subterranean forces of the will, a fixation rooted, in part, in the postwar vogue of Freudianism and existentialism, and one that ultimately served liberal propaganda purposes. Chapter two turns to a wider exploration of politics in the late 1940s and 1950s, especially the anti-Communism of the right. It suggests the way in which fears of Communism became entangled with anxieties about moral laxity and homosexuality. Such concerns added moral intensity and fuel to conservative anti-Communism, while the counteroffensive against Communism in turn gave urgency to moralists' attempts to "contain" the rising tide of unrestrained sexuality in American life. Moving from politics proper to culture, chapter three provides a broader cultural context with which to explore the sources of anxiety and the meanings of tropes and themes that surfaced in political discourse. It examines the concerns about social and political conformity, gender, and sexuality expressed by writers, social critics, filmmakers, psychologists, and psychiatrists in the late 1940s and 1950s. Bringing those concerns back to bear on the politics of the late 1950s and early 1960s, chapter four analyzes the psychologizing rhetoric with which centrist liberals represented the failures and deficiencies of their political rivals and reinvented the liberal as a manly cold warrior embodied in the figure of John Kennedy. The common thread that runs throughout the book is the sense of an American manhood weakened by the forces of a mass society and in need of rehabilitation to meet the challenges of a cold war world.

The dilemma posed by writing a book that focuses on and ascribes historical significance to such themes is that, in repeatedly calling attention to gendered and sexualized imagery in cold war politics, a narrative inevitably emerges in which sexuality appears ever-present and somehow decisive at every turn of events. While I do suggest that concerns about gender and sexuality were unusually pervasive in early cold war political culture and reveal themselves in sometimes surprising and unlikely venues, I always assume that first, there was a world beyond the fears and feverish imaginings of the anti-Communists treated here, and second, learned readers are familiar with that larger world from which anti-Communism was born. I do not make a claim for the "centrality" of gender in political history, even as I show how thoroughly anxieties about masculinity reappeared in cold war political and cultural discourse. Determining with any precision how decisive something as amorphous as masculinity actually was in the historical trajectory of cold war American politics is a difficult business, if only because gender is (here and elsewhere in political life) at once everywhere and nowhere—embedded in the way people mentally and rhetorically construct themselves and the world around them, and thus difficult to isolate as something "central" (or "secondary") in political life. I do argue, however, that the ideological polemics and partisan battles of the early cold war years were fought to an unusual extent on the terrain of manhood and sexuality, and thus the political dynamics of the early cold war years cannot be fully understood apart from the politics of manhood and the cultural tensions that nourished it. Nor is the Kennedy administration's view of itself, its liberal nationalism, and its conduct in foreign affairs fully intelligible outside of the currents that shaped the New Frontiersmen's cult of masculine toughness. To some palpable and yet immeasurable degree, their particular brand of virility encouraged the flexing of liberal muscle from Cuba to Vietnam.

CHAPTER 1

Postwar Liberalism and the Crisis of Liberal Masculinity

The curse of the age is its femininity, its lack, not of barbarism, but of virility. It is the age of woman-worship.

—Orestes Brownson (1864)

In the hard-driving, competitive, ruthless, materialistic world of the Gilded Age, to be unselfish suggested not purity but a lack of self, a lack of capacity for grappling with reality, a lack of assertion, of masculinity.

—Richard Hofstadter (1962)

When Arthur Schlesinger Jr. in his 1949 classic *The Vital Center* attempted to redefine a new anti-Communist liberalism and align it with the "vital center" of American politics, he replaced the old linear left-to-right ideological spectrum with a new circular model, where fascism and Communism would "meet at last on the murky grounds of tyranny and terror." Merging left and right extremist politics within the rubric of totalitarianism at the bottom of the circle, Schlesinger positioned—180 degrees opposite totalitarianism at the top of the circle—the vital center of American politics. It was an awkward reconfiguration of a linear model, for only if plotted on a straight line would this point really lie at the absolute center.[1]

In a political arena increasingly fractured by the charges against New Deal liberal and alleged Soviet spy Alger Hiss, properly distancing liberalism from Communism was no small concern, particularly for liberals like Schlesinger who assumed that Communism had "draped itself so carefully in the cast-off clothes of a liberalism grown fat and complacent." Crucial to reestablishing the integrity of liberalism was restoring order and meaning to a shifting political terrain in which the entire terminology of left and right had become unstable. Lest the differences between the vital center liberal and his political competitors to the left and right remain murky in Schlesinger's new circular model, the sexually tinged rhetoric that pervades *The Vital Center* served to draw the necessary boundary distinctions. In this remarkable cold war composition, left and right political extremes are both revealed as deficient in manliness, and the "vital center" emerges in the text not just as the locus of a tough-minded liberalism whose leaders bring a "new virility into public life," but also as the home of a secure and restored American masculinity.[2]

When historians discuss the emergence of postwar liberalism in the 1940s, they typically highlight a new realism born out of the experience of the Second World War. Postwar liberals appear sobered and disciplined by the global confrontation with totalitarianism, their politics shaped by a heightened awareness of the complexity and ambiguity of human nature, the shortcomings of an overly optimistic liberal rationalism, the dangers of ideology, and, in a word that permeates the new liberal discourse, the *reality* of the cold war world. Out of the historic wartime encounter with the "real" emerged a renewed appreciation for the virtues of a mixed economy and a pluralist politics, an appreciation now tempered by a "tough-minded" pragmatism which guarded against facile, utopian thinking. The new liberalism was thus suspicious of the naive sentimental politics of progressive and Popular Front era leftists, its ranks bolstered by the defection of dozens of repentant ex-Marxists and formerly radical New York Intellectuals who, along with New Deal liberals like Schlesinger, promised deliverance from the left-wing orthodoxies of the past and endorsed a new anti-Communist liberalism suited to the imperatives of a cold war world.[3]

Any kind of reliance on the historical actor's own self-description might have given even a postwar liberal historian like Richard Hofstadter pause. In relying on the same tropes and themes found within the liberal rhetoric of the 1940s and 1950s, most political and intellectual historians have missed, or perhaps dismissed as an idiosyncrasy, what may appear so conspicuous that it is ultimately rendered invisible: a preoccupation with—and an anxiety about—masculinity which infuses influential strains of postwar liberalism and finds its earliest and most dramatic expression in *The Vital Center*. An exploration of the nature of that anxiety, and the muscular politics that was its remedy, offers another vantage point from which to view the origins of a newly reinvigorated liberalism that would compete in the American political arena in the years following World War II. If the rhetoric that initially served as a "defense against 'extremists'" in *The Vital Center* later went on the offensive, adopting a "nationalistic strut and swagger" in the early 1960s, we need to look more closely at the affirmation of the vital center that inspired what has come to be known as postwar, cold war, or consensus liberalism.[4]

It would be disingenuous to suggest that liberals like Schlesinger simply "sold out" during the cold war, exchanging a commitment to social reform for a staunch anti-Communism that served as their ticket to political relevance and power. Of course there is truth to the idea that an unequivocal anti-Communist stance became compulsory in a political arena that would not tolerate anything less, especially during the tense years of the early cold war. But such an interpretation of liberal motivation reduces the liberal anti-Communist position to craven political opportunism at best, a failure of *radical nerve* at worst. Standing "tough" in the face of Stalinism was not merely a posture born of political necessity or liberal ambition; it was a moral and political imperative to many liberal anti-Communists for whom the lessons of Munich and the Moscow trials were deeply and inescapably real.

In any case, the question is not *why* liberals became anti-Communists in the early cold war years, for the answer is fairly clear, but rather *how* liberalism survived under the pressures that could have defeated it. Emerging from the war with a new sense of realism and robustness only to endure a vicious beating in the 1950s, liberalism not only endured the humiliation but triumphed in 1960. Sustained by nearly twenty years of economic growth, to be sure, it was a hybrid liberal-conservatism that evolved, one that had emerged in the 1950s as both Democrats and Republicans gravitated toward the center. Yet in a political arena in which partisan policy and platform became ever more indistinguishable as a broad ideological consensus blanketed the scene in the 1950s, it was image and posture that increasingly came under scrutiny, and here the liberal as a political figure—as a social *type*—continued to carry the taint of eastern establishment softness and more than a whiff of treason. If liberals withstood the blows of the decade only to claim victory by 1960 under the aegis of the New Frontier, they did so in large measure because they eventually succeeded in reinventing the liberal as a cold warrior and a redeemer of manly virtues.

Part political manifesto and part historical narrative, and arguably the most politically influential book of the postwar years, *The Vital Center* was primarily the blueprint for a new liberal self-image, one whose rhetoric laid the foundation for political styles and decisions which that rhetoric later seemed to necessitate in prosecuting the cold war. But *The Vital Center* also speaks to the overwrought political culture from which it emerged, and in this sense its language and imagery, its excesses and idiosyncrasies, are instructive. Imprisoned in polarities of thought and rhetoric that would come to permeate intellectual life in following decade, its sexually charged rhetoric a register of the sexual as well as the political tensions of the time, *The Vital*

Center may stand as the quintessential cold war intellectual work—a testimony to the "age of anxiety" that Schlesinger himself lamented in its pages and a remarkable piece of liberal propaganda.

The Vital Center may enjoy the dubious distinction of being one of the most oft-cited but rarely scrutinized books in American historiography. Habitually noted as a turning point for American liberalism in the twentieth century, the book tends to be discussed in passing, particularly by intellectual historians on their way to the more ideologically provocative left-to-right odysseys of the New York intellectuals, who by now have surely had their day.[5] But Schlesinger's work deserves the attention that has been given to intellectuals who had considerably less influence in political life. In short, Schlesinger is historically significant precisely in the way he saw men such as himself historically significant—as an intellectual *and* a political activist, one whose belief in the central role of the intellectual in government in the tradition of the New Deal brought him to Washington in 1961.

Schlesinger was not the first liberal intellectual to repudiate the left-wing Popular Front politics of the 1930s, yet he was one of the first to transform a repudiation of Communism into a new liberal politics. He advanced this reconstructed liberalism not only in *The Vital Center* and elsewhere in his voluminous public writings, but also within the organization he founded in 1948 with Reinhold Niebuhr, the Americans for Democratic Action (ADA), as a Democratic party activist and polemicist, as an advisor to two-time presidential candidate Adlai Stevenson, and later as a campaign advisor, speechwriter, and special assistant to John Kennedy. And while Schlesinger had much to do with giving form and voice to a new anti-Communist liberalism, he played a no less considerable role in shaping its legacy years later in his capacity as an official historian of the Kennedys.

Educated at Exeter, Harvard, and Cambridge, schooled in history and political statesmanship (and far from the heated sectarian–ideological debates that embroiled the radical left in the halls of the City College of New York), Schlesinger was always close, personally and politically, to the Democratic Party. The son of the eminent Harvard historian Arthur Meier Schlesinger Sr., the younger Schlesinger followed his father's trajectory: changing his middle name at age fifteen (from his mother's maiden name to his father's middle name, Meier) so that he could be properly known as Arthur M. Schlesinger Jr., studying history after entering Harvard at age sixteen, embracing a liberal politics, and eventually becoming a member of the Harvard history department. An intelligence officer in the Office of War Information (OWI) and the Office of Strategic Services (OSS) during the war, Schlesinger took a dim view of left-wing intellectuals who refused to get their hands dirty in the "real" political world.[6] Primed by his stint in the OWI and OSS, he was part of a new cohort of Ivy League liberals who returned from the war eager to discipline the intellectual world with some "hard" lessons from the real world.

"Politics in an Age of Anxiety"

Schlesinger began *The Vital Center* by stressing that mid-twentieth-century liberalism had been "fundamentally reshaped by the hope of the New Deal, by the exposure of the Soviet Union, and by the deepening of our knowledge of man." The New Deal showed that the excesses of capitalism could be curbed, and that a pragmatic, flexible liberalism could grapple with the problems of industrial capitalism without resorting to dogmatism, rigidity, or utopian appeals. The lesson of the New Deal was that there was hope in the ability of educated pragmatists to mitigate the problems of industrial society; the lesson of totalitarianism was that liberals must discard old assumptions about the rationality and goodness of man. The degeneration of the Soviet Union "broke the bubble of the false optimism of the nineteenth century," proving that the pragmatic democratic tradition (of which the New Deal was a part) had been too hastily abandoned by Depression-era leftists for naïve utopian fantasies. For Schlesinger, the rise of totalitarianism "reminded my generation rather forcibly that man was, indeed, imperfect, and that the corruptions of power could unleash great evil in the world."[7]

Schlesinger's depiction of a liberalism forced to confront the "real" displays one manifestation of what literary scholar Thomas Hill Schaub has called the "liberal narrative": the repeated accounts of a "Blakean journey from innocence to experience, from the myopia of the utopian to the twenty-twenty vision of the realist" found in so much of the literary criticism and fiction of the ex-Marxist intelligentsia. The narrative achieved a kind of mythic status in the discourse of "revisionist liberalism," informing a variety of cold war intellectual works and providing a means by which the formerly radical literary left came to grips with its Communist or fellow-traveling past. Never a left-revolutionary himself, Schlesinger reminded readers that his own generation had "escaped the lure of nostalgia." Still, the journey from youthful idealism to political maturity was a central theme in *The Vital Center,* infused with a new awareness of the fallibility of man and a steadfast rejection of facile notions of progress and human perfectibility. Echoing the liberal theologian Reinhold Niebuhr, who had criticized liberal rationalism and utopian secular humanism for failing to recognize the fears and irrationalities of human beings and their potential for corruption, Schlesinger emphasized the liberal awakening to "a new dimension of experience—the dimension of anxiety, guilt, and corruption."[8]

"Western man in the middle of the twentieth century is tense, uncertain, adrift," Schlesinger declared in the first chapter of *The Vital Center* entitled "Politics in an Age of Anxiety." Attributing this anxiety to the "global change-of-life" of the preceding three centuries, he stressed the "terrifying problem of adjustment" that had resulted. The waning of familiar institutions and kinship structures, the rise of industry, science, technology, and bureau-cracy, and new demands on the social structure had ushered in a civilization that is now "consumed by anxiety and fear." The impersonal industrial sys-tem had given "potent weapons to the pride and the greed of man, the sadism and the masochism, the ecstasy in power and the ecstasy in submission." And while the lone individual submerged within the "mass"—be it the cor-poration or the collective—need not assume responsibility for the exploi-tation produced by industrialism, a "sense of guilt" remained. "The result was to create problems of organization to which man has not risen and which threaten to engulf him."[9]

Like so many other American intellectuals in the postwar years whose attention had shifted from public problems of political economy and social institutions to private dissatisfaction and psychic malaise, Schlesinger as-sumed that the troubles of modern society were primarily psychological in nature. His assessment of the modern predicament ("frustration is increas-ingly the hallmark of this century") carried an urgency that reflects the un-certainties of the late 1940s, before the cold war had become, in a sense, more routinized. Schlesinger depicted a modern society in which "anxiety is the official emotion of our time" and the lure of extremist politics is nearly irresistible. In his view, the "reign of insecurity" and "fear of isolation" that modernity brought had the effect of encouraging "anxious man" to seek security in comforting utopian visions and the promise of order and cer-tainty that totalitarianism offers; thus does he embrace totalitarianism in a "frenzied flight from doubt," in a "flight from anxiety." But "security is a foolish dream of old men . . . crisis will always be with us," Schlesinger in-sisted. The obvious failure of utopian experiments proved that escape from crisis and anxiety was futile. "We must recognize that . . . the womb has irrevocably closed behind us."[10]

The essential problem for the modern individual, then, was *coping* with freedom. From Erich Fromm and Wilhelm Reich, both of whom studied the psychology of fascism, Schlesinger absorbed the concept of *mass man*— the twentieth-century by-product of a mass society who was psychologically vulnerable to totalitarianism. Freedom was a massive psychic burden for the modern individual, Schlesinger stressed: "The eternal awareness of choice can drive the weak to the point where the simplest decision becomes a night-mare. Most men prefer to flee choice, to flee anxiety, to flee freedom." The old liberalism had assumed that the individual longed to be free, but the rise of totalitarianism proved that "man longs to escape the pressures beating down on his frail individuality." Underlying the inclination to "surrender that individuality to some massive, external authority," Schlesinger emphasized à la Fromm, were "strivings for submission and for domination, the losing of self in masochism or sadism."[11]

The Vital Center's depiction of mid-century Western man, cast in the shadow of totalitarian horrors, was singularly dark and portentous. Schlesinger's use of physical imagery suggesting trauma to and invasion of the body vividly dramatized the crisis of free society, which has been "demoralized by the infection of anxiety, [left] staggering under the body blows of fascism and Communism." Here, industrial man is left with "savage wounds," "cuts and gashes," thus exposed to the "virus" of totalitarianism. As Schlesinger described it, "'Individualism' strips the individual of layer after layer of protective tissue. Reduced to panic, industrial man joins the lemming migration, the convulsive mass escape from freedom to totalitarianism, hurling himself from the bleak and rocky cliffs into the deep, womb-dark sea below." In a society in which "freedom has lost its foundation in community and become a torment" and "our lives are empty of belief," the future looked exceedingly grim. Schlesinger invoked Yeats: "the falcon cannot hear the falconer, the center cannot hold. Anarchy is loosed upon the world and . . . some rough beast . . . slouches toward Bethlehem to be born."[12]

If this depiction of mid-twentieth-century Western society was unduly bleak (and perhaps unrecognizably so—did readers in 1949 believe that freedom had become a "torment" and their lives were "empty of belief"?), it was because such a scenario functioned as a call for psychological regeneration. Schlesinger conceded that the problem of free society appears in the form of an external crisis—the international collision between the forces of democracy and totalitarianism. But he insisted that "in its essence this crisis is internal." Because democracy lacked an ability to draw upon the "profounder emotional resources" and thus had no defense against "the neuroses of industrialism," it appeared "pale and feeble" and was at a serious disadvantage next to totalitarian society, which had "scotched the snake of anxiety" (if only temporarily). While the enemy has the upper hand in his talent for relieving anxious man of his neuroses, Schlesinger reminded readers that totalitarianism is ultimately suited to weaklings, to "the invalids [who] throw away their crutches as they leave the Soviet Shrine" yet are later seen "whimpering and crawling a little way down the road." Democracy is suited to the strong; it must necessarily rely on man's courage and stamina, for if it "cannot produce the large resolute breed of men capable of the climatic effort, it will founder." Since insecurity and isolation are inescapable in a free society, the future of modern democratic man relied on mustering up the courage to be an individual, to resist the inclination to escape anxiety, to relinquish self to the collective and retreat into the "womb-dark sea."[13]

From the "forlornness, impotence, and fear" that man experiences as "organization towers higher and higher above him," to the "ineffectual escapists" who avoid military duty in the name of conscientious objection to war, to the retreat of big business into the "womblike comfort" of mergers and monopolies, to the progressive's need to immerse himself "in the broad maternal expanse of the masses," modernity's effect is to infantilize, enervate, and feminize. The womb is one of Schlesinger's favorite metaphors for collectivism. Its reappearance here and elsewhere in his work recalls T. S. Eliot's maxim that "totalitarianism appealed to the desire to return into the womb."[14]

Schlesinger was not the only twentieth-century thinker to represent modernity as a self-crushing, feminizing force, though he did so with an unusual degree of political and partisan intent. Popular writer and psychoanalyst Robert Lindner likewise underscored the importance of bolstering democratic individualism against the rising tide of totalitarian "mass manhood" in the United States when, in his 1952 book *Prescription for Rebellion*, he reminded readers that "where the right to protest is recognized . . . and no imperative to adjust is permitted to emasculate the culture, [mass man] will not appear." For Schlesinger, an emotionally recharged "fullness of faith" in democracy, maintained at a "high pitch of vibration," was apparently the only means by which the emasculating effects of modernity and its offspring—totalitarian mass man—could be warded off.[15]

Like many postwar writers and novelists in the late 1940s and 1950s, Schlesinger turned inward, toward the irrational, toward the "dark, slumbering forces of the will," as he put it. The wave of Freudianism and existentialism that swept through the postwar literary milieu here finds its expression in a political manifesto, and in many ways the sexually charged rhetoric in *The Vital Center* reflects the postwar fascination with the murky underside of the psyche that also inspired studies of the social–psychology of fascism. For Schlesinger, traditional categories of historical and sociological analysis that assumed rational political behavior were incapable of explaining the complex sources of left and right political extremism and the ghastly events of recent history. Apparent in *The Vital Center* are traces of Reich's argument in *The Mass Psychology of Fascism* that the psychic structure of the authoritarian personality type was formed early in the rigid, sexually inhibited family; thus, mass man's vulnerability to totalitarianism was rooted in sexual repression and dysfunction. The influence of both Fromm and Reich, the latter a proponent of sexual freedom whose work was much in fashion among postwar intellectuals, is as evident in Schlesinger's obsession with power, will, and sexuality (the "ecstasy" of power and submission) as it is in

Norman Mailer's preoccupation with the same and his idealization of the uninhibited, willful male rebel against mass conformity.[16]

Against the psychosexual deficiencies of mass man, the model of free individualist man was defined almost by default, as Schaub implied in his discussion of the relationship between the new "revisionist liberalism" and the work of writers such as Schlesinger, Mailer, and Paul Goodman. "Perhaps, inevitably," Schaub suggested, "the discourses of strong democratic individualism and sexual freedom that were essentially gender-neutral often produced a male-dominated rhetoric, in which society (totalitarianism, conformity) was associated with an emasculating femininity, and the rebel was always a man." And to be sure, the rhetoric of a robust democratic individualism, as Schaub noted, inevitably fell prey to "the gender biases latent in the sexual connotations of popular language."[17]

The model of mass man was no doubt conceived as gender-neutral, intended to explain the generalized implications of modernity. Yet the psychosexual rhetoric that animates *The Vital Center* registers more than the influence of Reich or Fromm. As a polemicist and a former intelligence officer attuned to the utility of political psychology, Schlesinger sought to create a new image of liberal man. His manifesto, above all, speaks to the intersection of partisan and propagandistic aims (restoring the image of the liberal) with real, palpable anxieties about sexuality and manhood specific to mid-century America, its language and imagery a defense against what the author himself called, in a later 1958 *Esquire* article, "The Crisis of American Masculinity." In this article, the problem of modernity is linked, not by the polarities inherent in psychosexual discourses or by the accident of language, but by explicit argument, to a decline in masculine identity and self-confidence. Underlying *The Vital Center*'s appeals to the beleaguered male self was perhaps the nascent assumption of a "crisis" in American masculinity long before Schlesinger explicitly addressed that issue.[18]

Masculinity in Crisis?

Concerns about a "crisis" in masculinity were a recurrent feature of modernity and already had a long history by the mid-twentieth century. In a myriad of venues, American men—writers, social commentators, politicians, adventurers, experts—showed an unusual obsession with manhood and its regeneration, beginning in the late nineteenth century. The workship of masculine toughness that was so conspicuous at the turn of the century grew in reaction to social and economic transformations that seemed to undercut older sources of masculine character. As urbanization, technological transformation, and commercialization changed the rhythms of life and leisure, as women made inroads into public life and brought female morals to bear on male behavior, and as the waning of small-scale entrepreneurship and the rise of corporate capitalism transformed the nature of work, many observers declared that American men had become emasculated. They worried that professional men were living a comfortable life of ease and self-indulgence; that large, impersonal bureaucracies relegated rising numbers of men to sedentary, managerial, or clerical careers of paper-pushing and deference to the firm; that educated bourgeois men who expended too much nervous energy were ever more prone to neurasthenia, the great affliction of the overcivilized; that urban middle-class boys were living a pampered, "namby-pamby" existence, surrounded by excessive female influences at home and at school and undisciplined by the rugged, outdoor lifestyle that had once turned boys into men.[19]

The quest for masculine renewal closely paralleled several of the antimodernist preoccupations that T. J. Jackson Lears discusses in his study of restless *fin-de-siècle* elites who searched for spiritual and psychological emancipation from bourgeois life and oppressive Victorian conventions. But it also transcended the world of the antimodernists and reflects more widespread anxieties about female power. If civilization itself was subverting manhood, so too, it seemed, were the women who embodied civilization's feminine impulses. By the late nineteenth century, the increasing presence of women in public life provoked a wave of dread as male critics denounced the feminization of the nation at the hands of moralizing, reforming women. In their multiple roles as wives, mothers, teachers, Christians, progressive reformers, or purveyors of a "sentimental" mass culture, American women appeared ever more determined to domesticate boys and men, shut down saloons and brothels, claim for themselves the franchise, and thereby force a feminine ethos onto the nation.[20]

That dread had been festering at least since the mid-nineteenth century, when male writers began to sneer at the feminine sensibility that had come to saturate American culture and literary life. Orestes Brownson's 1864 comment quoted in the epigraph of this chapter (Schlesinger published a biography of Brownson in 1939) was an early expression of a lament that would become familiar by the late nineteenth century: the loss of virility in American life (a by-product of the "woman worship" of his time, as Brownson saw it). The "separate spheres" ideology of the nineteenth century had idealized middle-class women as the moral guardians of the home sphere. But in the late nineteenth century, when reform-minded women increasingly began to move from the private to the public realm to exert their moral influence, the consequences were too much to bear for many men. Henry James's protagonist in *The Bostonians* (1886), Basil Ransom, a cultivated Southern gentlemen who finds himself cringing in the company of female reformers and feminists in Boston, denounces their influence in instructive terms:

The whole generation is womanized; the masculine tone is passing out of the world; it's a feminine, a nervous, hysterical, chattering, canting age, an age of hollow phrases and false delicacy and exaggerated solicitudes and coddled sensibilities, which, if we don't soon look out, will usher in the reign of mediocrity, of the feeblest and flattest and the most pretentious that has ever been. The masculine character, the ability to dare and endure, to know and yet not fear reality, to look the world in the face and take it for what it is—a very queer and partly very base mixture—that is what I want to preserve, or rather, as I may say, to recover.[21]

The use of the term "masculine" here (as something to be recovered rather than preserved) may subtly suggest the shifts in the ideology of manhood that were emerging in the late nineteenth century. According to Gail Bederman, the terms "masculine" and "masculinity" had only just begun to enter the national idiom in the 1890s. Moreover, these terms were not synonymous with the terms "manly" and "manliness," which were commonly used in the nineteenth century and carried distinct meanings rooted in Victorian ideals of manhood. The term "manliness" had moral connotations. In contemporary dictionaries the word conveyed "character or conduct worthy of a man"; it implied possession of the "proper" manly traits: "independent in spirit or bearing; strong, brave, large-minded, etc."; and was equated with the state of being "honorable, high-minded." Such a definition of manliness reflected the values that underlay the Victorian male ideal, including those historians have identified as "sexual self-restraint, a powerful will, a strong character." On the other hand, the new term "masculinity" (adapted from the French) was relatively neutral: it generally referred to the possession of any and all male characteristics, whether valued or not. As it began to appear in dictionaries, the word "masculine" conveyed the possession of "the distinguishing characteristics of the male sex among human beings, physical or mental. . . . suitable for the male sex; adapted to or intended for the use of males." The term was initially rather empty of meaning, at least until it gained wide currency in the twentieth century and eventually became wedded to male traits now associated with "masculinity"—aggression, dominance, physical strength, competition, and sexual potency. Its introduction into popular language was significant, Bederman suggests, for it reflects the need for a neutral, all-encompassing term for maleness shorn of some of the Victorian traits of manliness (e.g., self-restraint) that were being undercut by social and economic changes at the turn of the century.[22]

In some cases, those older "manly" traits were explicitly rejected by bourgeois men looking to shore up their "masculine" attributes. As the separate spheres doctrine eroded and the western frontier closed, many men responded by reasserting gender boundaries and turning what were previously male "vices" in need of restraint—aggression, passion, physical power, combativeness—into masculine attributes in need of active cultivation (hence the craze for martial arts, the warrior ideal, and competitive athletics at the turn of the century). As educated bourgeois men pursued the activities through which they could counteract the softening influences of an upper-class lifestyle, and thereby recover a healthy dose of the baser male impulses that Victorian values had squelched, educators sought to toughen up the body and the character of the nation's future generation of men by founding organizations such as the Boy Scouts of America. The most ambitious and controversial effort to masculinize boys was undertaken by psychologist G. Stanley Hall, who promoted the cultivation of boyhood "primitivism" as a means to combat neurasthenia and counterbalance the overcivilization of males. Hall's efforts to encourage a healthy savagery in boys did not go uncontested by observers at the time, many of whom found his embrace of primitivism barbaric. But the cumulative efforts to regenerate masculinity reflect the obsession with virility that surged around the turn of the century and found expression in many other areas of American life, including religion. Protestant ministers and evangelists such as Billy Sunday promoted a "muscular Christianity" (replete with its images of a virile, stern, brawny Jesus Christ) as an alternative to the sentimental, mushy Protestantism that had enfeebled religion and alienated men from its ranks of believers. Muscular Christianity restored a virile God to his heavenly throne and promised to remake male Christians in his image.[23]

Set against the social transformations occurring in the late nineteenth and early twentieth centuries, the search for masculine renewal had complex and overlapping impulses rooted in class, race, and gender tensions as well as national and imperial aims. No one better represents the complex sources of turn-of-the-century machismo than Theodore Roosevelt. Preeminent "Rough Rider" in the Spanish-American War, governor of New York, vice president and then president of the United States in 1901, Roosevelt became the most influential spokesman of his time for the recovery of masculine virtues. He called upon Americans to embrace the "strenuous life" as an antidote to the flaccid body and spineless character that not only unmanned men but sapped the will and strength of civilized Anglo-Saxon people. (Roosevelt also claimed that Anglo-Saxons, through their willful failure to breed adequately and thus keep pace with immigrants and the poor, were committing "race suicide.") In different rhetorical forms and guises, Roosevelt promoted "strenuous" endeavor as a means to masculine regeneration, national greatness, and imperial hegemony.[24]

The idea that civilization was unmanning men remained a theme in academic and popular culture throughout the twentieth century. After Roosevelt's "bull moose" virility impulse had run its course politically, the rise of the social and behavioral sciences meant that what Roosevelt and others scorned as "sissiness" would come under close professional and psychiatric scrutiny. Concerns among academics and experts about healthy parenting and the proper sex-role identification of children accelerated during the 1930s and 1940s as the Great Depression disrupted gender roles and the nexus between breadwinning and patriarchal identity, and then World War II brought rapid social transformations, including familial dislocation, father-absence, and massive female employment.

The social and economic trends that contributed to the "overcivilization" of men were not necessarily seen as exclusive to the United States. The problem was also cast as part of a broader feminization of the Western world that was said to be the consequence of modernization and women's rising influence in social life. In a 1940 article in *Harpers*, "Softness: Our Inner Threat," writer Roy Helton complained that while modernity in the West had brought unprecedented comfort, ease, and politeness, Westerners now live in a "far less virile world" in which female values and sensibilities have come to shape society and its ideals. Men can scarcely think of anything else except "women and their wants," he groused. Female influence has not been benign; it had weakened Western society in countless ways, Helton decried. "For twenty-five years," he wrote, "the feminine influence on Western life has mounted into dominance over every area of life but that of politics, and even there its power is absolute as to the direction of our purposes." Obviously the recent outbreak of war loomed over Helton's contempt for "inner softness." In fact he blamed the disastrous Munich Pact on the "female pattern" and "female philosophy" that inspired Great Britain's and France's "official appeasements and submissions . . . their lack of defensive aggression . . . their ability to struggle only when locked in the ravisher's arms, and then the complete and abject submission of France." With the onset of the Great Depression in 1930, the "wholly feminine dream of security for our domestic comforts" became Westerners' chief aim. "Security is the woman's wish," he stressed, and "its adoption as a goal by men and nations was the final signal of the turning point in the sex of our democratic civilization."[25] Helton, more explicitly than Schlesinger, expressed his dread that democracy itself had become emasculated.

By the mid-1940s public discussions of manhood and sexuality reflected not only the impact of the war and new global tensions, but also the growing influence of professional and academic psychology. As national defense assumed an unparalleled significance in the nation, the proper psychosexual role adjustment of American male youth became an imperative to some experts and social critics, lest democracy and its military defense be compromised. Many of the tropes and maternal themes that so often find their expression in *The Vital Center*—modernity as a "global change-of-life" that bred an anxious timidity and a retreat into the safe confines of the "womb," the language of engulfment and maturity (the latter the requisite quality of democratic man)—bear striking resemblance to those found within the psychiatric discourse of the 1940s and 1950s. Medical experts and psychiatrists attributed the growing problem of male timidity and immaturity—evidenced by the rising numbers of young men unable to withstand the rigors of war and thus rejected or discharged from the military—to the motherly engulfment they experienced growing up, a phenomenon clinically known as "maternal oversolicitousness." Whereas turn-of-the-century militarists had called for war as a means of masculine regeneration, cold war medical experts called upon parents to change their child-rearing practices in order to cultivate the masculine fiber that would prepare American boys to withstand hardship and fight wars in the first place.[26]

When we turn to the discussion of American manhood in the 1950s, the concerns that were expressed by experts and social critics were not wholly unlike those that had begun to surface in the late nineteenth century. Although the circumstances and lifestyles of middle-class American men had changed in crucial ways, in the mid-century discussion of manhood we see a continuum of themes that had been waxing and waning since the nineteenth century—corporatism and the decline of the self-made man; the effects of affluence and comfort; "civilizing," emasculating women; the power of a sentimental, feminine mass culture; and the excessive influence of women on boys and men. Yet, as old demons were recast and reconfigured in light of postwar economic and social trends, new demons appeared to undermine American manhood, and they could not be readily exorcized by beefing up male physical and constitutional stamina. Indeed, what marks mid-century discussions of American males and their predicament in an age of affluence and cold war is the assumption of psychic discontent and identity loss among middle-class white men. As we will see in chapter three, the ailments that plagued mid-century men, at least as far as they were diagnosed by experts and social critics, paralleled expressions of a wider cultural malaise and anxiety in the 1950s. Although male problems and grievances were configured in different ways and articulated in a variety of forums, some disconnected and some overlapping, they tended to coalesce around a central theme: the passing of the autonomous male self.

The notion of an *autonomous* male self is significant, for what may primarily distinguish mid-twentieth century discussions of American masculinity from those before is a growing awareness of the fragility of the male psyche—a sense that the male self was so malleable and unstable in a mass society that men were increasingly prone to relinquish masculinity altogether. Bederman was reluctant to call the obsession with masculine virility at the turn of the century a crisis because, she stressed, "there is no evidence that most turn-of-the-century men ever lost confidence in the belief that people with male bodies naturally possessed both a man's identity and a man's right to wield power."[27] Of course, the criteria (quantitative and qualitative) by which to adjudge a historical "crisis" is entirely subjective, and it might not be a useful historical designation at all. But Schlesinger's use of the term "crisis" is instructive, for at the very least a crisis of confidence appeared in the discourse of many mid-century experts, psychiatrists, and social critics. And though they did not profess loss of faith in a "male's right to wield power," they did reveal (implicitly or explicitly) nagging doubts that a male body naturally possessed a male identity, to use Bederman's formulation. As mid-century observers scrutinized the male psyche, there was a lurking sense, not explicitly developed but palpable enough, that male identity was to some degree a psychological and a social construct, and as such, pliable, brittle, and easily crushed by the anxiety, anomie, and insecurity that a mass society induced.

These assumptions form the basis of Schlesinger's argument in "The Crisis of American Masculinity." Here the author placed himself above the fray, as an interpreter of the "crisis" he proclaimed. "Today men are more and more conscious of maleness not as fact but as a problem," he wrote. "The ways by which American men affirm their masculinity are uncertain and obscure. There are multiplying signs, indeed, that something has gone badly wrong with the American male's conception of himself." One sign of men's deepening self-doubts and insecurities could be seen, he suggested, in recently published novels in which the male hero appears "increasingly preoccupied with proving his virility to himself." And while the merging of male and female roles and domestic duties within the home had obviously rattled many anxious men to whom demanding women appear as a "conquering army," there is "more impressive evidence," Schlesinger observed, that "this is an age of sexual ambiguity." Here he noted the example of Christine Jorgensen, the first well-known recipient of a sex-change operation, and the rising phenomenon of homosexuality which, he stressed, was "enjoying a cultural boom new in our history."[28]

At the root of this crisis, then, was men's growing anxiety about "whether they can fill the masculine role at all" (doubts which apparently accounted for both the fact of male homosexuality and homosexual anxiety, that is, the male's crippling fear that he *might* be homosexual). When Schlesinger posed the question, "What has unmanned the American man?" familiar themes abound in his answer—industrialization, technology, bureaucracy, economic pressures, anxiety, and anomie. Although he suggested that there was some truth to the idea that the emancipation of women had psychologically unmanned American men, the principal culprit, Schlesinger stressed, was mass society itself. Here again, the compulsion to flee from "the unendurable burden of freedom into the womblike security of the group" (the "group" is the peer group to whom the individual compulsively defers, but it is also a metaphor for a conformist mass society) is the central theme—now invoked to explain the crisis of masculinity. The self, upon which gender distinctions rely, was being undermined by the forces of mass society, Schlesinger warned. The first task for the American male was to "visualize himself as an individual apart from the group." He assumed that the coming of a mass society meant loss of self, which meant loss of gender identity, and while "most of us have not yet quite reached [a] condition of sexual chaos," the implication was that such a state of confusion was fast approaching.[29]

In placing so much emphasis on the *group*, Schlesinger drew upon the insights of the leading critics of mass conformity, but essentially returned to themes he had first articulated in *The Vital Center* ("as organization towers higher and higher above him, man grows in forlornness, impotence and fear"). But unlike the best of the 1950s conformity analysts, David Riesman and William Whyte, who examined the relationship between social forces and institutions (e.g., mass culture, the "organization") and the individual's tendency to conform to that which exists outside the self, Schlesinger saw more ominous forces working to obliterate male identity—an all-consuming *group* that was deviously seductive, its pressure on the individual to obey its dictates manipulative and even "vengeful," its doctrine of togetherness downright "sinister." The dire tone here suggests threats to the male self so subterranean and imperialistic that they seem remarkably totalitarian in nature. Against such sly and malevolent forces stood the besieged and insecure male self of the 1950s.[30]

"The key to the recovery of masculinity lies . . . in the problem of identity. When a person begins to find out *who* he is, he is likely to find out rather soon what sex he is," Schlesinger concluded. Masculinity (which presupposes male heterosexuality here) is thus dependent on something larger: an identity—a stable sense of self. But Schlesinger had insisted all along that identity was elusive, that the inner self was under "assault" in a mass society. Presumably, a male thoroughly lacking in masculinity (a homosexual) would have no sense of identity, or at least an arrested or distorted sense of self—an assumption that was widely accepted in psychiatric circles in the 1950s. Schlesinger never defined masculinity in this article, presumably because there was no way an enlightened liberal such as himself could reasonably affirm the qualities he called upon men to embrace in order to recover their masculinity—individuality, spontaneity, satire, appreciation of art, political activism—as the exclusive province of men. He could offer only a negative definition of masculinity by way of presenting "evidence" that it was in a state of crisis: male self-doubt, immaturity, and anxiety (which could take the form of hypermasculinity), as well as the rising tide of homosexuality. And while Schlesinger mentioned in passing that women, too, might now be a "lost sex" (a reference to the 1947 book, *Modern Woman: The Lost Sex*, which argued that American women were suffering from a debilitating neurosis because so many of them had rejected their "natural" feminine role), he failed to articulate precisely what might be "lost" about women (or found). Assuming that the essential qualities of masculinity and femininity were somehow fixed and understood by readers, Schlesinger evaded the problem of what constituted women's and men's identity, or what distinguished them from each other, by simply posing a rhetorical question: "How can masculinity, femininity, or anything else survive in a homogenized society, which seeks steadily and benignly to eradicate all differences between the individuals who compose it?"[31]

The sense of a growing sexual-identity confusion in American life that infuses Schlesinger's 1958 article, one that was largely absent in earlier discussions of masculine regeneration, helps explain the perception of a "crisis." For Schlesinger and other experts and social critics in the fifties, the male self was no longer a fortified, unified, autonomous entity. Rather, it was dependent, defenseless, impressionable, open to intrusion, prone to yield to the "other." Absent an identity, or at the very least a stable one, the American male is left, finally, unsure of "what sex he is." The heightened sensitivity to the psychological malleability of totalitarian mass man obviously found its way into Schlesinger's assessment of the state of American manhood. But in the end, it was not so much *mass* man but *homosexual* man who loomed over this declaration of a masculinity crisis, just as he loomed over the wider discussion about sexuality and the male self that we will return to in later chapters.

Not Left, Not Right, but a Vital Center

In *The Vital Center*, and more subtly in his 1958 *Esquire* article (which, in anticipation of the next presidential election perhaps, called upon men to embrace a "virile," "hard-hitting" political life as an antidote to emasculation), Schlesinger's depiction of modernity served his effort to present liberalism as redeemer of a "pale and feeble" democracy. Aligning the liberal tradition with the vital center of politics posed semantic difficulties, however. The term "liberal"—always slippery in terms of who could rightly lay claim to it—had crept too far to the left, thanks to liberalism's flirtation with the

Popular Front politics of the 1930s. Distinguishing liberalism from that which existed to the right was also crucial, for it was from here that the challenge to liberalism's legitimacy was increasingly voiced. Struggling to control the ambiguity of the term "liberal," Schlesinger psychologized right and left politics in a way that made the new liberalism correspond to the idea of a vital center in American politics. Whatever else the language of *The Vital Center* may suggest about the sexual contours of the "age of anxiety," the book is a magnificent case study of the way in which gendered dualisms can structure a historical narrative, delineate otherwise fuzzy ideological boundaries for partisan political purposes, and in this case reinvent the liberal by way of an appeal to the sexual anxieties of the time. Gender organizes *The Vital Center*; sexual and bodily metaphors—passions, climaxes, tears, thrusts, gashes, fluids, orgasms, outlets, tissues, wombs—animate its pages. Out of this admixture of eroticized imagery emerges the new virile liberal who rebels against the soft, collectivist-oriented tendencies of the extreme right and left.

The defense of the vital center began with an historical exposé of the "failure of the right," which Schlesinger traced back to the inadequacies of the businessman. The chief problem of conservatives was their plutocratic obsession with profit and their neglect of paternal responsibility. Although capitalism's accomplishments have rested on the businessman's "confidence, intelligence, and ruthlessness," these qualities soon dwindled, Schlesinger claimed. The businessman "rescued society from the feudal warrior, only to hand it over to the accountant. The result was to emasculate the political energies of the ruling class."[32]

To Schlesinger, the failure of the business class to govern well was in one sense a *fait accompli* since the self-interested plutocracy lacks a "family relationship with the nation" and the sense of "*noblesse oblige*" characteristic of aristocratic rule. Schlesinger stressed that "the plutocracy above all dreads violence and change. . . . Incapable of physical combat itself, it develops a legal system which penalizes the use of force and an ethic which glorifies pacifism." That this ruling class lacks "the instinct, will, and capacity to govern" was painfully evident at Munich, he noted. Britain and France developed a plutocratic foreign policy "founded on middle-class cowardice, rationalized in terms of high morality ('peace in our time') and always yielding to threats of violence." The plutocracy "enfeebled" France, "crippled its will to resist and hamstrung its means of resistance," while it left Chamberlain's Britain "impotent" in the face of Hitler.[33]

The discussion of plutocratic weakness (peppered with words like "instinct," "desire," and "will") speaks to the deep imprint that the appeasement of Hitler made Schlesinger's generation. The lesson of Munich hovers over *The Vital Center* and elsewhere in Schlesinger's work. As a historian and a polemicist, Schlesinger tended to see in every social, political, and historical issue the presence of hard/soft oppositions—bold statesmen and timid pretenders, political realists and naive sentimentalists, enlightened patrician leaders and plutocratic, frightened reactionaries. The theme of softness of character is nearly inescapable in his oeuvre; historical and political problems are repeatedly reduced to questions of psychology—to strength, will, instinct, heroism, confidence, and manliness in the face of individual or collective weakness, sentimentality, immaturity, timidity, and impotence. Certainly such dichotomies, whatever the precise language expressing them, have long been a staple of traditional political history. Moreover, their presence here is also indicative of the new scholarly penchant for political psychology. But for a new generation of liberals whose imagination was profoundly shaped by the experience of war and the failure of nerve at Munich, the dangers of individual or collective softness took on extraordinary significance. The themes of timidity and courage, appeasement and confrontation, whether on an institutional or individual level, also inform the fundamental questions of *Why England Slept* (1940) and *Profiles in Courage* (1956), the two published works of John Kennedy (two years behind Schlesinger at Harvard and also a junior officer in the war). Their inescapable presence in Schlesinger's work speaks to how deeply the experience of World War II (and the cold war) shaped the vision of a historian who throughout his career tended to see crises of confidence, failures of nerve, soft sentimentalism, or an absence of heroic leadership at the root of more than a few historical, economic, or political problems.[34]

While the specter of Munich looms large in *The Vital Center*, so does its corrective—an aristocratic masculine ideal that holds honor, culture, breeding, paternalism, knowledge of history, and an appreciation of the martial virtues as the essential attributes of statesmanship. Schlesinger's ideal model of a statesman was Winston Churchill. To Schlesinger, Churchill's "instincts were those of an imperial aristocrat, with power founded . . . on land and tradition." Churchill was "bold, vigorous, somewhat contemptuous of 'trade,' soaked in the continuities of history, schooled to standards and values alien to the plutocracy." He was "not afraid to fight. . . . He saved Britain."[35]

Schlesinger's representation of the history of American conservatism is essentially a story of emasculated new money, one that condemns plutocratic *arrivistes* for their chronic gutlessness. While the Federalists had been men of "robustness" and "tough-mindedness" who did not "shrink from" social conflict, the industrial revolution brought a new "raw class" to power that was "innocent of tradition" and "ignorant of history." They were "*parvenu* traders" who lacked the "sturdiness" and the "culture" of their predecessors; the insurgency of other classes "terrified them." These arrivistes regularly succumbed to fits of "*delirium tremens*" at the prospect of social reform and hid in the "womblike comfort" of tariffs and monopolies. They even took "the guts out of the idea of private property." Like their counterparts in Chamberlain's England, these "enfeebled" American plutocrats lacked the heroic virtues of "tougher breeds" like Churchill. Such a characterization of the "failure of the right" served *The Vital Center*'s political aims, for the conservatives depicted here look much like liberalism's enemies in the late 1940s—the "extreme right-wing" described in the book as "terrified of change, lacking confidence and resolution, subject to spasms of panic and hysteria."[36]

While the flattering depiction of Churchill was directed toward a liberal audience willing to be intellectually disciplined by a "responsible conservatism," Schlesinger's emphasis on class and breeding as the basis of a superior leadership celebrated a patrician ideal of elite manhood. Forged in Anglophilic male boarding schools in the early century, cultivated in Ivy League universities and other sex-segregated eastern institutions, and embraced by patricians like William James and Theodore Roosevelt, elite manhood stressed the virtues of male rites and rituals, athletic competition and the martial arts, self-sacrifice, civic virtue, and paternal social responsibility, all in the name of cultivating a responsible upper-class national leadership.[37] Schlesinger's endorsement of an aristocratic model of manhood helped shore up the manly credentials of a liberalism increasingly attacked by right-wing critics for its privileged and therefore effete eastern establishment origins.

It follows, then, that Schlesinger's model of patrician statesmanship in the U.S. would be that unequivocally masculine president, Theodore Roosevelt. Schlesinger saw in Roosevelt a "great political educator," a reformer with enough "vitality and vulgarity to impose himself on a timid and reluctant political scene." Others could merely write about "the greed and timidity of commercial life," Schlesinger noted, but it took Roosevelt to "invent the 'strenuous' life as the antidote and sell it to the American people." Although Roosevelt had the requisite "juices" that other Republicans lacked, Schlesinger complained that the conservative business community unwisely rejected his leadership, thereby ushering in an era of "political sterility (which presumably ended with the New Deal)." Always yielding to their "passions," driven by their "dark impulses" and "capitalist libido," business interests not only lack the "will" to govern; they sap the energies of the economy, allowing the "dynamism" to go "trickling out" of capitalism.[38]

The narrative of an exhausted, spent conservatism suggests the way in which Schlesinger adopted the pose of the virile reformer that had served Roosevelt so effectively. Roosevelt had endorsed the "strenuous life" not only to promote masculine rebirth, national greatness, and imperial might. He also sought to imbue the Progressive reform movement with a manly mission. Though Schlesinger's style is more metaphorical and erotic than

Roosevelt's raw, undiluted muscularity, the political aims underlying such posturing were essentially the same. Both Roosevelt and Schlesinger spoke an idiom that was actually rather defensive and compensatory in its muscularity, intended to counter the reputation for effeminacy that had hampered upper-class liberal reformers since the nineteenth century.

While the association of reform and feminine morality goes back to the heavily female Abolitionist movement, that association grew in the second half of the nineteenth century in tandem with the rise of reform movements that championed causes from civil service reform to temperance. When the liberal Republican reform movement organized in opposition to the spoils system and the corruption of the Grant administration, Republican party bosses attacked the reformers with rhetoric that helped to shape an enduring stereotype in modern American political culture: the effete liberal reformer—overeducated, cultured and aristocratic in demeanor, detached from the real rough-and-tumble political world, and naively idealistic. The reformers of the 1870s and 1880s were hardly aristocrats, but many of them were moderately well-off men of independent means and vocations who did not rely on politics for their livelihood. Republican Party bosses, angry at the reformers' lack of loyalty to their own party, assailed them in ways that called their manhood into doubt. The reformers were denounced as "namby-pamby, goody-goody gentlemen" who "sip cold tea" and spout the "gush" of ladies' magazines. Their advanced education and refinement was touted as a sign of effeminacy; so too was their "thin veneering of superior purity," since moral purity, after all, belonged to women. Underlying the attacks on the reformers' demeanor was always the sense that the reform impulse itself—what had long been derided as "snivel service reform," for example—was fundamentally feminine. Moreover, as Richard Hofstadter noted, even if the party bosses accepted the reformers' claim to be disinterested or selfless men whose aim was to cleanse politics of corruption and greed, their selflessness could be only understood as a masculine deficiency—proof of the reformers' inexperience in the "real" world of business and politics (which the gentlemen reformers did not directly depend upon for their livelihood), a male sphere not governed, party bosses decried, by feminine standards of morality. At the most fundamental level, selflessness in a man was simply suspect. "In the hard-driving, competitive, ruthless, materialistic world of the Gilded Age," Hofstadter observed, "to be unselfish suggested not purity but a lack of self, a lack of capacity for grappling with reality, a lack of assertion, of masculinity."[39]

The attempt to discredit one's political opponent by associating him with the values and pretensions of effete aristocratic gentlemen had its precedents in early American history, when republican attributes—simplicity, independence, and virtue—were touted as manly, and contrasted with idleness, love of luxury, and self-indulgence—vices that were derided as aristocratic and therefore effete. The Jacksonians, too, used a similar idiom to taint John Quincy Adams with stigma of aristocratic effeminacy. By the last quarter of the nineteenth century, the ideological dynamics of partisan politics (and gender relations) had shifted in ways too complicated to unravel here. By then, however, the rising presence of women in public life and in reform movements, and male reformers' alliance with female reformers, made the accusation of effeminacy less abstract and less purely symbolic than it had been in the past, and more resonant and portending. Thanks to a complex constellation of social changes, the charge of effeminacy could now stand as a general signifier of the gender disorder that modernity (and with it reform movements like female suffrage) seemed to be breeding. It could also stand as a vague yet resounding marker of an individual man's sexual *identity* (as opposed to simply his character or values, or those of the class to which he belonged).[40]

On occasion, Gilded Age politicians used the imagery of "sexual inversion" (the scholarly term for homosexuality and other forms of sexual deviance) to cast their political enemies as sexually suspect. At a time when opponents of female suffrage were predicting that allowing women to vote would forever "unsex" the sexes, such language had particular resonance. When several politicians descended to calling the male liberal reformers sexually tinged names—"man-milliners" (a reference to a man-woman in nineteenth-century parlance), "political hermaphrodites," "the third sex" doomed to "sterility"—they were ostensibly making the point that the reformers' disloyalty to the Republican Party now placed them in an indeterminate (or third) partisan location. But in translating the reformers' political ambiguity into sexual ambiguity, the politicians were appealing to the idea that when men closely associated with domineering female reformers, they not only absorbed a feminine sensibility, but somehow they *became* women themselves. The gender inversion could flow both ways. A common epithet for reformers in the late nineteenth century, especially temperance advocates—"long-haired men and short-haired women"—captures the oft-expressed notion that men would become feminized if they advocated reform, while women would be masculinized if they entered politics. The liberal male reformers, then, personified the loss of sexual polarity that modernity and waning of separate spheres seemed to augur, as well as the introduction of female standards of morality into political life, which the achievement of female suffrage promised to institutionalize forever.[41]

As for Roosevelt, he too regarded the gentlemen reformers as effete men who were, in his words, "wholly unable to grapple with real men in real life." Of course Roosevelt was personally sensitive to such issues. He had been a sickly, asthmatic child and a less than hearty young man, which his famous stint on a ranch in the Old West was intended to correct. And as an educated man of the patrician class, he was also vulnerable to the charge of aristocratic effeminacy. When he first entered politics, his political opponents in the New York press and the legislature mocked his "squeaky voice" and his unmanly, dandified demeanor, calling him "Jane Dandy," "young squirt," and "Punkin Lily." Critics even descended to some gay-baiting (one writer dubbed Roosevelt "our own Oscar Wilde"). Personally and politically, Roosevelt was highly attuned to the politics of manhood, and he realized early in his career that a demonstrably masculine reformer from the patrician class would have to champion the Progressive cause, lest the reform movement remain the province of moralizing women and educated men with their "emasculated milk and water moralities." In the end, Roosevelt's scorn for "parlor reformers" and his cultivation of a reputation as a manly imperialist and a trustbuster ensured that the Progressive tradition would correspond not to Jane Addams or "goody-goody" gentlemen, but to the "Rough Rider" himself.[42]

Just as Roosevelt expressed contempt for "parlor reformers," so Schlesinger heaped scorn on the progressive "wailers" whose femininity had sullied the manly reform tradition that Franklin Roosevelt and the New Dealers had inherited from Theodore Roosevelt. As patricians, as intellectuals, as reformers, cold war liberals had an almost desperate need to prove their militancy in foreign affairs, for it was here that mid-century Democrats were increasingly vulnerable to attack. The imminent fall of China lay in the background of Schlesinger's defense of liberalism, as did right-wing charges of Franklin Roosevelt's "sellout" of the United States at Yalta, Hiss's treachery, and Acheson's "blunders." And since these accumulated failures and betrayals were implied by critics to be the work of an effeminate eastern establishment entrenched in the White House and the State Department, the patrician ideal of manhood would counteract those charges.

In a mid-twentieth century culture that was increasingly struggling with a fear that Americans were growing too soft and self-indulgent next to their hard-driving, self-denying Spartan enemies in the U.S.S.R., Schlesinger could celebrate Roosevelt's cult of the "strenuous life," for it fit perfectly the needs of cold war America. He approvingly quoted Roosevelt:

> I preach to you . . . that our country calls not for the life of ease but for the life of strenuous endeavor. . . . If we seek merely swollen, slothful ease, and ignoble peace, if we shrink from the hard contests where men must win at the hazard of their lives and at the risk of all they hold dear, then the bolder and stronger peoples will pass us by, and will win for themselves the domination of the world.[43]

The imperative to resist an "ignoble peace" conjures up the failure of Munich; the call to confront "hard contests" and "risk" so that "bolder and stronger" people do not win world domination reminds readers of the dangers of softness in the face of a more determined Communist enemy. Kennedy would also eventually adopt the language of the strenuous life—the rhetoric of "vigor," of "confrontation" and "risk," of resisting a life of ease and "not shrinking" from conflicts and responsibilities.

If the right wing in *The Vital Center* embodied a kind of depleted masculine potency, the left-wing progressive never had a sufficient masculinity in the first place. The progressive, otherwise known as the "Doughface" with whom Schlesinger associated fellow travelers and Progressive Party members, is the principal "other" in *The Vital Center*. Any semantic confusion between the "real" liberal and his progressive-Doughface impostor is here resolved by a meditation on the latter's weaknesses. At best, the Doughface is a simpering, ineffectual "wailer"; at worst, he is a deluded accomplice of Stalin; in either case, he is an overemotional, immature, narcissistic, neurotic wreck. The Doughface is, as the pliability of his name suggests, hopelessly and irrevocably feminine, hence "the failure of the left."[44]

In the profile Schlesinger sketched, the Doughface's penchant for ideological abstraction and illusory utopian ideals constitutes an almost willful repression of the "real." Because he cannot face the "cruel complexities of life," he retreats into a fantasy world. His defining quality is his "sentimentality." The USSR still looks to him like an "enlarged Brook Farm community, complete with folk dancing in native costumes, joyous work in the fields, and progressive kindergartens. Nothing in his system has prepared him for Stalin."[45]

One reviewer of *The Vital Center* noted that Schlesinger was flogging a dead horse in his excoriation of the Doughface. The reviewer was right: the progressive left was hardly a force to be reckoned with, and Progressive Party presidential candidate Henry Wallace had been overwhelmingly defeated in the 1948 election. That dead horse, however, had great utility for Schlesinger, for it helped establish the necessary contrasts with which he shaped the new liberal self-image. Unlike the "radical democrat" (the liberal), the progressive is represented as sorely lacking, "endowed" only with "fatal weaknesses," including a "weakness for impotence, because progressivism believes that history will make up for human error," and "a weakness for political myth, since Doughface optimism requires somewhere an act of faith in order to survive the contradictions of history." The progressive is "soft, not hard" because unlike the Communist he "believes himself genuinely concerned with the welfare of individuals," and, unlike the radical democrat, he has "cut himself off" from the pragmatic tradition of men who, "from the Jacksonians to the New Dealers, learned the facts of life through the exercise of power under conditions of accountability."[46]

Invoking the idea that those who claim purity and remove themselves from the dirty business of political life in the name of remaining true to their ideals are therefore deficient in the experience and knowledge (the "facts of life") to speak authoritatively about politics, Schlesinger voiced an old complaint against armchair politicos. Yet it was not enough for Schlesinger to imply that those who lack the experience (or the proper *awe* for men of experience) have forfeited any claim to (or effectively castrated themselves from) the liberal tradition. Nor was it sufficient to suggest that even if the progressive could lay claim to a higher morality, he could do so only because he was an insulated, callow critic of a partisan political world within which he did not have to function thanks to his radical purity. And it was not even enough—as it should have been—to reproach fellow-traveling progressives for the intellectual dishonesty with which they continued to exalt the Bolshevik experiment in the face of mounting evidence of Stalin's crimes and the deterioration of the Soviet Union. Probing the progressive's inner psyche to explain the "failure of the left," *The Vital Center* delivered blow after blow to a Doughface who was hardly a political player at all, and in fact already knocked out cold in the first place.

Schlesinger took the progressive's political convictions as evidence of a particular emotional maladjustment—what postwar thinkers so frequently and indiscriminately called "neurosis." In a word, the progressive has *problems.* For him, politics functions as "an outlet for private grievances and frustrations." Throughout the book, the progressive is cast as a self-indulgent "wailer" who personifies the "self-love which transforms radicalism from an instrument of action into an expression of neurosis." Fearing the exercise of real power and responsibility, the progressive clings to mythologies that give him a feeling of empowerment, hence "the mystique of the proletariat." His attraction to the working class lies partly in "the intellectual's somewhat feminine fascination with the rude and muscular power of the proletariat, partly in the intellectual's desire to compensate for his own sense of alienation by immersing himself in the broad maternal expanse of the masses"; thus Schlesinger's conclusion that "worship of the proletariat becomes a perfect fulfillment for the frustrations of the progressive."[47]

There is much defensiveness and not a little buried self-contempt in Schlesinger's profile of the progressive intellectual, whose "guilt over living pleasantly by his skills instead of unpleasantly by his hands" also accounts for his attraction to working-class politics. Schlesinger presumed the ability to *see through* the left intellectual's worship of proletarian muscle, but what is striking is the absence of self-consciousness about *The Vital Center's* own unconcealed adulation of virility. Here the charge that the progressive's political stances serve as emotional compensation for his deficiencies as a mere intellectual more properly belonged to Schlesinger's critics. In a political milieu that was well on its way to experiencing a sharp bout of anti-intellectualism—the intellectual soon to suffer the indignity of being labeled an "egghead" in the popular press—the muscular rhetoric of a university professor looks like nothing so much as a rearguard action. Not a little incongruous, too, was the liberal's appropriation—*writ large* in *The Vital Center*—of what Christopher Lasch called the "hardboiled" style. The source of that style was, ironically, the unsentimental realist polemics of the old Marxist left, from which liberalism recruited more than a few tough converts.[48]

Of course, the Doughface of the late 1940s depicted in *The Vital Center* was scarcely the old, tough-talking Marxist polemicist of the Sidney Hook variety. Instead, he was a carping wailer cut right out of the Henry Wallace mold, and Schlesinger must have taken some delight in drawing this rather comical psychological portrait of the progressive as a dreamy adolescent. He reminded readers that however noble the progressive's dreams appear, they are "notable for the distortion of facts by desire." *Desire* is the operative word here, for the progressive embodies a frustrated, immature kind of desire: unlike the vital center liberal who has a healthy, mature "appetite for decision and responsibility" and gains "satisfaction" from exercising power, the progressive indulges in self-gratifying symbolic gestures, titillated by the "subtle sensations of a perfect syllogism," enjoying the occasional "emotional orgasm of passing resolutions against Franco." Thus does liberalism become, in the hands of the self-loving Doughface, a "mass expiatory ritual by which the individual relieves himself of responsibility for his government's behavior."[49]

The extraordinary incredulity with which Schlesinger viewed the progressive's political motivations was a reflex of the new liberalism's claim to political realism, one that presumed to understand the unconscious dimension of political behavior. Yet whatever legitimate grievances that could be laid at the door of fellow-traveling progressives in the late 1940s are here reduced to puerile caricatures, and it is not difficult to see how skepticism can turn to ultracynicism, how political analysis can turn to political posturing, for "softness"—the definitive quality of which is to "believe oneself genuinely concerned with the welfare of individuals"—and "neurosis" are never far apart in this view.

The effect of such rhetoric was to open up a new hiatus between modern liberalism and the social welfare tradition to which the former had been inextricably (if sometimes precariously) related since the ascendancy of reform movements in the nineteenth century. In cold war liberal circles, "social concern" became a tired cliché, the pursuit of social justice preachy and passé, a "concern for the welfare of individuals" the quality of the weak-minded and neurotic. And to liberals who returned from the war with an acute sense of their own relevance in the political world—not as mere intellectuals but as hardened men of letters armed with a war-bred realism and contemptuous of anything smacking of sentimentality—to be "socially concerned" implied (as in the Gilded Age) nothing so much as a lack of self, an inability to confront reality, a fear of power, a lack of masculinity.

When Schlesinger spoke of the "sentimentality" that has "softened up the progressive for Communist permeation and conquest," the likely model for such a caricature was once again Wallace, who had opposed Truman's containment doctrine and advocated a U.S. foreign policy that endorsed peaceful negotiation with the Soviets. Schlesinger cast Wallace as a witless dupe, a "well-intentioned, woolly minded, increasingly embittered man made to order for Communist exploitation." With his calls for unilateral disarmament and other fanciful humanitarian aims, Wallace perfectly embodied Schlesinger's caricature of the progressive whose "soft and shallow conception of human nature" blinded him to that which underlies all political behavior: *desire*. "The corruptions of power—the desire to exercise it, the desire to increase it, the desire for prostration before it—had no place in the progressive calculations."[50]

Desire—intractable, unwieldy, all-consuming, mature, immature, normal, perverse—underlies *all* political behavior in *The Vital Center*. Totalitarianism was always the model for Schlesinger, for its success in seducing millions of people was testimony to man's "darker impulses." The obvious case in point is the Communist: while the soft, easy-yielding progressive seems to invite domination and conquest, the bona fide Communist Party member actually longs for it: "America has its quota of lonely and frustrated people, craving social, intellectual, and even sexual fulfillment they cannot obtain in existing society. For these people, party discipline is no obstacle; it is an attraction. The great majority of members in America, as in Europe, *want* to be dominated." Members of totalitarian parties, Schlesinger stressed, "*enjoy* the discipline."[51]

If the central lesson of totalitarianism was how effectively ideology and propaganda mobilized the insecurities and emotions of beleaguered mass man, the former OSS officer responded to the challenge in *kind* (lest democracy continue "paying the price for its cultivation of the peaceful and rational virtues" and its failure to draw upon the "profounder emotional resources"). The most lurid imagery in *The Vital Center* served to mobilize those resources: while totalitarian leaders are cast as "hard" (shrewd realists with no aversion to the use of power or violence), the totalitarian masses appear not simply soft, but downright sexually perverse in their "totalitarian psychosis," in their "desire for prostration before power," in their "ecstasy in submission," in their need for "violent gratification," in their "masochistic delight in accepting correction." "No one should be surprised at the eagerness for personal humiliation," Schlesinger declared, for "the whole thrust of totalitarian indoctrination . . . is to destroy the boundaries of individual personality." Here, quotidian totalitarian man assumes the submissive role in *The Vital Center*, yielding repeatedly to "the thrust of totalitarianism," its "deep and driving faith," its "half-concealed exercises in penetration and manipulation." The concentration camp is "the culmination of dominance and surrender, of sadism and of masochism; it is the climax of the system of tension which keeps totalitarianism taut and triumphant." In case the reader has yet to grasp the point about Communism: it "perverts politics into something secret, sweaty, and furtive, like nothing so much, in the phrase of one wise observer of modern Russia, as homosexuality in a boy's school; many practicing it, but all those caught to be caned by the headmaster."[52] And here we come full circle on Schlesinger's schematic; totalitarianism thus conceived becomes the locus of complete demasculinization and sexual perversity, and exists 180 degrees from the vital center on Schlesinger's revamped political model.

Schlesinger's rhetoric suggests how the liberal imagination contributed to the notion that became commonplace in the 1950s of a nexus between political and sexual subversion. Otherwise normal and manly in a democratic society, politics under Communism becomes deviant. Like homosexual relations, the practice of politics under Communism becomes transgressive; perversely thrilling under the watchful eye of Big Brother; its excitement lies in the threat of punishment and humiliation that the sadist-schoolmaster–party leader takes pleasure in meting out. Musing on the "clandestine psychology" of Communist party members, Schlesinger compared the way Communists can instinctively identify other party members upon casual meeting to the ability of homosexuals to recognize other homosexuals: "by the use of certain phrases, the names of certain friends, by certain enthusiasms and certain silences. It is reminiscent of nothing so much as the famous scene in Proust where the Baron de Charlus and the tailor Jupien suddenly recognize their common corruption."[53] That "common corruption" was homosexuality, a perversity that the Communist shares in his attraction to clandestine life and his feminine fascination with the proletariat.

The association between Communist subversion and homosexuality, as we will see in the next chapter, was more than just metaphorical. What Schlesinger relied on as the basis of his allusions was a common presumption—voiced often enough by anti-Communists who had scarcely read Fromm, Reich, or Proust—that political and sexual unorthodoxy went hand-in-hand. In one variant of this view, the homosexual was assumed to be vulnerable to Communist ideology because he was a weak, neurotic social outcast, alienated from, or hostile to, "normal" society. In another variant put forth in the name of national security, the homosexual who worked in government was said to be vulnerable to Communist subversion because, by definition, he was weak-willed and self-indulgent, and therefore prone to extortion by foreign agents. However configured, moral weakness was the common denominator that typically linked the subversive and the homosexual. In 1950, Republican Senator Kenneth Wherry expressed that connection in the guilt-by-association logic of the time, explaining to the *New York Post* the threat posed by homosexuals working within the federal government: "You can't hardly separate homosexuals from subversives. Mind you, I don't say every homosexual is a subversive, and I don't say every subversive is a homosexual. But a man of low morality is a menace in the government, whatever he is, and they are all tied up together."[54]

Touting the twin threat of sexual and political subversion served the purposes of anti-Communists like Wherry who were determined to show how they could protect national security where others had failed. (Given the shortage of real Communists to be found in government during the McCarthy hysteria, the "menacing" homosexual served as the next best phantom.) In Schlesinger's case, beyond the defensive, manly, heterosexual pose of the anti-Communist liberal, we see how a fascination with the psychology of sexual will and transgression crept into his imagination of Communism, and especially his vision of its extraordinary power to seduce and then transform the individual's psyche. Moreover, in his representation of this seduction, once the individual's surrender of self to the party is complete, the psychological opposition between hard and soft necessarily breaks down, for enjoying the penetration of Communism (taking "ecstasy in submission") transforms the once soft and impotent individual into a hard and potent one, the masochistic individual into the sadistic one, however falsely empowered the latter is in reality. This collapse marks the psychic transformation that is totalitarianism's colossal and sinister triumph: thus formerly soft, "anxious man" is, in Schlesinger's imagination, turned into "a new man, ruthless, determined, extroverted, free from doubts or humility, capable of infallibility, and, on the higher echelons of the party, infallible."[55]

In such a world, liberalism had to redouble its will and strengthen its psychic foundations. Having fashioned a crude caricature of the Doughface, Schlesinger wrote the progressive *out* of the history of the American liberal tradition. Yet disavowing the Doughface tradition left an "activist" liberalism open to the charge of complacency and conservatism. Schlesinger therefore attempted to give the liberal tradition a radical heritage: the terms "liberal" and "liberalism," which appear in the forward of the book, are replaced in the text with the terms "radical democrat" and the "new radicalism."

Modern liberalism here becomes the legacy of a "radical," "pragmatic," "tough-minded" tradition embodied by men like Andrew Jackson, Franklin Roosevelt, and Nathaniel Hawthorne. Their tough-mindedness lay in the skepticism with which they viewed human nature; their radicalism evidenced by the willingness, in the case of Jackson and Roosevelt, to mediate social conflict by using government as a means to enlarge democracy while keeping business interests in check. Against the rising paradigm of consensus historiography, Schlesinger emphasized sharp ideological conflict in the American political tradition; to do otherwise would have left his radical democrats indistinguishable from political competitors. These radical democrats, as representatives of the "humble members of society," had historically engaged in a fight against "business domination." Here was, for Schlesinger, "the consistent motive of American liberalism."[56]

Demonstrating the liberal's eagerness to wield power was crucial in the cold war years. By reducing the issue to fundamental oppositions, Schlesinger made the essential point: "On the one hand are the politicians, the administrators, the doers; on the other, the sentimentalists, the utopians, the wailers." The "doer" has an "appetite for decision and responsibility" and gains his "fulfillment" from exercising power. Garry Wills has spoken of the distinction between one strain of American liberalism, which "feared power and trusted the people," and the cold war liberalism of the Kennedy administration, which thrived not only on a willingness to use power but an enjoyment of it.[57]

The ideological origins of the liberal celebration of power go back to *The Vital Center*. Though Schlesinger struck cautionary notes about corruptions of power and pointed to its dangers and its lure (the "ecstasy of power"), his emphasis on a liberal tradition that has the requisite thirst for power suggests precisely what he thought liberals needed to cultivate. Consider also the language of militant confrontation, tinged with the usual imagery of desire: "the new radicalism derives its power from an acceptance of conflict," "attacking" problems in order to secure "the freedom and fulfillment of the individual. It believes in attack—and out of attack will come passionate intensity."[58]

Schlesinger treated liberalism not as a set of political aims but rather as a state of mind, and by posing the fundamental dilemma of liberalism as a "conflict between doer and wailer, New Dealer and Doughface" ("a conflict within each of us" he added), Schlesinger framed the choice that liberals faced in dualistic psychological terms: "Only recently have we been forced to choose one side or the other," he emphasized, because "the rise of Communism transformed the wailer from a harmless and often beguiling character to a potentially sinister one." The reader's only choice was to relinquish anxiety and join the ranks of the new radicals. "The failure of nerve is over,"

Schlesinger proclaimed. Liberal political leaders have brought "a new virility into public life, a virility compact of humanity and not of ruthlessness." In one proclamation that sums up the problem and the proposed solution, Schlesinger declared portentously: "The campaign against social anxiety has just begun."[59]

That campaign, and the anxiety it sought to relieve, had an extrapolitical meaning. Schlesinger's hyperawareness of the power of totalitarian ideology and the means by which Communism played upon mass man's insecurities guided the way in which he fashioned the politics of the vital center. "We must somehow dissolve the anxieties which drive people in free society to become traitors to freedom," he announced. His solution was to reconstitute ideology at the same time he claimed to renounce it. Believing that he understood the psychology underlying one Communist's proclamation that "'I joined the struggle and I joined men,'" he also presumed that Communism was able to inspire a kind of quasi-religious devotion that secular democracy lacked. Attempting to cultivate an equally emotional devotion to democracy, he sought to imbue the new liberalism with a neo-Christian–tinged purpose that was self-consciously functional: "Our problem," he insisted, "is to make democracy the fighting faith." From one of the "prophets" of the new liberalism, Niebuhr, who throughout his ideological odyssey from liberal to Marxist to cold war liberal promoted a Christian realism that claimed to understand the irrationality and the weaknesses of man, Schlesinger absorbed an awareness of man's deep fears and insecurities, his desire for, as Niebuhr once put it, "confidence in his power over historical destiny."[60] *The Vital Center*'s relentless appeal to masculine self-confidence and virility is testimony to how that awareness of man's emotional vulnerability was here put into the service of a new liberalism.

The placement of liberalism in the "vital center" of American politics and the simultaneous insistence that it was a part of a "radical" tradition was fraught with historical, semantic, and conceptual difficulties. The obvious problem was the artifice in the liberal's claim to radicalism. And if the primary aim was, in the spirit of liberal realism, to reject anything resembling an "extremist" totalitarian reliance on ideology or illusion, what was the refashioning of liberalism as a "fighting faith" based on the "emotional energies and needs of man" but the construction of an ideology itself? In the last pages of the book, Schlesinger awkwardly struggled with the questions his liberalism posed: "The spirit of the new radicalism is the spirit of the center—the spirit of human decency, opposing the extremes of tyranny. Yet, in a more fundamental sense, does not the center itself represent one extreme?"[61]

Despite all the talk of pragmatism in *The Vital Center*, there is little discussion of political policy issues that might define the "vital center" of

American politics in concrete terms. Winston Churchill, Teddy Roosevelt, Andrew Jackson, Franklin Roosevelt, and other heroic statesmen are invoked as leadership models; substantive political issues receive vague attention. If the vital center is a place where non-extremist Democrats and Republicans can meet on the grounds of "human decency," upon what political policy issues might they agree? Truman's leadership is barely mentioned; nor is it clear whether his Fair Deal was in sync with the vital center liberalism that presumed itself heir to New Deal reform. Never well-liked among eastern establishment liberals, Truman—despite his tough-minded anti-Communism (also displayed by his famously hard-nosed Secretary of State, James Byrnes) as well as his efforts to carry on the New Deal agenda— did not apparently impress Schlesinger as embodying the manly patrician ideals of the vital center liberal. It was style that was ultimately at issue here; the "vital center" itself was always an abstraction.

Pitting the heart against the mind, the wailer against the doer, the utopian against the pragmatist, Schlesinger helped fix the terms for the future of liberal discourse. The result was to limit the kind of intellectual complexity, political realism, and deliverance from ideological orthodoxies that Schlesinger insisted were the virtues of the new liberalism. Rhetoric and abstraction substituted for searching social analysis and a real political agenda; ideology was refashioned in the form of a new faith in freedom and an adulation of muscularity; relentless dualisms precluded the kind of complexity of thought that liberals claimed as their special intellectual talent. As the hard/soft dichotomy took on a life of its own in cold war political culture, it became increasingly difficult to escape from the confines of the dichotomy—to condemn the results of the Bolshevik experiment and at the same time retain a meaningful commitment to "the humble members of society" at home; to be critical of the Soviet Union and simultaneously skeptical about the virtues of capitalist democracy in the United States; to denounce global Communist expansion and at the same time question the merits or the efficacy of an aggressive anti-Communist U. S. foreign policy.

Christopher Lasch observed the influence of ex-Marxists such as Niebuhr and Hook in the liberal camp, men who "brought to liberalism the same polemical gifts, the same sense of commitment, and the same intolerance of opposition which they had learned from the Bolsheviks—all of which . . . stood liberalism in good stead." As liberalism absorbed the "hardboiled" polemical style of the fiercely ideological Marxist left, it also absorbed the habit of thinking in overblown, zero-sum terms. In exchanging Communism for liberalism, cold warriors like Hook simply inverted the Marxist myth, exchanging one rival myth of history for another, adopting an exaggerated faith in the virtues of capitalist democracy—the same exaggerated faith that had earlier sustained their enthusiasm for the Communist experiment. Hook may have indeed made "a religion out of the defense of the 'free world,'" but what Lasch neglected to say was that the Marxist mythology was of a higher order and a different species, grounded in teleology largely absent in postwar liberalism. Still, his point remains valid: liberal political discourse grew increasingly artificial and abstract in the 1940s and 1950s. Obsessed with Soviet despotism and fixated on the refutation of Marxism above all else, cold war liberals were blind to an American society whose shortcomings, if they were acknowledged at all, could only be seen in the most dualistic and Manichean of terms. "When the adversary was 'total evil,'" Lasch avowed, "the 'imperfections' of democracy naturally faded from sight."[62]

As for Schlesinger, he absorbed the habit of rhetorical inflation and ideological mythmaking, but fashioned his own abstractions. In resting his entire case for the new liberalism on the debilitating anxiety of modern man—that which liberalism claimed to relieve and in fact vigorously combat—Schlesinger could not admit that the choices confronting mid-twentieth-century liberals were not those of a psychological nature; nor were they choices of allegiance to two rival political systems. The choices facing postwar liberals ultimately involved questions of political aims, strategies, and policies. As the leading liberal ideologue of his generation, Schlesinger could not acknowledge that turning freedom into a "fighting faith"—abstraction of all abstractions—was hardly the response of a pragmatic liberalism prepared to confront the unresolved social, political, and international problems that the nation faced during and after 1949. The troubles and grievances that would fester through the 1950s and implode, to the surprise of liberals, in the following decade—the efficacy or legitimacy of Communist containment efforts around the world, the arms race and covert paramilitary operations abroad, the growing power of an insufficiently restrained domestic and international security apparatus, the stubborn persistence of segregation and white Southern resistance, the dilemma of affluence and suburban flight amid poverty and urban decay—were all problems that, insofar as they might have warranted any attention at all, could be dismissed as preachy "Doughface" preoccupations. Having relinquished the overly sensitive Doughface "within us" and adopted an overblown faith in freedom, liberal realists like Schlesinger were blind to the realities of an America whose defects could hardly be reduced to psychological ailments like "anxiety" and "neurosis."

The emotional attachment to democracy—which Schlesinger claimed was sorely lacking in his bleak world where freedom was experienced as a "torment" and people's lives were "empty of belief"—was in fact alive and well, and fast transmuting itself, in the wider expanse of American life, into a shrill hyperpatriotism. So inflated did the "fullness of faith" in democracy become in the 1950s that the faith itself became part of the problem in American political culture, for it tended to distort the view of the "real" world and cloud festering problems at home and abroad. Speaking of the white southerners' bolt from the Democratic Party, for example, Schlesinger took the poor showing of the States' Rights Party in the 1948 election as evidence that "the South on the whole accepts the objectives of the civil rights program as legitimate, even though it may have serious and intelligible reservations about timing and method."[63] It is perhaps too easy in retrospect to view such an assessment as overly sanguine given the 101 members of Congress who signed the Southern manifesto in 1956 promising resistance to racial integration and the subsequent arrival of the first federal troops to the South since Reconstruction. But indications of white Southern intransigence and opposition were clear enough by 1949; here it is difficult to escape the conclusion that, had Schlesinger relied less on faith and more on the skeptical political realism touted to be the *sine qua non* of the new postwar liberalism, his appraisal of the white South might have been different. Liberal realism—a bulwark against fuzzy ideological thinking—was a contrivance of the cold war imperative to claim a view of the world that was unclouded by the uncontrollable vagaries of emotion and sentiment. Yet even if political realism was reserved primarily for foreign policy issues that garnered a higher priority in the eyes of cold war liberals, Schlesinger's optimistic view of the white South stands as a token of the increasing insulation of liberals from the "reform" issues for which they claimed a singular expertise and commitment. If vital center liberals in the fifties and the early sixties did not anticipate the gravity of the troubles that were germinating beneath the affluent society, neither did they anticipate the problem that would plague liberal foreign policy in the 1960s from the Bay of Pigs to Saigon: the fundamental incompatibility of political realism and an exaggerated faith in freedom, the latter becoming just one more sentimental, overly optimistic, distorting ideology.

As was so often the case with Schlesinger's polemics here and later in his career, his presentation of the nation's primary problems as fundamentally psychological in nature served the campaign to make liberal "heroism" the political remedy for cultural malaise. The persistent subordination of substantive political issues to matters of will, power, and self, and the appeal to the intellectual's need to see himself as manly and sexually willful, in the end gave Schlesinger's brand of liberalism the artificial quality of an identity politics. All of this would become more apparent when he got aboard the Kennedy campaign in the late fifties.

But in 1949—a year that saw Ernest Hemingway's heroic aura featured in *Life* magazine and the publication of Henry Miller's sexually explicit, male bravado–laced novel *Sexus*, a year after the release of Norman Mailer's much acclaimed tale of men at war, *The Naked and the Dead*—the concept of a virile vital center had unusual resonance. It promised that a liberal could be a centrist *and* a radical, a voice of the reasonable center *and* a hard, tough talking rebel at the same time. As if to underscore the virility of the center, the illustration accompanying Schlesinger's article on the "vital center" in the *New York Times Magazine* showed a huge clenched fist with an enormous torch rising above and between masses of frantic people, who were on each side toting banners signifying left and right.[64]

If the new liberalism was all about image and confidence, reviews of the book bear this out, for commentators were invariably struck by the style, the self-confidence, and the professorial tough talk of *The Vital Center*. Gerald Johnson's review in the *New York Times* noted the "energy, bold-ness, and certainty" with which Schlesinger proclaimed a "defiant confession of faith" in the liberalism whose name had become "if not exactly an epi-thet, at best a badge of futility and fatuity." In the *Saturday Review of Lit-erature,* Jonathan Daniels applauded Schlesinger's "brave eloquence," noting that "there is not one word of weakness or fear in the conviction with which Schlesinger faces the second half [of the century]." Henry Steele Commager's assessment of the book in the *New York Herald Tribune* praised "the pen-etration of its analysis, the lucidity of its presentation, the vigor of its argu-ment." The "vigor of [Schlesinger's] attack" likewise impressed the *Christian Science Monitor*, whose reviewer called upon readers to "recognize that Mr. Schlesinger has not given his answers to questions from the ivory tower. He had a previous engagement at the Hustings." Robert Bendiner in the *Nation* commended Schlesinger for his "gusto" and "virtuosity" as well as his "pen-etrating dissection of the alternatives to the 'vital center' in politics." The *Cleveland News* called the book a "battle cry;" the *Washington Star* praised it as "provocative and reassuring," while the *Springfield Republican* hailed its "surefooted sense of direction." Perhaps Jonathan Daniels best grasped the essence of *The Vital Center* when he stressed that "the spirit of the book is confidence. . . . It seemed to me one of those books which may suddenly announce the spirit of a time to itself."[65]

The confidence that impressed reviewers is inseparable from the manly idiom with which Schlesinger shaped the image the anti-Communist lib-eral. Liberal tough-talk was not only a habit of Schlesinger's, though it may have been his singular forte. From the liberal journal *The Reporter*, which boasted an allegiance to "a liberalism without tears," to philosopher and erstwhile Marxist Sidney Hook's call for liberalism to "toughen its fiber," to columnist Joseph Alsop's brash, Anglophilic machismo, to the Truman administration's defensive anti-Communist strut, liberal muscularity in the 1950s found a home in the liberal press and the academy, and, in a more problematic way (as we will see in the next chapter), in Washington. It would be exceedingly difficult, though, to find anything remotely comparable to the representation of liberalism that came from Schlesinger's pen. He was in many ways *sui generis* in his admixture of anti-Communism, Freudianism, existentialism, neo-Christian realism, and Jamesian pragmatism, in his habit of seeing in every single issue the opposition of fundamental "hard" and "soft" principles, and in his perpetual reduction of political issues to questions of psychology. Still, there is something illuminating about *The Vital Center*'s excesses and their appeal, something that speaks to the mood, the anxieties, and even the secret self-contempt of liberal intellectuals in the tense years of the early cold war. In the end, the crisis of American masculinity that Schlesinger proclaimed was never far apart from a crisis of *liberal* masculinity. The fixation on virility was the reflex of a liberalism struggling, in the shadow of the Hiss trial, to atone for its deficiencies and sins in a political culture growing increasingly suspicious of the liberal intellectual.

Schlesinger's effort to recast the liberal as a cold warrior and redeemer of manly virtues did not prevent a centrist Democratic presidential candidate from suffering two defeats in the 1950s; it did not even prevent Schlesinger himself from being attacked as a Communist sympathizer by Joe McCarthy. But *The Vital Center* did succeed in establishing a liberal discourse markedly different from that of the 1930s. In the process, it placed a ban on "soft," utopian thinking, reinvented the liberal's relationship to power, and in the name of liberalism seized the masculine high ground for a tradition too long associated with bleeding hearts, effete intellectuals, and striped-pants diplomats. The result was a liberalism that—save for its tendency to overcompensate for previous failures and lapses—was barely distinguishable from conservatism.

CHAPTER 2

Anti-Communism on the Right
The Politics of Perversion

[Those who call themselves liberals] present America exactly as the Communists want us to see it. And, by doing so, they destroy our faith, our hope and our love; they confuse our minds and hypnotize our wills; they subvert our morale; they soften us up for the easy kill.
—E. Merrill Root (1960)

When Reverend Billy Graham thanked God for the men who, "in the face of public denouncement and ridicule, go loyally on in their work of exposing the pinks, the lavenders, and the reds who have sought refuge beneath the wings of the American eagle," he spoke a language that had become commonplace in the early cold war years. The *pinks* were liberals, those who were close to, and thus tainted by, *red* Communists; the *lavenders* were homosexuals, otherwise known in the parlance of the era as "sex perverts" and linked to the former types by virtue of a shared moral laxity. Graham, who responded to the 1954 Senate condemnation of Senator Joseph McCarthy by comparing the Senate's action to Nero's fiddling while Rome burned, implied that liberals, homosexuals, and Communists posed a threat to American life, and that somehow political, moral, and sexual subversion went hand in hand. Of course, the association of Communism and sexual perversity was not unknown in the liberal imagination, as we have seen. But the idea of a pink, red, and lavender trinity undermining the nation was always more a fantasy of conservative anti-Communists, those whose resolute determination to root out godless Communism from American life involved combating, in Graham's words, the "easy-going compromise and tolerance that we have been taught by pseudo-liberals in almost every area of our life for years."[1]

If the hardboiled anti-Communist liberals of the vital center held "Doughface" progressives in contempt, the hardboiled anti-Communist conservatives of the time held liberals in a contempt that evolved, under the pressure of the cold war, into a political weapon underwritten by fear and paranoia. In the late 1940s and the 1950s, right-wing animus was aimed as much at liberalism as it was at Communism, for one begot the other in the imagination of arch-conservative anti-Communists. Despite the emergence of a strident liberal opposition to Communism as well as the "hard" anti-Communist stance of Harry Truman, James Byrnes, Dean Acheson, George Kennan, George Marshall, and other statesmen working in the Truman administration, Democrats were on the defensive throughout the 1950s, charged by the right wing with a host of deficiencies and offenses often encapsulated in the accusation that they were "soft on Communism." That open-ended phrase, employed indiscriminately and often with a willful disregard for the shades of meaning that the designation "liberal" had acquired since the onset of the cold war, could imply anything from advocacy of an overly "permissive" foreign or domestic policy insufficiently mindful of the Communist menace, to sympathy for the USSR or an appreciation of the virtues of a socialist state, to outright political subversion or espionage. While the ultra-conservative congressmen who fulminated against "soft" liberals may not have been the majority in the Republican party, the weightiness of their accusations, in the tense climate of the early cold war and especially after the onset of the Alger Hiss case, gave them an influence in political life out of proportion to their actual numbers on Capitol Hill. Reverberating in classrooms, pulpits, and American Legion halls, in national, state, and local political organizations, in books, pamphlets, and political journals large and small, the voices of conservative anti-Communism deplored the red menace and the liberals who left America vulnerable to it. The attack on soft liberals was not confined to right-wing Republicans or John Birch Society members. Graham, a Southerner and a registered Democrat, also espoused a conservative anti-Communism which shared the Republican conviction that the Roosevelt and Truman administrations were hopelessly soft on Communism and had in fact sold out America at Yalta and failed Chiang Kai-shek in China.[2]

Whatever the form or context, the accusation of softness always carried with it the insinuation that liberals lacked sufficient masculine toughness to rise to the occasion of the cold war, and were downright feminine in their New Deal political orientation. The epithet "bleeding heart," which gained wide usage in the 1940s and 1950s, epitomizes the feminization of liberalism in the early cold war years. Eleanor Roosevelt had long served as the archetypical do-gooding, fellow-traveling, liberal bleeding heart—"momism" politicized. It was not difficult for right-wing anti-Communists in the 1950s to turn the eastern establishment internationalists working under Democratic administration—men of affluent Ivy league backgrounds, cultured and vaguely aristocratic, cosmopolitan in thought and demeanor and thus suspiciously un-American—into the most sinister, effeminate figures. Cold war tensions inspired an extraordinary amount of rancor in partisan politics and brought to the fore old grievances against liberals, some of them ideological in nature, some of them intertwined with long-festering class antagonisms and "status anxieties"; indeed the right-wing, resentful of the old moneyed eastern establishment elites, exacted a price for nearly twenty years of Republican exile from the White House. The perceived failures of Democratic administrations to protect national security and halt Communist expansion in the world provided the right wing an opportunity for retribution against elite patrician liberals who had supported the New Deal and its insidious, creeping state socialism.[3]

Yet the nature of the invective heaped on liberals and Communists suggests that right-wing anti-Communism also became entangled with anxieties of a different sort. With its masculine bravado and its scorn for feminine attributes, with its language of sexual deviance and perversion, conservative anti-Communism speaks (less metaphorically and more genuinely than Schlesinger's self-conscious, stylish neo-Freudian imagery) to the convergence of anxieties about Communism, liberalism, and sexuality. Certainly the rhetoric that vilified "pinks," "lavenders," and "reds" was strategically and opportunistically employed as a weapon with which to stigmatize political opponents. But that rhetoric relied on (and mobilized) real anxieties about both Communism and sexual disorder in American life.

Given the obsession with national security, it is easy to underestimate the social issues that increasingly preoccupied conservative Americans in the early cold war years. As the liberal intelligentsia in the 1950s fretted about relatively abstract problems such as the erosion of self in a mass society or the "quality" of American culture, and while liberal politicians adopted a centrist politics that lacked the sense of moral purpose and social reform zeal that had stirred liberals in the past, right-wing conservatives in the 1950s were busy working up considerable fervor about a variety of social ills, which together seemed to signal the moral degeneration in America. They deplored the decline of traditional small-town American values, the advent of secularism, juvenile delinquency, sexual immorality, divorce, pornography, crime, apathy, welfare statism, the corrosive effects of commercialism, popular entertainment, and (for the most reactionary of conservatives) racial or ethnic integration. To a degree not seen in the prewar years, conservative Americans were stirred by a dread of internal moral degeneration, one that helped to give meaning and shape to their brand of anti-Communism.

Anti-Communists on the right were fond of saying that moral decay, just as it brought about the fall of Rome, paved the way for the Communist penetration of America. It was the liberal establishment that many conservatives began to hold responsible for the sorry state of American moral life, and thus the "soft" liberal was increasinly accused of moral laxity, an "easygoing" permissiveness (as Graham would have it) that invited a multitude of social evils, among them a creeping sexual immorality. In condemning the liberals who had weakened America and left it vulnerable to Communist infiltration from within and without, many conservatives, using anti-Communism as their vehicle, attacked modern liberalism on *moral* as well as political grounds. "McCarthyism" greatly accelerated the association between liberals and moral laxity, and that association would endure on the right. The repudiation of liberal tolerance and moral relativism would become, with varying degrees of intensity, a defining element of conservative politics for the rest of the century, remerging with renewed strength in the Reagan years.

The anxieties about morality, sexuality, and manhood that surfaced in conservative rhetoric and politics—the subject of the following chapter—had more immediate historical implications, however. Those anxieties helped to propel forward the phenomenon known as McCarthyism, whose demons drew upon heightened fears of sexual as well as political subversion of the nation. Adding to an already tense political atmosphere in early 1950 was the disturbing disclosure that ninety-one homosexuals had recently "resigned" from the State Department, a fact that provided McCarthy and his allies with useful substitutes for real Communist subversives in government service and put liberals and the entire Roosevelt-Truman foreign policy establishment under close scrutiny. The damage done by the McCarthyites' two-pronged red-lavender offensive against the "sissy" liberal establishment was suggested in 1955 by David Riesman and Nathan Glazer, who noted the sad fate of left-wing and liberal intellectuals in their time: those who "came forward during the New Deal and who played so effective a role in the fight against Nazism and in 'prematurely' delineating the nature of the Communist as an enemy, today find themselves without an audience, their tone deprecated, their slogans ineffectual."[4] The sexually charged accusations of softness that surfaced so often in the political culture of the 1950s were not inconsequential in the history of cold war American politics. Those charges helped to relegate liberals to a degree of political isolation and disrepute from which they would not fully recover until 1960.

"Twenty Years of Treason"

The event that would prove so damaging to American liberals and set the stage for the recriminations and suspicions that would plague American politics in the a decade to come was the Alger Hiss case. In 1948, just as some observers were predicting its demise, the House Un-American Activities Committee hit the political jackpot. In his testimony before HUAC, senior *Time* magazine editor and former Communist Whittaker Chambers named Hiss as a Communist party member. Hiss was a respectable liberal who had worked in the Roosevelt administration, and his rank and stature made the accusation singularly explosive. Urbane and sophisticated, Hiss was the perfect embodiment of the eastern establishment liberal of the kind the ultra-right loved to hate. A Harvard Law School graduate and former protégé of Felix Frankfurter, Hiss had clerked for Supreme Court Justice Oliver Wendell Holmes on Frankfurter's recommendation, and had then moved on to an impressive career in government service, first as a New Deal attorney in the Agricultural Adjustment Administration and eventually as a high-ranking official in Roosevelt's State Department. A liberal internationalist, Hiss had also been a delegate at the Yalta conference and had served as Secretary General at the inaugural meeting in San Francisco that established the United Nations. By the time the accusations against him surfaced in 1948, he was the president of the Carnegie Endowment for International Peace, a position to which he had been recruited by John Foster Dulles.[5]

When Hiss responded to Chambers's HUAC testimony by threatening to sue his accuser for slander, an incredulous Chambers opted to raise the stakes and tell all, confessing that both he and Hiss had worked in the Communist underground in the 1930s and had passed classified State Department documents to the Kremlin. Protesting his innocence, Hiss claimed only to have known a man in the 1930s named George Crosley to whom he had once rented a room—the same man who now appeared as Whittaker Chambers to implicate him in espionage. As first-term California congressman and HUAC member Richard Nixon led the effort to "get" Hiss prosecuted, many influential liberals rallied to Hiss's defense, while others, like Arthur Schlesinger Jr., sought to distance liberals from Hiss and the Communism that he had apparently more than flirted with in the 1930s. For anti-Communist liberals, the position one took on Hiss's guilt or innocence became a kind of ideological litmus test that sorted out the realists from the sentimentalists, or the "hards" from the "softs" (as some described the division) within the liberal camp.[6] For many on the right, Hiss's guilt was taken as an indisputable fact—one that proved both the legitimacy of the HUAC mission and the rumors of New Deal "treason" that had circulated for years.

The political impact of the Hiss trial is well known; the case made, compromised, and broke political careers, while Hiss's specter hovered over partisan politics for at least a decade, giving Republicans political ammunition against Democrats and hastening the end of their twenty-year hiatus from the White House. Yet the personal drama of the two principal actors in the case was in many ways paradigmatic for the era that was unfolding. Chambers, who was by 1948 both a devout Catholic and anti-Communist, privately confessed to the FBI that, following his induction into the Communist underground, he began to have homosexual experiences, telling agents that he finally "conquered" his homosexual "affliction" at the same time he broke with the party and conquered his Communist "affliction." Initially reluctant to reveal his sexual past to the FBI, Chambers decided that it was better do so at the onset of the trial, for the damaging information was bound to come out in the courtroom. Chambers confessed all to the FBI, and considerably more than he needed to—the promiscuous life he had secretly led as a "homosexual" and a married man, the parks and hotels he frequented, the compulsion with which he sought male sexual partners—in some kind of cathartic ritual of self-denigration that served to demonstrate both the depravity of his former life as a Communist/homosexual and his repentance for past sins and transgressions.[7]

Although Chambers's confessions to the FBI were confidential, his sexual past became widely known nonetheless. As the Hiss defense team cast about for information with which to damage Chambers's credibility, it accumulated some odd collaborators in the process. Chambers's former comrades provided the Hiss defense with information about Chambers's past sex life, as did "anonymous" sources. On the other side of the ideological divide, Joseph Alsop, influential Washington journalist, cousin of Eleanor Roosevelt, and eastern establishment icon known for his ultra-militant, anti-Communist foreign policy views, tipped off the Hiss defense team to homoerotic themes in a German novel that Chambers had once translated for publication, the narrative of which seemed to mirror Chambers's own "obsession" with Hiss. (That Alsop, himself a closeted gay man whose homosexuality was something of an open secret in his own inner circle, helped to discredit Chambers in this way adds a certain irony to the scenario, though not an altogether unique one in the strange history of cold war politics.) For his part, Hiss believed (or at least advanced privately) the utterly improbable theory that the man who was merely his former boarder had fabricated, over a decade later, the entire tale of their activities in the Communist underground because of his long-simmering resentment of Hiss. The source of that purported resentment was allegedly Chambers's unreciprocated infatuation with Hiss in the 1930s. In short, Chambers's "abnormal" advances to Hiss had been spurned. With the help of a prominent psychiatrist, the Hiss defense lawyers translated this explanation of Chambers's motives for making false charges against Hiss into what they called "a theory of unconscious motivation." Hiss privately called it "fairy vengeance."[8]

While Hiss's lawyers had developed a motive for Chambers's accusations, one that rested on his emotional and sexual instability, they advanced the "unconscious motivation" theory delicately in the courtroom, calling attention to Chambers's odd and excessive affection for, and seeming obsession with, Hiss in the 1930s. A homoerotic poem that Chambers had once written, "Tandaradei," was read aloud during the trial, and Hiss's lawyers brought psychiatrists into the courtroom who testified to Chambers's "psychopathic" personality (in the second trial, this included one reference to his "sexual abnormality"). But Hiss's lawyers were unwilling to push the issue further and make Chambers's homosexuality central to the defense, fearing that such a stunt could backfire in several ways. The FBI had gathered information about Hiss's stepson, Timothy Hobson, who had been previously discharged from the Navy for "psychiatric" reasons, including homosexuality. When the FBI questioned Hobson in the course of its investigation, a "broad hint" was dropped that the reasons for his discharge from the Navy would not be revealed if the Hiss defense did not make an issue out of Chambers's sexual past. In the end, the hint apparently prevented Hobson, a key witness in the Hiss defense, from testifying altogether. According to some accounts of the trial (especially those by Hiss partisans), Hiss's lawyers pleaded with him to let Hobson take the witness stand to refute Chambers's testimony about certain crucial facts at issue in the case. Hiss, however, fearing the consequences for the young man's reputation and well-being, nixed the only defense strategy—outing Chambers directly— that might have won him an acquittal. Hiss and his lawyers also seemed to worry about Hiss's own reputation, since outing Chambers directly could boomerang, causing an association between Chambers's homosexuality and Hiss in the jurors' minds. From the onset of the case, speculations had circulated that Hiss was himself homosexual, rumors whose basis need only have been Hiss's suave, well-coiffed, super-refined, urbane manner—the obscure mark of a gay man in the suspicious culture of the time. In any event, Chambers's sexual past became widely known to trial observers, and certainly Hiss's lawyers gave jurors more than a hint about the dubious character of Chambers, the "moral leper" and author of suspiciously homoerotic poetry.[9]

Underlying the most politically significant of the postwar political trials was a subtext that speaks to the sexually charged climate of anti-Communist cold war politics. Hiss's previous friendship with Chambers/Crosely, a man widely seen as unkempt, imbalanced, fanatical, and by his own confession sexually compromised, as well as Hiss's own explanation of this friendship— perceived by many observers as halted or strangely muted—made more than a few followers of the case wonder if something was missing from the story. While some thought Hiss was shielding his wife Priscilla, speculations also circulated about a previous sexual liaison between Chambers and Hiss, or Chambers and Hobson—something that would explain the inconsistencies in the accounts given by both the defendant and the accuser about their mysterious friendship in the 1930s.[10]

What is significant here is not the truth or falsity of the speculations, but rather the ideological fallout of the case's sexual subplot. Chambers's confessed homosexuality fed the imagination that linked Communism and "sexual perversion" together; his mysterious friendship with Hiss tainted the latter with Chambers's "sordid" past. *Witness*, Chambers's 1952 best-selling autobiography that established his legacy for a large audience, chronicled his metamorphosis from an underground Communist agent into a devoted Catholic, anti-Communist, husband, and family man. Reviewing *Witness*, Schlesinger wrote of the "ugly and vicious stories invented and repeated [about Chambers] by respectable lawyers and college professors which purported to 'explain' everything. . . . The anti-Chambers whispering campaign was one of the most repellent in modern history."[11]

If Chambers could be redeemed thanks to his willingness to renounce Communism and homosexuality, Hiss could never be redeemed, nor could those who came to his defense be forgiven easily. Tried twice after the first trial ended in a hung jury and convicted of perjury in January 1950 (since the statute of limitations precluded conspiracy charges), Alger Hiss became, in the conservative imagination, the embodiment of the weak-willed, effete, and ultimately treacherous eastern establishment liberal, whose "softness" left him prone to transgressions of a political, moral, and perhaps even of a sexual nature.

Of course, the Hiss case appeared to lend credibility to grievances that had been accumulating in right-wing circles since the 1930s. The charge that liberals were soft on Communism had its ideological roots in the idea that the New Deal had betrayed the classical, individualist, free-market liberalism upon which America was founded. Indeed, many conservatives in the 1930s and 1940s found it almost unbearable that the New Dealers had appropriated the term "liberal," for *real* liberals were enemies of statism (hence the repeated references to the "pseudo-liberal" or the "perversion" of liberalism in conservative rhetoric). If modern liberals' enlargement of government and establishment of a welfare state appeared to be the antithesis of classical liberal individualism and in fact smacked of creeping collectivism, their "tolerance" of Communism, evidenced in the "cozy" relationship between liberals and Communists during the Popular Front era, as well as Roosevelt's alleged appeasement of Stalin and "sellout" of United States at Yalta, fed the dubious idea of a nexus between liberalism and Communism. The Hiss case seemed to confirm what the ultra right wing had been saying for years: that the New Deal was fundamentally socialist and un-American, while Hiss's odyssey from New Deal liberal to Soviet spy gave new credence to the belief, as an intelligence officer once told a congressional subcommittee, that "a liberal is only a hop, skip, and a jump away from a Communist. The Communist starts as a liberal."[12]

The two Hiss trials had spanned a year and a half, and by the time Hiss was hauled off to federal prison in January 1950, a series of events—the establishment of the People's Republic of China, the Soviet detonation of an atomic bomb, the arrest of Justice Department official Judith Coplon for espionage, the arrest of KGB agent Klaus Fuchs in Britain (who would implicate the Rosenbergs)—had converged with the Hiss case to create a political climate that allowed Republicans to seize the anti-Communist high ground (the Rosenbergs were arrested in the summer of 1950). When Dean Acheson, Truman's Secretary of State, vowed on the day Hiss was sentenced not to turn his back on Hiss in a gesture of Christian loyalty to his old friend, the pledge was taken by critics as brazen disloyalty to America. Nixon insisted that Acheson must be suffering from "color blindness—a form of pink eye toward the Communist threat in the United States." Conservatives went on the offensive and called for Acheson's head, blaming his leadership for the suspicious blunders and failings that resulted in the Maoist victory in China. In 1950, as the vilification of Acheson as an Anglophilic "pink" accelerated in right-wing circles, his aristocratic pretensions and waxed moustache became fraught with symbolic meaning, his loyalty to Hiss indicative of a larger conspiracy of effete eastern establishment foreign policy elites. The very image of Acheson was capable of provoking extraordinary revulsion in some right-wing circles. About the Secretary of State, Republican Senator Hugh Butler of Nebraska thundered: "I look at that fellow. I watch his smart-aleck manner and his British clothes and that New Dealism, everlasting New Dealism in everything he says and does, and I want to shout, Get out! Get out! You stand for everything that has been wrong in the United States for years."[13]

As the Truman administration came under increasing assault, congressional races grew ugly by late 1950 as Democratic candidates found themselves vulnerable to singularly vicious smear campaigns. Nixon obviously recognized the great utility of his "pink" epithet, employing it to discredit and defeat his Democratic opponent in the California Senate race, incumbent Helen Gahagan Douglas, whom Nixon dubbed "the pink lady." Warning audiences that Douglas was "pink right down to her underwear," Nixon circulated the "pink list"—her congressional voting record which allegedly demonstrated that she followed the Communist Party line.[14] It wasn't the first time Nixon had baited a political opponent in this way, but Nixon's campaign against Douglas (as well as his later tactics against Adlai Stevenson, whom he also smeared as a "pink") speaks to the ease with which conservatives were able to stigmatize Democrats in the aftermath of the Hiss trial as "pink," feminine, suspiciously soft.

McCarthy, to cite the most obvious example, shaped his personal identity and his political mission around a contrast between the privileged, effete Ivy League liberals from the eastern establishment, and the sturdy, self-made, patriotic men—*real* men—from the heartland of America. Several weeks after Hiss was convicted, McCarthy officially began his crusade in Wheeling, West Virginia, where he gave his famous speech to the Republican Women's Club, claiming to have a list of 205 Communists in the federal government. McCarthy insisted that the United States was now in a global "position of impotency" and blamed Communist gains in the world on those "bright young men . . . born with silver spoons in their mouths" who worked in the U.S. State Department, men who had presumably been weakened by lives of ease, privilege, and luxury. To McCarthy, American impotence in the face of global Communist expansion could only be the work of aristocratic, effeminate statesmen, most notably Acheson, that "pompous diplomat in striped pants, with a phony British accent . . . [who] endorsed Communism, high treason, and betrayal of a sacred trust." Here was the same man who was steadfastly loyal to his Harvard classmate, Alger Hiss, and presided over the State Department that had previously betrayed America at Yalta, lost China to the reds, and was now, McCarthy charged, infested with Communists.[15]

McCarthy's rhetoric was relatively tame among the genteel ladies of the Republican Women's club, but it soared to new and rude heights in venues where rancor and vulgarity were less offending. Soon after the Wheeling speech, he began a campaign to impugn the manhood and thus the political legitimacy of Democrats. McCarthy ranted about the "left-wing bleeding hearts," the "pitiful squealing" of "egg-sucking phony liberals," those who held "sacrosanct those Communists and queers" in the State Department who had sold China into "atheistic slavery." Assailing the "dilettante diplomats" who "cringed," "whined," and "whimpered" in the face of Communism, McCarthy vowed to rid the State Department of "the prancing mimics of the Moscow party line." General and former Secretary of State George Marshall was a tool of the Soviets, a "pathetic thing," McCarthy proclaimed. But it was always Acheson who evoked the greatest fury in McCarthy, and he repeatedly called attention to the suspicious femininity of the "Red Dean" of the State Department, the "Dean of Fashion," the man who could only speak out against Communism "with a lace handkerchief, a silk glove, and . . . a Harvard accent." Styling himself "Tail-gunner Joe," McCarthy posed as the antithesis of the "pretty boys" from the East, a real *man's man* who went straight for the "groin," as he boasted, and would "kick the brains out" of his political enemies. The lines were thus drawn, and in a crude version of the choice between being a soft, Doughface wailer or a manly, , anti-Communist doer, a swaggering McCarthy posed his own ultimatum to several reporters: "If you want to be against McCarthy, boys, you've got to be a Communist or a cocksucker."[16]

Even when spared the rude insinuations of a McCarthy, liberals could still be assailed for their lack of masculine toughness in highbrow circles. Conservative intellectuals often emphasized how fundamentally timid liberalism was, philosophically and psychologically. Postwar conservatives, like liberals, had developed a penchant for political psychologizing in the 1950s, and thus the liberal "habit of mind" came under new scrutiny. Richard Weaver, professor of English at the University of Chicago, suggested in the *National Review* what less erudite conservative politicians often implied when he compared the liberal's softness of mind to the hardness and rigidity of more able men. Seeking to expose the "roots of liberal complacency," Weaver suggested that underlying the liberal's wishy-washy denial of the existence of "either-or choices" and rejection of "logical rigor" was a sentimentality born of a weak, timorous psychological disposition: "It is the sentimentality of the new liberal which leaves him incapable of accepting rigid exclusion. And this propensity to moral and intellectual flabbiness leads to an inordinate fear of a certain type of man, of which MacArthur and Taft are good examples. Such men reveal, by the very logic of their expression, that they think in terms of inclusion and exclusion. Their mentality rejects cant, sniveling, and double-talk." Weaver pointed to the liberal's "almost hysterical reaction" to the "man of Plutarchian mold," his outpouring of "supercilious dismissal" when he encounters an "individual of clear mind and strong personality."[17]

Weaver's portrait of the modern liberal shared the rhetorical flavor of Schlesinger's depiction of the frightened, neurotic, intellectually dishonest Doughface who, unlike the tough-minded Jacksons and Roosevelts of the world, rejected hard facts and choices in favor of sentimental fantasies. But Weaver's targets were New Deal liberals and their allies who, having actually held political power, could be held responsible for the lethargic, complacent state of the nation. Like James Burnham and other conservative thinkers, Weaver implied that the modern liberal had weakened the nation and its once strong, self-reliant citizenry. His rhetoric reflects conservative's mounting critique of liberal welfare statism (and the torpor it bred) in the late 1950s. To Weaver, "the complacency of this often financially well-to-do liberal" was rooted in his materialist philosophy and his "idealization of comfort." Having made comfort the primary aim for which society strives (and, presumably, having made government responsible for ensuring that all citizens have access to it), modern liberals, Weaver implied, had encouraged the advent of the soft, self-indulgent, low-achieving, indolent, spiritually and intellectually empty modern individual. Softness, Weaver insisted, was at the core of the liberal's materialist philosophy, which "now shows a definite antagonism toward all strenuous ideals of life," hence the liberal's rejection of "the code of the warrior, of the priest, and even the scholar, [which denies] the self for transcendent ends. . . . The liberal preaches an altruism that is sentimental, and therefore he is hostile to all demands that the individual be something more than his natural, indolent, ease-loving, and complacent self." Yet complacency, Weaver stressed, is the very attribute the liberal denounces in the conservative. "It is not an unknown thing to have the very vices one is denouncing slip up on one from the rear in some pleasing disguise. This the liberal has done by not being truly circumspect, and by giving into certain weaknesses that disqualify him for leadership."[18]

More often than not, however, the attack on "soft" liberals who give in to weaknesses came not from the professoriat but from the oft-noted groundswell of anti-intellectualism in the 1950s, nearly all of which was directed at left-wing or Ivy League liberal intellectuals. In a 1952 article in *Freeman* devoted primarily to demonizing New Deal liberalism and its "lachrymose sentimentality and shriveled academic abstractions," novelist Louis Bromfield responded to the introduction of the term "egghead" into political discourse by offering his own definition of the typical "egghead," which merged intellectuality, femininity, and liberalism into a single ridiculous caricature:

> Egghead: a person of spurious intellectual pretensions, often a professor or the protégé of a professor. Fundamentally superficial. Overemotional and feminine in reactions to any problem. Supercilious and surfeited with conceit and contempt for the experience of more sound and able men. Essentially confused in thought and immersed in a mixture of sentimentality and violent evangelicalism. A doctrinaire supporter of middle European socialism. . . . Subject to the old-fashioned philosophical morality of Nietzsche which frequently leads him into jail or disgrace. A self-conscious prig, so given to examining all sides of a question that he becomes thoroughly addled while remaining always in the same spot. An anemic bleeding heart.[19]

Bromfield welcomed the defeat of Adlai Stevenson, regarding it as a sign of the "remoteness" of the egghead from the masses of ordinary Americans.

The animus that the "egghead" evoked in the 1950s, which reflected and overlapped with the aversion to the eastern intelligentsia inflamed by the Hiss case and McCarthy's crusade, made for a potent brew. By the end of the decade, after the worst excesses of the red scare were over, the ultra-right could still fulminate against left-wing intellectuals as the most menacing of figures in American life. E. Merrill Root, a poet and a scholar himself (professor of English at Wheaton College in Illinois), told the Texas Society Sons of the American Revolution in 1959 that the "greatest danger" confronting the United States was not military attack from outside the nation, but rather "inward cultural subversion" at the hands of liberal intellectuals, those "witless dupes and tools who call themselves 'liberal' in the ironic modern sense of that perverted term." Through their domination of higher education, "avant-garde" liberal professors "soften us spiritually" and "render us impotent." When they criticize the founding fathers and "sentimentalize collectivism and even Communism" in the textbooks they write, they "subvert our faith" in America.[20]

If it seemed to Root that the liberal had "perverted" the original meaning of the term "liberal," this was in part because modern liberalism appeared so hopelessly soft, so obviously contrary to the rugged, manly, hard individualistic values that had once defined the term in its classical sense. Like Schlesinger's Doughface, the liberal was—in much 1950s right-wing rhetoric—feminine in principle, effeminate in embodiment, and emasculating in effect.

Panic on the Potomac

The perversion tropes, the language of weakness and impotence, of inclusion and invasion, and the scorn for effeminacy and timidity that surfaced so often in conservative anti-Communist rhetoric of the 1950s surely speak to anxieties about national defense against an implacable Communist enemy that seemed to threaten the nation from within and without. But that language also had a more specific context. It was born of a political culture that confronted a new demon in American political life: the homosexual. The explicit link between political, moral, and sexual subversion surfaced in national politics a few weeks after McCarthy charged that the State Department was infested with Communists, and a month after Hiss was convicted. On February 28, 1950, members of the Senate Appropriations Committee, after grilling Dean Acheson about security protocol in the State Department, aggressively questioned Undersecretary of State John Peurifoy, who disclosed that the ninety-one employees who had departed from the State Department since 1947 were homosexuals. The result was to unleash what historian John D'Emilio has called the image of the "homosexual menace" in government. That image rested upon the fundamental assumption that homosexuals were by definition morally bankrupt and, as such, politically suspect.[21]

Politicians of both parties expressed alarm at what had long been rumored about the State Department, but never publicly confirmed. Conservatives quickly pounced on the issue to attack the Truman administration. Republican Party national chairman Guy Gabrielson circulated a letter to seven thousand party members claiming that "sexual perverts . . . have infiltrated our Government in recent years" and they were "perhaps as dangerous as the actual Communists." He spoke of the new "homosexual angle" in Washington and implied that party members had a duty to express their outrage, especially since moral "decency" constrained the media from "adequately presenting the facts" to the American public. Republican floor leader Kenneth Wherry (R-Nebraska) called for a full-scale investigation of the matter after the chief of the District of Columbia vice squad, Lieutenant Roy E. Blick, informed a Senate committee that "thousands of sex deviants" prowled around the nation's capital, and a large percentage of them worked for the federal government. Wherry insisted that Blick had "in his possession the names of between 300 and 400 Department of State employees suspected or allegedly homosexuals." Wherry became the most outspoken Republican on the issue of "perverts" and the dangers they posed to national security, declaring that the government "must be cleansed of its alien-minded plotters and moral perverts. Moral rearmament, frankness, and honesty with the people must be restored."[22]

Republicans had already been staking their political fortunes on the issue of national security and denouncing the Truman administration's security lapses and foreign policy failures, as well as its alleged corruption. The Peurifoy revelations provided more ammunition against Democrats. Other Republicans joined in the fray. Senator Styles Bridges of New Hampshire not only attacked the Truman administration for its tolerance of subversives and homosexuals within the federal government, but also implied that the Roosevelt administration had nourished a cabal of pinks, lavenders, and reds within its ranks. In a speech before the Senate entitled "Who is the mastermind in the Department of State?" Bridges demanded to know: "Who put Hiss and Wadleigh [a confessed member of the Communist underground whom Chambers also identified] in our State Department? Who put the 91 homosexuals in our State Department? . . . We must find the master spy, the servant of Russia who moved the puppets—the Hisses, the Wadleighs, and the others—in and out of office in this capital." Bridges called for an investigation that would reach back to the Roosevelt administration and put William Bullitt, the first American ambassador to the USSR, on the stand. Bridges demanded to know who persuaded Roosevelt to recognize the Soviet Union, and who convinced former Soviet ambassador Joseph E. Davies to write *Mission to Moscow*.[23]

Always the opportunist, McCarthy understood the political utility of the scandal, hence his "Communist and queer" epithets. After the Peurifoy disclosure, the image of the homosexual menace became most useful to the Wisconsin senator. When the Tydings Committee convened in March 1950 to investigate McCarthy's charges of Communist infiltration of the State Department, a defensive McCarthy, lacking evidence for his allegations, at one point fell back on the lavender threat. He stressed that some of the individuals he had previously counted as Communists were actually homosexuals, a fact that demonstrated, he told the committee, the "unusual mental aberrations of certain individuals in the department." McCarthy proceeded to quote "one of our top intelligence men in Washington," who believed that "practically every active Communist is twisted mentally or physically in some way." Tipped off with information and names of alleged homosexuals by his allies in the FBI, McCarthy later informed the Tydings Committee that he had evidence of a "convicted homosexual" who had resigned from the State Department in 1948 and now held a "top-salaried, important position" within the Central Intelligence Agency, despite the danger he posed to national security. That official was Carmel Offie, a former member of the diplomatic corps in the Roosevelt administration who had served in the first American embassy in the Soviet Union under Bullitt and eventually found his way to the CIA. Offie, one of the earliest victims of the purge of suspected homosexuals from the federal government, was quickly forced out of the CIA after McCarthy outed him.[24]

While Wherry led the crusade against "sex perverts" in government, the scandal also worked both to legitimize "McCarthyism" and to increase McCarthy's own popular appeal. For many observers, the revelations of the presence of so many homosexuals in the State Department provided a smoking gun. It didn't really matter whether the infiltrators were homosexuals *or* Communists—it was taken as self-evident that homosexuals, like Communists, endangered the security of the nation. The pro-McCarthy *New York Daily News* reported that, of the first 25,000 letters that McCarthy received about his campaign against subversion in the State Department, "a preliminary sampling of the mail shows that only one out of four of the writers is excited about the red infiltration into the higher branches of the government; the other three are expressing their shocked indignation at the evidence of sex depravity." Whether or not these figures are at all accurate is unknown, but *The New York Daily News* certainly did as much as it could to inflame readers about the homosexual menace, repeatedly calling attention to "a State Department infiltrated by sex perverts and Kremlin agents of the Alger Hiss type." *Daily News* columnist John O'Donnell wrote about the scandal at every opportunity, and repeatedly depicted McCarthy as a bold and manly patriot, a "blue-jawed ex-marine" who bravely combated a conspiracy of effete, overeducated traitors and sex perverts in government. When faced with criticism, McCarthy "calmly rolled with the punches [and] picked off his opponents," one of whom was Millard Tydings, who, O'Donnell noted, had "perverted the Senate directions to investigate State Department Reds into a political investigation of . . . McCarthy." Referring to the presence of so many homosexuals in the State Department, O'Donnell wrote that "no situation such as this has ever confronted the Republic. And because it is something new, none of the boys is certain how to handle it. Complete revelation will mean the blasting of reputations which go back to the early days of the New Deal." O'Donnell's comments prompted this letter to the editor from a woman in Long Island:

> The homosexual situation in our State Department is no more shocking than your statement that "they are uncertain what to do about it." Let every American who loves this country get behind McCarthy or any committee which will thoroughly investigate and expose every one of these people by name no matter who or how highly placed they are. Let heads fall where they may. This is no time for compromise. Democrats or Republicans—we must rid our Government of these creatures.[25]

Though Republicans had made the "sex pervert" issue their own weapon with which to discredit past and present Democratic administrations, there was in fact a bipartisan consensus on the necessity of removing homosexuals in government service. In June 1950, a Senate subcommittee headed by Clyde Hoey (D-North Carolina) began its official investigation of "homosexuals and sex perverts" in government.

Nowhere was the image of the "homosexual menace" more clearly delineated than in the report authored by the Hoey subcommittee entitled "Employment of Homosexuals and Other Sex Perverts in Government." The report declared that "those who engage in acts of homosexuality and other perverted activities are unsuitable for employment in the Federal Government." Persons who indulge in such "degraded activity are committing not only illegal and immoral acts, but they also constitute security risks." The operative assumption of the report, bolstered by the testimony of psychiatrists, was that "those who engage in overt acts of perversion lack the emotional stability of normal persons." Because the homosexual's "moral fiber" had supposedly been weakened by sexual gratification, the authors concluded that homosexuals were serious national security risks highly susceptible to extortion by foreign espionage agents.[26]

In charging that "one homosexual can pollute a Government office," the report also implied that homosexuality was a kind of contagious disease that spread through the government and contaminated the entire body politic. The authors noted that the homosexual has a "tendency to gather other perverts about him" because "he feels uncomfortable unless he is with his own kind." Thus does he "attempt to place other homosexuals in Government jobs." According to the report, the other (and perhaps more disturbing) way that a homosexual could corrupt a government office was by spreading his contagion to otherwise heterosexual employees: "These perverts will frequently attempt to entice normal individuals to engage in perverted practices. This is particularly true in the case of young and impressionable people who might come under the influence of a pervert." Moreover, the authors of the report stressed that homosexuals were ever more difficult to identify since their outward appearance did not necessarily correspond to the stereotype of the male homosexual with "feminine mannerisms" or the female homosexual with "masculine characteristics." Because homosexuals now seemed increasingly able to pass as straight, the authors called for more effective methods of detecting homosexuals in government service.[27]

The report established an official rationalization for what was already the consensus in Washington: homosexuals were unfit for government employment. According to the report, blackmailers looking to extort information from a government employee made a "regular practice of preying upon the homosexual." Heterosexual indiscretions had long been considered a means by which foreign agents extorted confidential information from government employees. But homosexual relations were assumed to be far more dangerous because the social taboos against homosexuality were so pronounced. Thus the homosexual, when threatened with exposure of his "perversion" by an agent provocateur, would be more inclined to betray his country rather than endure public exposure of his homosexuality. Moreover, the report stressed the prevailing psychiatric judgment that "indulgence in sexually perverted practices indicates a personality which has failed to reach sexual maturity." Depicting homosexuals as weak-willed, immature, and narcissistic, the authors noted that perverts were "vulnerable to interrogation by a skilled questioner and they seldom refuse to talk about themselves." Implicit in the entire report was the fundamental assumption that the homosexual was more likely to engage in subversion because, by virtue of engaging in homosexual acts, he had already proven himself prone to succumbing to weakness, that is, to perverse desires that a well-adjusted individual would resist. In D'Emilio's words, the report assumed that homosexuals, "immature, unstable, and morally enfeebled by the gratification of their perverted desires . . . lacked the character to resist the blandishments of the spy."[28]

Central to the assumption that homosexuals were extraordinarily vulnerable to blackmail was the stereotype of the male homosexual as slave to his sexual passions. Representative Arthur L. Miller (R-Nebraska) helped to encourage that stereotype. A physician who sponsored legislation to increase penalties for sex crimes and in effect regulate homosexuality in the District of Columbia, Miller proffered his own "medical" opinion on the subject of homosexuality to two reporters from the Hearst-owned *New York Mirror*. His comments were originally part of a speech he gave to the Nebraska State Medical Association, a speech which he entered into the Congressional

Record in May 1950. Congressman Miller drew a connection between class, intellectuality, and homosexuality, insisting that "perversion is found more frequently among the higher levels [of society] where nervousness, unhappiness, and leisure time leads to vices." Miller stressed that while "the homosexual is often a man of considerable intellect and ability," he is driven by organically based, uncontrollable sexual impulses that drive him to satisfy his urges at any cost. In what has to stand as one of the most absurd medical opinions advanced by any physician, Miller warned that "the cycle of these individuals' homosexual desires follow the cycle closely patterned to the menstrual period of women. There may be 3 or 4 days each month that this homosexual's instincts break down and drive the individual into abnormal fields of sexual practice." Yet Miller saw a glimmer of hope for the homosexual: with "large doses of sedatives and other treatments during this sensitive cycle . . . he may escape performing acts of homosexuality." Miller cautioned, however, that we are still "far from a solution" to the problem of sexual maladjustment in government and the military.[29]

Against the backdrop of such egregious misinformation about homosexuality, the "homosexual menace" became entangled with national security concerns. Senator Wherry and Congressman Miller helped to circulate the idea that Stalin had come into possession of Hitler's "master list" of homosexuals around the world who could be enlisted for the purposes of subversion. Miller pointed out in his speech that "the Russians and the Orientals still look upon the practice [of homosexuality] with favor." Lack of any citable cases of homosexual blackmail in American government did not stop Miller from insisting that "espionage agents have found it rather easy to send their homosexuals here and contact their kind in sensitive departments of our government." Nor did it prevent Wherry from calling for new laws to guarantee the "security of seaports and major cities against sabotage through a conspiracy of subversives and moral perverts in Government establishments."[30]

Like conservatives from the Midwest, Republicans on the East Coast spoke out about the "homosexual menace" in government. In a May 1950 speech to the Republican State Committee in New York, Thomas Dewey, governor of New York and Truman's opponent in the 1948 presidential election, "accused the Democratic national administration of tolerating spies, traitors, and sex offenders in the government service," according to the *New York Times.* Some observers saw a smoking gun in the disclosure of large numbers of homosexuals in the State Department. The *Brooklyn Tablet,* the weekly Catholic newspaper with the largest circulation in the nation, applauded McCarthy's efforts to cleanse the government of traitors on the grounds that "the presence of close to a hundred perverts in the State Department—even though Hiss has been forced out and convicted and the perverts fired—justify [*sic*] a complete and thorough search for further evidences of the Communist conspiracy within the departments of our government." The front page editorial called upon readers to write to their congressmen and senators and demand answers. "What are YOU doing about it?" the editorial asked readers. The excitable O'Donnell of the *New York Daily News* considered the problem of homosexuals in the federal government the "primary issue" of the 1950 congressional race. At issue in the campaign was the "truth or falsity of the charge that the foreign policy of the United States, even before World War II, was dominated by an all-powerful, supersecret, inner circle of highly educated, socially high-placed sexual misfits, in the State Department, all easy to blackmail, all susceptible to blandishments by homosexuals in foreign nations."[31]

The tendency to link homosexuality with the State Department of the Roosevelt administration in fact went back to the 1930s and 1940s. The notion of a "supersecret" circle of aristocratic "sexual misfits" undermining U.S. foreign policy was clearly a reference to Sumner Welles, Roosevelt's Undersecretary of State. The Harvard-educated Welles, who was close to the Roosevelt family and came from a similar patrician background, and upon whom Roosevelt relied in matters of foreign policy (to the displeasure of Cordell Hull, Roosevelt's Secretary of State), became suspected of homosexual indiscretions by members of the administration in early 1941. When J. Edgar Hoover's FBI confirmed the validity of the rumors, reporting that Welles had made "lewd" sexual advances to several railway porters and was also observed looking for homosexual partners in parks and public restrooms, Welles's enemies in the administration, Hull and Ambassador Bullitt, urged the president to fire Welles. Roosevelt refused, perhaps heeding pleas from Eleanor Roosevelt on Welles's behalf. But the Undersecretary's opponents pressed the issue, and circulated the idea that Welles's homosexuality made him a "pawn" of the Soviets. After a three-year cover-up of the allegations of homosexuality, the increasing possibility of a congressional investigation into Welles's personal life moved Roosevelt to request his resignation on the eve of the 1944 election. It was not the first time a New Dealer had been the object of such an investigation by the FBI, but Welles was the first high-ranking government official whose career was ruined by one. The sexual allegations against the Undersecretary were well-known in Washington, though not officially acknowledged. The reports on Welles would add to Hoover's ever-growing file of "sex deviates."[32]

The Welles incident had passed quietly in the war years, but it was resurrected in the early 1950s to cast doubt on the Roosevelt and by extension the Truman administration. Combined with tales that had circulated for years about the decadent, libidinous atmosphere of the first U.S. diplomatic mission to Moscow (the tales were not entirely untrue—the embassy in the thirties apparently experienced more than its share of partying and sexual carousing of all forms), the Welles story only added fuel to the notion that Democratic administrations—full of urbane, aristocratic, bohemian, dissolute internationalists—had for decades been infiltrated by sexual and political subversives. Sniffing out sex perverts wherever they could be found, McCarthy, Wherry, Bridges, and their allies, including Senators Pat McCarran, Karl Mundt, and William Jenner, eagerly followed up on leads secretly fed to them by Hoover's FBI and friends in the security division of the State Department. They also followed tips from anonymous letters sent to them which identified certain individuals in government agencies as homosexuals. The onset of the Korean War in June 1950 shifted public attention away from the scandal, but the dismissal of suspected homosexuals continued unabated as the Truman administration sought damage control and a restoration of the reputation of the diplomatic corps before McCarthy and his cronies did any more damage. In addition to the State Department, other federal government agencies, including the Civil Service, the CIA, and the Secret Service, began to investigate and dismiss suspected homosexuals from their ranks.[33] What became known on Capitol Hill as the "purge of the perverts" had begun.

Max Lerner, a journalist of the "vital center" variety, expressed what could be considered a liberal point of view on what he called the "Panic on the Potomac." In a twelve-part series on the scandal in the then-liberal *New York Post*, Lerner attempted to present a cooler, more reasonable assessment of the issue, one that sought to steer clear of "the exploitation of the morbid, the cheap and easy attack on sexual deviants, [and] the sentimental defense of them as an oppressed minority." Lerner denounced the "homosexual panic" in government encouraged by Wherry and others who exploited the issue for their own political purposes. In his lead article, Lerner called readers' attention to the "hunted," the victims: "They are human beings, we must assume: they do get hurt, they lose their jobs, their lives are shattered" by allegations of homosexuality. Of special concern to him was the typical casualty of the purge—the man in the State Department who had no Communist or radical associations, who was doing a good job and lived quietly, and whose only sin was that at some point in his life he "had some kind of homosexual relations." In light of the hysteria that pervaded the discussion of homosexuals in government, Lerner showed unusual sympathy for the accused (especially for the men who had apparently only dabbled in homosexuality). Lerner stressed that the victims of the purges (the "pink-slipped") understood that they had little recourse against such charges. The accused could attempt to win an acquittal, but "they never appeal" because they "would never live down the publicity and the whisperings."[34]

Lerner conceded, however, that the presence of homosexuals in government did pose a national security problem, and like a true liberal he called upon the authority of experts to illuminate it. "The hunting down of job-holders on a mass scale for their private sexual life is something new in Washington. . . . I want to help take the problem [of homosexuality] out of the darkness of rumor, into the open," he wrote, "out of the wild procession of hunters and hunted into the area of fact and science…the problem of homosexuals is primarily one for doctors, psychiatrists, psychoanalysts, social statisticians." Lerner pointed out that anxious and ill-informed government officials made no distinction between casual, harmless homosexuals and compulsive, dangerous ones; nor did they distinguish sensitive posts in the government, where potential blackmail could be considered a legitimate concern, from lesser, nonsensitive posts. Lerner insisted that the government needed disinterested scientists to illuminate the nature of homosexuality and the varying gradations of homosexual proclivities. "*We need to put the whole problem in the hands of the scientists,*" he repeatedly stressed—only then could the innocuous homosexuals be sorted out from the dangerous ones. Most homosexuals, Lerner thought, could control their urges, and thus their sexual proclivities were irrelevant to their ability to function as government officials. But a small percentage, he said, were "compulsive homosexuals" who were in fact security risks. "There are some men whose sex impulses involve them in criminal tendencies. There is no room for the criminal in the government. He is not merely a security risk, but a form of disease in society. The disease must be isolated, and an effort made to cure it."[35]

Lerner's call for scientific expertise fell on deaf ears, for Washington inquisitors had no interest in splitting hairs over who was a homosexual and who was not, who was a true security risk and who was not. Lerner doggedly pursued politicians and government officials in an effort to force them to confront how unreasonable and even pointless such an indiscriminate purge of the federal government actually was. In an interview with Wherry, Lerner asked the senator whether the purge of the State Department could prove endless, given the Kinsey report's statistics on the widespread existence of homosexual behavior among American men. Wherry wasn't interested in Kinsey's statistics, which in any case he highly doubted, nor would he define in concrete terms precisely what constituted a homosexual. "A homosexual is a diseased man, an abnormal man," he replied, summarily dismissing the question. Lerner also pursued State Department officials, Civil Service Commission officials, senators, and FBI officials in an effort to determine whether there were any cases of homosexuals actually being blackmailed by foreign agents, but was not able to track down "a single case." The panic was heightened, Lerner noted, by the oft-told story in Washington of Hitler's "master list" of homosexuals, which Stalin now possessed and was poised to use for the purposes of blackmail and subversion of American officials. Lerner agreed that the Nazis had in fact used people's vices for the purposes of extortion, and the Russians could do the same, but he could find no actual cases supporting the theory that the Russians were using this list to blackmail officials in the U.S. government.[36]

For some observers of the purge, however, there were legitimate reasons other than those involving blackmail and security (strictly speaking) that were grounds for disqualifying a homosexual from employment in the State Department. Lerner summed up this rationale by describing it as "a theory of the relation between virility and the needs of diplomacy in the age of the atom bomb." The theory, he said, was told to him by a "Harvard professor with considerable government experience." According to the unnamed professor, "it takes a virile man . . . to be able to meet Russian diplomacy today. It requires the kind of toughness that an effeminate man simply would not have." Lerner rejected this "he-man theory of government" and cited it as an example of the "militarization of our thought." But it was no doubt a common sentiment in Washington at the time, especially since—in the absence of real cases of homosexual blackmail that anyone could cite—an alternative rationale for the purge was necessary.[37]

Lerner's view of homosexuality, while much more tolerant than that of the Wherrys and the Millers of the time, was in many ways characteristic of the 1950s liberal intelligentsia—an admixture of sympathy, pity, and condescension for the "afflicted," infused with a faith in scientific expertise to solve the "problem." Though Lerner emphasized the gradations in homosexual behavior and continually made distinctions between "compulsive homosexuals" ("police blotter" cases) and innocuous homosexuals (the "random, occasional or even latent kind") who posed no danger as government officials, he spoke in general terms of homosexuality as a pathology, one that with proper psychiatric treatment could be "cured." Lerner's attitude reflected the assumptions of the medical profession in the 1950s, which tended to support the decriminalization of homosexuality *and* to regard homosexuality as a pathology, one rooted not in congenital or biological traits but rather induced by psychological, familial, or social forces (assumptions that made possible the notion of a "cure"). The Washington sex scandal, Lerner wrote, "may prove a healthy development. It has broken the tabu [*sic*] on the discussion of sexual deviations." Lerner agreed with Democratic Senator Lister Hill of Alabama, who had stressed that "we now have the chance for an educational job [*sic*] about sexual deviations and inversion comparable to what the Surgeon General's Office has done on venereal disease." In the last article in the series, Lerner expressed a kind of lesser-of-two-social-evils sentiment, concluding that, "while homosexuals are sick people, the ruthless campaign against them is symptomatic of an even more dangerous sickness in the social atmosphere."[38]

Lerner speculated about the possible implications of the use of sexuality as a political weapon. "When you try to use the twisted sex issue as a weapon for twisted political purposes," he wrote, "there is a danger of a boomerang." He meant that political exploitation of such a prickly issue could eventually bring everyone under scrutiny; no politician was immune. After all, he stressed, if the incidence of male homosexual behavior was as widespread as Kinsey's studies indicated, no group, party, or region of the nation was without its homosexual element.[39]

What Lerner did not say was that there was also a danger of "boomerang" for those who spoke out against the "Panic on the Potomac." Just as few politicians were willing to challenge McCarthy and his brethren on the Communist issue lest the taint of "softness" damage them, even fewer wanted to tangle with the right wing on the issue of perversion in government. Indeed, in the 1950s any politician's seeming "defense" of homosexuals in government service would have been a political kiss of death. Two journalists and well-connected members of the foreign policy establishment, brothers Joseph and Stuart Alsop, did speak out in general terms against what they called the "mental illness" that had overcome Washington. No doubt the right wing's unprincipled attack on the Roosevelt administration and the foreign policy establishment—men of the Alsops' own patrician background, education, and breeding—was especially offensive to the brothers (the sentiment that led Joe Alsop, presumably, to help the Hiss defense team discredit Whittaker Chambers with the taint of homosexuality). In a July 1950 article in the *Saturday Evening Post* ("Why Has Washington Gone Crazy?"), the Alsops spoke of the "miasma of fear" and "creeping neurosis" that was infecting Washington. Nearly everyone seemed to be looking over their shoulder, wondering if their phones were wiretapped and growing ever more distrustful of their government. Two "mental images," the authors noted, explain the national nervous breakdown: the image of the "handsome young man with high cheekbones" in governmental service who stands accused of betraying his government, and the image of "a large, mushroom-shaped cloud." Resentment of traitorous elites spurred by the Hiss case, and general anxieties about nuclear war, underlay the McCarthy phenomenon, the authors implied. But the claim that "the government is now in the hands of perverts and traitors" was baseless, the Alsops insisted. They mocked the ridiculous antics of McCarthy, who could be observed in his office shouting "cryptic instructions" to mysterious allies on the telephone, and in whose anteroom lurked "furtive-looking characters" who might be "suborned State Department men." In another column, Joe Alsop ridiculed Wherry's move to elevate homosexuality to the level of "serious issue" and a "clear and present danger" to national security, calling it "vulgar folly." To a hard-line cold warrior like Alsop, the real danger to national security was not internal but external: Communist expansion in Korea, Vietnam, and elsewhere in the world, the battle against which the McCarthyites only undermined with their self-serving, foolish crusade.[40]

The Alsops' article enraged McCarthy, who responded by gay-baiting Joe Alsop. The senator wrote a letter to the editors of the *Saturday Evening Post*. The letter noted that the Roman Empire had fallen because its leaders became "morally perverted and degenerate." Any intelligence officer knew, McCarthy claimed, that a "moral pervert" was vulnerable to blackmail, and he professed to be incredulous that Wherry's call to remove "perverts" from our government, a "long overdue task," would be considered "vulgar" and "nauseating" to the *Saturday Evening Post*'s editors. In an obvious innuendo aimed at Joe Alsop, McCarthy stressed that "I can understand, of course, why it would be considered 'vulgar' and 'nauseating' by Joe Alsop." McCarthy took another shot at the journalist, noting that "certainly the *Post* knew what it was doing when it hired Joe Alsop to write this article for it" (omitting Stuart Alsop from authorship). Naturally, McCarthy added some old-fashioned red-baiting, insisting that the article was "almost 100 percent in line with the official instructions issued to all Communists and fellow-traveling members of the press and radio by Gus Hall, national secretary of the Communist Party."[41]

Joe Alsop was nearly impervious to red-baiting. ("Not a sparrow fell during the cold war that Joe Alsop did not believe was shot by Moscow's cannon," Leslie Gelb once wrote.) But Alsop *was* vulnerable to gay-baiting, and McCarthy had delivered a low, barely oblique blow. Outside of the official inquisition in government, professional protocol and legal liability typically made explicit charges of sexual impropriety unacceptable or unwise to voice directly; thus innuendo, "code-talk" and rumor-mongering often served as informal tools with which to damage the reputation of an individual. Suggestive, coded language was commonplace; terms like "cookie pusher" and "striped-pants diplomat," for example, had been used for years to denote homosexuals in the diplomatic corps. McCarthy ensured that the "private," innuendo-laden letter to the *Post* was made "public"; indeed he read it into the *Congressional Record*, as if the issues at hand had extraordinary significance. Despite the Alsop brothers' proposals for subsequent anti-McCarthy articles to the *Saturday Evening Post*, its editors didn't publish another piece by the Alsops critical of McCarthy—a testimony, perhaps, to McCarthy's success in bullying the press. Yet the Wisconsin senator ultimately failed to intimidate the Alsops, for the brothers didn't stop criticizing McCarthy and his allies in their syndicated newspaper columns.[42]

McCarthy, however, continued to make political use of the homosexuality issue. When he became chairman of the Permanent Subcommittee on Investigations in 1952, the parent body to the subcommittee that had authored the report on the "Employment of Homosexuals and Other Sex Perverts in Government," he became privy to a considerable amount of information that he and his allies frequently deployed to smear government officials. McCarthy's staff included some figures of unlikely partisanship. Young Robert Kennedy, thanks to his father's intervention, landed his first official job in Washington as general counsel to McCarthy's Subcommittee on Investigations. Kennedy's first task—a dubious beginning to a career that would become the stuff of history—was to examine the influx of homosexuals into the State Department. Kennedy's superior was McCarthy's chief counsel, Roy Cohn, the former assistant U.S. attorney who had helped prosecute the Rosenbergs and remained a closeted gay man until he died of AIDS in 1986.[43]

McCarthy used the findings of the Senate's report on "Employment of Homosexuals and Other Sex Perverts in Government" in his 1952 political manifesto, *McCarthyism: The Fight for America.* He quoted the report extensively in this election-year broadside, highlighting its conclusions that many homosexuals were permitted by the Truman administration to resign for undisclosed reasons and then promptly relocated to other departments of government. McCarthy added that, "in addition to the security question, it should be noted that individuals who are morally weak and perverted and who are representing the State Department in foreign countries certainly detract from the prestige of this nation." McCarthy proceeded to denounce the State Department's conduct of foreign policy, implicating members of the Roosevelt administration, including Hiss and Sumner Welles, in a conspiracy to "sell out" China to the Communists. Much of the broadside was devoted to attacking Acheson, who, McCarthy emphasized, had vouched for Hiss's character in his first trial, facilitated Hiss's rise in government, and secured for Hiss his position of secretary at the Dumbarton Oaks meeting. Obliquely, the broadside implied a conspiratorial connection between elite pinks, lavenders, and reds.[44]

To the ultra-right, the pink-red-lavender trinity was inseparable from its affluent male breeding grounds—the eastern establishment, the Ivy League, and the diplomatic corps. While the image of the State Department liberal internationalist—overeducated and worldly, enfeebled by wealth and refinement, tainted by exposure to suspicious foreign ideas, an appeaser of Communism and quite possibly a red dupe—belongs to McCarthy and his brethren, the image of the suspiciously effeminate "striped-pants diplomat" was not McCarthy's invention. The belief that the State Department's effectiveness and prestige had long been compromised by feckless, feminized diplomats could be heard in many quarters, even before the 1950 "sex scandal" became public news. Schlesinger had made reference in *The Vital Center* to the State Department that "Americans had reasonably regarded as a refuge for effete and conventional men who adored countesses, pushed cookies, and wore handkerchiefs in their sleeves," hailing their replacement by more able and expert men. By the early 1950s, the State Department had become an object of scorn and ridicule, its reputation marred by the image of the "striped-pants" diplomat as well as its perceived security lapses and foreign policy gaffes. While the polite *Saturday Evening Post* ran an article in 1950 entitled "Why Americans Hate the State Department" that spoke in euphemisms about the "cookie pushers" who had made the State Department a "favorite whipping boy" for Americans, the *New Yorker* ran a cartoon the same year that satirized the reputation of the diplomatic corps. The cartoon depicted a former State Department official applying for a new job and assuring his prospective employer that he was fired from State *merely* for "incompetence." Elsewhere, conservative journalists mused that "until the recent purges of the State Department, there was a gag around Washington that you had to speak with a British accent, wear a homburg hat, or have a queer quirk if you wanted to get by the guards at the door."[45]

Others took the reputation of the State Department more seriously. In 1953 Secretary of State John Foster Dulles, responding to "rumors," instructed recently appointed American ambassador to the Soviet Union, Charles Bohlen, to travel on the same plane with his wife to the Soviet Union. After an extraordinarily nasty confirmation battle, such a gesture would presumably quell lingering doubts that Bohlen was anything but a "normal" family man. The Harvard-educated Bohlen had worked in the Roosevelt and Truman State Departments, had served in the much-maligned first American embassy in Moscow in 1934–35 under Ambassador William Bullitt, and had been a member of the Yalta delegation, a résumé that rendered him positively diabolical in the eyes of the right wing—a symbol of the elite liberal softness and decadence that the State Department had come to represent. Worse still, Bohlen refused to accede to demands that he repudiate the ill-conceived policy of "appeasement" at Yalta. Bohlen's vast experience in Soviet diplomacy had earned him Eisenhower's nomination, but the president was then unaware of his nominee's skeletons, since Bohlen had never undergone a full loyalty-security investigation. In the end, Bohlen's confirmation was viciously fought—through the usual smear and innuendo—by McCarthy and his cronies, who exploited rumors about Bohlen and the results of the FBI security-clearance inquiry into his private life, which alleged that he associated with sexual perverts.[46]

The allegations leveled against Bohlen seriously damaged his reputation and came close to destroying his career. Others in government service accused of homosexual indiscretion, including Bohlen's own brother-in-law, were not so fortunate. Unlike Bohlen, who had the support of Eisenhower and whose bitter confirmation process played out a mounting tension between the McCarthyites and the Eisenhower administration, the vast majority of governmental officials suspected of homosexuality were unable to salvage their careers. As Robert Dean's impressive research into the internal machinery of the sex inquisition has shown, its victims were either dismissed or forced to resign from their positions, typically after humiliating investigations into their private lives that could be initiated on as little grounds as an anonymous letter, a report of a suspiciously "effeminate" voice or demeanor, gossip and hearsay, or simple guilt by association (i.e., with a known homosexual). Personal grudges, age-old feuds, or professional rivalries could motivate such accusations, while the accused had few rights traditionally associated with due process. The sex inquisition mirrored the Communist inquisition in its form and methods.[47]

The purge of homosexuals from government accelerated under the Eisenhower administration. Eisenhower revised Truman's loyalty program to include "sexual perversion" as grounds for disqualification or dismissal from all federal jobs, while Dulles and his subordinates policed the State Department aggressively, lest Dulles suffer the fate of his predecessor at State. The purge, the intensity of which was driven by the assumption of a closely knit homosexual "cell" within the State Department, eventually brought down several high-ranking men in the diplomatic corps, including Charles W. Thayer (Bohlen's brother-in-law), former director of the Voice of America who had previously served, along with George Kennan, Bohlen, and Carmel Offie in Bullitt's Moscow embassy in 1934–35. Thayer was also accused by informers of harboring Communist sympathies (allegedly cultivated during his wartime liaison with Tito's partisans as an OSS officer in Yugoslavia), thus encouraging the idea of a secret international network of reds and lavenders with allied cells in the State Department. Another prominent member of the Foreign Service whose career was ruined by charges of homosexuality was Sam Reber, Deputy High Commissioner of Germany and, like Bohlen and Thayer, a product of the eastern establishment. Yet hundreds of lesser-known employees in the State Department—from attachés to clerks to ambassadors—were forced out of government service on the grounds of suspect sexual orientation in the late 1940s and the 1950s. The "lavender purge" of the State Department, combined with the "red" purge of those with suspect political affiliations—including "China hands" John Paton Davies, John Stewart Service, and John Carter Vincent—demoralized the State Department, depleted the Asian and Eastern European divisions of some of its ablest officers, and did incalculable personal harm to its victims, several of whom committed suicide.[48]

As D'Emilio and Dean's research has suggested, more federal government employees were dismissed as security risks in the "McCarthy era" on the grounds of sexual deviance than were dismissed on all other grounds, such as Communist sympathies, suspicious affiliations, or generic misconduct (e.g., alcoholism) of a compromising nature. They were overwhelmingly but not exclusively men. According to Dean, more than 400 suspected homosexuals were dismissed from the State Department under the Truman administration between January 1947 and January 1953, a number nearly double the number of individuals dismissed as security risks for all other reasons. Such statistics likely underestimate the number of victims of the purge, since many employees "quietly" resigned for undisclosed or contrived reasons. Hundreds more were fired or forced to resign under the Eisenhower administration, whose new loyalty-security guidelines resulted in the dismissal of homosexuals from government service at a rate of forty per month in their first sixteen months of implementation. Moreover, the purge of homosexuals extended to many other federal government agencies, and the armed services dismissed homosexuals with a new urgency. Discharges from the military on the grounds of homosexuality had averaged slightly more than 1,000 per year in the late 1940s, but by the early 1950s dismissals for homosexuality averaged 2,000 per year and by the early 1960s had risen by another 50 percent. Finally, the federal government's example encouraged state and municipal governments to dismiss suspected homosexuals through loyalty-security investigations, gave tacit permission to federal agencies like the FBI to gather information on suspected sex deviants, and gave local police forces free rein to harass gays and lesbians in their communities.[49]

The principal rationale for the purge—the security risk posed by homosexuals in government—appears to have been something of a lavender herring. No cases of genuine "homosexual blackmail" of government officials by foreign agents were uncovered (or have been uncovered by historians). The only example that the Hoey subcommittee could cite as justification for the purge was an incident in 1913 involving an Austrian intelligence officer who betrayed the Habsburgs after he was blackmailed by agents of the Russian czar, who threatened to expose his homosexuality. Another tale circulated in Washington concerning the Prince Eulenburg affair in early twentieth century Imperial Germany, which involved a secret cell of aristocratic homosexuals who had formed a "state within the state" under the kaiser's nose.[50] Unless genuine cases of homosexual blackmail of American government officials were hushed up to avoid the exposure of embarrassing lapses in national security protocol, none were ever touted as proof of the legitimacy of the purge.

In one known case of an American civilian who was the victim of a homosexual extortion plot by Soviet agents during the cold war, the denouement did not play out the scenario that government officials would have predicted. In 1957, Joe Alsop took a trip to the Soviet Union and found himself the target of a set-up by NKVD agents, who rigged his hotel room and photographed him in a sex act with a young Soviet agent provocateur. When the NKVD demanded that Alsop become a Soviet agent or endure the humiliation of the photographs being made public, the steadfast anti-Communist journalist treated the Soviet agents with contempt, mocking their plan and telling them that he refused to be blackmailed. But Alsop was deeply shaken by the incident, and ashamed that he had allowed himself to fall prey to an extortion attempt. He sought the advice of Ambassador Bohlen, who advised Alsop to leave the U.S.S.R. immediately and make a full disclosure of the extortion attempt to the CIA. Alsop was later debriefed by the agency, and in what was professed to be routine counterintelligence protocol, the agency forwarded a report of the incident, and an accompanying history of Alsop's self-confessed sex life, to Hoover's FBI (the scrupulous director already had a file on Alsop with incriminating information on the journalist's private life). The Moscow incident, which caused Alsop immense pain and humiliation, did not die there. Alsop had been a vocal critic of the Eisenhower administration's military defense cost-cutting, and, as his FBI file indicated, a critic of the bureau itself. Hoover wasted no time relaying the news of the sex-extortion attempt to Alsop's enemies in the White House. News soon spread through the administration and to one member of the press that Alsop was a confessed "fairy." If the desire was not simply to exact revenge on Alsop but to intimidate him, such subterfuge wasn't successful, for the journalist continued to be a critic of the administration, harping on an alleged missile gap and other failings in Eisenhower's timid foreign policy. The extortion incident continued to haunt Alsop for the rest of his life, even fifteen years later when the photographs mysteriously reappeared in circulation and reached the desks of several prominent members of the press.[51]

While Alsop's Groton–Yale pedigree, Anglophilic leanings, and less than closeted homosexuality made him a fitting symbol of the eastern establishment in the eyes of men like McCarthy, his blustering anti-communism might have made him a singularly satisfying challenge for the Soviets. Throughout his career, Joe Alsop remained an unreconstructed hawk who waged his own cold war with his typewriter. A grossly exaggerated estimation of Soviet military capabilities led him to espouse several reckless positions, including the idea of launching a preemptive nuclear air-strike against the U.S.S.R. The double life that this consummate cold warrior led for so many years, the skirmish with McCarthy, the extortion attempt in Moscow and its political fall-out at home, captures on multiple levels the ironies, the inanities, and the political opportunism underlying the entire panic about homosexuality in government.

Ironically, Alsop's enemies at home, nourishing grudges and exploiting the incident for their own purposes, were able to make more effective use of his homosexuality than were the Soviets. The Alsop incident also demonstrated how the national security state machinery and Hoover's FBI could vindictively turn on an American—even a hard-line cold warrior like Alsop—for reasons that had nothing to do with the protection of national security. But perhaps the larger significance of the incident, which evidently escaped the notice of government officials, was that Alsop had proven the conventional wisdom of the national security state wrong; his actions contradicted the image of the enfeebled homosexual who would sooner become a traitor to his country than suffer public exposure of his homosexuality.

While the federal government's purge of politically and sexually suspect "security risks" from its ranks and the phenomenon known as McCarthyism were distinct (yet overlapping) manifestations of anti-Communism, it was the radical right that pushed the political/sexual inquisition to its limits, mobilizing fear and paranoia in the American public with allegations of "twenty years of treason" and baseless accusations and smears against individuals in government. Fears of homosexuality and sexual disorder were not at the root of anti-Communism or McCarthyism. But neither can such fears be disentangled from the constellation of troubling social changes and tensions that made Americans feel so vulnerable to Communist subversion at home, and therefore made them tolerant of the excesses of anti-Communism, or sympathetic to the McCarthyites' crusade. In exploiting and shaping Americans' fears and longings for an older, simpler, unspoiled America—before the arrival of internationalism, New Deal statism, commercialism, secularism, and urban cosmopolitan values had infected it— McCarthy and his allies promoted an anti-Communism that served as an ideological buffer against the evils of modernity. "Elite" liberals came to embody those evils, among them sexual immorality.[52]

Richard Hofstadter made the point many years ago that McCarthyism reflected a broader, longstanding "revolt against modernity," though he confined that revolt largely to McCarthy's base in the heartland of the nation and did not recognize its moral/sexual dimension. The dangers of moral leniency and the "drift toward sex anarchy" in American life were expressed often in the 1950s, and not just by folks from America's heartland. The sense of moral decline often intersected with anti-Communism, both in its virulent (McCarthyite) form and its more moderate manifestations. Moral disorder bred political disorder. When Pitirim Sorokin, the founding chairman of the Harvard sociology department, warned in a 1956 book that "fertile soil for the development of social and political anarchy is provided by our incipient sex anarchy, which breeds a cynical transgression of all moral and social imperatives," he voiced from the ivory tower a concern that was shared by many conservative moralists at the time.[53]

Pinks, Lavenders, and Reds

The obsession with political and sexual subversion did not, strictly speaking, reflect cold war national security imperatives only—that is, the possible blackmail of homosexual government officials who could be *forced* through extortion to aid the Communist cause. On occasion, a more direct association between Communist subversion and sexual disorder was made in anti-Communist rhetoric.

Weak, lonely, maladjusted, alienated, neurotic conformists lacking a sense of self: the typical psychological profile of the Communist recruit that emerged in academic and popular discourse contained a virtual catalogue of the same psychic ailments that were so often said to plague ordinary Americans in the 1950s. That these ailments appeared *writ large* in the shadowy figure of the Communist made them all the more disturbing. And not always, but often enough, lurking somewhere in the Communist's (or fellow-traveler's) attraction to proletarian politics was also the individual's misguided sexuality, another preoccupation of the mid-century psychiatric profession. The link between political and sexual subversion, therefore, could also rest on the assumption that Communism, as an ideology and a way of life, somehow appealed to maladjusted individuals' psychosexual weaknesses, frustrations, and perversities, even offering an enticing life of freedom from—or rebellion against—bourgeois sexual constraints.

Nowhere was the link between Communism and sex deviance more explicit that in the myths that sometimes circulated in right-wing circles that envisioned a homosexual-Communist conspiracy. R. G. Waldeck, a political writer, novelist, and self-proclaimed expert on homosexual-political intrigue in world history, described the nature of that link in an article that appeared in a weekly Washington publication, *Human Events*, entitled "Homosexual International." The author claimed that the homosexual threat was increasingly worldwide in scope, and that homosexuals were joining forces with the Communist movement in the U.S. and elsewhere. Waldeck's obscure article would be rather unremarkable had it not circulated on Capitol Hill. In May 1952, after the Truman administration announced that it had removed another 119 homosexuals from the State Department in the previous year and the "purge of the perverts" issue was renewed, Representative Katherine St. George (R-New York) read the article into the *Congressional Record*. St. George introduced Waldeck's article by stating that "the dangers to our own country and our whole political structure from this kind of international ring is [*sic*] dangerous in the extreme and not to be dismissed lightly." Waldeck's article warned that the problem facing the government was not simply sexually compromised blackmail-prone government officials: "Members of one conspiracy are prone to join another conspiracy." In other words, since (by definition) homosexuals are "enemies of society," they naturally become "enemies of capitalism," Waldeck claimed. "Without being necessarily Marxist they serve the ends of the Communist International in the name of their rebellion against the prejudices, standards, ideals of the 'bourgeois' world."[54]

Waldeck offered no current evidence of an international homosexual-Communist conspiracy and relied on myths about Communist sexual freedom as well as her own vivid imagination. She claimed that "the alliance between the homosexual International and the Communist International started at the dawn of the Pink Decade. It was then that the homosexual aristocracy—writer, poets, painters, and such—discovered Marxism." "Why did this bleak doctrine charm people who up to now had posed as decadent aesthetes?" she asked. In addition to the usual reasons that typically explained intellectuals' attraction to Communism, Waldeck stressed the particular emotional and sexual vulnerabilities of sexual deviants: the homosexuals' need to purge themselves of "guilt concerning their forbidden desires" by altruistically participating in a worker's liberation movement. But homosexuals also joined the Communist movement, she noted, for self-serving reasons: to get "closer to their proletarian ephebes." Also attractive to homosexuals was the clandestine nature of underground Communist rituals, which fed the homosexual's need for secret, perverse thrills. Ultimately for Waldeck, it was the realization of a "classless society where everyone would be free" that appealed to the homosexual's "need for freedom from bourgeois constraint."[55]

The idea that Communism promoted free love or sexual immorality went back to the early days of the Bolshevik revolution, when tales began to circulate about the new Communist regime's aim to abolish marriage and the family. In 1956, Russian émigré sociologist Pitirim Sorokin explained that the Soviets, after the 1917 revolution, sought to "eliminate 'capitalistic' monogamy and to establish complete sexual freedom as a cornerstone of the Communist economic and social regime." Such statements exaggerated the nature of the Bolshevik's new socialist policies: marriage was made a civil institution, but it was hardly abolished; gender equality was promoted with new policies such as state-sponsored child-care, but the family was scarcely abolished; divorce was made easy, as was state-funded abortion, but this was not "free love," which was a matter of individual choice. If the Soviet government in the early years was in fact relatively permissive on matters of sex and homosexuality, things changed when Stalin later declared the Soviet Union's allegiance to monogamy and the family and repudiated the policy of tolerance toward homosexuals. In fact, he began to persecute them viciously in the 1930s. Yet tales of Soviet free love continued to circulate in the 1950s, despite the fact (as Sorokin pointed out) that mid-century Soviet society was rather starchy and conservative in its attitude toward sex and marriage. Had Waldeck or St. George read Arthur Koestler's recollections of the strict "bourgeois" morality and behavior expected of Communist Party members, they might have recognized how dubious was the notion that Communism promised "freedom from bourgeois constraint" in matters of sexuality.[56]

Waldeck's notion of an international homosexual-Communist alliance that threatened American national security may have been extreme even for the time, but it was not that much more far-fetched than the theories that emerged in national security circles that linked men like Charles Thayer to secret international cells of lavender-red conspirators. Waldeck's tendency, however, to blame "liberal laxity" for both the homosexual infiltration of the State Department and what she called more generally the "homosexual invasion of American life" was not so atypical among conservative anti-Communists. For what Waldeck really seemed to deplore was the "pseudo-liberal" attitude of "tolerance'" toward the "homosexual invasion." Waldeck called on Americans to "combat the 'love-and-let-love' line which, peddled by the pseudo-liberal fringe, claims that sexual perversion does not prevent a man from functioning normally in all other contexts, and it was just like Senator McCarthy to 'persecute' the poor dears in the State Department. This line is fatal in that it lulls society into a false sense of security."[57]

The McCarthyites' self-serving deployment of the homosexuality issue and their move to collapse the threat of Communism and homosexuality in the public mind was seemingly obvious to critics who were paying attention, even if the use of sexuality as a political weapon against liberals was rarely publicly commented upon or criticized. But in their 1955 essay, "The Intellectuals and the Discontented Classes," Nathan Glazer and David Riesman discussed its obvious political utility to the right. They recognized the power of the rhetoric used against eastern-bred, ultra-educated men of the Democratic administrations who, the authors stressed, had ironically ascended to the top of the list of groups despised by the radical right: "How powerful," the authors asked rhetorically, "is the political consequence of combining the image of the homosexual with the image of the intellectual—the State Department cooky-pusher Harvard-trained sissy thus becomes the focus of social hatred and the Jew becomes merely one variant of the intellectual sissy—actually less important than the eastern-educated snob!" Riesman and Glazer saw the sexually tinged charges against over-educated "sissy" liberals as the product of the radical right's status anxieties and resentments. They also viewed those charges as both a reflex and an exploitation of the growing fear of homosexuality in American life. The authors pointed out that "the sexual emancipation which has made the Negro less of a feared and admired symbol of potency has presented men with a much more difficult problem: the fear of homosexuality. Indeed, homosexuality becomes a much more feared enemy than the Negro."[58]

What political scientist Michael Rogin has more recently called "political demonology" has a long and complex history in American political life; sexual fear and fantasy have often underlain the demonization of those imagined as threats to order and civility in America—from "licentious" Catholics to Indian "cannibals" to black male "rapists." As Rogin theorized, in the counter-subversive imagination, the subversive signifies disorder, a loss of restraint, boundary invasion; his attributes are wildly exaggerated, his power magnified, and thus he is transmuted into an alien, hideous, monstrous figure—a reflexive caricature of the counter-subversive's own buried anxieties and obsessions. According to Rogin, the demonization of political enemies serves strategic propaganda aims, but it also permits the counter-subversive imagination to indulge in thoughts and fantasies forbidden by the culture.[59]

Riesman and Glazer were right to suggest a historical parallel between the fear of the homosexual male and the black male—both were perceived threats to the social and sexual order, and both were "demonized" in the manner that Rogin suggests. During and after Reconstruction, the black male was transformed by white Southerners into a figure of frightening sexual potency—a rapist and a threat to white womanhood. Such an image was part and parcel of the effort to enforce racial segregation and maintain economic exploitation of African Americans through terror and violence, but it also reflected white Southerners' fear and loathing of the breakdown of racial barriers that had previously (under slavery) precluded open (acknowledged) miscegenation. In contrast, the image of the homosexual as an oversexed, insatiable, preying sex-deviant in the early cold war years served efforts to uphold sexual and gender conformity in the nation, and reflected growing anxieties about a disintegration of sexual boundaries in a rapidly changing nation. And like the black male who was figured as a sexual predator, at once repulsive and irresistible, the homosexual was imagined as a predatory sex-deviant whose perverted practices were simultaneously appalling and seductive, so much the latter that his sexual contagion was dangerously easy to spread to otherwise "normal" individuals.[60]

Fears of homosexuality and sexual deviance were not new in American life; what *was* new was the perception that male homosexuality was dramatically on the rise. Riesman and Glazer, in attempting to explain the unparalleled political exploitation of homosexuality in their time, speculated that "homosexuality is itself spreading, or news of it is spreading, so that people are presented with an issue which formerly was kept under cover." Other social critics, medical authorities, and opinion makers were more unambiguously confident of its statistical rise. Psychiatrist and popular author Abram Kardiner spoke in 1954 of the enomous rise in male homosexuality in America, noting a 100 percent increase in homosexuality over the previous thirteen years and dating the onset of the increase to U.S. entry into World War II. While the first Kinsey report in 1948 (unintentionally) did much to encourage the idea of a growing incidence of male homosexuality in American life, the Washington sex scandal also played a significant role in bringing the issue to the attention of the public. A 1950 article in *Coronet* magazine noted that the congressional investigation into homosexuals in government had brought the formerly unspeakable topic of homosexuality into the national headlines. It was now time to break the "longstanding taboo" against talking about the problem, the author declared. Americans are unaware of the magnitude of the danger: "homosexuality is rapidly increasing throughout America today," he warned. Whether the rise of homosexuality was real or imagined, the perception of an "epidemic" of homosexuality was expressed repeatedly in social commentary and psychiatric discourse in the 1950s.[61]

Despite the deserved reputation of the 1940s and 1950s as a repressive era for gay Americans, homosexuality may have been more visible in American life than ever before. According to historians, the Second World War was a turning point in gay and lesbian history, a nationwide "coming out" experience for many gay members of the military. Uprooting men and women from their homes and local communities, the war brought them together in sex-segregated institutions and provided a space within which to pursue same-sex relationships. To be sure, the majority of gays and lesbians remained closeted in their public lives, lest they be subject to discrimination, fired from their jobs, and/or confronted with harassment or violence. But the rise of gay and lesbian urban enclaves and communities in the postwar years suggests the extent to which the war, and the accelerated social and economic changes it provoked, helped to establish a larger or at least more noticeable gay subculture in America.[62] The real or imagined presence of increasing numbers of homosexuals in American life was felt by many anxious heterosexual observers, whose visceral response was often an inflated, brittle, hyper-allegiance to the traditional heterosexual family.

The establishment of one of the first homosexual advocacy organizations in the United States, the Mattachine Society, offered anxious observers evidence of both a newly open homosexuality in American life and an unambiguous link between Communism and homosexuality. Founded in 1951 by several former Communist Party members, most notably Henry Hay, the organization was initially secretive and its structure was modeled after the Communist party. The Mattachine Society gradually became more open and activist in challenging sexual discrimination in the early fifties and distanced itself from its radical origins, but not before a Los Angeles newspaper took notice of the organization and discovered that Mattachine legal advisor Fred Snider had previously been an "unfriendly witness" before HUAC (he had taken the Fifth Amendment). In March 1953, Los Angeles *Mirror* reporter Paul Coates informed readers of the society's ties to the Communist party and reminded them that homosexuals were known national security risks. Coates speculated that "sex deviates," scorned by the heterosexual majority, "might band together for their own protection" and "swing tremendous political power." He warned his readers of the imminent danger of such a scenario: there were roughly 200,000 homosexuals in the Los Angeles area alone, he estimated, and a "well-trained subversive could move in and forge that power into a dangerous political weapon." Hoover's FBI must have concurred; the bureau infiltrated the Mattachine Society in the 1950s, and through its informers kept the organization under FBI surveillance.[63]

Like other anti-Communists, J. Edgar Hoover spoke of Communism as an ideology and a lifestyle that spread like a disease and would subvert moral life and the American family. Communism, he believed, was an "evil and malignant way of life . . . that eventually will destroy the sanctity of the home . . . [thus] a quarantine is necessary to keep it from infecting the nation." In his 1958 anti-Communist tract, *Masters of Deceit*, Hoover characterized American Communist Party members as weak-minded, emotionally unstable social outcasts who became Communists because they were unable to cope with normal society. Communists, he wrote, were "twisted, mixed-up neurotics" whose stated reasons for joining the Communist movement masked deep-rooted personal problems and inadequacies. Americans joined the Communist Party, Hoover said, for a variety a reasons—a need for belonging, a sense of guilt attributable to their "well-to-do" backgrounds, a "persecution complex," a feeling of personal failure, or for "sexual pleasure." Hoover did not explain precisely what he meant by "sexual pleasure," but by 1958 it was almost taken as a given that the party provided a social outlet for frustrated sexual misfits. Hoover added, however, that those who join solely for reasons of sexual pleasure often drift out of the party eventually, since self-indulgent individuals are not the disciplined stuff from which "hard-core," self-denying Communists are made.[64]

While *Masters of Deceit* did not make the explicit connection between homosexuality and Communism, Hoover elsewhere paired the demons of moral and political subversion together. His pledges that the FBI would stamp out "Communists and sex perverts" in government (including the FBI itself), his surveillance of the sexually and politically deviant Mattachine Society (whose leaders enraged Hoover by placing him on their regular mailing list), his undercover steps to discredit alleged Communists and fellow-travelers as sexually "deviant"—all suggest that for Hoover, the "enemy within" was both ideological and sexual. That Hoover was himself gay—a plausible conjecture but one that has not been established with ample evidence—is a subject better left to biographers. Whatever the director's sexual orientation, Hoover's FBI was the primary intelligence-gathering instrument upon which the purge of homosexuals and Communists from government relied, and the institution that—in the name of national security—gathered, maintained, and deployed information on the sexual indiscretions and "deviations" of countless individuals as a means to intimidate and neutralize political enemies, especially (but not exclusively) leftists and Communists.[65]

Though Hoover attempted publicly to steer clear of partisan politics, he was of course an arch-conservative who openly supported and covertly aided McCarthy and his allies, privately railed against "phony" liberals, and did much in his long career as FBI director to stigmatize them as both soft on Communism and morally compromised. In the 1940s and 1950s, his preferred target was Eleanor Roosevelt, whom he seemed to revile with an intensity that bordered on obsession. (When asked why he never married, Hoover was reportedly fond of saying that it was because "God made a woman like Eleanor Roosevelt.") Like many on the ultra-right, Hoover regarded Roosevelt as the insidious overbearing force behind her husband's leftist politics (she too had committed the unforgivable sin of initially coming to the defense of Alger Hiss). Hoover also blamed her for protecting Sumner Welles and interceding on his behalf when the allegations of homosexuality came to the attention of her husband (she did so because Welles's "softness toward Russia served the interests of the Communist party," Hoover told his aides). Convinced that Eleanor Roosevelt was a degenerate, negro-loving Communist sympathizer who had numerous male and female lovers, including at least one black man, Hoover kept her private life under bureau surveillance and maintained a voluminous file on the activities and sexual indiscretions of Roosevelt and her friends.[66] Hoover's FBI was no doubt one source of the tales that circulated in right-wing circles of decadent, morally corrupt liberal elites who undermined the moral fiber of America.

The majority of Americans, to be sure, weren't privy to Hoover's internal world of debased leftist and Communists, but millions of American readers encountered similar ideas in Lee Mortimer and Jack Lait's 1951 book *Washington Confidential*. The book, which climbed to number one on the *New York Times* bestseller list a month after its publication, was written by two conservative journalists as a kind of tell-all exposé of Washington life. It depicted the nation's capital (the "district of confusion") as a den of inequity, riddled with corruption, gambling, drunkenness, prostitution, and all manner of sexual immorality and deviance. The authors' primary targets of contempt, however, were the loose liberals of Democratic administrations whose twenty-year reign in the White House had helped to turn Washington into "the dirtiest community in America." Mortimer and Lait devoted an entire chapter to the homosexuals they claimed were so ubiquitous in Washington, "a garden of pansies" where so many of them "make love under the equestrian statue of the rugged Andrew Jackson, who must be whirling on his heavenly horse every time he sees what is going on around his monument." The authors were especially fixated on the Civil Service and the State Department, where "homos," they said, tend to flock like birds of a feather: "Like immigrants from foreign lands, for these people are aliens in their own . . . they attract those who speak their language and live their kinds of lives." Mortimer and Lait resurrected the Sumner Welles incident, and without naming Welles told the story of the Undersecretary's indiscretions in the Pullman car in ample detail ("one high State Department official was a notorious homo who preferred young Negro boys . . ."). Quoting extensively from Congressmen Miller's "expert" views on homosexuality and blackmail, Mortimer and Lait deplored the lax policies of the Truman administration and insisted that 6,000 homosexuals remained on the government payroll.[67]

Washington Confidential made explicit the connection between political and sexual transgression that had been implicit in so much political discourse. The authors vilified the "parlor pinks," the "reds," the "lavenders," the "negrophiles," the "lesbians," the "decadent" diplomats—those who together constituted the liberal left that had arrived in Washington in the 1930s, when it became "fashionable to be 'liberal' [and] to love all radicals including revolutionaries." Singled out for special excoriation were the aristocratic left-wing elites in "Gorgeous Georgetown," the trendy Washington enclave that was home to Eleanor Roosevelt (who conceived of it as "a genteel bohemian community" for she and her "sandal-shod" friends"), Dean Acheson, actress Myrna Loy (she "played enough spy roles in the movies"), Felix Frankfurter, Henry Hopkins, and scores of rich New Dealers and debauched leftists. The authors noted that when Roosevelt and her equally rich and hypocritical leftist friends "discovered" Georgetown, they drove out of the neighborhood the poor, "gentle Negroes" who had lived there for over a century. Home to "many rich fairies and lesbians," Georgetown, the authors claimed, might lack "the streetwalkers who plague every other section" of Washington, yet "what it lacks in ambulant magdalens is more than made up for by homosexuals of both indeterminate sexes. It seems that nonconformity in politics is often the handmaiden of the same proclivities in sex."[68]

Mortimer and Lait revealed just how feverish the anti-Communist imagination could become when they described the sexual means by which leftists and Communists entice people into their depraved political world. "Wealthy left-wingers with mansions in Georgetown" invite "humble government employees" to their "exotic, erotic parties." Of course, "this sudden entrance into a world of wealth, taste, refinement, liquor, and libido is irresistible to hoi polloi." To lure the dispossessed into political subversion, "the reds and bleeding hearts play up their 'love' for negroes at every opportunity." "Most negroes are patriotic," the authors pointed out, but a few are taken in by the "crocodile tears of the Eleanor Roosevelt brand of reformer" and the "white gals" of the Communist party, whose superiors urge them "to give themselves to colored men." American left-wingers learned these tricks from their Soviet masters, who regularly infiltrate "perverted circles" in foreign countries, and entice people into "acts of adultery and abnormality" at lavish parties replete with "pornographic exhibitions, unlimited liquor, and every form of dope—and a hidden talking moving picture camera recording it all." Mortimer and Lait claimed to have seen some "stills" from one such "drunken, depraved orgy," which involved a gossip writer who had become a "transmission belt for the Communist line" thanks to his degeneracy (and the film's record of it). "The use of sex as a means of recruiting is a basic [red] tactic," Mortimer and Lait warned.[69]

With its shameless tabloid sensationalism, *Washington Confidential* would be difficult to treat seriously if it were not for the bestselling book's massive readership (the paperback edition sold millions). Mortimer and Lait, both of whom wrote for the Hearst-owned New York tabloid, the *Daily Mirror*, had just enough "respectability" to be regarded by readers as legitimate journalists, and just enough latitude as Hearst reporters to raise unsavory "issues" that were beyond the boundaries of more reputable journalists. With its lurid descriptions of criminals, prostitutes, drug dealers, sex perverts, corrupt and whoring government officials, bohemian leftists, and twisted Communists, as well as its tendency to blame soft New Dealers for the lawlessness and dissipation of the nation's capital, *Washington Confidential* satisfied the same appetite in the American public that made so many of Mickey Spillane's novels bestsellers in the 1950s. Mortimer and Lait, of course, presented the link between liberalism and moral disorder as fact, not fiction.[70]

The idea that leftists and Communists led morally dissolute lives and used sex as a means of enticing weak-willed, maladjusted, or young vulnerable individuals into their ranks appeared in much tamer form in popular magazines and publications. A 1948 *Life* magazine article, "Portrait of an American Communist," profiled a young man, "Kelly," who was lured into the party at twenty years old. Kelly found the party appealing for a number of reasons, especially the intellectual prowess of its members (whom he desired to emulate), the social life and sense of camaraderie that the party offered, and its sexual intrigue. Kelly, young and inexperienced, was literally seduced by the women in the party "who went to bed in the same way they carried placards—as a service to the party." While Mortimer and Lait had portrayed female Communist party members as near prostitutes for the cause, the *Life* writer reported that, according to Kelly, new party prospects received "encouragement, adulation [and] sexual satisfaction," especially Negroes, whom "party girls were assigned to enfold." (Kelly soon found, however, that life in the Communist party was no party; after he became a full-fledged member, he found that his was a life of "boredom and grim discipline.") As in other depictions of Communists, the individual's sexual needs or frustrations, while not always the principal motivation for joining the party, typically figured into the general psychological profile of the maladjusted Communist recruit.[71]

Scholars also noted the sexually charged allure of Communism. John Kosa, author of *Two Generations of Soviet Man*, included within his psychological profile of the Communist the "neurotic" type, most prevalent in "countries where Communists make up a small deviant minority." Forlorn, alienated, perhaps even prone to write romantic poetry that idealizes Communism, the neurotic's lack of a "love object" leads him to concentrate his "tender emotions upon the party and gain an almost sexual satisfaction from his relationship to the Communist movement." As we have seen, Arthur Schlesinger Jr. also cast the Communist's attraction to the party in psychosexual terms, stressing the erotic appeal of clandestine party rituals and the opportunity to satisfy homosexual or sadomasochistic impulses.[72]

The idea that Communists in the United States were psychologically maladjusted or emotionally unstable people gained wide currency in the fifties, and provided the "rationale" for the notion that they were therefore prone to be sexual misfits. Two intersecting assumptions were usually prominent in the stereotype of the American Communist that appeared in popular books and magazines, government propaganda, and scholarly works: first, Communist recruits were social outcasts who, having been rejected or scorned by society because of their inability to "fit in," developed a latent or manifest hostility toward "normal" society and thus joined the ranks of the Communist Party as a form of rebellion. Second, Communist recruits were feeble-minded, self-less, alienated individuals adrift in society and incapable of making decisions or asserting themselves on their own; thus they longed to be told "what to do" and "what to believe" by an external authority (the party). As one *New York Times Magazine* writer noted in 1953, these individuals flee from the "hard duty of decision" into a "closed system of thought" that offers them a psychologically comforting and authoritative "truth." For both sets of reasons, which often converged in popular analyses, the maladjusted individual—prone to blame "society" for his problems, idealistic insofar as he seeks an external "cure" (revolution) for what ails him internally—is easily seduced by the feeling of empowerment that the party offers him, even though the party actually controls him. And with this newfound sense of empowerment, he is easily duped by the lies, myths, and utopian promises of Communism, an ideology that ultimately serves as a kind of therapeutic religion for the individual. Popular representations of Communists in magazines and books such as *Masters of Deceit* often reflected the basic assumptions of scholars and psychoanalysts, who stressed the party members' individual and collective "neurosis"—the byproduct of a mass society. However the psychological malady was presented, it was generally assumed by both popular writers and scholarly experts that no sane, well-adjusted individual in the mid-twentieth century would ever embrace Communism. In *One Lonely Night*, when Mike Hammer explains to Oscar Deamer, a Communist whom he is about to strangle, "you were a Commie, Oscar, because you were batty. It was the only philosophy that would appeal to your crazy mind. . . . You saw a chance of getting back at the world," Spillane echoed many social critics whose primary explanation for the appeal Communism was the psychological instability of its devotees.[73]

Morris L. Ernst and David Loth, two self-styled experts on American Communists, published their *Report on the American Communist* in 1952. Using anecdotal "profiles" of party members, the report depicted Communists as "damaged souls." The authors suggested that the party was "heavily populated with the handicapped—some of them physically, but more of them psychologically." These weak, emotionally crippled, or physically unattractive people find the Communist Party appealing "because their handicap is neither so noticeable nor so much of an obstacle in the party as it has been in the world outside." Communists, they claimed, tended to be pessimistic, humorless people in whom "intellectual preoccupations predominate rather than athletics" (Paul Robeson was the exception to the rule, they noted). Ernst and Loth claimed that people joined the party because of emotional disturbances as well as sexual needs, but the authors sought to dispel the popular myth that "life in the Communist party was one long sexual orgy." The party encouraged monogamy, they noted. Moreover, like Hoover, these self-styled experts on Communism pointed out that the party expected self-discipline and fidelity from its all members. The party leadership "frowns on excessive intimacy, even in marriage," since "tenderness for a sexual partner might diminish the profound devotion which must be reserved for Stalin and Russia."[74]

Life in the party may not have been especially licentious, but sexual relations and marriage between party members looked perverse and abnormal to Ernst and Loth. The sex life of the Communist, they wrote, was "casual, rather random, somewhat less monogamous than the average of their income and education in the country, and also less sentimental or even intimate." The impersonal, blasé attitude toward sex was in part the product of the Communist Party members' "declaration of independence from the morals of bourgeois society." Citing the Kinsey report as a standard by which to measure, the authors also claimed that there is "a reasonable . . . quota of homosexual or suppressed homosexual tendencies" in the party. They pointed out that (unnamed) psychoanalysts see common psychological traits in the Communist and the homosexual, since both "want their shame and enjoy the guilt of lying, cheating, and deceiving their friends." (The authors also noted that "there is not the degree of impotence among men" in the party, again mentioning Kinsey's data as a standard.) Moreover, Ernst and Loth observed a gender role reversal in the Communist marriage: "the tendency seems to be that in Communist marriages the wife is the more dominant partner." This relationship is more prevalent in the top echelons of the party, the authors said, noting the common assumption among party members that CPUSA leader Earl Browder was "henpecked." (The source of such an idea was apparently "Red Spy Queen" Elizabeth Bentley, who told federal investigators that Raissa Browder took her orders from the Kremlin, one of which was to keep her husband in line.) A similar point was made about Ethel Rosenberg. A psychological profile that reached Hoover's desk and circulated within the federal government claimed that "Julius is the slave and his wife, Ethel, the master." Ernst, a friend of Hoover's, was the author of the report.[75]

The idea that Communism somehow unsexed the sexes and stripped women of their femininity was reinforced in popular magazine articles in the 1950s, which often portrayed women in the Soviet Union as masculinized workhorses for the Communist machine. Images of physically hefty women, unadorned and unattractive and toiling away in industrial occupations that required heavy labor, summoned pity from American commentators. So deficient in femininity and charm were Russian working women that they appeared to be barely women at all. A *Look* magazine writer pronounced in 1954 that "nowhere in the world is female beauty held in such low esteem— needless to say, there is no Miss U.S.S.R." The writer also noted the exceptional opportunities Russian women had to become educated professionals— doctors, scientists, engineers, high party officials. But she could only lament in the end that "a woman in Russia has a chance to be almost anything—except a woman." While American observers reported that Soviet Communism scorned housewifery as a bourgeois heresy, they also noted the absence of consumer goods in the U.S.S.R., which meant that Russian women were deprived of the accoutrements necessary for their feminine beautification. Seen through the lens of American domesticity and consumerism, Communism in practice appeared to erase masculinity and femininity in the process of making men and women equal in their enslavement to the Soviet state.[76]

Such perspectives on Soviet women are unsurprising given the domestic ideology of the time and the revulsion for Communist tyranny. But the idea that Communism reversed somehow the natural order of gender relations and even empowered women at the expense of men is a more complex reflex of deep anxieties rooted in American life, not Soviet reality. In another of Mortimer and Lait's wildly successful exposés, *USA Confidential*, the authors claimed that Marxian teachings encouraged (along with other social trends) female dominance and a matriarchal order in which "men grow soft and women masculine." The perils of a society breeding soft men and hard women was becoming a recurrent theme in popular and psychiatric discourse in the 1940s and 1950s, and their expression here and elsewhere in anti-Communist rhetoric reveals the way in which cold war anxieties intersected with growing concerns (as we will see in the next chapter) about the problem of "momism" in American culture. Moreover, as Rogin has shown, science fiction novels by Philip Wylie such as *Tomorrow* (1954), as well as cold war era films such as *My Son John* (1952) and *Kiss Me Deadly* (1955), obliquely blamed misguided women and parasitical mothers for atomic devastation or Communist malfeasance.[77]

The most well-known of these films is John Frankenheimer's *The Manchurian Candidate* (1962), based on the bestselling Richard Condon novel (1959) in which a U.S. senator and anti-Communist crusader, Johnny Iselin (an undisguised Joe McCarthy figure), becomes a dupe of his imperious wife, who is actually a secret agent working for the Kremlin. Central to Mrs. Iselin's plot to take control of the U.S. government is her son, Raymond Shaw, a former Korean War POW who has been psychologically programmed while in captivity to robotically obey the directives of the Communists, including his mother, and to kill on command. In this surreal nightmare of Communist perfidy, Mrs. Iselin (played by Angela Lansbury in the film) appears as a Communist dragon lady and an oversolicitous mother who controls her weak and foolish husband, nearly seduces her brainwashed son, and comes close to turning the American government over to the Kremlin.[78]

This is a narrative of Communist cunning, to be sure, and that cunning has a maternal face. Mrs. Iselin's incestuous desire for her son Raymond consciously disgusts him, yet it is the source of her grip on his unconscious. While momism *is* the source of Communist subversion here, Rogin's conviction that *The Manchurian Candidate*, as "a Kennedy administration film," sought to "reawaken a lethargic nation to the Communist menace" misreads the film's sardonic perspective and misplaces its political preoccupations. Warning the public about the sinister machinations of reds intent on infiltrating the U.S. government by secretly boring from within was an obsession of the early 1950s. By the late 1950s, domestic subversion as an immanent threat was regarded, at least by cynical liberal anti-Communists of Condon's type, as an outmoded and destructive preoccupation of the recent past. In many ways, *The Manchurian Candidate's* darkly comedic narrative aimed to disrupt the cold war conventions of the early 1950s. But its primary theme—the programming of Raymond's psyche—speaks above all to the obsession with mind control and brainwashing that grew in American culture after the Korean War, and was followed by the "psywar" vogue that peaked in national security circles in the late 1950s and early 1960s. Indeed, if *The Manchurian Candidate* reflects the Kennedy administration's anti-Communism at all, it is in its fascination with psychological coercion and warfare.[79]

If *The Manchurian Candidate* satirized momism in its depiction of Mrs. Iselin as a destroying mother by taking it to its absurd extreme (open incestuous lust for her son), it clearly parodied McCarthyism—the dopey, sleazy, alcoholic Senator Iselin announces that fifty-seven Communists have infiltrated the U.S. government, a number he has determined by staring at a catsup bottle. Condon's novel was published in 1959 and the film produced in 1962, long after the political excesses of the early fifties were widely scorned. The Communist threat to the United States does appear very real and portending in the narrative. But *The Manchurian Candidate* points to perils that emanate from the far right as much as the far left. Its twisted, disorienting conspiracy plot mirrors for the viewer the calculated distortions and schemings of those whose aim it is to confuse, condition, and control people's minds. That Senator Iselin becomes a tool of the Communists ultimately suggests that the dim and unprincipled right wing is capable of doing the kind of damage to democracy that would only serve to further Communist aims in the end—thus Condon's collapse of the two sets of "totalitarian" forces (Johnny Iselin/McCarthyism and Mrs. Iselin/Communism) into a single force that would subvert American freedom. The politics of *The Manchurian Candidate* lay in the vital center; so too, perhaps, does its anti-Communist style. Frank Sinatra, an honorary member of the Kennedy clan, played the role of Major Ben Marco, the army officer who successfully resists the psychological conditioning that has debilitated his fellow soldiers, and whose savvy intelligence finally allows him to crack the enigma of Raymond's brainwashed state.

The popular interest in subliminal psychological conditioning and mind control was heightened by a series of widely read books in the 1950s, from

Fredric Wertham's 1954 *Seduction of the Innocent* (on the corrosive influence of symbol-laden comic books on youth) to Vance Packard's 1957 book *The Hidden Persuaders* (on subliminal messages in advertisements). But the obsession with *ideological* brainwashing for the purposes of political subversion became acute during the Korean War, when some American POWs were subjected to psychological conditioning by their Communist captors. The issue made headlines in 1953 when twenty-one American soldiers who had been captured in Korea refused repatriation to the United States after the war ended. Here is the source of *The Manchurian Candidate's* interest in mind control. That American GIs would reject their homeland, choose to live in "Red China" and even sing the Communist *Internationale* shocked American observers, many of whom concluded that these "traitors" had been "brainwashed" (with Chinese techniques). Other American POWs confirmed that their captors did in fact attempt to brainwash them with repetitive indoctrination and humiliation tactics. Much public discussion ensued, as American military officials, experts, and journalists debated the motives, the intelligence levels, and the mental stability of the "turncoat GIs." Some observers spoke of the turncoats' visible "girl-lessness" [*sic*] before they left for Korea. A 1954 article in *Newsweek*, "Korea: The Sorriest Bunch," cast the men who refused repatriation as a sorry bunch of losers and misfits, and even suggested that half of the men were "bound together more by homosexualism than Communism."[80]

Though some observers isolated the "turn-coats" as the dregs of the military, the controversy inevitably raised the larger, nagging problem of the soft, conformist American self, weakened by affluence and all that came with it, including smothering mothers. The failure of the United States to achieve a clear victory in Korea brought more hand-wringing about the questionable performance of American soldiers in this war. Their allegedly poor preparedness for military duty and combat, combined with the twenty-one "brainwashed" GIs—seemingly weak-willed, malleable, and unable to withstand the ordeal of captivity and the enemy's manipulations—confirmed the warnings of several leading psychiatrists. Since World War II, they had been insisting that too many American servicemen were psychologically ill-equipped for the emotional and physical rigors of military service, a symptom of being coddled and over-mothered. If "moms" were ever truly considered "subversives" in the conscious life of Americans in the 1940s and 1950s, it was largely for the sin of maternal overbearance.

To many Americans, Communism as a way of life seemed frighteningly oppressive, depressingly bleak, and vaguely perverse in the way it coldly corrupted human relationships. To others, Communism represented more than an Orwellian nightmare; it appeared so deeply immoral and fiendish that it had to be exorcized from American life through ritualistic excoriation.

No one promoted the idea of Communism as intrinsically wicked more than the Reverend Billy Graham. Ranked as the fourth most admired man in the world in a 1958 Gallup Poll, Graham's successful career as an evangelist would be "unintelligible outside of the milieu of dread and anxiety" that marks the culture of the cold war, as historian Stephen Whitfield has suggested. Rarely did Graham preach a sermon that did not condemn the red menace, often in the most apocalyptic of terms; redemption itself became a defense against Communism. So long as Communism was understood by Graham and his audience as "Satan's religion," it had to stand, above all, for sin and immorality. To Graham, Communism wasn't so much an anti-capitalist movement or even an imperialist movement, but rather a "great anti-Christian movement." "My own theory about Communism is that it is masterminded by Satan," Graham said in 1957, for "there is no other explanation for the tremendous gains of Communism in which they seem to outwit us at every turn, unless they have supernatural power and wisdom and intelligence given to them." In a cold war climate of anxious hyper-masculinity, Graham could hail the great enemy of Satanic Communism—Jesus Christ himself—as "every inch a 'He-man.'" Indeed, "Christ was probably the strongest man physically that ever lived," Graham told his audience. "He could have been a star athlete on any team. He was a real man."[81]

In a 1949 sermon entitled "The Home God Honors," delivered in Los Angeles ("the wickedest city in the world"), Graham claimed that Communists sought to sabotage America by striking at the very heart of Christian values—the home. He told his audience that "a nation is only as strong as her homes," and warned of the impending boundary invasion by fifth columnists: "One of the goals of Communism is to destroy the American home. If the Communists can destroy the American home and cause moral deterioration in this country, that group will have done to us what they did to France when the German armies invaded the Maginot line."[82]

Like Hoover, Graham left it up to the imagination of his listeners the precise means by which Communists could destroy the home, and thus bring moral and political collapse to the nation. But Graham's message was no doubt understood viscerally by audiences as they listened to sermons detailing the many sins of Americans—adultery, divorce, wives who "wear the trousers" in the family, loose talk, teen promiscuity, suggestive clothing, orgies and wife-swapping, sex maniacs and perverts, dirty books and magazines—all of which, insofar as they too were masterminded by Satan, could be imagined as part of the same diabolical plot to undermine the family and thus weaken Americans to Communist infiltration.[83] If there is still something missing in this absurd logic that connected Communists with the moral degeneration of America, we might consider the man whom Graham accused of doing more to undermine American morals than any other individual: Alfred Kinsey. The sexologist, whose studies of sexual behavior in the United States showed that Americans were hardly virtuous and sexually restrained, personified the liberalism that weakened the nation's morals—the murky "missing link" between Communism and the deterioration of American morality.

The Kinsey reports were perhaps the most important catalysts in the rising perception of a breakdown in sexual order in American life. Kinsey's first study, *Sexual Behavior in the Human Male*, published in 1948, examined the sexual behavior of a sample group of American men, revealing that 50 percent of married men surveyed had committed adultery, 85 percent had sexual intercourse prior to marriage, and 69 percent had at least one sexual encounter with a prostitute. Few of the statistics, however, violated conventional sexual norms so much as those on homosexual behavior: a full 50 percent of American men surveyed admitted they had been sexually attracted to other men; 37 percent had at least one postadolescent homosexual experience leading to orgasm; 10 percent of men had been "more or less" exclusively homosexual for at least three years of their lives between the ages of 16 and 55; and 4 percent of men were exclusively homosexual throughout their lives. Of the men who remained single at age 35, the report found that 50 percent had overt homosexual experience leading to orgasm. The unexpectedly high rates of homosexual activity among men, along with the suggestion that homosexuals were not always outwardly identifiable by their demeanor and thus did not typically conform to the prevailing stereotype of the effete homosexual, implied to readers that there might be more homosexuals in American life than previously thought. Taken together, Kinsey's data appeared to show a glaring disparity between what Americans professed to believe in and what men actually did in their private lives.[84]

Sexual Behavior in the Human Male was an immediate bestseller, much to the embarrassment of the cautious *New York Times*, which had refused to advertise or review the book (and later reviewed it favorably), and to the horror of moralists who accused Kinsey of condoning the sexual behaviors that he rather dryly described. Conservatives were not by any means alone in criticizing Kinsey; influential liberal intellectuals like Reinhold Niebuhr and Lionel Trilling also did so, while plenty of other critics attacked Kinsey's statistical methodology. But the most strident voices of protest—the ones that questioned Kinsey's right even to publish the book regardless of its accuracy—came from the right, and especially the religious right. The most common charge was that Kinsey, by failing to denounce the sexual behaviors he described, had lowered the moral standards of the nation. An editorial in the *Catholic Mind* attacked Kinsey for being at war "against purity, against morality, against the family." In a *Reader's Digest* symposium on the book entitled "Must We Change Our Sex Standards?" (the uniform answer was "No"), minister Norman Vincent Peale denounced Kinsey's approach because it implied that statistics were indicative of what is normal. Peale assailed Kinsey for his failure to use the term "abnormal" when describing (unspecified) sexual behaviors. "No matter how many murderers there are, murder will never be normal," he decried. Clearly, critics' preoccupation with Kinsey's normalization of the abnormal had much to do with his statistics on male homosexuality, as opposed to his data on adultery, premarital sex, masturbation, or sex with prostitutes, all of which may have been considered generally immoral, but were hardly so "abnormal." In the same symposium, J. Edgar Hoover also weighed in on the report and also rebuked Kinsey for presenting the abnormal as normal. Hoover insisted that "man's sense of decency declares what is normal and what is not." Descending to oblique red-baiting, the FBI director warned that "whenever the American people, young or old, come to believe that there is no such thing as right and wrong, normal and abnormal, those who would destroy our civilization will applaud a major victory over our way of life."[85]

It was Kinsey's second study, *Sexual Behavior in the Human Female* (1953), also an immediate bestseller, that inspired Billy Graham to denounce Kinsey as public enemy number one. "It is impossible to estimate the damage this book will do to the already deteriorating morals of America," Graham insisted. If it was profoundly unsettling to discuss men's sex lives, it was an "affront to womanhood," as the *Schenectady Union Star* put it, to discuss female sexuality openly. Twenty-six percent of wives surveyed by the Kinsey research team reported that they had committed adultery before age forty; 50 percent of women said they were non-virgins before marriage; 90 percent of women had engaged in premarital petting; 28 percent said they had been sexually attracted to other women; and 13 percent had at least one homosexual experience resulting in orgasm. Kinsey's statistics on women who were primarily or exclusively homosexual were "only about a half to a third" of the corresponding male figures.[86]

Sexual Behavior in the Human Female was perhaps more disconcerting than was Kinsey's previous study of males. Aside from the general objection to discussing female sexuality publicly, the statistics themselves were more than upsetting. Men, "being men," were no doubt expected to transgress the boundaries of official sexual norms, to some extent (especially in the areas of premarital sex or adultery, for example). Thus the data on male sexual behavior, while deeply troubling to many observers and shockingly high in some categories (e.g., male same-sex attraction), were perhaps less disturbing than were the statistics on female sexual behavior. Much more restraint was expected of women, especially in the areas of chastity and fidelity. Representative Louis Heller (D-New York), whose admission that he had never read Kinsey's study didn't preclude his call to ban the book, scolded Kinsey for suggesting that the "bulk of American womanhood [had] sinned before or after marriage." Heller pronounced Kinsey's statistics "highly questionable" on the basis of interviews with fewer than 6,000 women, "many of them frustrated, neurotic outcasts of society." To Heller, women were not *just* women, individuals in their own right; they were "our mothers, wives, daughters, and sisters," against whom Kinsey had hurled "the insult of the century." Henry Pitney Van Dusen, head of Union Theological Seminary, said the worst thing about the report, if Kinsey's facts were correct, was that it revealed "a prevailing degradation in American morality approximating the worst decadence of the Roman Empire."[87]

It was inevitable that some moralists would accuse Kinsey of "aiding the Communists' aim to weaken and destroy the youth of your country," as one writer of hate-mail to Kinsey put it. On several occasions, religious critics stained the implications of Kinsey's research with the color red. A Presbyterian minister in Indianapolis told his congregation that there was "a fundamental kinship between that thing and Communism. . . . The influence of this report, though it may seem to be a thousand miles from Communism, will in time contribute inevitably toward Communism, for both are based on the same basic naturalistic philosophy." An editorial in the weekly newspaper of the Indiana Roman Catholic Archdiocese claimed that Kinsey's studies "paved the way for people to believe in communism and act like communists." While its editors acknowledged that Kinsey wasn't himself a Communist, they added that "we couldn't for sure tell you in what respect the Kinsey view of nature and human morality differs from the communists."[88] Such pronouncements were extreme, just as the Roman Catholic Church's anti-Communism was extreme. But they do suggest the way in which the collective sexual sins of America—which Kinsey had merely revealed, not invented or explicitly endorsed—could become enmeshed with, and even displaced onto, Communism.

In his sermons on the "Sin of Tolerance," Graham explained that the word "tolerant" was synonymous with "liberal" or "broadminded." It meant a willingness to "put up with beliefs opposed to one's convictions and the allowance of something not wholly approved." Warning his audience about the sins of immorality, alcohol, divorce, delinquency, Godlessness, and "wickedness in high places," Graham insisted that "over tolerance in moral issues has made us soft, flabby, devoid of convictions."[89] In the imagination of Graham and other conservative anti-Communists, it was liberal permissiveness and moral relativism that invited the subversion and perversion of all that was normal and sacred in America: freedom, private property, God, the patriarchal family, and sexual purity. Communism, insofar as it was to be the final, hideous denouement of a naïve liberal softness and

permissiveness, promised to turn asunder all "natural" hierarchies and relations completely: free man and the state, God and mankind, the individual and the collective, the spiritual and the carnal, and at the most
elemental level, man and woman. Popular images of mannish Soviet women
and slavish emasculated Soviet men provided one negative referent against
which America could be defined, its moral superiority imagined, its order
and civility restored.

Those who sought to stifle or smear Kinsey's controversial sex research
did some damage to the sexologist, but they were largely unsuccessful in
halting the currents that were bringing a greater degree of sexual openness
in mid-century American life—currents that Kinsey's work symbolized.
Representative Heller's effort to sponsor legislation that would have, in effect,
banned the Kinsey reports went nowhere. After the publication of *Sexual
Behavior in the Human Female*, the Rockefeller Foundation cut off further
funding to Kinsey's institute when its president, Dean Rusk, yielding to pressure from politicians and religious leaders, concluded that the foundation's
underwriting of the controversial sexologist's research would leave it open
to attack by congressional right-wingers. But by then the two Kinsey reports
had already done their cultural work.[90]

Critics on the right were correct in ascribing major cultural significance
to Kinsey's reports, for they unleashed a wide-ranging, unprecedented dialogue about sexuality in American life that was largely immune to the forces
of sexual containment. The Kinsey reports permitted previously buried or
unmentionable issues to be discussed and debated everywhere from college
campuses to coffee shops to cocktail parties. And despite Kinsey's arguably
disinterested "scientific" style, his studies did have the effect of normalizing,
if not all sexual *behaviors*, at the very least a more open *discussion* of the
range and nature of sexual behaviors in American life. The Kinsey reports
and the controversy they unleashed also had the unintended effect of increasing anxiety and unease in many quarters, whether or not observers
were fully conscious of it. The tensions that emerged as a result of the Kinsey
studies, as well as other cultural and demographic tides of change—the increasing presence of women in the workforce, the incursions of sex into
popular culture, the rising visibility of homosexuals in American life—help
explain the urgency and artificiality with which the sanctity of the family,
rigid gender role ideals, and sexual restraint were promoted as a defense.

Sexuality was in fact becoming far more present in American cultural
and commercial life than ever before, a fact that makes comprehensible the
anxieties about sexual disorder that surfaced in political culture. To say that
this was a transitional era would be rather meaningless, inasmuch as any
era could be considered culturally transitional. Clearly, though, social, cultural, and market forces were unleashing new currents of sexual change

that both helped to inspire, and then bumped fitfully against, an official ideology that insisted on allegiance to the nuclear child-centered family and sexual chasity. These currents brought new and unsettling developments, some of which (arguably) would have been scarcely imaginable before the war. From the publication of *Lolita* (1955) and *Peyton Place* (1956), and the arrival of the first *Playboy* magazine in 1953, to the proliferation of ever more explicit sex and marriage manuals and the willingness to discuss male impotence, female sexual needs, and homosexuality more frankly, from the public discussions about Christine Jorgensen's sex change operation (1952) to the establishment of the Mattachine Society (1951), mid-century American culture raised previously repressed, unspeakable, or unconfronted issues and phantoms for many Americans.

An emphasis on the pressures to contain or stifle expressions of sexuality in the 1950s masks the extent to which American culture was becoming considerably less rigid and more permissive. "The surging circulation of *Playboy* exposed how flimsy the floodgates of traditionalism were becoming," historian James Patterson noted. Moreover, although Hollywood had adhered since the 1930s to Production codes that banned sensitive subjects from being depicted in motion pictures, the codes began to break down with films like *From Here to Eternity* (1953), which featured the theme of adultery, and *Baby Doll* (1956), probably the "dirtiest" movie ever legally permitted, according to *Time* magazine. "Not even the Holy Mother Church could stem the tide," Patterson observed. Certainly by current standards, Hollywood studios still engaged in censorship in the 1950s, especially when it came to the subject of homosexuality.[91] Indeed, films like *Compulsion* (1958) or *Tea and Sympathy* (1956) clearly had homosexual themes, but never were characters explicitly identified as such, nor was the "issue" of homosexuality or its relationship to the plot lines ever made explicit. Nevertheless, the Hollywood codes were losing their force, and so too were the guardians of American morality like the Catholic Church, losing their power to "contain" sexuality in American cultural life.

In the end, the images of decadent leftists and Communists that surfaced in conservative anti-Communist discourse reveal anxieties that were less about Communism and more about a changing America—an America that appeared to be nourishing ever more neuroses and a creeping sexual disorder. While anti-Communism became a vehicle for the expression of extra-Communist concerns, the specter of sexual immorality and chaos, projected on to red and pink enemies, added a potent and subterranean dimension to anti-Communism. It helped to lay the basis for what Daniel Bell called "the equation of Communism with sin," thereby elevating a serious national security issue into a *moral* issue worthy of extraordinary fervor.[92]

Adelaide

The ultimate political casualty of the multiple anxieties and resentments of the time was Adlai Stevenson. Governor of Illinois and a cold war liberal Democrat, Stevenson was embraced by the liberal intelligentsia as its candidate in the 1952 presidential election. Stevenson had served as special counsel in the Roosevelt administration in the 1930s and as a special assistant to the Secretary of the Navy and the Secretary of State during the war; he had also been a delegate to the foundational meetings that established the United Nations. Ivy League pedigreed, urbane, articulate, witty, and often verbose, Stevenson had all of the eastern establishment credentials that the right wing detested, among them a previous "association" with Alger Hiss (whom Stevenson had known at the U.N.). Stevenson had vouched for Hiss's character in the first Hiss trial, a fact that the right wing parlayed into the most sinister of relationships, expressed in the absurd prediction by Republican Senator William Jenner that "if Adlai gets into the White House, Alger gets out of the jailhouse." Anti-Communism was at its high point in 1952, and the fallout from the Hiss and Rosenberg cases, the loss of China, the first Soviet explosion of an atomic bomb, and the onset of the Korean War—all of which had occurred under a fifth successive Democratic administration—surely meant that any Democratic candidate would have been at a considerable disadvantage. Yet, at a time when homophobia was running high and Republicans like Everett Dirksen from Illinois were vowing that, if elected, a Republican administration would "kick the lavender lads" out of the State Department, Stevenson was vulnerable to a determined campaign to impugn his masculinity.[93]

Perhaps in no other presidential election was the hard/soft dichotomy more exaggerated or pronounced. The conservative press frequently called attention to Stevenson's effete liberal demeanor and assailed his "gentlemen" supporters, who were deemed equally suspect. The *New York Daily News* called the governor "Adelaide" and claimed that he "trilled" his speeches in a "fruity voice." His "teacup words" were said to resemble nothing so much as a "genteel spinster, who can never forget that she got an A in elocution at Miss Smith's Finishing School." Stevenson's liberal supporters were "Harvard lace-cuff liberals," "pompadoured lap dogs," and "lace-panty diplomats" who, in the face of McCarthy's accusations, wailed in "perfumed anguish" and sometimes "giggled" about anti-Communism.[94]

"Tail-gunner Joe," more a partisan of Nixon than Eisenhower, touted Nixon's manliness against Stevenson's effeminacy. Predicting that Nixon's election would be "a body blow to the Communist conspiracy," McCarthy elsewhere implied that the "pinkos" in Stevenson's campaign were so effete that they needed a good manhandling. McCarthy told a Wisconsin audience,

"If you will get me a slippery elm club and put me aboard Adlai Stevenson's campaign train, I will use it on some of his advisors, and perhaps I can make a good American of him."[95]

Eisenhower held fast to his tough-minded "Korea, Corruption, and Communism" platform. Although he generally steered clear of vulgar red-baiting and hyperbole, he was not immune to harping on the issue of Communist infiltration of government and the failures of the security-compromised State Department, which, he publicly proclaimed, "weakly bowed before the triumph in China of Communists." His vice-presidential running mate continued to use the strategy that had served his political career so well in the past, mixing masculine bravado with charges of softness and timidity against his opponent. Nixon called Stevenson "Adlai the appeaser," the man with a "PhD from Dean Acheson's cowardly college of Communist containment." Five successive Democratic administrations were responsible for, as Nixon put it, "the unimpeded growth of the Communist conspiracy in the U.S." Therefore, a Democratic victory would surely "bring more Alger Hisses, more atomic spies, more crisis." Alluding to the compromised reputation of the State Department and Stevenson's prior service within it, Nixon told audiences that he would rather see "good old army khaki" in the White House than "State Department pink."[96]

Though Stevenson employed a good deal of anti-Communist toughtalk in the campaign, his eloquent speeches did more to contribute to his popular reputation as an effete intellectual. Eisenhower's "plain talk" differed considerably from Stevenson's flowery rhetorical style. "When an American says he loves his country," Stevenson proclaimed in a speech, "he means not only that he loves the New England hills, the prairies glistening in the sun, or the wide rising plains, the mountains, and the seas. He means that he loves an inner air, an inner light, in which freedom lives and in which a man can draw the breath of self-respect." Stevenson's acceptance speech to the Democratic National Convention no doubt projected weakness or insecurity more than the humility and integrity that he wanted to project. "I accept your nomination—and your program," Stevenson said, adding that "I should have preferred to hear these words uttered by a stronger, a wiser, a better man than myself." As Hofstadter noted, "It was not the right note for the times; it made for uneasiness, and many found it less attractive than Eisenhower's bland confidence." Nor, perhaps, did Stevenson's concession of defeat to Eisenhower bode well for his next campaign; he said he felt like the "little boy who had stubbed his toe and was too grown-up to cry but too hurt to laugh."[97]

A surge of anti-intellectualism was everywhere evident during the 1952 campaign. General Eisenhower's stern paternal image, his military, matter-of-fact style, and his homespun Americanism contrasted sharply with

Stevenson's intellectuality, style, and cosmopolitanism, leaving the latter at a serious political disadvantage. The erudite, "abstract" knowledge that marked Stevenson as an intellectual was played up by conservatives, who posed it against Eisenhower's superior, practical, "real world" knowledge. An Eisenhower campaign biography spoke of "Ike" as a man of "rural simplicities rather than urban sophistications," a "typical," "practical" Kansan whose youth was spent close to the land, performing the hard chores of an austere, virtuous rural life. Drawing an obvious contrast to Stevenson, the biographer noted that Eisenhower "is not one to shoot his mouth off. . . . Indeed he is a little suspicious of highfalutin' theory and abstraction. He has grown up in a world of deeds and hard facts. . . . He has an inbred distrust of the 'big talk' of intellectuals."[98]

Such an image of Eisenhower—a sturdy, down-to-earth, plainspoken man from the heartland of America—appealed to many Americans longing for a sense of security and wary of worldly ivory tower liberals whose "highfalutin'" knowledge and exposure to foreign ideas rendered them, at best, unfit for leadership, at worst, politically suspect. Next to plain men of "proven ability"—and here Ike's war heroism was always the ultimate testimony to his real world experience—an intellectual like Stevenson was at a disadvantage from the beginning. By 1952, intellectuals were being scorned for precisely the same attributes that Schlesinger had derided in the progressive Doughface—a dreamy, bookish, self-indulgent intellectuality, a lack of familiarity with the "hard" facts of life, and a fetish for rhetoric.

In the words of one partisan, "Eisenhower knows more about world conditions than any other two men in the country, and he didn't obtain his knowledge through newspapers and books either." A midwestern newspaper proclaimed that "Stevenson, the intellectual, must share the views of his [leftist-professor] advisors or he would not have selected them. A vote for Eisenhower, the plain American, is a vote for democracy." McCarthy and his allies had laid fine groundwork for an Eisenhower landslide; it is hard to imagine the *Chicago Tribune*'s sarcastic headline "HARVARD TELLS IN-DIANA HOW TO VOTE" without the previous two years of McCarthyite assaults on the eastern establishment. Moreover, while Stevenson had served in the military only in an administrative capacity, General Eisenhower had, after all, led the D-Day invasion of Normandy, and in the political climate of the early fifties, the fact that Ike had never even registered to vote might have been less of a liability than one might imagine.[99]

Liberal observers sympathetic to Stevenson articulated privately what other Americans must have perceived. Newsman Eric Sevareid recognized the high-minded moralism that Stevenson projected at the expense of creating a sense of unquestionable paternal confidence. Sevareid wrote to an associate, "in his almost painful honesty, [Stevenson] has been analyzing, not asserting; he has been projecting not an image of the big competent father or brother, but the moral and intellectual proctor, the gadfly called conscience." Among his own partisans, Stevenson's acceptance speech at the Democratic National Convention raised specific concerns about his seeming "dread" of power and responsibility:

> I would not seek your nomination for the Presidency, because the burdens of that office stagger the imagination. Its potential for good or evil, now and in the years of our lives, smothers exultation and converts vanity to prayer. I have asked the Merciful Father—the Father of us all—to let this cup pass from me. But from such dreaded responsibility one does not shrink in fear, in self-interest, or in false humility. So, "if this cup may not pass from me, except I drink it, Thy will be done."

Joe Alsop, a supporter of the governor, professed to be driven "literally to drink" upon hearing this speech in which Stevenson "compared his agony in deciding to run with Christ's agony in the garden following the last supper." Stevenson's stated reluctance to imbibe the cup of presidential power—"Let this cup pass from me!"—apparently struck a hard-line cold warrior like Alsop as pretentiously humble and ridiculously weak.[100]

Yet the reputation for effeminacy that Stevenson acquired was not the inevitable result of the persona he himself projected with his "tea cup" words and gentlemanly pretensions. Stevenson's reputation for "softness" also rested upon a determined effort to call into question his sexuality. The 1952 presidential election may have been a high-water mark in the history of dirty politics in America. While Eisenhower maintained his dignity, Senators McCarthy, Nixon, and Jenner played dirty, circulating rumors, stories, and innuendoes about Stevenson. What journalist Marquis Childs called the "ugly whispering campaign" about Stevenson revealed itself in a report that came to Democratic headquarters, which claimed that McCarthy was going to deliver a television attack on the Stevenson campaign in which he would say that the Stevenson campaign staff was made up of "pinks, punks, and pansies." On October 27, 1952, McCarthy appeared on television and smeared the entire Stevenson campaign, as well as the liberal organization Americans for Democratic Action and its spokesman and Stevenson advisor, Arthur Schlesinger, Jr., as Communists. Two times McCarthy made the apparent slip "Alger—I mean Adlai." But the "pinks, punks, and pansies" innuendo, part of a larger strategy to discredit Stevenson with damaging "information" about his personal life, was not used by McCarthy in this speech (Democrats had threatened a nasty retaliation that would embarrass Eisenhower).[101]

The source of the information about Stevenson was the FBI. According to Hoover biographer Kurt Gentry:

> The FBI had supposedly obtained, from local police, statements alleging that Adlai Stevenson had been arrested on two separate occasions, in Illinois and Maryland, for homosexual offenses. In both cases, it was claimed that as soon as the police had learned his identity, Stevenson had been released and the arrests expunged from the record, though not from the recollections of the arresting officers. Through a devious route which hid the bureau's complicity, Crime Records had channeled this and other derogatory information to Nixon, McCarthy, and members of the press. Although most newspaper editors had the story, none used it. But it was widely circulated, as anyone who worked in the campaign could attest.[102]

Hoover, receiving reports alleging that Stevenson and Bradley University President David Owen were the "two best-known homosexuals" in the state of Illinois and that Stevenson was known in the homosexual community as "Adeline," used the law-enforcement grapevine and his associates in Washington to spread the rumors about Stevenson's homosexuality that dogged his campaign. Hoover placed the reports in one of his special files marked "Stevenson, Adlai Ewing—Governor of Illinois—Sex Deviate."[103]

The national political unconscious is surely impossible to measure. Stevenson's two successive defeats cannot be blamed on the sexual aspersions cast on him; liberalism was clearly on the decline given not just what conservatives were calling "twenty years of treason" but what cooler heads were calling "a time for a change" after five successive Democratic administrations. Stevenson could have also been hurt by his divorce and rumors that he was a womanizer. Although the press refused to report Stevenson's alleged arrests on morals charges because no police record could be officially documented, Stevenson's enemies, if only by innuendo, stigmatized him anyway by calling him "Adelaide" or "Adeline," and ridiculing his "fruity voice," among other suspiciously feminine attributes. If the allusions did not cost him the election, they did earn him a reputation as the consummate effete liberal "egghead." Lacking a record in military combat, sports, or anything that might have shored up his manly credentials, Stevenson was only "a gentleman with an Ivy League background," as Hofstadter delicately noted, "and there was nothing in his career to spare him from the reverberations this history set up in the darker corners of the American mind."[104]

Stevenson's defeat sparked a debate about the relevance of the intellectual in American political life that popularized the term "egghead." Eisenhower's landslide victory was taken by some members of the press as evidence of a popular repudiation of intellectuality in America. *Time* magazine, for one, announced that there appeared to be a "wide and unhealthy gap between the American intellectuals and the people," while other critics (including Bromfield, quoted earlier) depicted intellectuals like Stevenson as "eggheads," "oddities," and "bleeding hearts" who were completely out of touch with the mainstream of America. (The idea that Stevenson was a bleeding heart was rather disingenuous, politically speaking. Although he was criticized for advocating a cut-back of the draft and a halt in the testing of the hydrogen bomb, he was no reluctant cold warrior. Ideologically, Stevenson was hardly distinguishable from his opponent and cautiously conservative on domestic issues. His vice-presidential running mate, John Sparkman, a segregationist from Alabama, ensured that their platform would take a position on civil rights that was to the right of Truman's.)[105]

The image of the bleeding-heart-liberal-egghead had superseded the image of the pragmatic, well-educated manly liberal bureaucrat of earlier years. That shift in imagery dramatized the fact that the era of the liberal-intellectual-as-expert had come to an end. When the new Republican administration arrived in Washington, and that "plain American," General Eisenhower, settled into the White House—staffing his administration with business leaders from General Motors and other American corporations, reading the fiction of the Old West, watching football games, and playing regular games of golf in his considerable spare time—it seemed to liberals that, in Stevenson's words, "the New Dealers had been replaced by car dealers." After twenty years of uninterrupted Democratic rule, in which the educated, liberal reformer had come to enjoy an unprecedented status and respectability in American political culture, the funeral march for the egghead-in-government seemed to smack of a low-blow, philistine attack on the manly credentials of the liberal braintrust. Liberals more defensive than Stevenson bristled at the disrepute they were said to be in, and the loudest voice was Schlesinger's.

"Now business is in power again," Schlesinger announced in a 1953 *Partisan Review* article, and it would no doubt bring "the vulgarization which has been the almost invariable consequence of business supremacy." With the usual rhetorical flourish, Schlesinger observed the "rise to climax of the hatred of intellectuals which had long been stewing and stirring in various sections of American society," a hatred that now "burst forth in full violence. By early November the word 'egghead' seemed almost to detonate the pent-up ferocity of twenty years of impotence." Schlesinger may have overstated his case when he concluded that the intellectual is "on the run today in American society," but he understood the grounds upon which Stevenson and his supporters were maligned.[106]

For liberals unencumbered by Ivy League propriety, the lesson of McCarthyism (and the smears against Stevenson) was to fight fire with fire.

Max Lerner had been right about the "boomerang" effect, for McCarthy himself proved not to be immune to the lavender taint and the guilt-by-association smear. When the liberal *New York Post* ran a series of articles entitled "Smear, Inc.: The One-Man Mob of Joe McCarthy" in 1951, the writers, Oliver Pilat and William V. Shannon, called attention to, among other things of a suspicious nature in McCarthy's life, the appearance of a homosexual on McCarthy's staff in 1947. "The man who flamboyantly crusades against homosexuals as though they menace the nation employed one on his office staff for many months," the *Post* writers proclaimed. Other journalists, activists, and congressional enemies of McCarthy searched for and accumulated information on his past improprieties, including those of a sexual nature. Occasionally, liberals actually vented their hatred of McCarthy with a hefty dose of the senator's own medicine, as did the famous liberal journalist Drew Pearson, who not only made some of the same charges in his newspaper column about the presence of a convicted homosexual on McCarthy's staff, but maintained a file of affidavits from men who claimed to have had sex with McCarthy.[107]

Pearson preferred to circulate his affidavits about McCarthy's homosexuality within insider circles rather than put them into print, but others were not so cautious. Pearson's dubious testimonies found their way into the hands of the publisher of the *Las Vegas Sun*, Hank Greenspun, who had been nursing a grudge against McCarthy (McCarthy had previously called Greenspun an "ex-Communist"). In October 1952, as the presidential election neared, the *Las Vegas Sun* identified McCarthy as a homosexual in its pages, named one of the Senator's "illicit" sex partners, and claimed that McCarthy was a well-known patron of gay bars in Milwaukee. Readers were informed that "Joe McCarthy is a bachelor of 43 years. He seldom dates girls and if he does he laughingly describes it as window dressing. It is common talk among homosexuals in Milwaukee who rendezvous at the White Horse Inn that Senator McCarthy has often engaged in homosexual activities." Disturbed by the "homo stories," McCarthy consulted the director of the Anti-Defamation League about suing the paper, but in the end decided against a criminal-libel suit. By then rumors of McCarthy's homosexuality freely circulated on Capitol Hill and fueled the speculations that he finally wed his secretary, Jean Kerr, in 1953 to quell public doubts about his sexual orientation.[108]

It was the drama of the 1954 Army-McCarthy hearings, however, that fueled the festering rumors about McCarthy and his staff members—chief counsel Roy Cohn and aide G. David Schine. The rumors contributed to the Senator's increasing disrepute. Cohn and Schine, who had previously embarked on a much-publicized junket in Europe to investigate Communist influence in the Voice of America, had long been targets of ridicule by

McCarthy-haters in the press, as well as objects of whispers about their suspiciously close relationship. When Schine was drafted into the army in 1953, Cohn attempted to use his leverage—and McCarthy's power—to secure for Schine certain privileges in his military service. At issue in the hearings was the validity of McCarthy's investigation and charges of Communist infiltration of the U.S. Army (an unlikely hotbed of reds and an unwise target for the Senator), and the Army's countercharges—that McCarthy and Cohn had bullied the Army in order to obtain favors for Private Schine. The Army's documented account of McCarthy and Cohn's repeated interventions on Schine's behalf, raised, as the Alsop brothers obliquely put it in their syndicated column, "certain suggestions as to the nature of the McCarthy-Cohn-Schine relationship." Referring to the "sordid tale of Senator McCarthy, Committee Counsel Roy Cohn, and their pet, Pvt. David Schine," the Alsops questioned, like other observers, Cohn's "feverish desire to be of service to Schine," as well as Cohn's seeming possession of "a peculiar power over McCarthy." During the Army-McCarthy hearings, enemies of McCarthy relished the unseemly spectacle of "Tail-gunner Joe" flailing about, on the defensive, repeatedly calling "point of order," flanked by his two sexually suspect young minions. "Bonnie, Bonnie, and Clyde," Lillian Hellman later called the trio. To more than a few observers and enemies of McCarthy, homosexuality explained much of what underlay the actions and abuses of power that were at issue in the Army-McCarthy hearings.[109]

The suspicions about the three men—genuine, inflated, or manufactured—surfaced dramatically when Senator Ralph Flanders (R-Vermont) delivered to the Senate a devastating, innuendo-laden attack on McCarthy. Likening McCarthy to both Hitler and Dennis the Menace, Flanders spoke of the "mysterious personal relationship" between Cohn and Schine. "It is natural that Cohn should wish to retain the services of an able collaborator [Schine], but he seems to have an almost passionate anxiety to retain him. Why?" Flanders then raised the question of McCarthy. "Does the assistant [Cohn] have some hold on him, too? Can it be that our Dennis . . . has at last gotten into trouble himself? Does the committee plan to investigate the real issues at stake?" Given Senate protocol, Flanders had broached the subject of homosexuality as clearly as he could. He subsequently received letters from American citizens congratulating him for raising the issue "that had to be raised." The sexually charged dialogue about "pixies and fairies" that arose during the hearings was in many ways a fitting denouement to the sexual undertones of the entire spectacle, the undoing of McCarthy and the waning of the peak red scare years.[110]

The sexual innuendos about McCarthy, Cohn, and Schine certainly helped to heap disgrace on McCarthy, and his critics will no doubt see some sort of poetic justice at work here, especially in the guilt-by-association logic that rendered him sexually suspect by virtue of his association with Cohn and Schine. Yet the frequency with which the innuendos against McCarthy were deployed immediately before and during the Army-McCarthy hearings was more a symptom of McCarthy's increasing disrepute than the cause of his downfall. McCarthy undid himself by foolishly attacking the Eisenhower administration and the U.S. Army; no sexual smear was necessary to bring the senator down. He had become a serious liability to the Republican Party and his antics had begun to call into question the legitimacy of anti-Communism itself. Of course, McCarthy's fall did not end the purge of homosexuals from the federal government, but his censure by the Senate did put to an end the worst excesses of anti-Communist partisan politicking. By then the damage had been done. The sexual smears and accusations of homosexuality that were leveled against government officials in the name of national security worked to the advantage of the far right and the Republican Party and did considerable harm to the liberal establishment. They also brought incalculable career injury and personal pain to the victims.

The conviction that homosexuals were security risks and should be removed from the government was generally bipartisan, but it was the Republican right that led the "purge of the perverts" and used it (given the dearth of real Communists in government) to create powerful images of a soft and morally corrupt liberal foreign policy establishment. Ironically, the fierce political brawls of the early fifties belie the fact that a broad ideological consensus had been emerging at least since the late 1940s. Yet if liberals had become "hard" on Communism in the fifties, they were still not demonstrably hard enough to escape the image of the soft liberal that had been established in the fallout from the Hiss case and the McCarthyite hysteria. In 1956, Stevenson would suffer another crushing defeat in the presidential race against Eisenhower.[111] The lesson of the red scare and two successive Democratic defeats—that an unquestionable manliness was the essential prerequisite for a Democrat—was not lost on the most ambitious of liberals, who would turn the very attributes that had rendered Stevenson soft and suspect in the 1950s—wealth, an Ivy League pedigree, style, cosmopolitanism, intellectuality—into the virtues of a new liberal manhood. The origins of that new image of liberal manhood lay not only in cold war political imperatives but also in the cultural preoccupations and intellectual styles of the 1950s, the subject of the next chapter.

CHAPTER 3

Conformity, Sexuality, and the Beleaguered Male Self of the 1950s

> To the psychiatrist, both the craving for Utopia and the rebellion against the *status quo* are symptoms of social maladjustment. To the social reformer, both are symptoms of a healthy rational attitude. The psychiatrist is apt to forget that smooth adjustment to a deformed society creates deformed individuals. The reformer is equally apt to forget that hatred, even of the objectively hateful, does not produce that charity and justice on which a utopian society must be based.
>
> —Arthur Koestler, *The God That Failed* (1950)

If one were to judge mid-twentieth century American culture by a selected assortment of popular books, novels, and films, it would appear singularly preoccupied with the self and its fragility. In these works, many of which might seem to share little in common—David Riesman's *The Lonely Crowd* (1950), William Whyte's *The Organization Man* (1956), Leslie Fiedler's *An End to Innocence* (1955), Paul Tillich's *The Courage to Be* (1952), Erich Fromm's *Escape from Freedom (1941)* and *Man for Himself* (1947), Arthur Schlesinger Jr.'s *The Vital Center (1949)*, and Sloan Wilson's *The Man in the Gray Flannel Suit* (1955); books by popular psychiatrists and psychoanalysts: Edward Strecker's *Their Mothers' Sons* (1946), Robert Lindner's *Prescription for Rebellion* (1952) and *Must You Conform?* (1956), and Abram Kardiner's *Sex and Morality* (1954); and films such as *12 Angry Men* (1957) and *Rebel Without a Cause* (1955)—variations on a theme reappear: *the surrender of self.* Like many others in the postwar era, these narratives, each in its own way, reveal a self in danger of engulfment by forces larger and more power-ful—the group, the organization, the Communist Party, ideology, the mother, totalitarianism, a mass society. Whether it is the "organization man" engulfed by the committee and its "groupist" ethos; the Communist who relinquishes self to the party and its all-consuming collectivist ideology; the juvenile delinquent all too eager to surrender self to the "pack"; or the army-reject whose self has been so weakened by a smothering mother that he is left unfit for military service—the lone, pliable self stands in opposition to some seductive, overwhelming force that squashes individual will and autonomy.

Never before had the self come under such scrutiny, a measure of the growing influence of professional psychology and psychiatry as well as its popularization for a mass audience. The concern with the besieged American self also registers a shift in the principal concerns of leading intellectuals in the 1940s and 1950s. While Depression era thinkers had been largely con-cerned with issues of class, poverty, exploitation, and social justice, mid-century social critics and intellectuals turned their attention to psychological discontent and cultural malaise. In part, the shift away from public institu-tions and their shortcomings toward private ailments and inner dissatisfac-tion reflected the postwar economic recovery and the arrival of an affluent society. But it was not just that economic deprivation was no longer the pressing issue of the time. Once fears of economic crisis were put to rest once and for all in the boom years of the 1950s, affluence itself became a problem. The great retreat into private life was accompanied by chronic worries about the psychological effects of consumerism, materialism, suburbanization, leisure, and self-indulgence on the American character. As white-collar men increasingly filled the managerial ranks of large insti-tutions and corporations to bankroll the orgy of consumption for their fami-lies, social commentators worried that these men had exchanged their souls for the good life. Whether middle-class Americans knew it or not, they were psychologically plagued by the very prosperity that seemed to promise them freedom and security. The more sated and comfortable they grew, the more conformist and self-*less* they became; such was the price of affluence.[1]

Yet it was not only prosperity and its cultural implications that gave pause to mid-century social critics and intellectuals. Fear, neurosis, retreat, con-formity, erosion of the self—these were the debilitating byproducts of a "mass society" in which the individual, unloosed from traditional social, kinship, or spiritual moorings, left rootless and adrift, became ever more overwhelmed by the impersonal, self-crushing forces of modernity—bureaucracy, organization, technology, and a mass-produced homogenous culture. The psychological implications of a mass society, and the difficulty of achieving autonomy—an independent, well-fortified sense of self within that society—became the single most compelling problem for postwar intellectuals and social critics.[2]

Although the term "mass society" had lost its exclusive attachment to fascism by the 1950s, the origins of the term lay in the work of European social theorists who had initially sought explanations for the willingness of large numbers of people in Germany and Italy to submit to fascism. Wilhelm Reich's *The Mass Psychology of Fascism,* published in 1933, rejected the idea that fascism's success in mobilizing millions of people could be attributed to the personal power of Hitler or Mussolini. Reich argued instead that what made the masses susceptible to fascism was the "psychic structure" of mass man, formed early in life within the sexually repressed authoritarian family. Here the individual internalized the repression of parental authorities and developed a personality that was fundamentally reactionary and conformist. Frankfurt School theorist Theodor Adorno and other theorists augmented the growing body of discourse on mass psychology in *The Authoritarian Personality* (1950). In this influential collection of studies, several psychologists argued that the prototypical authoritarian male exhibited a hypermasculinity ("pseudo-masculinity") that was psychologically cultivated to compensate for his deep-rooted insecurity and passivity.[3]

Another intellectual byproduct of the Frankfurt School analysis of fascism absorbed by American intellectuals was the concept of "mass culture." It was developed by Adorno, Max Horkheimer, and other theorists as a corrective to the deficiencies of orthodox Marxism, which could not adequately explain the political behavior of the masses. The concept of mass culture highlighted the means by which modern instruments of culture, including radio, film, and mass circulation publications, created a homogenous cultural experience for millions of individuals that ultimately encouraged ideological conformity and passivity. In the work of these theorists, culture was the primary source of domination, less the social relations of production.[4] Originally conceived as an explanation of fascism's success in indoctrinating and tranquilizing the masses, the concept of mass culture was absorbed by American intellectuals eager to explain the cultural dynamics of American society.

Of all the works of social psychology imported from European thinkers and émigrés, Erich Fromm's 1941 *Escape from Freedom* had the greatest impact on American intellectuals, influencing the work of Schlesinger, Riesman, Tillich, Lindner, and others. Like Reich, Fromm argued in *Escape from Freedom* that human beings tend to fear freedom and welcome the order and certainty that authoritarianism offers. Yet Fromm's work focused more on the ambiguities of freedom: the anxiety, fear, and terrifying sense of powerlessness that freedom inspires in the individual. For Fromm, acting as an individual in a free society involves confronting the existential anguish of making choices and exercising responsibility; hence the individual's inclination to escape the burdens of freedom by surrendering to an external authority. Such a surrender allows him to hide in a hierarchy within which his place and his role are certain. In Fromm's analysis, submitting passively to the power of others was one manifestation of the escape from freedom; another was the desire to wield power over others and impose structure on them. Of course, these were the lessons of authoritarian systems in Europe, but Fromm's fundamental observation—that people avoid freedom by fusing themselves with others—was intended to suggest a more general problem facing free societies. Both *Escape from Freedom* and Fromm's 1947 book, *Man for Himself* (a wider exploration of the existential crisis of the besieged modern man) inspired a new interest in the psychodynamics of character formation.[5] Fromm's work appealed to postwar American intellectuals' desire to understand the problems and paradoxes of American society—the anxiety, the apathy, and the conformity of individuals living in the freest society in the world and yet unwilling or unable to accept their freedom or embrace their individuality.

Long before postwar social critics began to voice their concerns about the conformist nature of American society, philosopher John Dewey implied in 1939 that the United States was vulnerable to the phenomenon of mass man. "The serious threat to our democracy," he wrote, "is not the existence of totalitarian states. It is the existence within our own personal attitudes and within our own institutions of conditions similar to those which have given a victory to external authority, discipline, uniformity, and dependence upon The Leader in foreign countries." Fromm, who quoted Dewey's comments in *Escape from Freedom*, essentially agreed, arguing that the frequency with which people avoid freedom and relinquish their self was a problem confronting all modern nation-states. "Compulsive conforming," he averred, "is prevalent in our own democracy."[6] Most American intellectuals and social critics did not argue that American society was veering headlong toward totalitarianism, but its phantom loomed over the postwar discourse on the self.

It would be difficult to overestimate the impact of totalitarianism on postwar American intellectual life. The questions that now engaged intellectuals called for an exploration of the psychological dynamics of character and culture. If freedom is the ultimate aim for which man strives, why do so many people surrender their freedom? Why was the working class so obviously *un*revolutionary? Why were middle-class people so miserable in a society of abundance? Why were Americans so apathetic and conformist in a free, democratic society? Could capitalist democracy produce yet another version of mass man? The older categories of analysis—class as the agent of historical change, alienation as the condition of the worker under industrial capitalism, the systemic crises of overproduction and underconsumption in a capitalist economy—hardly seemed to address the questions raised by a mass (and increasingly affluent) society.[7]

When postwar American intellectuals and social critics turned their attention inward toward the self, the nature of intellectual discourse shifted markedly. Disposing of old Marxian categories that failed to explain the complex and irrational dimension of human nature and political behavior, postwar intellectuals placed America—past and present, real or fictional—under psychological scrutiny. Historians and sociologists declared America a consensus society and transmuted class conflict into "social stresses" and "status anxieties" as sources of historical or social change; conflict now lay buried deep in the psyche, not in the social structure of the society. While scholars examined the Puritans, the Populists, and the McCarthyites as archetypes bearing particular characterological and psychological attributes, the search for an organic American "national character" engaged leading figures in the academy. Literary critics disavowed the proletarian aesthetic of the Depression years and declared their allegiance to complexity, ambiguity, and "reality"—that which the excessively ideological thinking of the thirties had elided or denied. Reality was redefined in psychological terms, and in the name of the new realism, Huck Finn and Alger Hiss both ended up on the psychoanalytic couch of the literary critic. Fiction writers and novelists probed the private self, turning to Freud and existentialism and the subterranean recesses of the psyche. Theologians, too, peered into the psyche and bemoaned the epidemic of anxiety in mid-century life and the irrationality, guilt, and sense of meaninglessness that plagued modern man. Across intellectual disciplines in the 1950s, Communism was now discussed less as a *system*, whose political economy was to be debated or critiqued, and more as a psychological *affliction*, born of man's neurosis, anxiety, fear of freedom, or lack of self.

Popular writers and social commentators, influenced by a rising army of postwar experts, also scrutinized the psyche, and were all too eager to diagnose America as chronically maladjusted. That the Communist was said to suffer from the same psychological ailments (loss of self, anxiety, neurosis) that, according to popular writers and experts, plagued white-collar businessmen, middle-class country clubbers, and juvenile delinquents, marked the triumph of therapeutic culture in the 1950s. As the obsession with the besieged American self found its expression in both middlebrow and highbrow culture, the state of the American psyche began to look exceedingly grim. Nearly everyone seemed to be "fleeing," "escaping," "surrendering," or "retreating" from something, all the "flights" and "retreats" and "surrenders" summed up in a single word: *anxiety*, the great psychic scourge of a mass society, only to be rivaled by its close clinical kin, *neurosis*, the ubiquitous affliction of the 1950s.

In his influential 1952 book, *The Courage to Be*, theologian Paul Tillich, arguing for a spiritual reawakening that would conquer the pervasive anxiety of modern man, spoke of the national obsession with anxiety:

> Sociological analyses of the present period have pointed to the importance of anxiety as a group phenomenon. Literature and art have made anxiety a main theme of their creations, in content as well as in style. The effect of this has been the awakening of at least the educated groups to an awareness of their own anxiety, and a permeation of the public consciousness by ideas and symbols of anxiety. Today it has become almost a truism to call our time an "age of anxiety."[8]

Historically, anxiety had taken multiple forms, Tillich explained, becoming generalized when "the accustomed structures of meaning, power, belief, and order disintegrate." The primary anxiety that plagued twentieth-century man was existential and spiritual in nature, characterized by a profound sense of guilt, meaninglessness, despair, and fear. Fromm's influence looms large in Tillich's work, as does the image of man surrendering to totalitarianism:

> Doubt is based on man's separation from the whole of reality, on his lack of universal participation, on the isolation of his individual self. So he tries to break out of this situation, to identify himself with something transindividual, to surrender his separation and self-relatedness. He flees from his freedom of asking and answering for himself to a situation in which no further questions can be asked and the answers to previous questions are imposed on him authoritatively. In order to avoid the risk of asking and doubting he surrenders his right to ask and to doubt. He surrenders himself in order to save his spiritual life. He "escapes from freedom" . . . he is no longer lonely . . . but the self is sacrificed.

To Tillich, overcoming anxiety required the spiritual and psychological regeneration of the individual confronting his own being, lest he succumb to fanaticism, "the correlate to spiritual self-surrender." In counseling his audience not simply "to be as oneself" but to develop "the courage to be as oneself," Tillich struck a familiar note of the time.[9]

As theologians looked for insight in psychology and existentialist philosophy, psychologists absorbed existentialism. In *Man's Search for Himself* (1953), psychologist Rollo May (who had published *The Meaning of Anxiety* in 1950) echoed Tillich's emphasis on courage: "In any age courage is the simple virtue needed for a human being to traverse the rocky road from infancy to maturity of personality. But in an age of anxiety, an age of herd morality and personal isolation, courage is *a sine qua non.*" À la Fromm,

May located the source of anxiety within freedom: "Courage is the capacity to meet the anxiety which arises as one achieves freedom. It is the willingness to differentiate, to move from the protecting realms of parental dependence to new levels of freedom and integration." Psychotherapy, then, would have to facilitate the development of the individual's maturity, the prerequisite for living in a free society and a bulwark against anxiety. Maturity and courage in the face of anxiety were themes that in one form or another reappeared in countless psychiatric and psychological texts.[10]

Intellectuals were not alone in suggesting that Americans lived in an "age of anxiety," a phrase that had gained wide currency after the 1947 publication of W. H. Auden's poem, "The Age of Anxiety," and the 1949 premiere of Leonard Bernstein's symphony based on that poem. The "discovery" of anxiety made possible the sale of an endless array of self-help books published by psychologists and self-styled experts in the forties and fifties. Dale Carnegie's 1948 *How to Stop Worrying and Start Living* anticipated the slew of books to follow, the titles of which—*Relax and Live, How to Control Worry, Cure Your Nerves Yourself, The Conquest of Fatigue and Fear*— suggest that a national nervous breakdown was in the works. In the 1950s, Americans flocked to see psychiatrists and psychoanalysts as never before; admissions to mental hospitals doubled between 1940 and 1956; and, by the end of the 1950s, one out of every three prescriptions was a tranquilizer. So prevalent was the idea that an epidemic of anxiety was unnerving the nation that a Harvard sociologist and former president of the American Sociological Association, Samuel A. Stouffer, conducted a study of public opinion in 1954 which sought to answer, among other questions, "Is there a National Anxiety Neurosis?" Stouffer, who published his findings in book form in 1955, concluded that there was not (interestingly, the number of respondents who worried about the threat of Communists in the United States was less than 1 percent). Whether or not Stouffer's findings accurately measured the extent of "anxiety neurosis," the question itself is symptomatic of the nagging sense that Americans lacked inner tranquility.[11]

One commentator after another in the 1950s lamented the anxious, beset state of the American psyche. Writing in the *Atlantic Monthly* in 1957, Herbert Gold summed up the postwar sense of disquiet:

> We are a disappointed generation. We are a discontented generation. Our manner of life says it aloud even if discreetly our public faces smile. The age of happy problems has brought us confusion and anxiety amid the greatest material comfort the world has ever seen. Culture has become a consolation for the sense of individual powerlessness in politics, work, and love. With gigantic corporations determining our movements, manipulating the dominion over self which alone makes

meaningful communion with others possible, we ask leisure, culture, and recreation to return us to a sense of ease and authority. But work, love, and culture need to be connected. Otherwise we carry our powerlessness with us onto the aluminum garden furniture in the back yard. Power mowers we can buy, of course.

Gold did not believe that a truly "autonomous personality" was possible to maintain in a mass society. The only advice he could offer readers in these "crowding times" was to stoically "cultivate your own garden." It was another way of saying that the most one could do was struggle privately to overcome anxiety and resist the pressures to conform, "so that we can give the world more than a graceless, prefabricated commodity."[12]

However the problem of the modern self was cast in the diverse cultural works explored in this chapter, the antidote was always the same: to embrace individualism, to muster up the courage to be free, the ability to be alone in a world hostile to the individual. The obsession with strong character that permeates the cultural works of the 1950s was in part a response to unprecedented prosperity and dramatic social and cultural changes (including the rise of therapeutic culture itself) unleashed by the war and accelerated by the postwar economic boom. But those concerns were also the product of the wartime encounter with mass man and the cold war that followed, both of which raised concerns about the ability of the American self to withstand the forces of a mass society that would overwhelm and crush it. The problem of the beleaguered self in mid-century American life was fraught with ideological tension.

It was also fraught with sexual tension. If the mid-century self was so frail, so was the gender identity upon which the self rested. The crisis of the self in the 1950s was distinct from, but overlapped in significant ways with the "crisis of masculinity" that was expressed both explicitly and implicitly in so many cultural productions in the 1940s and 1950s. Insofar as most male critics assumed women didn't have a self in any meaningful sense, at least an autonomous one in need of rehabilitation, most of the fretting about conformity of thought and behavior in American life was *about* men. If women had a place in the crisis of masculinity discourse at all, it was as the oppositional archetype against which a healthy autonomous male self could be measured, or as the purveyor of feminizing values and forces that emasculated the culture or crushed the male ego.

Anxieties about an erosion of masculinity, shifting gender norms and behaviors, and the perception of a breakdown of sexual boundaries were inextricably bound up with the growing dread of the "soft," malleable American psyche. The nation might not have been drifting toward a "social structure made up of he-women and she-men," as psychologist Irene Josselyn insisted.[13] But such claims, while hyperbolic, were not without some sort of wellspring. Their immediate source lies in the undercurrents of change in gender roles and sex relations that were rippling through postwar American culture. They also reflected almost a century of concerns about a breakdown of sexual barriers in American life.

Imprisoned in Brotherhood

The decade of the fifties opened with the publication of David Riesman's influential collaborative work, *The Lonely Crowd*, a book that set the terms of discussion and debate for so much of the cultural criticism of the next ten years. The product of academic sociology, *The Lonely Crowd* nonetheless landed a place on the bestseller list in 1950 and made "other-direction" a familiar phrase in the national lexicon. By the time journalist William Whyte's *The Organization Man*, another bestseller, was published in 1956, a series of novels, magazine articles, social-psychology books, and films (notably *The Man in the Gray Flannel Suit*, *12 Angry Men*, *High Noon*, and *Rebel Without a Cause*) had already given diverse expression to the problem of the beleaguered American self.

That problem was captured in Riesman's astute portrait of the "other-directed" personality type—a pliable, likeable, socially attuned person whose definitive quality was his need to gain the approval of others. Excessively sensitive to the opinions and attitudes of his peers, the other-directed person suffered from a "diffuse anxiety" at the possibility of their disapproval. Riesman contrasted the other-directed personality type increasingly prevalent in mid-century American society with both the "tradition-directed" personality type characteristic of the Middle Ages and the "inner-directed" personality type of the nineteenth century. The rise and decline of such personality types corresponded with major economic, social, and demographic forces and shifts: from a rigidly class-structured feudal society in which the individual deferred to centuries-old customs and whose identity was immutably grounded in family, class, or caste (the "tradition-directed" personality); to an expanding, capital-accumulating, production-oriented economy in which social mobility and achievement were valued over obedience to tradition, and success lay in individual drive, initiative, and competition (the "inner-directed" personality type); and finally to a consumption-oriented affluent society in which the pursuit of goals and work itself became less important than the rewards of work, and individual success was tied to social gregariousness, that is, how well one could market a likeable personality (the "other-directed" personality type). While Riesman observed that the other-directed personality type was not yet dominant in the United States, he noted that, if social trends continued, "the hegemony of other-direction lies not far off."[14]

Riesman primarily contrasted the new other-directed personality type with the inner-directed personality of the nineteenth century, whose inner voice guided him as he blazed new trails and ventured into unexplored frontiers in business and industry, and whose internalization of parental authority left him with a "psychological gyroscope" upon which his driven character relied. The other-directed personality type of the twentieth century, on the other hand, took his social "cues" from others—friends, bosses, teachers, advertisers, celebrities, peers, and the most significant thing he absorbed from his parents was their own "highly diffuse anxiety." Absent an inner gyroscope, the other-directed person was left only with highly attuned "radar" with which to detect the styles and attitudes of others whom he would compulsively emulate. The other-directed type's character was molded by schools, peer groups, and a mass-produced culture, all of which imprinted upon him not drive and ambition (as with the inner-directed type), but rather the imperative to *get along* with others.[15]

Riesman's contrasting archetypes were not meant to suggest that the other-directed type was the lone conformist in history. The tradition-directed person of the Middle Ages scarcely saw himself as an individual; he had no choice but to conform to the rigid social role prescribed to him by class, custom, and tradition. The inner-directed type of the socially mobile nineteenth century unconsciously yielded to external imperatives; his inner "gyroscope" was shaped by parental authority and the cultural norms of industrial society appropriate to his status, and in this sense he too sought the approval of others. But the other-directed individual, Riesman implied, had succumbed to a qualitatively different kind of conformist behavior, for he was at once more liberated *and* more psychically imprisoned—the product of a free, democratic society and yet an unwitting captive of its progeny, mass culture. Indeed, he appeared as thoroughly inauthentic as the mass culture within which his personality was shaped.[16]

The other-directed man may not have self-consciously pledged his faith, like *Death of a Salesman*'s Willy Loman, to the "power of personality" ("be liked and you will never want"), but early in his life he had absorbed the lesson that getting along meant getting ahead. Socialized in schools where progressive educational ideals encouraged children to "cooperate" with others, the other-directed person learned to value popularity over the achievement of goals. As a result, the mature other-directed person's forte was not boldly pursuing new enterprises and innovations but rather in selling his affable personality. Riesman's model of the other-directed personality type obviously drew from Fromm's sketch, in *Man for Himself,* of the hollow "marketing personality" born of commercial capitalism, the salesman who lacked any individual traits or idiosyncrasies that might conflict with the requirements of the market. Riesman, however, focused not just on the lack of self but the lack of drive exhibited by the other-directed type. With no deeply held beliefs or inner obsession to compel him forward to achieve some aim, the other-directed type sought largely to "fit in" and be liked by others; instead of the achievement of a goal, the payoff was a comfortable life of consumption and leisure. The other-directed person channeled his energy into the "ever-expanding frontiers of consumption," unlike the inner-directed person who channeled his energy "relentlessly into production."[17]

For Riesman, a postindustrial society of abundance provided the seed-bed for the growth of other-directedness, the perfect specimen of which could be found at the managerial level of American corporations. Unlike the inner-directed type, who could be a highly effective leader as well as a ruthless opportunist, the other-directed type sacrificed self-initiative and trailblazing for the promise of affection from the group. As he submerged his competitive instincts underneath an outwardly genial manner, he suffered immense "anxiety" at the possibility of exercising initiative or achieving success at the cost of alienating those around him. Repressing "all 'knobby' or idiosyncratic qualities and vices" lest he alienate others, the other-directed person essentially feared being alone. In this sense, he was not unlike William Whyte's "organization man," whose primary psychological affliction was also his "need to belong."[18]

Though there were significant differences between Riesman's other-directed personality type and Whyte's archetypical "organization man," both authors shared a concern about the frequency with which middle-class Americans appeared to engage in what Riesman called "submission to the group." Like so many professional men in the postwar era, Whyte's "organization man" worked in middle management within a large corporation, government bureaucracy, or large-scale scientific, educational, or technological institution. He was a new species of man who, unlike the entrepreneurs and pioneers of earlier times, sought to work for—and closely with—others. Whyte's typical organization man was essentially a "committee" man, one who assumed as a matter of habit that "the group," a committee of like-minded individuals dedicated to cooperation with each other in the pursuit of some mutually conceived project, could accomplish more in the way of progress, efficiency, and creativity than the individual struggling alone. Whyte attributed such an assumption to the "social ethic," a "body of thought" defined by its three central propositions: "a belief in the group as the source of creativity; a belief in 'belongingness' as the ultimate need of the individual; and a belief in the application of science to achieve the belongingness."[19]

Despite Whyte's gestures of impartiality, he clearly had contempt for the social ethic. It worked to reward conformity and mediocrity, while stifling individual creativity and genius. In the name of consensus and harmony, the social ethic endorsed team-playing and cooperation while it discouraged competition, divisive debate, and intragroup conflict. Loyalty to the company was privileged over independent thought and bold initiative. In Whyte's judgment, the social ethic had succeeded in demonizing the lone individual. Pursuing ideas and action apart from the group was now understood as selfish, while "conflict, change, fluidity" had become "the evils from which man should be insulated." Whyte's belief that the organization was psychically oppressive and his barely concealed preference for old-fashioned ways resounds in his declaration that "what [the old boss] wanted primarily from you was your sweat. The new man wants your soul."[20]

If the organization man—ill-equipped to see anything but "beneficence" in the social ethic—was sadly "imprisoned in brotherhood," the executive within the organization could be driven almost schizoid by it. In Whyte's view, the executive is the man who is most suspicious of the organization; he is attuned to its "velvety" grip and resents yielding to it; "he wants to dominate, not be dominated." But he cannot "act that way." Outwardly accommodating and sociable inasmuch as he sees "utility" in projecting the spirit of brotherhood, the executive in Whyte's book looks much like an instinctual inner-directed man struggling in an other-directed environment, to use Riesman's formulation. In having to display traits that run counter to his personality, he develops the "executive neurosis," a complex of "frustrations," "psychoses," and "tensions." The origins of that neurosis lie in a collision between old and new, between the executive's own inner drive to "control his own destiny" and the dubious imperative toward cooperation, team work, and good fellowship, which ultimately "bores him to death."[21]

Whyte came close to blaming the rising tide of "organization men" on the incursions of a progressive do-gooder liberalism—with its communitarian ethos, bureaucratic proclivities, and therapeutic ideals—into the organization. Indeed, his critique of the "social ethic," peppered with words like "collectivization," "surrender," and "utopian" and explicitly linked to the twentieth century rise of progressive reform and social engineering, bears a remarkable resemblance to the postwar intelligentsia's indictment of the leftists and revolutionaries of the 1930s. Whyte revealed the social ethic for what he believed it was: a manipulative "ideology," a bogus "utopian faith," one that appealed to the weak-minded, to man's "need to belong," his need to be "soothed" by a comforting doctrine of "togetherness." To Whyte, the social ethic was far from benign; it lured men into "surrender" (much the same way Communist ideology was said to induce self-surrender), not by means of naked coercion but by a deceptively benevolent ethos of "progress" through "cooperation," and "social harmony" through the "science" of human relations. The social ethic (ideology) was the weapon of the organization (the collective): the means by which the organization invaded the psyche, destroyed the boundaries between self and group, and thus succeeded in stealing a man's very "soul." And like Communism, the social ethic was utopian in that it assumed the perfectibility of man; his nature could be "adjusted" to exist in complete harmony with the collective. In essence, the social ethic represented the merging of the therapist, the middle manager, and Big Brother. Finally, like many critics of the left, Whyte focused not on the legitimacy, integrity, or the structure of the institutions at issue, but on the organization man's willingness to surrender to something external to the self. He assured readers that "the fault is not in the organization," but rather "in our worship of it." Indeed, the real danger was "not man being dominated but man surrendering."[22]

Whyte was describing a kind of corporate collectivism; Riesman had already analyzed something akin to its broader cultural counterpart, mass conformity. Riesman did not tend to employ politically tinged terms like "collectivist" in *The Lonely Crowd*, but he was a centrist liberal who clearly shared Whyte's scorn for the communitarian ideal (the problem for mid-century individuals was not "the material environment," Riesman observed, but "*other people*").[23] While Riesman attributed the trend toward other-direction and groupism to the rise of a consumption-oriented mass society, rather than a particular ethic or seductive ideology, the new other-directed society looked, if not quite like totalitarianism, at least suspiciously vulnerable to it.

Riesman's *The Lonely Crowd* and Whyte's *The Organization Man* were trenchant and resonant critiques of mid-century American society. In an era of national self-congratulation and complacency, both men revealed an America that had pledged its allegiance to "individualism" and then relinquished it in exchange for the good life, or what passed for it. Riesman's work elided the difficult problem of female "other-direction"—a serious omission by a sociologist who otherwise typed people scrupulously. Given the domestic ideology of the time, if anyone was a victim of the mass culture that pressured individuals to be attuned to the "other," to surrender self, it was the middle-class American woman. Nonetheless, as public intellectuals, both Riesman and Whyte initiated considerable debate about the problem of individuality in American culture and some much needed national self-criticism. If they recoiled from the radical implications of their conclusions, maintaining their focus on the private (male) self and refusing to call for change in the institutions and the social order that encouraged and rewarded conformity, it was because they could not imagine, as Richard Pells observed, any alternative to the present order—except socialism, which was already discredited for affirming the very collectivist attitudes they disdained.[24] Unable to deliver any real answers to the problem of mass conformity, Riesman and Whyte could only recommend that people become more self-aware and attuned to their predicament. Yet their fundamental ideas continued to encourage debate about the problem of individuality in American life well into the 1960s and helped inspire the radical critiques of Paul Goodman and other social critics.

Riesman and Whyte were political centrists, and save for their obvious dislike of the communitarian ethos, they were not overtly political in their work. Yet their common theme, the tension between the self and the other and the need to rescue the former from the latter, had immense ideological import. *The Lonely Crowd* was published in 1950, the same year that Alger Hiss was convicted of perjury and Julius and Ethel Rosenberg were indicted for conspiracy to commit espionage. Ever more sensitive to the failures and transgressions of the left, many mid-century intellectuals viewed these and other radicals through the lens of social psychology and pronounced them conformists of a sort: leftists whose communitarian ideals or allegiance to the Communist Party were symptoms of the need to belong, the compulsion to submerge identity in a group, and to play out a social role shaped by ideology and dictated by the party "organization."

This kind of critique of the Communist left had been germinating for over a decade. Like Fromm, postwar social critics assumed that Communism, like fascism, was a totalitarian ideological system that exalted the collective mass at the expense of the individual. Never before had political systems depended so much on the psychological appeal to and manipulation of the masses' anxieties and fears; never before had political parties and their leadership sought so deliberately, in Arthur Koestler's words, "the transformation of character and of human relationships" within their ranks. One Communist Party defector after another proffered personal narratives that validated these assumptions and stressed self-deception as the *sine qua non* of the Communist Party recruit. In *The God That Failed*, Koestler, a former member of the Communist Party in Germany, revealed the inner workings of the party and the determination with which it enforced ideological uniformity among members. Why did so many people submit? Koestler acknowledged the generosity of spirit that motivated so many revolutionaries to fight injustice and exploitation in the name of the proletariat, as well as the thirst for faith that brought people such as himself into the party—the same faith that allowed so many of them to sustain the utopian dream even after the Soviet experiment had degenerated into gulags and show trials. Koestler also suggested that there was some truth to the idea that "most revolutionaries and reformers" were people who had "neurotic conflicts" with family and society (though he stressed, using Marx's idiom, that this proved that a "moribund society" produces "its own morbid grave-diggers"). Whatever the public or private origins of the revolutionaries' malaise, Koestler's account of the Communist Party experience, like others that emerged in the 1940s and 1950s, speaks to an assumption that became axiomatic to the postwar American intelligentsia: the typical Communist revolutionary had a deep, "neurotic" need to rebel and conform to something external to the self.[25]

In his 1955 reappraisal of the radicalism of 1930s America, *Part of Our Time*, journalist Murray Kempton depicted the American revolutionaries of his generation as lonely people who sought to escape the unbearable "burden of solitude." "We were, most of us, fleeing the reality that man is alone upon this earth. We ran from a fact of solitude to a myth of community." Kempton was not speaking of solitude solely in an abstract, existential sense. Communist recruits, he suggested, were often weak-willed people who easily yielded to authority ("an appalling number came into the movement and stayed in because they could be bullied by someone who could muster the illusion of decision") or lonely and desperate hangers-on like Elizabeth Bentley (it was not politics or religion that was "the mainspring" of Bentley's life "but the fact of being alone"). Kempton cast Bentley, the Soviet espionage agent turned FBI informant, as a foolish "old maid." He noted the research of Herbert E. Krugman, whose psychoanalytic case studies of Communists claimed to show the high incidence of psychological maladjustment and sexual deviance in the ranks of party members. In Krugman's case studies, as Kempton put it, "the average *neurotic* male Communist would thus appear to be a person who has talent without genius. The average *neurotic* female Communist would seem to be unafflicted with either. . . . The special frustrations of modern women, [Krugman] concluded, made them altogether better haters than men."[26]

Kempton's least pleasant recollection of the Communist experience, he said, was that "so many people whimpered so often." The revolutionaries of the 1930s desperately wanted to feel themselves a part of a great historical movement, to belong to something larger than themselves. But they were not rebels at all, Kempton concluded. They were "persons desperate to conform or to enforce conformity." The true rebel, he insisted, was "the radical who dared to stand alone, to whom no man called out in vain, to whom the lie was dishonorable and the crawl degrading."[27]

For many ex-radical critics like Kempton, the great sin of the revolutionaries was not so much their "escape from reality" into a naïve utopianism—a sin for which Depression era idealists could be forgiven—but rather their abject personal inauthenticity. Kempton's contempt was directed at the many American revolutionaries who "pursued their function in disguise. Their inner and their outer selves were alike a mask." The argument that leftist revolutionaries could best serve their causes by remaining covert party members (whether in organized labor or the movement for racial justice) did not impress Kempton. Open party membership would have been hardly "fatal" for these revolutionaries in most instances. In fact, the disguise suited the individual's desires more than party objectives. The truth was that "the Communists are the only political party in our history with a great body of members consistently embarrassed to admit their allegiance."[28]

In Kempton's judgment, the "great lie" was the only crime most revolutionaries committed, and it was no small offense. In misleading others as well as themselves, in trying "at once to possess their dream and live outside of it," they did "terrible violence" to their nature, "adding that much more to the burden of solitude which had made so many of them Communists in the first place." In a slightly more caustic indictment, Harold Rosenberg, writing in *Dissent* in 1955, depicted fellow-travelers and Communist intellectuals as disingenuous, self-satisfied social-climbers, attuned to securing the "Good Spot" in Hollywood, academia, publishing, or government while imagining themselves revolutionaries on "The Stage of History," worthy of a post in "the future International Power" when the revolution came. To Rosenberg, they were essentially "middle-class careerists, closed to both argument and evidence, impatient with thought, psychopaths of their 'radical' conformity."[29]

As Pells observed, in the intellectual climate of the fifties it was not inconceivable to see Alger Hiss—with his neatly pressed suits, well-groomed look, and smooth, false exterior—as a fifties-style conformist, "the radical as organization man." Literary critic Leslie Fiedler, in a 1950 piece on the Hiss-Chambers case in *Commentary*, represented Hiss as such a conformist. As Fiedler saw it, Hiss was the antithesis of the old-style Bolshevik, the scruffy romantic bohemian poet who chanted protest songs, lived a life true to his radical allegiance, and openly rebelled. Hiss was rather the "new model Bolshevik," a creation of the Popular Front imperative to make peace with liberalism while secretly "boring from within." In Fiedler's eyes, this was an appealing role for Hiss, a divided man who could pursue his revolutionary ideal and at the same time exist so comfortably outside of it. Needing to protect himself from "a merely selfish kind of success" as he climbed the career ladder, needing to rationalize his spectacular rise as a government bureaucrat, he moonlighted as a Soviet agent—proof to himself that he had not completely "sold out" to the bourgeois world from which he "profited immensely." Every promotion to a higher governmental position could thus be considered as yet another opportunity for "infiltration." Hiss appeared in Fiedler's essay as the consummate left-wing phony, as "other-directed" as any gray-flannel suit businessman, though the "other" from whom he took his cues obviously had two faces. In Fiedler's exegesis, it was Hiss's disheveled and eccentric nemesis, Whittaker Chambers, who looked truly authentic, first in his incarnation as the genuine social outsider/old-fashioned "romantic" Bolshevik, and later as a self-critical, self-denouncing Communist apostate.[30]

It was not sufficient for Fiedler to argue that a man like Hiss was self-deceptive and ambivalent about the bourgeois society he ultimately betrayed. Seeing Hiss as the epitome of "the Popular Front mind at bay, incapable of honesty when there was no hope in anything else," Fiedler probed Hiss's inner psyche as an object lesson in the psychology of the left. Why did Hiss lie, Fiedler asked, as if the instinct to deny the charges and thus salvage some remnant of his reputation could not explain Hiss's plea of innocence in the face of a lesser perjury charge. For Fiedler, Hiss's lies could only be viewed as symptomatic of the collective neurosis of the left. Echoing Schlesinger's earlier diagnosis of the Doughface-turned-Stalin-accomplice, Fiedler concluded that Hiss was neurotic and narcissistic (witness his need to "pose as The Victim") and also hopelessly immature, for the "qualifying act of moral adulthood is precisely this admission of responsibility for the past and its consequences." Maturity demanded that one relinquish idealism and face the "hard facts of life" (in Schlesinger's idiom); it required the acceptance of complexity, ambiguity, and reality, which in turn demanded not just the acceptance of anti-Communism, but a bold show of one's renunciation of Communism. In this view, maturity required atonement for past sins. Timid and duplicitous, Hiss, in refusing to confess, could thus stand for the childishness of the left, its refusal to grow up.[31]

If Hiss became a symbol of left-wing timidity, immaturity, and conformity, Julius and Ethel Rosenberg came to represent much more. For Fiedler and other critics, it was not so much the gravity of the Rosenbergs' crime (passing atomic secrets to the Kremlin) but rather their wholesale relinquishment of self and their lame, transparent Communist theatrics that made them perfect case studies in radical conformity. In a 1953 essay in *Encounter*, Fiedler argued that the real "tragedy" of the Rosenbergs was their inability "to think of themselves as real people," their willful transposition of themselves into props for the revolution. Unlike Hiss, whose "double allegiance" allowed him to play both sides (without truly ever having to believe in *anything*), Julius and Ethel Rosenberg had so thoroughly surrendered their identities to the cause that they had no guilt whatsoever. Assuming that "sharing the atomic secret" meant they were striking "a blow for world peace," the Rosenbergs could imagine themselves "innocent, more innocent than if they had never committed espionage."[32]

The letters of Julius and Ethel Rosenberg, written to each other while they were in prison and published in 1953, shaped these impressions. Looking at this correspondence, Robert Warshow, a writer and editor at

Commentary, came to nearly the same conclusions as Fiedler. Warshow argued that the Rosenbergs were prisoners of the role they had constructed for themselves—two people almost pathologically inauthentic. Like Fiedler, Warshow saw the Rosenbergs' letters to each other as so absurd and formal—a mixture of progressive banalities, pretentious intellectual posturing, and coded revolutionary doublespeak—that they sounded like parodies of the Communist mindset. It seemed almost unfathomable that Ethel, facing capital punishment along with her husband, could write to Julius from her jail cell and cheer the Brooklyn Dodgers for their recent victories on the baseball field as well as "their outstanding contribution to the eradication of racial prejudice." Julius and Ethel Rosenberg, Warshow concluded, seemed to have no identity or experience that truly belonged to them, and inasmuch as they thought and felt anything, it was only what their "political commitment required them to think and feel." On the eve of their execution, they were quite incapable of expressing anything but the most programmed of thoughts, written less for each other than for public consumption. To Warshow, the Rosenbergs inhabited a mental world in which they were only able to see themselves as they believed *others* would see them—as perpetual victims, selfless humanitarians, devoted Jews, martyrs, cultivated highbrows, Brooklyn Dodgers fans, even American patriots. "It is as if these two had no internal sense of their own being but could see themselves only from the outside, in whatever postures their 'case' seemed to demand."[33]

Of course, the Rosenbergs' seemingly outward normality and social conformity was inseparable from the charge of inauthenticity, and here they were being assailed, as Andrew Ross and others have noted, for what was perhaps their worst offense in the eyes of critics—their dreadful middlebrow habits, their embarrassing petit-bourgeois affectations, Ethel's self-conscious attempt at a serious "literary" style. As a purported member of the Communist underground, Ethel's exterior could strike observers as incongruous. It may have been difficult to believe, as one historian noted, "that someone who chose to wear hats with six-inch high flowers sticking straight out of them—as Ethel did the day she was arrested—could fully represent the international Communist menace." Postwar intellectuals had long been assailing mass culture and its endless diet of empty sentimentalities, and here those banalities could meet the conformist, petit-bourgeois Communist mind. The couple's published letters (lauded by the editors of the second edition as "world classics in democratic eloquence and inspiration") were a "godsend," as Morris Dickstein observed, for they enabled critics to turn Julius and Ethel Rosenberg into unreal people, comic bood caricatures of party members, types to be intellectually ransacked for signs of banality and inauthenticity.[34]

To critics eager to exorcize the vulgar Popular Front progressive from their intellectual universe, Hiss and the Rosenbergs were not simply the miserable casualties of a failed revolution, dissemblers caught in a monumental historical tragedy from which they could not, in the end, manage to extricate themselves. Rather, in their steadfast refusal to claim responsibility for their crimes, or, more importantly, to defend their actions by bravely stating the convictions that justified them—the only act that could have rendered them authentic people—they became personifications of all that was psychotic about the left. Each represented variants of revolutionary inauthenticity and conformity: Hiss, the genteel, suave Ivy Leaguer, a classic Popular Front bureaucrat whose "double allegiance" allowed him to take full advantage of the system he pretended to want to overthrow; and Julius and Ethel Rosenberg, petit-bourgeois party hacks, the purest specimens of Communist self-abnegation and delusion, their identities so psychologically submerged within a role that they ultimately opted for martyrdom and death over confession and life.

Whatever their differences, Hiss and the Rosenbergs proved to critics that when individuals ceded self to the collective, they were robbed of identity, autonomy, and intellectual integrity. The crime of espionage was almost beside the point. The lesson of Hiss and the Rosenbergs extended to all those Communists and fellow travelers who, in substituting sentimentality for intelligence and ideology for truth, in refusing to relinquish a dream that had long been betrayed by the hideous reality of Stalinism, had committed the crime of intellectual dishonesty. Harold Rosenberg insisted that the prototypical Communist intellectual was primarily guilty of "intellectual crimes," and insofar as he could be judged innocent of these offenses, it could only be by reason of something akin to mental incapacity: "The Communist intellectual, *as a distinct figure produced by the movement,* was innocent in one sense only: the *non sui juris* of pathology. He had been taken over completely by a false or assumed 'we'—which is the basis of mystification in our century. But the spurious 'we' is also the basis of modern terrorism."[35]

Postwar social critics and intellectuals interpreted left-wing politics through the lens of social psychology, while psychiatrists and pop psychologists interpreted the political and social world with their eyes cast also on the ideologically noxious "we." In his 1956 anticonformist treatise *Must You Conform?* psychoanalyst and popular author Robert Lindner presented the mid-twentieth century conformist as a prototype of mass man, and warned of his "increasing presence" in American life. Such a conformist was a "mechanized, robotized caricature of humanity . . . a lost creature without separate identity in the herding collectivity . . . a mindless integer of the pack." Whether he was a member of a juvenile youth gang or the Communist Party, he was just one of the hordes of weak and frightened people who, yielded to the imperative to "adjust" and "conform" to roles prescribed by the collective. To Lindner, Communism was the ultimate manifestation of psychological conformity. In promising relief from the loneliness of mass society through a comforting pseudoreligious doctrine, the party becomes "a haven for neurosis and a refuge for neurotics—actually a great organized, systematized, ready-made neurotic defense." It takes a "total surrender to adhere to the Party and to submit to its discipline, but for the distraught neurotic even the abandonment of his birthright of individuality and personal freedom is not ordinarily a price too expensive to pay for the relief thus obtained."[36]

In *Must You Conform?* Communists were not the only mindless conformists who exemplified the "herd" mentality. But in the "struggle between man and Society over the issue of conformity, Society is winning," Lindner proclaimed, and such a victory threatened to turn America into a neo-totalitarian state. "To combat the rising tide of psychopathy must become a task to which citizens of a democratic society have to dedicate themselves if they want their civilization to continue." In his 1952 book *Prescription for Rebellion*, he had declared that "in our own United States, especially, we are confronted with a demand for conformity that not a single agency or institution opposes . . . the making of Mass Man is in the process." In *Must You Conform?* Lindner upped the ante, warning that "our civilization appears to have entered its terminal phase."[37]

The excitable Lindner must be distinguished from the more thoughtful critics of conformity and mass man. Few of them saw real totalitarian apocalypse approaching in the United States; even fewer got as much mileage out of the issue as did Lindner, whose many books dealing with conformity, rebellion, and psychopathy, including *Rebel without a Cause*, earned him a considerable windfall.[38]

Even for more thoughtful critics, however, the problem of conformist thought and behavior in American society had serious political implications. In his book *The Courage to Be*, Tillich discussed the conformity crisis, making a distinction between the "courage to be as oneself," which he associated with a free individualist democracy, and the "courage to be *as a part*," which he associated with Communist collectivism. Of course, it was the former that needed to be cultivated in America, and while Tillich was primarily concerned with spiritual life, he shared Schlesinger's assumption that modern man's success in overcoming the fear of being a free individual required a profound emotional and spiritual regeneration. That regeneration had political import for Tillich as it did for Schlesinger. "Conformity is growing," Tillich wrote, "but it has not yet become collectivism."[39]

Tillich attributed the conformity crisis in American and Western life to the arrival of modernity. The industrial and technological revolution had imposed fixed patterns on the production process; the more standardized production became, the more it demanded the conformity of individuals in order to facilitate "the smooth functioning of the big machine of production and consumption." More original among the conformity critics of the time was Tillich's conviction that the battle against totalitarianism encouraged a growing behavioral conformity: "World political thinking, the struggle with collectivism, forced collectivist features on those who fought against them. This process is still going on and may lead to a strengthening of the conformist elements in the type of the courage to be as a part which is represented by America [sic]." Tillich did not elaborate on what those features were, saying only that "conformism might approximate collectivism," not so much in a political or economic sense but rather "in the pattern of daily life and thought." In short, cold war imperatives and anxieties had increased the pressure on the individual to conform to prevailing norms of thought and behavior, resulting in a kind of cultural collectivism that made individual autonomy all the more difficult to achieve.[40]

In the early years of the cold war, this positing of the opposition between the individual and the collective, the self and other, the "I" and the "we," served to further undermine the "communitarian" values of the American left, which had been on the defensive politically since the late 1940s. Even the rhetoric of the American intelligentsia shifted accordingly. Pells observed so perceptively how the connotations of words and tropes used by the 1930s intelligentsia had shifted, and even reversed themselves, by the 1950s:

> What the writers of the 1930s called "community," the postwar intelligentsia labeled "conformity." Cooperation now became "other-direction"; social consciousness had turned into "groupism"; solidarity with others implied an invasion of privacy; "collectivism" ushered in a "mass society"; ideology translated into imagery; economic exploitation yielded to bureaucratic manipulation; the radical activist was just another organization man.[41]

Taking this shift further, even alienation, once considered the scourge of capitalist society, might now be cultivated as a defense against the suffocating "togetherness" of a mass society. It was surely a sign of the times when Daniel Bell declared in his influential treatise, *The End of Ideology*, that "alienation is not nihilism but a positive role, a detachment, which guards one against being submerged in any cause, or accepting any particular embodiment of community as final."[42]

From the narratives of George Orwell to those of Ayn Rand, from *The Vital Center* to *The Organization Man*, the "we" became the disease against which man must innoculate himself, while the embattled "I" took on new significance. In more than a few postwar dramas that exalted the alienated individual struggling against the dictates of the group, there stood Riesman's individualist hero. Like the protagonist in the 1957 film *12 Angry Men* whose lone dissent on a jury in a murder trial ultimately served to uphold the rights of the individual against the unthinking group, the genuine autonomous individual had the ability to endure solitude, to assert his convictions even at the cost of alienating others, to stand alone and above the lonely crowd, to muster up the courage to *be*. And like the protagonist in *12 Angry Men*, the autonomous individualist hero was always a man.

Manhood and Conformity

Riesman employed broad, gender-neutral terms to describe the new character types born of the shift from production to consumption, from the Protestant ethic to the social ethic. Yet both *The Lonely Crowd* and *The Organization Man* were keyed to men. Whyte's subjects were those who held management positions within the organization; his claims were necessarily limited to males. Though Riesman's archetypes were apparently intended to be loosely applicable to both men and women, they were obviously conceived with normative male behavior in mind. Despite the apparent flexibility of Riesman's types, the older "inner-directed" person embodied qualities (self-possession, will, drive, an "inner gyroscope") which would be difficult to reconcile with female roles in the nineteenth (or the mid-twentieth) century. In his later book, *Individualism Reconsidered*, Riesman described (not uncritically) the typical older "inner-directed" types as unmistakably male: they were "hardy men who pioneered on the frontiers of production, exploration, and colonization," paternalistic men who, despite the disreputable pirates or slave traders among them, "were more likely to subscribe to high moral principles (e.g., the elder Rockefeller)."[43]

The absence of any extended discussion of women in Riesman's broadly conceived book suggests the difficulty that was inescapable here and elsewhere in the conformity discourse. Riesman had little to say pointedly about women, save, for example, that as chief consumers and shapers of domestic life, they were complicit in the rising tide of other-direction that permeated middle-class life. Other-direction manifested itself first in men and later in women, Riesman noted, without further explanation. Although he occasionally made distinctions between the social roles of men and women in his elaboration of the "other-directed" personality, lapsing into the phrase "other-directed man" (as opposed to "person") when he was clearly speaking exclusively of men, he could hardly bring himself to use the term "other-directed woman." Indeed, Riesman could not draw a portrait of an "other-directed" woman; to do so would have been unthinkable, even awkwardly redundant, for the qualities which together signified "other-direction" were those traditionally built into the definition of wife and mother. To construct a meaningful, archetypical "other-directed female" would have required Riesman to confront a body of cultural norms which had long assumed, and in fact required, women to be selfless and therefore self*less*.

Barbara Ehrenreich pointed out that the character traits that Riesman assigned to the "other-directed" personality type were essentially feminine. "The perpetual alertness to signals from others, the concerns with feelings and affect rather than objective tasks . . . were precisely those that the patriarch of mid-twentieth century sociology, Talcott Parsons, had just assigned to the female sex." Ehrenreich noted that "in Parson's scheme, the male (breadwinner) role was 'instrumental'—rational and task-oriented—and the female role was 'expressive'—emotional, attuned to the feelings of others."[44]

Those gender roles rested on behavioral norms that were sanctioned in the nineteenth century and reappeared in altered form in the domestic ideology of the 1950s. Insofar as woman—innately passive, maternal, and emotional—was expected to put herself in the service of others, to define herself in relation to others, and to sacrifice her "self" to husband and family, she was in a fundamental sense the first "other-directed personality type." That her character traits had begun to appear in mid-century men made "Riesman's sweeping characterological transformation look like nothing so much as the feminization of American men," in Ehrenreich's words. If the other-directed man was, in essence, "a Parsonian *woman*," so too was Whyte's "organization man." In his need for "belongingness," in his deference to the group, in his acceptance of the therapeutic ideals of cooperation and conflict resolution, the organization man looked remarkably feminine in psychological predisposition.[45]

Both Riesman and Whyte generally avoided expressions of nostalgia for a more competitive, ruggedly individualist bygone era. Riesman admired some of the qualities of the inner-directed man, yet he recognized that it was difficult to celebrate the days of slavemasters and robber barons. He was aware of the flaws of the inner-directed type; such a man could be opportunistic, compulsive, and plagued by guilt, and given that his personality was formed by an uncritical internalization of parental authority, he was never genuinely autonomous himself. In *Individualism Reconsidered*, Riesman imagined a new type of individual who could successfully negotiate a balance between self and other. The true autonomous individual, self-aware and alert to the pressures surrounding him, would value warm interactions with his peers but would not defer to them out of some mindless craving for acceptance; he would be both aware of those around him *and* self-possessed, a captain of his own self; he could successfully function both "alone and with others." Like Whyte's self-aware organization man, who knows how to "fight" the organization but would not resist it reflexively just to make an empty, equally conformist statement, Riesman's autonomous man would not feel a compulsion to rebel against conformity for its own sake. Rather, his sense of personal security and heightened self-consciousness left him "free to choose" whether to conform or rebel. Which choice he made was less important than the psychic liberation that allowed him to choose. Echoing existentialist philosophy, Riesman suggested that modern individuals attempting to find a way out of alienation must "'choose themselves', in Sartre's phrase."[46]

If Riesman and Whyte were reluctant to celebrate the individualist male of the nineteenth century, their depictions of twentieth-century conformist society could not help but contrast sharply with the days of yesteryear, when *men were men*, when they confronted the conflicts and tasks of a rough, competitive world and had no irrational craving for approval from their peers. Both authors used the familiar hard/soft idiom. To Whyte, the Protestant ethic was "hard-boiled"; those who deny the conflict between the individual and society were "softminded." For Riesman, the "inner-directed" man was "hard"; he confronted the "hard" material world with a "hard enduringness." "Today," Riesman noted, "it is the 'softness' of men rather than the 'hardness' of material that calls on talent and opens new channels of social mobility."[47]

The sexual implications of the conformity crisis ran deeper than the use of these descriptive terms, however. Riesman's and Whyte's analyses appeared to confirm male critics' declaration of a "masculinity crisis" in American society. Riesman did not speak directly to such issues, but *The Lonely Crowd's* discussion of parenting in an other-directed society seemed to suggest problems for the mid-century child, especially the male child. Riesman's assumption that other-directed parents, lacking certainty and self-assurance, transmitted their own "highly diffuse anxiety" to their children complemented a body of "expert" discourse that held the dysfunctional or matriarchal American family responsible for the problem of "soft" male children. For Riesman, the older inner-directed family had been "patriarchal"; it had instilled in male children an inner gyroscope and the drive, not to get along with one's peers, but to be *better* than them. The new other-directed family, by contrast, was extremely child-centered, its parents permissive and highly sensitive to the wants of the child to whom they often deferred. While Riesman did not address the issue of a declining patriarchal authority or excessive mothering that was so often said to plague male children, he seemed to regard the trends of the new other-directed society as especially detrimental to the male child. Later quoted in a *Look* magazine article, Riesman lamented that, these days, "boys can be boys only from six to ten" years of age, implying that afterward it was questionable whether a boy would adopt a traditional male role. It may be only a coincidence that *The Lonely Crowd*'s single example of an earlier other-directed society was fifth-century Athens, a culture known for its acceptance of male homosexuality.[48]

Riesman did, however, speak directly to the sexual anxieties that characterized the other-directed society of his time. As women increasingly become "peer-groupers themselves," consumers of "'aids to romance,'" and, with men, "pioneers" on the "frontier of sex," Riesman observed that "the anxiety of men lest they fail to satisfy the woman also grows." In an earlier era, a man's "unemancipated wife and socially inferior mistresses could not seriously challenge the quality of his sexual performance," Riesman noted. Yet the modern woman is now able to do so with the help of mass culture: women's magazines, self-help books, sex and marriage manuals, and an army of experts who determine ideals of normative, mutually satisfying sexual relationships. Given that such a woman can now respond to men "in a way that only courtesans were supposed to in an earlier age," given that the "mystery" of the brothel can now be reproduced in the suburban bedroom, the emergence of the sexually emancipated women added to the insecurities of other-directed men, Riesman implied. Indeed, he had obliquely approached the problem of male performance anxiety and sexual impotence.[49]

To be sure, Riesman framed this discussion of sexual anxiety in broad gender-neutral terms. In the other-directed society of the time, both men and women, he suggested, were highly attuned to the approval and judgment of each other as well as their peers. Dating had become "a test" of one's ability to rate highly in the dating game and thus attract desirable mates. Sexual relationships were now laden with unprecedented fears and insecurities. "Sex today carries too much psychic freight," Riesman declared. But for whom? Women had long been sexually other-directed—socialized to please the other, to be attuned to his gaze and approval, to stake her entire self-worth on her marriageability and success in securing and maintaining the attraction of the male "other." The "psychic freight" that Riesman noted seems a more apt description of the experience of the mid-century male who appears ever more pressured, in an increasingly therapeutic culture, to be "sensitive" to the other. If the "new" other-directed woman appeared to be clutching the latest sex manual in triumph, what Riesman called other-directedness, and the mass culture that nourished it, had in one sense been liberating for women at the expense of the sexual security of the male.[50]

Perhaps it was inevitable that women would occupy such an awkward and mostly invisible place in the entire discussion of conformist behavior in American life, for their role remained full of contradictions that could not be easily reconciled with the mid-century revolt against conformity. In his commencement speech at Smith College in 1955, Adlai Stevenson didn't seem aware of those contradictions. Stevenson, an icon of mid-century liberalism (and a year away from a second Democratic candidacy for president), invoked the familiar themes of contemporary social thought in his address to Smith graduates. A modern mass society, he emphasized, encouraged conformity, overspecialization, narrowness of personal identity, dehumanization, lack of wholeness of mind, and group-think. In such a society, "individual freedom is wholly submerged." Mass society, Stevenson stressed, had given way to the great twentieth-century collision between individualism and collectivism; hence the need to restore the individuality, the sense of purpose, the wholeness of Western man. Otherwise, Stevenson warned, the individual will be "absorbed" by his specialized function.[51]

Hearing these generalities, listeners must have wondered how Stevenson would reconcile such problems with the predicament of women—after all, he was speaking to an audience of female graduates. Lest anyone assume that he was referring to Western "man" in a gender-neutral sense, Stevenson made it clear that these were the identity problems of men, the "typical Western man—or typical Western husband!" he declared. "You may be hitched to one of these creatures we call 'Western man,'" he told Smith graduates, and "part of your job is to keep him Western, to keep him truly purposeful, to keep him whole." It was an educated woman's duty, as Stevenson saw it, to restore her man's sense of purpose, to humanize him, cultivate his "mature values," and help keep him on guard against group-think and conformity. "[What] you young ladies . . . have to do [is] rescue us wretched slaves of specialization and group thinking from further shrinkage and contraction of mind and spirit." When Western man's life lacks "valid purpose," then the "life of the society he determines will lack valid purpose." Educated women, Stevenson stressed, "have a unique opportunity to influence us, man and boy, and to play a direct part in the unfolding drama of our free society."[52]

If there was an obvious lapse in Stevenson's failure to acknowledge to an audience of females that modern women might just be "wholly submerged" by their own "specialized" functions as housewives and mothers—that women might have "sacrificed wholeness of mind . . . to the demands of their specialties"—it completely escaped him. In fact, the dismissal of any female claim to individuality, to a sense of her own self, purpose, or wholeness, implicit in so much of the anticonformist discourse, is here explicit. While Stevenson expressed his distaste for "conformers and groupers" ("While I am not in favor of maladjustment, I view this breeding of mental neuters, this hostility to eccentricity and controversy, with grave misgiving"), his speech elided the issue of female individuality, which he could not reconcile with the role he expected these women to fulfill, inevitably. As he put it, "the humble role of housewife . . . [is] statistically . . . what most of you are going to be whether you like the idea or not just now—and you'll like it!" As for the Smith graduates who might feel that housewifery was a waste of their lives and education, he emphasized that "women 'never had it so good' as you do." He reminded them of their "very special responsibility for Western children," suggesting that their "primary task" to make homes and therefore "whole human beings in whom the rational values of freedom, tolerance, charity, and free inquiry can take root" was noble and completely self-justifying. The implication was that women would be selfish for wanting anything more. In advising women to "help others—husbands, children, friends" to see "life steady" and "whole," he was essentially affirming female other-directedness.[53]

The rallying call for women to humanize others and foster maturity and personal growth in their husbands (and children) was a variation on an older ideology of Republican womanhood. By the early nineteenth century, the female role as wife and mother was politicized: selfless women were granted special moral power in the home in tacit compensation for their political and social subordination. They would serve the political needs of the early republic by cultivating its moral values within the family. Stevenson likewise invested the educated housewife of the 1950s with political import; he cast her stabilizing role in marriage and the family as crucial in a cold war world. Stressing the "dire trouble" that people in free society were experiencing and the "powerful drive . . . toward totalitarian collectivism" in the twentieth century, Stevenson made the woman's special duty to restore her husband's sense of self and purpose an urgent political aim. As he told his audience, you must "help to integrate a world that has been falling into bloody pieces. History's pendulum has swung dangerously far away from the individual, and you may, indeed you must, help to restore it to the vital center of its arc."[54]

The "vital center," as we have seen, was the locus of a reinvigorated masculinity. In essence, it was masculinity that Stevenson sought to restore, plagued as it was by "shrinkage," "shriveling," and "contraction"—words that permeate this speech. Moreover, Stevenson's view of the role of educated wives and mothers was hardly surprising, given the domestic ideology of the fifties. What is more significant about his speech is that, in an address that one might reasonably expect to be about *women*, the image of the beleaguered, victimized male overwhelms all else (battered by "violent pressures," he is reduced to "subordinate status" in a mass society, his "range of choice" limited; he is a "slave of specialization and group thinking").[55]

The sense of male victimization that Stevenson expressed was a familiar theme in the work of male writers in the 1950s, many of whom were considerably less sanguine than Stevenson in their assessment of womens' influence in the family and society. To Stevenson, women were to be the saviors of men besieged by a groupist mass society. But for many male critics convinced of what *Look* magazine called the "Decline in the American Male," women were part of the problem, not the solution—the dreaded feminizing forces lurking behind the pressure on men to conform and adjust. Inasmuch as these critics saw any female attempt to civilize man—to shape his psyche and instill in him "mature values"—as oppressive and manipulative, they would have regarded Stevenson's speech as *proof* of the decline of masculinity itself.

The Unmanning of American Men

Riesman and Whyte did not explicitly call attention to the gendered implications of their broad character types. Other observers, however, took their conclusions as added evidence of a masculinity crisis in America. In 1958, a series of articles in *Look* magazine appeared, collectively entitled "The Decline of the American Male." So popular was the series that it was published in book form by *Look* editors later that year. In one article, "Why Is He Afraid to Be Different?" author George Leonard drew a fictional composite of a mid-century American man named Gary Gray. The character distilled for a popular audience the themes of leading postwar social critics like Riesman, Whyte, Schlesinger, Lindner, and Vance Packard. The narrative began with a grim scenario that recalls Schlesinger's "sinister" doctrine of togetherness: "One dark morning this winter, Gary Gray awakened and realized he had forgotten how to say the word 'I,'" the narrator told readers. "Struck with terror," Gary forced himself to repeat the word "I," but "its force and meaning were gone." Recognizing that it was more "reassuring" to say "we," Gary came to the sad realization that he "passed his days and nights not in the bright glow of personal conviction, but under the vague gray shadow of uneasiness and doubt." Gary had in fact "lost his individuality. In the free and democratic United States of America, he had been subtly robbed of a heritage that the Communist countries deny by force." Perhaps it was his own tendency to assume that "The Group was always right" that had debilitated his individuality, he thought.[56]

Gary's self-reproach was mixed with a profound sense of victimization. He had no "private inner self." "Who had taken it?" he asked. He began to see the power of "The Group" everywhere: the corporation he worked for, which required junior executives to "adjust" their behavior to its norms and values in the name of "teamwork," and whose company psychiatrists "rape[d] his privacy and integrity" by using a battery of psychological tests to pry into his "inner self," including his sex life, to discover his hidden weaknesses, just as it routinely identified the consumer's weaknesses in order to subliminally market its products; the schools Gary's kids attended and his suburban neighborhood, which had imposed standards of behavior on his family who, eager to fit in, had anxiously yielded to its watchful eye; the government agents who conducted a "security check" on Gary's neighbor and asked questions about the man's personal life; and even on the streets, where loud, faceless voices shamed those who jaywalked, a conditioning technique one would expect to find in Russia or China, Gary thought. Suburban America looked suspiciously totalitarian. But "the enemy who had robbed Gary had neither name nor face . . . the subtle poison of adjustment and conformity was what had taken away Gary's ability to say 'I.'"[57]

If the culprit who robbed Gary of his individuality was only vaguely identifiable, for other observers of the "Decline of the American Male," the enemy did have a name and a face—one that was unquestionably female. Since the end of World War II, the American male has changed "radically and dangerously," *Look* writer J. Robert Moskin declared in his article, "Why Do Women Dominate Him?" Citing "scientists," Moskin claimed that the male "is no longer the masculine, strong-minded man who pioneered the continent and built America's greatness. . . . The experts pin most of the blame for his new plight squarely on women." While some of the authorities Moskin cited were harshly critical of women's growing dominance over men, Moskin twisted the findings of other "experts" (Alfred Kinsey, Margaret Mead, David Riesman) into a devastating indictment of American women.[58]

Like other spokesmen for male discontent in the fifties, Moskin emphasized modern women's control over the male, which begins from "the moment he is born." Coddled, doted upon, and made dependent by feminine forces—mothers, nurses, and teachers—the American boy is domesticated at an early age, especially by his mother who uses a "subtler technique for bossing her son": the "withholding of love" as a means of reward and punishment. Thus it is no wonder that soon the adolescent male easily falls prey to "'going steady'" and other "girl's schemes" to impose early monogamy on him, then to women who control premarital sex, and finally to wives who set the patterns of sexual relations. Citing (and distorting) Kinsey's conclusions, Moskin attributed these changes to "the developing emancipation of the female." By withholding and meting out approval, love, and sex at their will, manipulative women, wives, and mothers crush men's instinctual drives toward dominance, autonomy, and (sexual) freedom. Thus were women able to maintain a hold over men's psyches for the rest of their sad lives.[59]

Moskin cast the American family as hopelessly matriarchal. In many homes the male is "pushed out of any significant role in rearing his son." Either he works so hard that he has little time to spend with his son, or he is domesticated, forced to do so many household chores that his son never sees him in "strictly masculine pursuits." It is this kind of dad that "experts worry about most of all," for he is reduced to "a mother-substitute or nursery assistant," Moskin wrote (quoting sociologist Helen Hacker). The home had become so oppressive that men were prone to "escape [into] the pleasures and fraternity of corporate life." Moskin declared that "female dominance may, in fact, be one of the several causes of the 'organization man' who is so deplored today."[60]

To Moskin, women's power transcended the home. Not only were women outnumbering men in the population, living longer, and by extension exercising greater political power in the voting booth; they were pouring into the workforce in record numbers and "an increasing proportion . . . will hold authority-wielding jobs in the future." While women exercise their economic power as the chief consumers in American life, they also own a remarkable amount of securities and stock. "By numbers alone," Moskin warned, "the American woman has the means to dominate her men."[61]

One measure of male success in the postwar era was the breadwinner's ability to satisfy his family's desire for material things. Some male critics reacted to this burden by turning the critique of conformity and consumerism back upon women. In a *Coronet* magazine article, one sociologist claimed that men were becoming "economic serfs" to their wives, who demanded comforts and conveniences that chiefly benefited *them*. When *Look* writer William Attwood posed the question "Why Does He Work So Hard?" in his article of that title, he answered that husbands were victims of "the steady, if tacit, pressure by wives to keep up with those Joneses . . . next door." Attwood suggested that the desire to impress others with the accumulation of material possessions emanated from the wife, who then infected the family with her mindless consumerism. Moreover, incessant female demands for status, prestige, and material possessions led to the problem of the overworked male, which in turn led to his tendency to die at an earlier age than his wife, both Attwood and Moskin suggested.[62]

This kind of rhetoric echoed Philip Wylie, whose widely popular social commentary and science fiction novels over several decades blamed women for everything from nuclear holocaust to homosexuality to the student radicalism of the sixties. His 1942 book, *Generation of Vipers*, selected by the American Library Association in 1950 as one of the major works of nonfiction in the first half of the twentieth century, launched an attack on American women and mothers that was culturally resounding and remained so well into the 1950s. *Generation of Vipers* denounced "megaloid momworship" in American life. "Momism" was a phenomenon that Wylie attributed to the arrival of modernity. Having lost her labor-intensive pre-industrial duties in the home, the modern mother spent her considerable spare time eliciting the adulation of men and smothering her children, particularly her boys. To Wylie, mom's outward display of love for her children disguised her self-interest and love of herself. Middle-aged and self-righteous, infantile and narcissistic, mom reduced the males in her family to psychic bondage while the entire culture deferred to her overwhelming power.[63]

In Wylie's punishing portrait of mom, she was the "destroying mother," the perfect blend of a ball-busting female castrator and a mind-controlling totalitarian tyrant whose use of propagandistic techniques to elicit adulation of herself could rival that of Hitler or Stalin. Through an insidious campaign to sentimentalize herself in the eyes of men and the culture at large, thereby establishing a kind of perpetual Mother's Day, the American mother drew her power from the cult of mom. She did so with the skill of a Hitler and the force of his Brown Shirts (Wylie's "mom" commanded allegiance to "her Party" with her devious "shirtism"). But her gravest sin was that she emasculated her husband and engulfed her son, leaving the former mealy and henpecked and the latter hopelessly immature, "a lifelong suck-ing-egg" who has "sold his soul to mom." The psychological damage she did to her son and future generations was enormous, for she forced her son to transmute the desire that ought to be properly directed toward other fe-males into love of *her*. By always protecting her son and interceding on his behalf, she precluded the essential father-son conflict that would establish the latter's maturity and independence (while she turned her daughters into harpies—replicas of herself). To Wylie, momism constituted nothing less than slavery, for "possession of the spirit of a man is slavery also, because his body obeys his spirit and his spirit obeys its possessor." Thus does the "destroying mother" annihilate the male self, leaving American society "a matriarchy in fact if not in declaration."[64]

Other widely read social commentators denounced the overwhelming influence of the "feminine" in American life. In 1946, the English anthropologist Geoffrey Gorer, in his book *The American People*, observed that "the overriding fear of all American parents" was that "their child will turn into a sissy." Gorer regarded this a singular obsession of Americans, apparently failing to recognize that his own depiction of "the clinging mother [as] the great emotional menace in American psychological life" could help to generate the anxiety he observed as unique to Americans. Gorer's mother—provincial, foolish, meddlesome, affected, doggedly clinging to stylishness and youthfulness, "unlovable and unloved," and at her peak "social influence" at menopause—was the key to understanding American culture, for it was her influence that defined the values of the nation, including that particular American predilection for "idealism." Gorer may have been slightly more generous than Wylie in his portrayal of mom as a necessary (albeit problematic) civilizer of men. Yet his notion of the "encapsulated mother"—the internalization of maternal morality that constitutes the individual and collective American conscience—and its impact on males ("the little boy has doubts about his masculinity") has Wylie's hideous, moralizing, emasculating mom written all over it.[65]

Tangled up within the image of the destroying mother were many of the same grievances that appeared in the critique of American conformity. In the demonic version of momism, the American mother embodied all the attributes of mass society that Wylie, Gorer, Attwood, and other male critics deplored—consumerism, materialism, moral rigidity, sentimentality, mass-produced commercial banalities, psychic manipulation, even the dreaded organization. (By the fifties, Wylie had joined the crusade against conformity, endorsing Lindner's *Must You Conform?* on its dust jacket: "the grimmest demon of our day—the demand for conformity set up by the frightened men, the men George Orwell said would triumph by '1984.'") Mom personified this insidious pressure to conform in *Generation of Vipers,* which collapsed the organization, its deceptively benevolent social ethic, and mom's controlling maternalism into a single ominous image. "Mom is organization-minded," Wylie insisted. "Organizations, she has happily discovered, are intimidating to all men, not just to mere men. They frighten politicians to sniveling servility and they terrify pastors; they bother bank presidents and pulverize school boards." Mom loves organizations and committees because through them she can "compel an abject compliance of her environs to her personal desires"; thus her communitarian social projects, undertaken in the name of "social service, charity, care of the poor, civic reform, patriotism, and self-sacrifice." Underneath the guise of maternal (and liberal?) selflessness always lay mom's demented desire to control and intimidate.[66]

In Wylie's 1942 *Generation of Vipers,* mom's influence had lurked vaguely behind the menacing "liberal" organization and its emasculating social ethic. In his writings of the 1950s, mom *was* the organization. Indeed, his earlier caricature of the bureaucratic-minded mom reached its logical culmination when Wylie declared that it was women who ran corporate America. In a 1956 *Playboy* article, "The Abdicating Male . . . and How the Gray-Flannel Mind Exploits Him Through His Women," Wylie estimated that women controlled corporate America because they controlled 80 percent of the nation's capital wealth. Clutching the national purse strings, mom not only kept the corporations obedient to her every whim in her role as super-consumer, but she also assumed control of the economy through the "abdicating male," who ceded to her control of household finances. Worse, when husbands die after years of slaving away for their wives, "the insurance is made out to the gals and the real estate is in their name. They own America by mere parasitism," Wylie proclaimed. Later, in a 1958 *Playboy* article, he again deplored the abnegation of males, and claimed that what "started as feminism" had "matured into wanton womanization" of American society.[67]

The absurdity of Wylie's idea of an American matriarchy might be generously read as an expression of anxiety about a loss of control or a sense of powerlessness in the face of impersonal corporate and organizational forces which seemed to undercut male initiative, an anxiety that Wylie (and other male critics) displaced onto women. But to see his image of parasitical, destroying women as a form of displacement, to interpret it as a manifestation of some other grievance or anxiety, runs the risk of minimizing Wylie's visceral animus toward women. His misogyny was surely entangled with other grievances, but it needn't be symptomatic of something else. To Wylie, women were leeches and gold diggers, first and foremost (he had been the subject of a wrongful paternity suit in 1924, which he appealed and won).[68] Obsessed with psychologically freeing men from the old ball and chain, Wylie was one of the forerunners of the male rebellion against commitment in the 1950s and 1960s, the expression of which was increasingly voiced in the magazine (*Playboy*) to which he contributed in the fifties.

Momism would be easy to write off as the rantings of a marginal crank if it were not for Wylie's considerable popularity as well as the more respectable writers and medical professionals who gave his basic assumptions about "momism" intellectual legitimacy. In 1943, David Levy's book *Maternal Overprotection* suggested that excessive mothering was the cause of a host of adjustment problems for children. Like other critics and medical professionals, Levy's focus was almost exclusively on boys who were infantilized by overprotective moms. Obviously World War II had much to do with elevating momism into a serious psychiatric problem. During the war there were plenty of concerns voiced about absentee fathers serving abroad and a lack of paternal authority at home. But it was Edward Strecker's 1946 book, *Their Mother's Sons: The Psychiatrist Examines an American Problem,* that turned mom and her influence on the male self into a threat to national defense.[69]

A psychiatrist employed by the army during the war, Strecker studied soldiers rejected at induction or discharged from the army for psychiatric reasons. He concluded that the failure of unprecedented numbers of young men to meet induction criteria or cope with military discipline and hardship in the armed forces suggested a growing immaturity in American life, and a corresponding "psychoneurosis" among males. "We consider ourselves among the most mature of the world's nations," Strecker stressed. But America's current and future soldiers are hopelessly infantile, victimized by mothers who keep their children "paddling about in a kind of psychological amniotic fluid rather than letting them swim away with the bold and decisive strokes of maturity from the emotional maternal womb." Using Wylie's idiom, Strecker declared that "momism is the product of a social system veering toward a matriarchy." Momism wasn't the only cause of male immaturity, Strecker claimed, but extinguishing it was crucial, for mom's tendency to smother her children prevented them from being able to properly distinguish between self and other. He framed the problem in political terms: "The survival or death of our democracy depends on a clearer understanding and a more accurate delineation of the 'I and You' relationship" (which smothering mothers subvert). It followed that restoring father, a *real* father (not a mom-like "pop") in the family would help to counteract excessive maternal influence, foster boys' maturity, preclude the rise of homosexuality (overly solicitous mothers stifled mature heterosexuality, he claimed), and thereby protect the nation from external perils. Male maturity, which would become a central theme in the psychiatric discourse of the 1950s, was a national imperative to Strecker. "Only if peace is handled by mature people will it succeed; only if nations reflect maturity can the peace endure," he insisted. The fate of the free world hung in the balance. "There is nothing of which Psychiatry can speak with more confidence and assurance than the danger to our democratic civilizations and cultures from keeping children enwombed psychologically and not permitting them to grow up emotionally and socially. Here is our gravest menace."[70]

Political concerns found their way into professional and popular psychology, while the language and preoccupations of professional and pop psychology found their way into political discourse (as *The Vital Center*'s rhetoric of maturity and womblike retreat suggests). Other mental health experts weighed in on the problem of momism. Psychologist Ralph Wentworth-Rohr studied veterans of World War II and came to conclusions similar to Strecker's. In a 1956 article originally delivered as a lecture at Cooper Union in New York City, he proclaimed momism an "insidious disease." Since mom was the dominant force in the family, and since male children always identify with the strongest figure within it, American boys were dangerously mother-identified. Wentworth-Rohr held mom responsible not only for weakening the nation's present and future soldiers, but also for "the great increase in homosexuality in America" (which he assumed the Kinsey report proved), as well as a myriad of other ailments including the generalized "neurotic syndrome" in children, the rising divorce rate, and even the problem of "fat or obese people" who suffer from a "neurotic eating" syndrome thanks to doting moms who use food to manipulate family members.[71]

Influential journalist Max Lerner even included a discussion of momism in his sweeping two-volume study, *America as a Civilization* (1955), isolating the problem of excessive mothering as one of the American family's most striking features. Citing Gorer and Wylie, Lerner wrote:

> The American mother . . . becomes the child's rearer, cajoler, censor. Her ways are less authoritarian than manipulative. She is a matriarch not in exercising firm power but in managing the family. Since she is the chief socializing agent—along with the usually female school teacher—the American boy comes to identify moral codes with women, and thus either to think of them as "sissy stuff" or else to associate the sexual life with an impossible goal of purity. If she proves too possessive the result is shown in the psychiatric records of battle-shock cases in World War II, when boys from mother-sheltered families found the transition to the realities of an all-male world too sharp. In cases where she is the dominant adult the boy may find it hard to establish his own later role, having no effective masculine model.

Lerner raised delicately the issue that always hovered over the wider discussion of momism: the sexual maladjustment that resulted from the mother-engulfed male child's unconscious association of chastity and femininity. The mother-smothered boy, it was assumed, was predisposed to homosexuality.[72]

Respected psychologist Erik Erikson proffered a sketch of mom that could have given credence to Wylie's depiction of the middle-aged mom as hopelessly batty and narcissistic. "'Mom' is a woman in whose life cycle remnants of infantility join advanced senility to crowd out the middle range of mature womanhood, which thus becomes self-absorbed and stagnant," Erikson claimed. In her 1963 book *The Feminine Mystique*, Betty Friedan recast Erikson's diagnosis of mom and, in the name of feminism, turned it into an argument against the "feminine mystique." Momism was the price to be paid for confining women to the home, Friedan implied; domesticity infantilized women and they in turn infantilized their offspring (hence the shocking passivity and weak egos seen in our Korean War POWs, she noted). Since a woman's mature psychological development was stunted by housewifery, and any ambition she had for a career or a life outside the home was thwarted by a near-compulsory domesticity, the frustrated housewife turned her attention to her son. She lived through her son, and passed on to him her own childlike immaturity, smothering him with "parasitical mother-love" and using her femininity to seduce his affections. Friedan accepted uncritically the Freudian model implicit in many other critiques of momism: the boy so smothered is kept from growing up, sexually or otherwise; thus "he can never mature to love a woman." Suffering from arrested psychosexual development and an unhealthy fixation on his mother, he becomes a homosexual. In Friedan's judgment, "his love for men masks his forbidden excessive love for his mother; his hatred and revulsion for all women is a reaction to the one woman who kept him from becoming a man." Even when overt homosexuality is not present, the male's love-hate relationship to his smothering mother inspires a "sublimated revulsion for women," or more open misogyny—"an implacable hatred for the parasitical women who keep their husbands and sons from growing up." To Friedan, the overbearing mother and the corresponding misogyny of the time were the toxic by-products of compulsory domesticity; both helped to explain why homosexuality was "spreading like a murky smog over the American scene."[73]

The attempt to make domesticity all the more odious to her audience by linking it to parasitical mothers and homosexuality speaks to Friedan's prejudices as well as her political agenda. Friedan was not alone in using the "destroying mother" to advance arguments for female liberation. Feminist Della Cyrus also recognized momism as a social problem and cited it as proof that women must be emancipated from the home.[74] The political aims of feminists aside, the acceptance of momism as a cultural phenomenon by a diverse array of social critics, writers, and experts raises questions about the cultural obsession with mom and its relationship, as suggested by recent scholars, to "the age of anxiety" within which it was nourished.

In the 1940s and 1950s, American mothers were both idealized *and* vilified. The paradox is rooted in the contradictions and tensions inherent within domestic ideology, which played themselves out in the discourse on momism (as Friedan's rhetoric suggests). Political theorist Michael Rogin has stressed that in domestic ideology, women were conceded a heightened, if oblique, authority within the home in tacit exchange for their political and economic subordination; when that authority was experienced as too powerful, mothers could become menacing figures in the male imagination. Rogin's analysis of mid-century science fiction novels and films places momism in the context of the global threats, and links anxieties about atomic warfare and Communist subversion to heightened fears of female and maternal power.[75]

The ideology that idealized mothers and sanctified their role within the home produced its antithesis in a kind of "return of the repressed," in Rogin's formulation. Momism was the "demonic version of domestic ideology," for it "uncovers the buried anxieties over boundary invasion, loss of autonomy, and maternal power generated by domesticity."[76] In a culture anxious about ideological manipulation, mom's invasion of the male psyche and her ability to whittle away at the male self and elicit adulation rendered her something like the domestic counterpart to "the group"—the totalitarian political party, the organization, the mass. Wylie, who had been obsessed with Communism long before the onset of the cold war, gave mom extraordinary transformative power. Like the Communist ideological apparatus, she entered the self, formed, cajoled, punished, and manipulated it; like the party, she built around her image a "cult," one that demanded surrender of self to her hypnotic, sexually charged authority.

At a time when so many critics worried about the "soft" American self, anxieties about maternal power easily intersected with cold war fears, especially the notion (advanced by some experts) that children reared in dysfunctional families may grow up to be psychologically vulnerable to alien ideologies like Communism. But momism was accepted as a reality by such a wide array of critics—male and female, chauvinist and feminist, liberal and conservative alike—that it cannot be attributed to anxieties about Communism. In any case, the obsession with "momism" predated the cold war. Nor can it simply be attributed to hysterical male critics who sought to restore some sort of retrograde patriarchal order. Wylie's 1942 *Generation of Vipers* opened the floodgates of contempt for mom, but concerns about excessive maternal influence on boys had been increasing steadily throughout the twentieth century. Certainly World War II, the Korean War and the cold war gave new urgency to these concerns.[77]

It would be a mistake, however, to overestimate the political underpinnings of momism. Given the extraordinary vitriol hurled at mom from all sides, we might consider what Rogin missed in his otherwise perceptive reading of the cold war political imagination and mom's penetration of the male psyche. While momism was one manifestation of the wider concern with the malleability of the American self, what primarily drove the preoccupation with momism was an anxiety that, while certainly not disconnected from politics or the imperatives of national defense, would have been manifest even in the absence of the totalitarian threat: the fear of an epidemic of male homosexuality, a subject to which we shall return. Both obvious and implicit in so much of the discourse on the American mother, the growing fear of a rise in male homosexuality was the single most important reason for the dread of momism in the 1940s and 1950s.

Not all participants in the masculinity debate were so openly contemptuous of women. Schlesinger denounced those male critics who blame women for the crisis in masculinity as immature, hysterical, and just plain silly. "Masculine supremacy, like white supremacy, was the neurosis of an immature society," he informed his readers in the psychologizing idiom characteristic of the time. "It is good for men as well as women that women have been set free. In any case, the process is irreversible." Schlesinger scolded men for whining about female aggressiveness, which was tantamount to an admission of defeat. Women had made only modest and uneven gains in any case, he noted: "Those amiable prophets of an impending American matriarchy (all men, by the way) are too pessimistic."[78]

As we have seen, Schlesinger's answer to the "Crisis in American Masculinity" lay not in an unseemly humiliation of the female, but rather in psychological resistance to the lure of "the group." Yet here, too, the group looks remarkably maternal: it appeals to man's need for "womblike security"; it renders him incapable of thinking or acting on his own; finally, it leaves him unsure of his sexual identity. The "cult of the group" and the "cult of mom" look strikingly similar in the way they work to absorb and conquer the male psyche through "subconscious" means:

> Men no longer fulfill an inner sense of what they *must* be; indeed with the cult of the group, that inner sense itself begins to evaporate. Identity consists not of self-realization but of smooth absorption into the group. Nor is this just a matter of passive acquiescence. The group is aggressive, imperialistic, even vengeful, forever developing new weapons with which to overwhelm and crush the recalcitrant individual. Not content with disciplining the conscious mind, the group today is even experimenting with means of violating the subconscious. The subliminal invasion represents the climax of the assault on individual identity.[79]

Hovering over this sense of a "violated" subconscious is also the influence of Vance Packard, whose bestselling 1957 book, *The Hidden Persuaders,* analyed the means by which advertisers psychologically manipulated consumers and used subliminal messages to sell products.[80] A former OSS officer, Schlesinger had long been interested in issues of covert psychological manipulation; in his view, the male psyche was being assaulted on all fronts.

The plight of the American male—trapped, manipulated, struggling against the forces that robbed him of his freedom, his individuality, his will, his sexual potency, and his soul—became a central theme for many postwar cultural critics, novelists, and filmmakers. He was Sloan Wilson's *The Man in the Gray Flannel Suit,* whose only true excitement in life occurred during the war, when he killed and made love and had not yet succumbed to the rat race, the tract home, and the family. He was Frank Wheeler in Richard Yates's novel, *Revolutionary Road,* another war veteran and corporate drone, the captive of a not-so-revolutionary suburban home awash in a "bath of sentimentality" and "togetherness," who imagined escaping to Paris and recovering the bohemian life he had once led. He was Alan Harrington's corporate automaton in *Life in the Crystal Palace,* lured by the "utopian drift" and beneficent private socialism of the corporation into trading his soul for the safety, comfort, and congeniality of the organization. He was Willy Loman in *Death of a Salesman,* the lower middle-class version of the other-directed type whose belief in the power of personality ("personality always wins the day") fails him so miserably. He was the "country husband" in John Cheever's eponymous short story, invisible and unappreciated by his wife and kids and infatuated with the family babysitter whom he absurdly preys upon.

Indeed, he was the stock white-collar businessman in countless postwar narratives—restless, fatigued, oppressed by the job, the wife, the mortgage, the PTA, and the irritating neighbors in a nightmare of suburban middle-class conformity.[81]

In other media, he was Mr. Stark, the hopelessly henpecked organization man and antifather in *Rebel Without a Cause*. He was the always hilarious domesticated dad—Ozzie Nelson or Danny Thomas—in numerous television sit-coms, or the ridiculously diminutive husband whose wife towered over him in so many James Thurber cartoons. He was *The Incredible Shrinking Man* in Richard Matheson's allegory of male powerlessness and emasculation. He was the abdicating male—everyman—in so many of Wylie's fictional and non-fictional tales of twisted matriarchal subversion. He was the ensnared American husband to whom Hugh Hefner offered *Playboy*, the "bible of the beleaguered male," trapped in the prison that is marriage and a sexual free spirit, if only in his dream life. He was the antihero who lurked between the lines of more than one Norman Mailer composition, a symbol of the emasculated status quo that Mailer's literary prowess would subvert. He was the beleaguered American male.[82]

Whether explicitly or implicitly expressed, the perception that American manhood was in crisis was real. But was the *crisis* real? Was masculinity really in a state of decline? Masculinity is an ideal, and insofar as there was a growing disparity between the ideal itself and the avenues available for white middle-class men to realize that ideal, there was something like a crisis, hyperbole aside. For better or worse, the sources of an older nineteenth-century male identity—based on individual achievement and initiative, self-discipline and self-denial, autonomy and mastery, male prerogative in public life and patriarchal authority in the home—*were* eroding. By the 1950s, the shift in middle-class values that had begun in the nineteenth century—from self-denial to self-indulgence, from self-discipline to self-realization, from the Protestant ethic to the social ethic—was nearly complete.[83] The older ideal of manhood no longer corresponded with the realities of men's lives, and while mid-century male critics were reacting to trends that were over half a century in the making, those trends were vastly accelerated in the 1940s and 1950s, magnified at the very moment when easy military security became a faint memory.

That disparity between ideals and reality had been widening for at least half a century, as we have seen. What was so new, then, in the 1940s and the 1950s about male concerns and anxieties? Certainly many of the same themes that appeared in turn-of-the-century male discourse—the effects of affluence, leisure, white-collar work, corporatization, excessive female influence in the family and the culture, the waning of a rugged rural life, the decline of the self-made man—resurfaced with new twists and turns in mid-century expressions of a crisis in masculinity. The bureaucracy—now the "organization"—had evolved in a way previously unimaginable; the issue now was less the sedentary, impersonal, or deferential nature of corporate work and more the *personality* it demanded of men—likable, groupist, and false. Postwar prosperity provided the engine for a baby boom, and as the middle class expanded, so did consumption, suburban living, leisure, and narrow gender-role expectations, all of which appeared to destabilize male autonomy and inner-direction. With a more extensive reach than ever before, mass culture—advertising, paperback books, mass circulation magazines, film and television, pop psychology—proffered the universalized values and images often experienced as mawkishly feminine or psychologically coercive.

Turn-of-the-century men had focused on the twin problem of physical and characterological flabbiness: bolstering the former would discipline the latter. Yet the problem for mid-century males could not be so readily addressed by the cultivation of outward physical manliness, for what was at issue now was a wholesale loss of *self*. As mid-century critics and experts scrutinized the male psyche, man became a victim as never before, his psyche malleable and unstable—the captive of a "togetherness" ethos that seemed to smack of collectivism. That the forces responsible for this loss of self were elevated to the status of "isms" ("groupism," "momism") speaks to the new ideological context in which men's problems were often framed. No longer were men simply defending their manhood against the coddled sensibilities and false delicacies that Henry James's hero Basil Ransom ranted about when he declared his generation sadly "womanized"; they were up against conformity's new mid-twentieth-century corollary, totalitarianism.[84] As such, the mid-century crisis in masculinity, while stemming from an admixture of old and new trends, dislocations, and fears, was now a problem inseparable from national defense.

Of course, it was not the first time that the problem of American manhood became entangled with ideological needs and global aspirations, as the case of the Spanish-American war and the expansionist impulse at the turn of the century suggests. But World War II ushered in a new internationalism and a sustained global tension that made the United States the world's policeman and placed the nation under endless watchfulness and vigilance. The aim was no longer simply imperial expansion abroad as an exercise in promoting national greatness and masculine regeneration, as it had been during the earlier masculinity "crisis." National safety and survival was now at issue. Militarization reshaped almost every area of mid-century American society. The imperatives of war transformed the economy, fueled technological development, dominated political debate, and helped to shape a broad ideological consensus, while symbols of war proliferated in American cultural life. Military defense became an ongoing function of the state and national security a consuming source of anxiety.[85]

Militarization exacted its own kind of conformity; the assertion of American global superiority created its own burdens and frustrations; national security and the threat of nuclear war encouraged a sense of dread, impotence, and powerlessness. But male critics largely ignored these issues in their discussion of men's sense of self-doubt and crisis. Even Schlesinger, who elsewhere was preoccupied with issues of war and global conflict, did not explicitly consider them possible sources of the masculinity crisis— perhaps to do so would have seemed too judgmental coming from an academic. Still, while most male critics attributed men's problems to the effects of an affluent mass society, the assumption that the latter was softening the nation's men always coexisted alongside doubts that American men were prepared to meet the demands of a hypermilitarized nation. As we have seen, the Korean War and the failure to achieve victory brought the problem of American soldiers' poor performance in war (and their vulnerability to indoctrination) into sharper focus. Doubts about the fiber and fortitude of young men continued to be voiced at the end of the 1950s, when critics could assess the effects of over a decade of prosperity and abundance on American youth. In 1959, Pulitzer Prize-winning author and *New York Times* military correspondent Hanson W. Baldwin warned readers that the physical and constitutional "softness" of American males left them ill-prepared to fight America's "harder" enemies: "Can American man—after years of protective conditioning—vie with the barbarian who has lived by his wits, his initiative, his brawn? Will he retain the will to fight for his country?" Baldwin doubted that "slow-witted," unmotivated, sedentary, comic-book reading male adolescents, enfeebled by material comfort and excessive leisure, could provide the muscle, the will, and the brains necessary to fend off the barbarians.[86]

The pressures and burdens placed on mid-century American men as breadwinners and cold warriors were real. In the national celebration of private life in the postwar years, middle-class men were expected to satisfy their families' desires for the good life and to be proper husbands and fathers, according to the prescriptive norms of a therapeutic society. Books such as H. A. Overstreet's 1949 bestseller *The Mature Mind* set the standards for male behavior in the decade to come by judging any life trajectory other than acceptance of the responsibilities of work, marriage, and family to be hopelessly immature.[87] In the workplace, white-collar men were likewise compelled to adjust to the institutional norms of the organizations for which they worked, while, in the shadow of the cold war, they were expected to measure up as *men*, defenders of the free world in an increasingly militarized society. Shorn of the kind of authority, prestige, and unfettered male prerogative that had once functioned as psychological rewards of white manhood, the male role, as it appeared to mid-century critics, had been reduced to that of a simple breadwinner, a slave to the family. Male writers' sense of victimization was often overblown and often histrionic, to be sure, and their grievances were all too often projected onto women. But their sense of un-ease and discontent was genuine, even if their grievances were arguably no less serious, their masculine "tasks" no less burdensome, and their military service no less taxing than those of American men in the past.

Indeed, American men had always been husbands, breadwinners, and soldiers, compelled to uphold family and nation under circumstances which could be considered more difficult and demanding than those of the mid-century. Yet the male complaints and problems articulated in the 1940s and 1950s involved an experience of *psychological* oppression more than any-thing else. In this sense, the crisis of masculinity discourse can be seen as the reflex of a culture in which expectations for "self-realization," shaped in part by therapeutic culture and in part by middle-class affluence, were greater than ever before. But prosperity, far from delivering a sense of personal liberation from the constraints and deprivations of the past, seemed only to augment the psychic burdens of being a man. So did therapeutic culture, which helped to generate a feeling of individual "entitlement" to self-fulfillment at the same time it increased the sense of male oppression by promoting normative, "mature" male role expectations. To be sure, only some American men openly longed to be more than corporate drones and breadwinners bankrolling split-level homes, swimming pools, and family vacations. Yet mid-century therapeutic culture pathologized the man who sought a lifestyle outside of the conventions of the time. Moreover, the in-creased awareness of the (invisible) male homosexual in every walk of Ameri-can life added to the sense that a man was compelled to fulfill the life trajectory that experts deemed "normal" and "mature," lest he be tainted by the stigma of homosexuality. When the narrator in Philip Roth's *My Life as a Man* complained that the bourgeois men of his generation who dared to reject marriage and family life thereby laid themselves open to the charge of immaturity, selfishness, an inability to "love," fear of responsibility, and of course homosexuality, he spoke to both the perception that men's options had diminished *and* the new sense of entitlement to personal freedom and self-fulfillment. While longings for personal emancipation were of course not entirely novel, in earlier eras they would have been difficult or unac-ceptable for most men to openly express.[88]

Greater expectations for individual fulfillment were also experienced by women, and so too were the cultural constraints, which were much more pronounced for women than they ever had been for men, and thoroughly different in quality. Whether they knew it or not, male critics who decried a "decline in masculinity" were also responding to women's increasing expectations for self-satisfaction and self-realization. Indeed, they were reacting to undercurrents of change in sex and gender relations that would come to a head in the 1960s but whose impulses lay in the 1940s and 1950s.

The tendency on the part of mid-century critics to blame women and mothers for men's emasculation had its precedent too in nineteenth-century attacks on domineering female reformers. But in the mid-twentieth century, the enemy for many male critics was less the female reformer proper (the ominous image of Eleanor Roosevelt notwithstanding) but rather self-assertive, "civilizing" women in the private sphere, and a looming matriarchy radiating outward from the home. The claims made by mid-century male critics that women maintained a matriarchal grip on the family and society were absurd, yet they reflect new and unresolved tensions about women's mid-century roles. Elaine Tyler May's work has gone a long way toward revealing the complex relationships between the Great Depression, women's entry into the wartime workforce, anxieties about gender and (female) sexuality, and the rise of a cold war—all of which encouraged the postwar rush into marriage and family life and the revival of domestic ideology. That ideology sanctified the home and the family, insisted on narrowly defined gender roles for men and women, and encouraged women to devote their lives to homemaking and motherhood.[89]

But domesticity was not a monolith even within the white middle class. Its postwar ideological revival coexisted uneasily with other trends, including the continued entry of women (and married women) into the workforce throughout the fifties, women's active participation in politics, labor unions, and reform movements, endorsements of female achievement and capability in popular publications, and an increasingly therapeutic mass culture which expressed and affirmed female needs and aspirations at least as often as it discouraged or denied them. Despite Betty Friedan's emphasis on the feminine mystique of the 1950s that suppressed women's ambition for any other role but housewifery (and the subsequent historiography that her work influenced), it is becoming more apparent to scholars that domesticity was less than pervasive in postwar American culture, either as ideology or reality. Joanne Meyerowitz's research suggests that there was much more variation, ambiguity, and complexity expressed in popular magazines, which did not consistently endorse female subordination, sexual passivity, and male domination (as Friedan would it) but frequently acknowledged, and even celebrated, female ambition and achievement. William Chafe long ago emphasized the social and cultural crosscurrents of the time: not only was "the revolution in female employment continuing" in the 1950s, but it was "spearheaded by the same middle-class wives and mothers who allegedly found new contentment in domesticity." Moreover, the feminine mystique was counterbalanced by another competing body of popular, expert, and academic discourse that articulated a broad range of ideas about women's "nature" and role in society that did not uniformly endorse female domesticity or submission.[90] In terms of both the experiences of women and the gender values and images promoted in American culture, the complexities of this era make easy generalizations, especially about a consistent and universal "ideology" of gender, problematic.

If domestic ideology within the middle class was so pervasive and effective as a means of ensuring male domination, female passivity, and acceptance of housewifery—if it was so successful in "containing" postwar women—male critics didn't seem to notice the results. There was a common assumption, voiced often in men's writings, that American women were now personally, politically, and even sexually emancipated. In retrospect it is tempting to write off such an idea as more imagined than real; after all, the second wave of feminism had yet to begin, and we are accustomed to thinking of the 1950s as a profoundly limited, conservative era for women. Yet we might take male critics at their word and consider the possibility that they were reacting to something very real, albeit immeasurable: a heightening female self-assertiveness, nourished by World War II and the new space for female autonomy it created, and by postwar affluence which brought Americans of both sexes greater expectations for individual self-fulfillment.

As the distinguished psychoanalyst and popular writer Abram Kardiner stressed in 1954, "the influence of feminism is not limited to those women who enter careers. All women today are feminists in that their expectations for themselves from marriage have changed."[91] Certainly organized feminism was on the wane in the 1940s and 1950s, but observers at the time perceived a decline in patriarchal authority in the middle-class home and a growing sexual egalitarianism in private and public life that should not be dismissed as male paranoia. An exclusive focus on domesticity, with its implicit assumption of female subordination and passivity, as the essence of middle-class women's postwar existence obscures other aspects of women's public and private lives and changes in relations between the sexes—developments currently being unraveled by revisionist historians.

Many postwar writers and social critics assumed that their generation had witnessed not the suppression of feminism but its *fulfillment,* or at least its noxious aftereffects. In 1956 *Life* magazine predicted that historians would someday see the 1950s as the "era of the feminist revolution." John A. Schindler, author of the 1957 book *Woman's Guide to Better Living,* conveyed a sense of postwar women's new confidence when he declared that "the American woman is a new thing. She's like a vice-president who has suddenly become president." He predicted that men would not become accustomed to her for at least three generations. Such an historic female victory, it was often assumed, had come at the expense of men. Schlesinger described (not uncritically) the "standard indictment" of women by his male contemporaries:

> In the last part of the nineteenth century women won their battle for equality. They gained the right of entry into one occupation after another previously reserved for males. Today they hold key positions of personal power in our society and use this power relentlessly to consolidate their mastery. As mothers they undermine masculinity through the use of love as a technique of reward and punishment. As teachers, they prepare male children for their role of submission in an increasingly feminine world. As wives, they complete the work of subjugation.[92]

Clearly such an indictment exaggerates and grossly distorts female power, and it is not necessary to elaborate each and every way it does so. Nonetheless, it is possible—distortions aside—that what male critics experienced as wifely "subjugation" and female "personal power" was in fact a growing female self-assertion in private life and a corresponding decline of patriarchal authority in the home? While it is impossible to measure the former, the erosion of patriarchy as a middle-class ideal is clearer to historians. The 1950s witnessed the acceleration of a cultural trend that had begun in the 1920s, when older modes of patriarchal authority in the family were no longer considered so acceptable within the white middle class. As Robert Griswold's study of American fatherhood suggests, postwar husbands and fathers were now encouraged by experts and opinion makers to develop self-expressive and warm relationships with their wives and children, to abandon outdated modes of paternal dominance and yield to what *McCall's* magazine called "togetherness," a catchword that became an anathema to countless male writers in the 1950s. In Griswold's study, many American men accepted and lived the reality of the "new fatherhood" (even while others responded by demanding that father be restored to his throne). Historians of the family have also stressed how companionate ideals of marriage, previously held by upper middle-class families in the early twentieth century, became widespread by the 1950s. Although these ideals did not endorse a truly equal partnership between husband and wife, they nonetheless served to soften male dominance and make an older form of patriarchal authority seem anachronistic. If American men had in fact become more "domesticated" in private life, it should not be surprising that postwar male critics reacted to it with varying degrees of scorn and animus.[93]

Even when traditionalists called for women to embrace feminine ideals as a defense against modern heresies—the careerist woman, or the overly demanding, self-possessed wife—those critics were acknowledging (and lamenting) the fact that male domination and female submission were no longer pervasive in marriage and family life. In 1947, Marynia Farnham and Ferdinand Lundberg, a psychiatrist and a journalist respectively, published *Modern Woman: The Lost Sex*. The book's primary argument was that modern woman was "lost" because she had become alienated from her inner femininity, her innate impulses to be a dutiful wife and mother. To the authors, the most obvious manifestation of this pathology was feminism, a "neurotic" response to male domination and a "deep illness." Farnham and Lundberg traced the problem of mid-century women back to the industrial revolution, when women lost their traditional productive functions within the home and became increasingly idle. Left purposeless and adrift, women increasingly attempted to compete with men, both in private and public life. At home, the result was overbearing women who rode roughshod over their husbands and overmothered their children, turning them into maladjusted authoritarian personality types. In public life, the result was "masculinized" career women whose futile effort to imitate men left them ever more neurotic, while men grew ever more hostile to women. Farnham and Lundberg blamed all major social ills—alcoholism, juvenile delinquency, crime, male sexual impotence, female frigidity, the epidemic of mental illness, and homosexuality—on the neurotic women who rejected their natural role. Psychotherapy, they believed, was necessary for the "army" of frustrated, miserable, bitter, mentally ill women in the United States.[94]

To Farnham and Lundberg, one major casualty of the modern woman's relinquishment of her feminine self was male sexual confidence and virility. In insisting on the goal of "sexual, orgiastic equality with men," modern women perverted the natural dynamics between the sexes and undermined male sexual superiority. A true woman accepted with joy her dependence on men; she relished her own feminine distinctiveness and achieved her ultimate happiness by yielding to men. The sex act itself was a metaphor for the role she plays in her entire life, the authors claimed. The woman assumes the prone, receptive role in sexual intercourse; all she had to do to achieve her own satisfaction was to welcome the male passively and then "deliver a masterly performance, by doing nothing whatever except being duly appreciative" (which is "easier" than "rolling off a log for her. . . . It is as easy as being the log itself"). But the woman who refuses to be a log, who is "unable to admit and accept dependence on her husband as the source of gratification and must carry her rivalry even into the act of love . . . will seriously damage [a man's] sexual capacity." "'The Battle of the Sexes' is a reality," the authors claimed, "and one of its results has been rather extensive psychological castration of the male." [95]

Published but two years after the war ended, *Modern Woman: The Lost Sex* in many ways reflects particularly acute anxieties about wartime female employment and independence, sexual and otherwise. The book is often cited by scholars to demonstrate the rise of the feminine mystique. But it could also be read, conversely, as a telling cultural register of the rise of the very trends the authors abhorred: female independence, self-assurance, sexual assertiveness, and the reality of an ever larger female and married labor force. Always driving the authors' shrill call for women to embrace the feminine within themselves was the author's deeply unsettling (and not wholly unwarranted) suspicion that female dependence on men, motherhood, and domestic life was in fact less than fulfilling for many American women. As early as 1947, the signs of female discontent were surely plain enough to a psychiatrist like Farnham. Indeed, the book's discussion of the profound discontent of modern women—their nervousness, sleeplessness, frustration, depression, and misery—in one sense foreshadows Friedan's later description of the "problem that has no name." Of course, Farnham and Lundberg's diagnosis of that discontent (neurosis stemming from a failure to yield to the female role, as well as "penis envy") and proposed treatment (joyful acceptance of feminine dependence and passivity) were not only virulently antifeminist, but ridiculously outmoded, even to readers in the late 1940s who observed how retrograde such prescriptions were. As Meyerowitz has noted, the sentiments expressed in *Modern Woman: The Lost Sex,* a book that generated much criticism and controversy when it was published, did not reflect mainstream thinking about women at the time.[96]

The perception that women were expecting and demanding more in marriage and private life was not just a theme struck by antifeminists and anxious male critics eager to denounce overbearing women. In 1955, psychiatrist Lena Levine observed uncritically that women were asking for more in marriage than they ever had before, demanding sexual satisfaction from their husbands and often seeking therapeutic help to obtain it. Women, Levine noted, "want a reaction like their husband's—a completely mutual response." One popular chronicler of American sexual mores, John McPartland, observed in 1947 that women were "beginning to be outspoken in expecting men to be satisfactory lovers." In marriage manuals, according to Deirdre English and Barbara Ehrenreich, "the experts were not only acknowledging female sexuality, but welcoming it as they insisted it was the husband's *duty* to satisfy it."[97]

In the name of extinguishing momism, some experts advised women to cultivate their sexuality, to shed their sexual inhibitions in their relations with husbands. Enhancing the sexual relationship was judged a means of demonstrating to herself, her husband, and even to her children that mom was a *real* woman, with her feminine identity intact and her sexuality directed appropriately toward her husband (unlike the pathological "moms" of the time, whose frustrated sexuality played a role in their unhealthy relationships with their sons).[98] The problem in the tense sexual milieu of the era was that women could never win. If they were perceived as insufficiently sexually responsive, they were deemed repressed or frigid; if they were seen as sexually assertive, they were guilty of damaging male sexual performance. Either way, women could be blamed for undermining male sexual confidence.

Moskin's *Look* article speaks to the male anxieties generated by the advent of therapeutic culture and the perception of a rising female sexual assertion endorsed by the experts. While Wylie's moms of the early 1940s were plump, hideously made-up, and sexually repressed, Moskin's wives of the 1950s were aggressive sex seekers, eager consumers of sex aids and negligees, and "pioneers, with men, on the frontier in sex" (quoting Riesman). Noting the research of Kinsey and other authorities, Moskin insisted that something akin to sexual revolution was taking place, and women were in its vanguard. Now in full possession of birth control, women were freer than ever to enjoy sex, and they increasingly demanded to be sexually satisfied. Quoting one expert, Moskin claimed that women have been shown to possess "a far greater sex potential than men."[99]

The price to be paid for women "taking charge of sexual relations" was not negligible, according to Moskin. "If the experts are right," he said, the American male has "even lost much of his sexual initiative and control; some authorities believe that his capacity is being lowered." Marriage advisors were partly to blame, for they "warn him that he is no longer to concentrate on his own pleasure; he must concern himself with primarily satisfying his wife." ("He might as well reach for the moon," Moskin complained). No longer able to focus on his own pleasure, Moskin's prototypical male becomes ever more soft and emasculated. Moskin's anger at "marriage advisors" who create unattainable standards of sexual normalcy echoed the views of a 1955 book, *Paradoxes of Everyday Life* by psychoanalyst Milton Saperstein, that claimed marriage manuals were creating unrealizable expectations in marriage and sexual life and thus severe "emotional strains" on those couples who use them as their guides.[100]

Like Farnham and Lundberg, Moskin saw female sexual assertiveness as an immense threat to a man's confidence. When he asked "what are the results of women's new aggressiveness and demand for sexual satisfaction?" he listed "fatigue," "passivity," "anxiety," and "impotency." He claimed women were responsible for "the decline of male potency that doctors observe," and regretted that, "if men are not to be the aggressors in sex, they must be the receivers." To dramatize the dangers posed by female sexual willfulness, Moskin stressed statistics showing the increase of bachelorhood, family desertion, and homosexuality in the nation. "Domineering women" were driving men away, he warned, provoking them to escape not only into "the organization" (now a "refuge" from women), but also into sexual relationships with other men. Citing one unnamed "scientist," Moskin depicted the rising trend of homosexuality as a "flight from masculinity." The Kinsey report's statistics on male homosexuality, he implied, proved this "flight from masculinity" a sad reality.[101] Moskin's view of women as emasculators and castrators, like that of Wylie, Farnham, and Lundberg, may seem extreme. It was certainly strong stuff for upbeat *Look* magazine. But the dreaded "flight from masculinity" always loomed over the crisis of masculinity discourse as well as the critique of momism, and assumed its place among all the other "escapes" and "flights" and "retreats" in 1950s cultural criticism.

The Flight from Masculinity

The Second World War accelerated multiple cultural, political, and economic currents that made the fear of a "decline" in manhood especially acute. Aside from ushering in an unprecedented concern with military defense and an uneasy sense of national vulnerability, the war was a catalyst for rapid social and economic change that disrupted sexual and racial relations. The glorification of the family and the revival of domestic ideals after 1945 emerged in part as a check against an unrestrained (female) sexuality and the rising tide of working women in the 1940s and the 1950s, especially during the war when women poured into the labor force and experienced a relative sense of autonomy. In several ways, the war also accelerated the movement for racial equality, and when civil rights activists challenged white superiority and paternalism, they indirectly and directly challenged white male authority. Taking into account the sense of mastery over one's world and paternal authority over others that the white masculine ideal had always assumed, clearly the cumulative trends of the era, including a burgeoning civil rights movement, meant that an older ideal of Anglo-American manhood no longer corresponded to the social, political, economic, and sexual realities of postwar America.

Yet something else was at stake here that accounts for the shrillness of male rhetoric and the new emphasis placed not just on masculine strength and virility (à la Teddy Roosevelt) but on male heterosexuality: the fear of homosexuality. Although experts and authorities since the nineteenth and early twentieth centuries had considered male homosexuality a scourge that was exacerbated by urbanization and other social dislocations, it was generally assumed to be a social problem confined to select urban deviants and social misfits, not a subculture into which most "average" respectable American males could be easily seduced. By mid-century, however, the possibility of an expanding homosexuality in American life loomed over the perception of a crisis in masculinity. In 1955, Max Lerner noted the "uneasy sense," apparent early in the decade, that homosexuality was increasing in the United States, an assumption voiced by countless writers, social critics, and experts at the time.[102] Whether a homosexual orientation was attributed to the effects of an impersonal, self-crushing mass society, a dysfunctional matriarchal American family, or the growing secularism and moral decay of the nation, the idea that male homosexuality was on the rise distinguishes the sexual anxiety of this period from others before it.

Homosexuality was undoubtedly more visible than ever in America, legal and cultural efforts to contain it notwithstanding. The notion that male and female homosexuality was increasing in American life was not wholly unwarranted. As we have seen, World War II was a crucial moment in gay and lesbian history. By mobilizing so many individuals into sex-segregated military units, encouraging a massive geographic relocation of Americans, and bringing about an economic recovery, the war hastened the establishment of a larger or at least more perceptible gay subculture in the United States. If World War II did encourage a nationwide "coming-out" experience for so many Americans, as some historians have stressed, then such a watershed could not have gone unnoticed by tense heterosexual observers, whose definition of manhood had always rested on the tacit assumption— so axiomatic it hardly needed articulation *until now*—of male heterosexuality.[103] It is no accident that this national "coming-out" experience coincided with the popularization of the term "momism" in the early 1940s.

Maturity and immaturity were major themes and tropes in cold war political rhetoric, as were "flights" and "escapes" from reality and responsibility, as we have seen. The same tropes and themes saturated psychiatric discourse in the 1950s. As Ehrenreich noted, maturity was the definitive attribute of the "well-adjusted" male in the 1950s. Psychiatrists and psychologists assumed that male maturity was nearly synonymous with fulfilling a particular life trajectory: attaining a respectable job, getting married, maintaining a home, and establishing a family. Men who remained unmarried well into their thirties were assumed to be suffering from a kind of perpetual adolescence signified by their fear of commitment and evasion of responsibility. Here the experts' diagnoses of the bachelor and the homosexual were strikingly similar: having failed to adjust to normative male role requirements, both were assumed to suffer from some combination of the same afflictions: infantile fixations, dread of responsibility, a deep attachment to the mother, or fear of the opposite sex. Of course, the lines between the irresponsible bachelor and the deviant homosexual were always fuzzy, and they could easily break down. In psychiatric judgment, the male homosexual and the bachelor were both fundamentally immature and maladjusted, but unlike the bachelor, the homosexual had supposedly given up entirely on fulfilling a normative masculine role in society.[104]

Psychiatrist and popular author Abram Kardiner popularized the "flight from masculinity" as an explanation of the apparent rise in male homosexuality. Homosexuality, he claimed, "grows from a social condition that strikes those who have a developmental vulnerability and an acquired weakness in masculinity." Men can arrive at homosexuality through a variety of "routes," he explained. But the male's failure to adapt to normative male role expectations, thus provoking an "escape" into homosexuality, was a route that seemed increasingly pervasive in American and European society. Kardiner asked:

> What is the failure of those men with the neurotic "homosexual component" in personality development? They have a deep sense of impoverishment of resources. They cannot compete. They always surrender in the face of impending combat. This has nothing to do with their actual ability, for many of them have extraordinary talent. It does have to do with assertiveness and pugnacity and the way in which they interpret the cultural demands for accomplishment. These are the men who are overwhelmed by the increasing demands to fulfill the specifications of masculinity and who flee from competition because they fear the increased pressure on what they consider their very limited resources.[105]

The belief that male homosexuality constituted a "flight from masculinity" reflects a new paradigm among psychoanalysts in the 1940s and 1950s that located the catalyst for male homosexuality in external sociological factors, as opposed to innate biological or libidinal drives, or developmental dysfunction rooted exclusively in familial dynamics. While Kardiner, like other adaptational theorists, assumed that there were common attributes ("the homosexual component") and developmental problems that gave particular men a predisposition to homosexuality (e.g., oversolicitous mothers), he emphasized the "large indeterminate group" whose sexual patterns were not permanently fixed earlier in life and thus could vary according to the success or failure with which these men met male role expectations. Since social factors (e.g., economic depression, war) could affect a man's ability to fulfill male role specifications, those factors could in turn influence his "voluntary" sex-object choice.[106]

The notion that homosexuality was an acquired trait that could be socially induced was intended to explain the apparent increase in the incidence of homosexuality. Kardiner rejected the idea that such an increase could be explained in purely biological terms ("no biological variant can increase one hundred per cent in a period of thirteen years"). Shifting the focus away from biology and toward society, Kardiner argued that the social trends and disorders of the times were the basis for this large-scale "flight from masculinity." He pointed to external circumstances that could affect a man's sense of himself: economic depression (unemployment, failure in business), affluence ("inability to keep up with the Joneses"), and war (male camaraderie under the stress of combat). Yet he repeatedly stressed that the excessive demands women place on men, as well as the rise of feminism, were major factors in the "flight from masculinity." Feminism destabilized the male self by making the female a "competitor" to the male; not only did the emergence of the female competitor generate familial dysfunction and male resentment of women, but it decreased the "social opportunities" of men (for employment, apparently). Kardiner's use of the phrase "flight from the female" suggests the significant role he assumed that women played in the male's "flight from masculinity." He summarized the more general trends that encouraged men to seek refuge in homosexuality: "the stepping up of the expectations of masculinity; the predominance of the instrumental use of human beings . . . the disintegrative influences operating on the family; the ideal of effortless achievement of comfort and status; the presence of universal anxiety and the fear of annihilation." These were the same conditions, Kardiner noted, that were responsible for the increase in schizophrenia and juvenile delinquency.[107]

Like Kardiner, leading psychoanalyst and New York University professor Hendrik M. Ruitenbeek assumed that sociological factors could explain the "rising prevalence of male homosexuality in contemporary America." For Ruitenbeek, it was the "radical social mobility" of the United States—the "alienation and loneliness" that men suffer in such a large, fluid, anonymous society—along with the "disorganization of the family" that were the causes of the dramatic rise in homosexuality. Ruitenbeek stressed that the modern father had lost the hard-driving, productive occupations that his forebears' sense of manhood once rested upon. The result was the decline of paternal authority in society and the family. Moreover, changing sex and gender roles, including the increasing independence and earning power of the wife (who could become a competitive threat), added to the tensions that plagued men. Combined with the social pressure placed on men to conform and marry early, it was no wonder, Ruitenbeek lamented, that so many American men were opting for a "way out."[108]

The shift in emphasis toward sociological factors as an explanation for the apparent rise in male homosexuality meant that the line between latent and overt homosexuality was always a shaky one. In 1954, psychoanalyst Lionel Ovesey created a category called "pseudo-homosexuality" for men who straddled that line. Ovesey reasoned that the purely "sexual component" of same-sex attraction was less important in understanding such men than the emotional dynamics that ensue when the male experiences "adaptive failures":

> In our culture, the premium is on self-assertion, and the man who lacks it and fails to meet success-goals is plagued with doubts about his masculinity. Thus any adaptive failure—sexual, social, or vocational—may be perceived unconsciously as a failure in the masculine role and, which is worse, may be symbolically extended through an equation that is calculated only to intensify the anxiety incident to the failure. The equation is the following: *I am a failure = I am castrated = I am not a man = I am a woman = I am a homosexual.*

A man experiencing adaptive failures wasn't necessarily a true homosexual, Ovesey stressed, since the intense anxiety he experiences due to his adaptive failures (which have nothing to do with his sexuality) may lead him to misidentify himself as one. But for Ovesey, adaptive failure was one of three major components in the "homosexual conflict" that afflicted homosexuals of the latent or overt variety (the other two components were sexuality and dependency). By focusing on adaptive failures and rejecting the notion of an irreversible physical, biological, or psychological predisposition to homosexuality, mental health professionals like Ovesey could treat male homosexuality as a pathology, subject to a therapeutic "cure." Indeed, Ovesey remarked that, since Freudian libido theory had been challenged by the adaptational approach, "this made possible the reclassification of homosexuality as a neurosis and opened the pathways to psychotherapy."[109]

Recovering a sense of masculine identity, then, could mean a good deal more than recovering a sense of autonomy or inner-direction that had waned along with the frontier. It meant protecting oneself from the temptations of masculine "flight" in a world that placed monumental burdens upon men. The basic assumptions of adaptational theory found their way into popular culture, as Moskin's *Look* article suggests. Moreover, the 1956 film *Tea and Sympathy*, one of many anti-conformity films of the fifties (adapted from a Broadway play), implied the adaptational theorists' conviction that excessively rigid masculine roles and norms of behavior could provoke males to escape from masculinity. The film suggested to viewers (as overtly as was possible in a motion picture at the time) that male norms were so ridiculously competitive, the pressure on males to conform so excessive, that a young man might flee from manhood and begin a slide into homosexuality. If one took adaptational theory too seriously, it might seem that any adaptive failure—getting sacked at work, rejected by the army, an episode of sexual impotence—could bring on the self-doubt that unconsciously encouraged a "retreat" into homosexuality. The beleaguered males represented in 1950s theater and film productions like *Tea and Sympathy* and

Look Back in Anger appeared to be inching toward the homosexual "way out."[110]

There was no solid consensus among mental health experts in the post-war years about the root cause of male homosexuality, although the majority of psychologists and psychiatrists attributed it to some form of arrested psychosexual development, often provoked by powerful, smothering mothers and weak, detached, or absent fathers (patterns that could themselves be socially induced). But the notion that homosexuality was a *learned* trait that could be provoked by social factors and men's "adaptive failures" to cope with modern life gained a new audience. In the work of adaptational theorists discussed here, the focus was primarily on male homosexuality. While Ovesey wrote that adaptational theory could be applied to female homosexuality, other theorists tended to assume that because women's gender role expectations were less demanding, they were not prone to a corresponding "escape" from femininity.

In an era in which heterosexual men were chafing at their prescribed role and all that came with it—the constraints of breadwinning and family life, the togetherness ethos, the social conformity encouraged by the organization, and overly demanding women—it is not all that surprising that the image of the homosexual loomed large over the crisis in masculinity discourse. A terrifying figure of loathing and fear, and perhaps even the object of buried envy, the homosexual appeared to have what male critics seemed to long for: freedom from marital responsibility, ease of sexual relations, and a kind of autonomy within his private life that conventional masculine roles precluded.

Before the popularization of adaptational theory, writer John McPartland, author of the 1947 book *Sex in Our Changing World,* depicted homosexuality (both male and female) as an "escape" from the emotional tensions of marriage and normal sexual relations into homosexual relationships "unencumbered by responsibilities" and laden with "powerful attractions." McPartland stressed how seductive the homosexual relationship was: for those fleeing from problematic heterosexual relationships, "the new tensions of an unnatural love are something of a novel relief." Among homosexuals, the feeling of "'belonging'" is "greater," "the abandon . . . is apt to be greater [and] the release more complete than in many of our bound and harassed heterosexuals." McPartland did not discount "physical and endocrinological factors" as causal factors in a homosexual orientation. Moreover, he articulated a host of reasons for the rise in "reversion to homosexuality," including urbanization, the complexities of economic life, and excessive mother-love. But McPartland seemed most preoccupied with those whom he believed were not hopelessly inclined toward inversion: the "unnecessary homosexuals" who could have been "happy in a normal life" but were driven into "unhappy homosexuality" because of the ignorance of parents, teachers, and society (despite its many attractions, homosexuality could only be "unhappy" in the end to McPartland). Americans' discomfort with the topic of homosexuality, McPartland wrote, stifled open discussion of the problem and thus actually permitted the "growth of invert tendencies."[111] The idea that a lack of discussion of homosexuality served to encourage its spread was a note often struck by commentators at the time.

In so much of the popular and psychiatric literature on sex and homosexuality in the 1940s and 1950s, there is a tangible concern with certain types of male homosexuals—not the feminine "fairies" or inveterate urban "sex deviants" of the past, but rather the beset males who "escape" from masculinity, the latent homosexuals (experiencing "homosexual conflict"), the covert homosexuals (e.g., the married men who secretly indulge in gay life on the side), the "pseudo-homosexuals" (experiencing "adaptive failures"), or the "unnecessary homosexuals" of the kind McPartland discussed. Such a preoccupation suggests an acute fear that heterosexual relations, marriage, and family life had, in fact, become too onerous for American men. It was an anxiety no doubt aggravated by the lack of options for men: divorce remained unacceptable to many Americans and extended bachelorhood still carried more than a hint of suspicion. The presumption that these men, the escapists, were now joining the ranks of homosexuals (thus the perception of an "epidemic" in homosexuality) was not, however, borne out by the Kinsey report. Contrary to popular opinion, Kinsey's findings did not show that overt homosexuality was statistically on the rise in the population. But the Kinsey report did reveal that 37 percent of men surveyed had at least one postadolescent homosexual experience leading to orgasm; 50 percent of men who remained single until age 35 had overt homosexual experience leading to orgasm; and 50 percent of men admitted to experiencing sexual attraction to other males. The report's unexpectedly high rates of same-sex male attraction and behavior, combined with its suggestion that homosexuals often appeared as straight, raised the possibility that there were more male homosexuals than previously thought.[112] Indeed, the Kinsey report may have unintentionally encouraged the idea that many outwardly heterosexual males could in fact be invisible or latent ("experimental") homosexuals, potentially en route to a homosexual life.

Orthodox psychiatrists and psychoanalysts still placed primary emphasis on developmental psychosexual factors and especially the homosexual's strong attachment to the mother as the basis of a homosexual orientation. Unlike adaptational theorists, who stressed as a corrective to the deficiencies of Freudian theory the social factors that can induce a homosexual orientation, more orthodox psychiatrists and psychoanalysts tended to accept Freudian libido theory and emphasize internal conflicts such as unresolved

Oedipal dilemmas and oral fixations as the psychological source of a homo-sexual orientation. But by mid-century, nearly all mental health professionals in the United States agreed that homosexuality was an acquired as opposed to an inborn trait—a pathology that called for "treatment" or "prevention." The American Psychiatric Association continued to include homosexuality in its diagnostic inventory of mental illnesses until 1973.[113]

A typical mid-century medical view of homosexuality was expressed by psychiatrist Frank S. Caprio in his 1952 book *The Sexually Adequate Male.* Homosexuality, he claimed, "is very often a symptom of some deep-rooted neurosis that can be traced to the development of a neurotic relationship to certain members of the family who were more than likely neurotic. It is neither an inherited condition nor a disease entity. Medical evidence tends to disprove the existence of any glandular cause for homosexuality. It is an *acquired* form of sex behavior, resulting from *psychological* rather than physical causes." The neurotic relationship to which Caprio referred was the familiar momist one: the suffocating mother who tries to turn her son into a substitute-husband, and the male child whose attachment to the mother forever infantilizes him. Hence the "homosexual pattern" that such men exhibit in adolescent and adult life, marked, according to Caprio, by feelings of inferiority, infantile regression, sexual immaturity, narcissism, and fear of the opposite sex. "There appears to be developing an epidemic of homosexuality as evidenced by recent statistics," he observed.[114]

Must You Conform?

Adaptational theory aside, the idea that smothering mothers caused boys to grow up to become sissies at best, homosexuals at worst, was so self-evident to many Americans that it hardly needed the theoretical imprimatur of ex-perts. The debate in the late forties and fifties about the "troubled" American family reflected these assumptions; the problem of "sissiness" in children was no small source of anxiety for American parents. The term "sissy," while not synonymous with the word "homosexual," had become a kind of murky code word for a would-be male homosexual. A sissy male child did not neces-sarily grow up to be a homosexual, but the inverse was frequently assumed: that the male homosexual began as a sissy boy-child—overly coddled, pal-pably feminine, frightened of competition, and neurotic. Girls were some-times said—parenthetically—to be prone to such a problem, if a "sissy" was defined, as one psychologist put it, as "a boy (or girl) who gets too much satisfaction from what his mother does for him and not enough from what he does for himself." But sissiness was primarily seen as a male problem. A girl sissy may grow up to be a feeble, neurotic woman, a poor candidate for wife and mother, an inept or overly permissive mother who might fail to instill proper values into her children; but her role in society was less crucial than that of a male. The danger for the boy "sissy" was infinitely greater: he could become a poor soldier, a failed breadwinner, sexually maladjusted, a homosexual.[115]

In popular magazines, one mental health commentator after another called for more effective fathering to counteract excessive maternal influence and cultivate proper heterosexual identity-formation in children. "Being a father is not a sissy business," one psychiatrist insisted in *Parents* magazine in 1947 as he urged men to take on "the most important occupation in the world." Experts influenced by functionalist sociology assumed that producing children with proper sex-role identification was crucial to the social order. Having discovered that an ultramasculine father did not necessarily reproduce masculine sons (in fact, such a father might produce his opposite), and that a stern, punishing father could reproduce maladjusted authoritarian personality types (as in the German family), many child-rearing authorities became convinced that boys were more prone to develop healthy masculine traits if they had close relationships with emotionally open, companionate fathers. As one child-rearing expert put it, boys are "more likely to identify with fathers whom they perceive as rewarding, gratifying, understanding, and warm, than with fathers who are not perceived in these ways." Another concurred: "A boy who admires his dad and cherishes the happy hours they have spent together can accept his masculine role smoothly and easily," whereas his sister "will be forming, half-consciously, her ideal picture of what a man should be and the kind of relationship she will one day have with her husband." Nurturing, involved fathers would foster proper sex-role socialization in children and cultivate tolerant, nonauthoritarian children as a bulwark against mass man. The "new fatherhood" of the 1950s was rooted in a set of ideals that germinated in the early decades of the twentieth century and were fitted to the imperatives of postwar American life.[116]

The importance placed on a more willful, activist fatherhood that would serve to preclude the feminization of boys by mothers and female teachers presented a paradox. The "new fatherhood" required American fathers to spend quality time with their children, especially their boys, in order to foster proper sex-role development. The companionate dad would be a "pal" to his son, cultivating a close, affectionate relationship that would eventually instill in the boy a sense of the values and behaviors appropriate to a well-adjusted American male. Such a role required dad to help his boy accept smoothly his masculine role in life. What were those values and attitudes that dad was imparting to his son? According to two experts, the effective father would demonstrate his "emotional maturity" to his son by embodying the values of patience and self-responsibility. The model father is forward looking and realistic in his worldview; he "accepts the unavoidable in life" and does not use "escape mechanisms such as drinking" to ignore problems. He demonstrates enthusiasm for his work, and his greatest reward is the "fun" he has when he exercises his abilities. He "gets along and cooperates with others" and shows that he can "love someone other than himself" and "be patient and wait where the greater good for himself and others is concerned." In short, the effective father, like the ideal middle manager, is flexible, sober in temperment, likeable, enthusiastic, respectful of others, understanding, and cooperative.[117]

The paradox was that the new American father began to look a little *too* domesticated, a little too feminine and conformist. Therapeutic culture had told him to relinquish the ways of his own father, to serve as a nurturing mentor to his son, to share hobbies and have lots of fun with his son. Yet, as Griswold pointed out, "the new father was a team player"; he embodied the values of the organization and its social ethic, values that were often said to be emasculating. Shorn of any idiosyncrasies or rough edges that were unacceptable in the white collar world, the warm, easygoing sympathetic dad began to look like nothing so much as an "organization man" who had surrendered to the ideal of togetherness. Having abandoned the old patriarchal mode of fathering, he was reduced to being a buddy to his son, not an authority figure who could impart a sense of leadership, self-possession, ambition, and individual will. The essential problem in mid-century fatherhood, then, was finding a balance between paternal warmth and nurturance on the one hand, and paternal leadership and authority on the other. Like Riesman's ideal autonomous male who can successfully negotiate the tension between self and other, the American father would have to negotiate the appropriate balance between "soft" and "hard" fathering.

Nowhere were the interrelated crises of masculinity, fatherhood, conformity, and the American self more dramatically expressed than in the 1955 film, *Rebel Without a Cause*. Via Hollywood, psychiatric authority here weighed in on the "problem" of the American family, so maligned at the time that Max Lerner complained about its reputation as "an unstable neurotic chaos." The screenplay for *Rebel Without a Cause* was based on the work of psychoanalyst Robert Lindner, whose 1944 case study of criminal psychopathy, *Rebel Without a Cause*, was the source of the film's title and inspiration (though the film's narrative was adapted from an unpublished story by Lindner, "The Blind Run").[118] *Rebel Without a Cause* speaks to the assumptions and therapeutic aims of experts who shaped so much of the discourse on manhood and fatherhood in the 1940s and 1950s.

Juvenile delinquency rose to the level of a major social problem when it became a phenomenon of the white middle class in the 1950s. Studies of juvenile delinquency proliferated in the disciplines of social science and social psychology in the fifties. Like Talcott Parsons and other experts, the film

Rebel Without a Cause locates the source of juvenile delinquency in the maladjusted American family, placing weak fatherhood and maternal overbearance under indictment. The film is usually remembered as a cautionary tale about the problem of affluent, troubled youth and the need for proper parenting. But in highlighting the unhealthy psychosexual dynamics between fathers and mothers, parents and children, the film meditates on the complex relationships between affluence, conformity, gender roles, and sexual identity-formation.[119]

Central to the drama is the teenage son of an affluent, middle-aged couple. Jim Stark (James Dean) is a rebel "without a cause" because he comes from a comfortable middle-class family and apparently wants for nothing—except, as the film implies, understanding and guidance. Jim's history of getting into trouble is repeated when the Stark family moves to a new suburban community and he immediately lands himself in the custody of the local police. Jim is clearly immature; in the film's opening scene he appears in a drunken stupor, looking infantile as he lies in the street in a fetal position clutching a toy animal. His problem—the problem of troubled youth like him—is established early on when Jim confronts his hypocritical, self-absorbed, bickering country club parents at the police station. It turns out there *is* a cause for Jim's rebellion—his parents and the empty, conformist, middle-class culture they personify.

Mr. Stark, a gregarious, affable, backslapping businessman, displays the artificial personality that one would associate with an "organization man" imprisoned in brotherhood. Eager to please and even more eager to avoid conflict, the well-meaning Mr. Stark appears almost deferential toward his drunk and rebellious son. Worse, Mr. Stark shrinks in the grips of his nagging and severe wife. Clad in mink and jewelry, Mrs. Stark hounds her husband and simultaneously dotes on and reproaches her son for getting into trouble. Her "solution" to this crisis is for the family to relocate once again in order to spare themselves the embarrassment of yet another family scandal. In the film's judgment, Mr. and Mrs. Stark, so false, so morally corrupted by affluence, so mired in their troubled relationship that they are hardly capable of listening to Jim, let alone understanding him, have failed miserably as parents.

The impact of this crisis of parental authority is registered in Jim's own crisis of selfhood, which forms the basis of the film's narrative. Jim is alienated and alone, groping for his own identity in a world hostile to the lone individual and in a matriarchal family which offers no positive male role models. Jim's tendency to waver between the "need to belong" and his desire to establish an autonomous self is dramatized in his relationship to the "group," a gang of rebellious teenagers at his high school. Jim's personal and moral dilemma centers on whether to resist or succumb to the lure of the gang, symbolized by the seductive and equally troubled Judy (Natalie Wood). Clearly, Jim's potential to allow himself to be lured into the groupist behavior of the gang is also a statement about his parents, troubled groupists themselves who are ill-equipped at instilling in Jim a sense of the proper boundaries between self and other.

Such a lack of boundaries carried immense dangers, the film implied. *Look* magazine writer George Leonard might have been speaking of Mr. and Mrs. Stark when he observed in 1958: "when you teach a child undue conformity to the group, when you take away his respect for the unique characteristics that make him different from all other human beings, then you create an automaton, ideal fodder for juvenile gang—or later, a totalitarian mass movement." *Rebel Without a Cause* reminds viewers that man is alone in the world (most obviously in the notable scene in the observatory) and, furthermore, that his ability to endure loneliness and alienation, his ability to be an individual apart from the group, is the only thing that will save him from psychopathy (or, by extension, totalitarianism). In his 1944 book, *Rebel Without a Cause*, Lindner defined "the psychopath" as "a rebel without a cause, an agitator without a slogan, a revolutionary without a program; in other words, his rebelliousness is aimed to achieve goals satisfactory to himself alone; he is incapable of exertions for the sake of others."[120]

Just as Whyte's organization man wanted to "get along" rather than assert leadership and independent initiative at the risk of offending others, Mr. Stark wants to be a pal to his son instead of a real father. When Jim is confronted with a dare by the gang's leader, Buzz, to engage in a dangerous drag race, Jim is unable to recoil from this challenge to his manhood because he dreads looking like a sissy. His instinctive misgivings about joining the pack, however, lead him to seek the advice of his father. But Mr. Stark is a dud as a dad; while nurturing and sympathetic, he is unable to offer any paternal guidance. When Jim asks his father what he should do in response to a challenge to his manhood, Mr. Stark pathetically waffles back and forth, unable to give his son a definitive answer. In consummate "committee man" form, Mr. Stark finally suggests that together they make "a list" of the pros and cons of the issue, which further frustrates Jim. Thus it is Mr. Stark's indecisiveness, his staggering failure of paternal leadership, that is responsible for Jim's decision to participate in the gang's drag race known as the "chickie run." The "chickie run" is a test of masculinity, and clearly a bogus one in the film's judgment, for the mark of a true man would be to stand alone and apart from the group and its mutually validating behavior. But Jim's other-directed father is, of course, hardly in a position to point out that his son's desire to be a man would better be realized by resisting the herd mentality, not by succumbing to it.

In explicating the causes for Jim's crisis, *Rebel Without a Cause* does not let mom off the hook, not by a long shot. The film more than implies that the source of Jim's need to belong, the source of his entire crisis of self, lies not only in Mr. Stark's failures as a father, but in the reversal of gender roles within the Stark family. Mrs. Stark is a domineering woman and mother, and while young Jim is not quite a sissy, he desperately fears being perceived as one, thanks to his dad's obvious emasculation at the hands of mom. When Jim encounters his hopelessly domesticated dad submissively crouching down in the hallway, sporting a frilly apron over his businessman's suit and fearing the wrath of a disapproving Mrs. Stark whose dinner he has just clumsily dropped, Jim recognizes all that is wrong in his matriarchal family, and castigates his timid father for not standing up to mom.

Rebel Without a Cause does, however, offer hope for the future of American manhood, and by extension the future of American society. Mr. Stark's fecklessness and inability to listen to his son is contrasted with the surefooted and empathetic juvenile officer Ray, the film's model of an autonomous masculine self. The alternative male father-figure affirmed in the character of Ray is a careful, shrewd listener, smart and decisive; he *understands* the kids. Most importantly, Ray is *authentic*. He is neither a conformist nor a pal-father; nor is he rigid or authoritarian. He is the man who has the appropriate mixture of empathy and authority, understanding and masculine toughness, and he knows how to deploy these qualities in order to counsel Jim effectively. It is Ray's "type" who promises to reproduce well-adjusted children and properly inner-directed sons who could safely be unleashed in the world.

The crisis within the family that results in maladjustment and groupist behavior in youth is played out in a variety of ways in *Rebel Without a Cause*, but it always returns to the recovery of appropriate masculine roles, implying that feminine roles and behaviors would then fall into place. (The film implies that if Mr. Stark were a stronger, more self-aware man, he could keep mom in check, and she'd not only yield to him, she'd like it.) While Jim's father is too "soft," Judy's father is too "hard"—a sexually repressed, stern, old-fashioned patriarch who presumably dominates his wife; Judy's mom is so inconsequential a force that she barely appears in the film. Uncomfortable with showing affection for his daughter and uneasy with her budding womanhood, Judy's tense father grows cold and detached, at one point repulsing a kiss from his daughter that he views as inappropriate for a young woman her age. His reaction is not wholly unwarranted, the film suggests; Judy *is* too sexed-up and obsessed with her dad. But his puritanical hang-ups are to blame, for he cannot see that his own sexual anxieties only encourage her need to be (sexually) recognized; so long as he remains distant and unable to negotiate an appropriate relationship with his daughter, he will remain the object of her misguided desire.

It is this paternal rejection that leads Judy not only into the arms of the group—within which she can elicit the attention that her father cannot give her—but to real or potential prostitution. Indeed, she is picked up by the police at the beginning of the film (it is vaguely suggested) for streetwalking. Her identity crisis is most clearly manifested in her sexually charged relationship to the gang. As a confrontation between Jim and the kids heats up outside the observatory, the alluring, tight-sweatered Judy licks her lips at the imminent competition for masculine dominance of the group (and hence possession of her). In fact, it is she who raises her arms to signal the commencement of the doomed "chickie run." By highlighting Judy's inappropriately directed sexuality, Rebel Without a Cause speaks to the dangers of the older, repressed model of the patriarchal family.

Judy and Jim's troubled family dynamics are the cause of their psychological malaise, but Plato's (Sal Mineo) lack of any visible mother and father at all suggests a worst-case scenario. Plato is the son of wealthy, divorced, and absent parents; the breakdown of his family suggests the dangers of affluence run amok. While Plato's selfish, uncaring parents are absent in the home, he is left in the care of the black housekeeper (and in a female-dominated household). Plato is thus the consummate misfit, so pitifully soft and needy, so lacking in sense of self that he clings to Jim and Judy as ersatz parents. But Plato is more than immature. As his name not so subtly hints and his effete demeanor implies, Plato is a latent homosexual, and his adoration of Jim—so exaggerated in the drama that it cannot help but slide into homoeroticism—is central to the film's depiction of him as sadly psychotic (he is initially arrested for shooting a litter of puppies.) Plato's sanity might have been recovered had his uncaring mother not put an end to his psychotherapy, but in the absence of a "cure" for what ails him, he becomes ever more disturbed. Rebel Without a Cause becomes a tragedy when Plato is shot dead by the trigger-happy establishment, which has misunderstood him, and like his parents, failed him disastrously.

Rebel Without a Cause endorsed the therapeutic cure as an antidote to the problem of maladjusted children and poor fatherhood. Ray represented the preferred model of fatherhood; by virtue of his ability to understand so astutely the kids' grievances against their parents, he also symbolized the therapeutic culture of the experts. (Ray is an "agent of the therapeutic state," as one critic of the film suggested.[121]) In his expertise as a social worker/therapist/juvenile officer (he was a plainclothes officer whom the film carefully distinguished from the other establishment cops who seemed gruff and unsympathetic), Ray reproduced the psychiatric judgment that understood juvenile delinquency not as a problem of spoiled brats in need of stern punishment (the establishment view), but the consequence of neurotic, dysfunctional families in need of therapeutic help. Inasmuch as the film criticized the establishment—and the affluent, suburban lifestyle and middle-class conformity that nourished juvenile delinquency—it also passed judgment on the "new fatherhood." Personified in the figure of Mr. Stark, the new fatherhood ideal reproduced the soft, social ethic of the organization.

Like other critiques of American conformity, *Rebel Without a Cause* in the end affirmed a more enlightened kind of conformity. As a cautionary tale about the affluent family and the crisis of paternal legitimacy within it, the film revealed the dangers of producing maladjusted children, and especially vulnerable sons, who, lacking proper paternal authority, might become rebellious groupists at best, misfits unsure of their sex role at worst. If the film sympathized with the kids against their screwy parents, it could not recommend rebellion against either the establishment or traditional gender roles within the family. Rather, *Rebel Without a Cause* presented an alternative vision of a nuclear family, one that Jim and Judy would hopefully reproduce: nurturing and authentic, self-expressive and morally sound, and navigated by a properly inner-directed man at its helm. After all, it is Jim who has achieved the all-important psychological breakthrough that will result in his establishment of an autonomous self. Judy's dilemma is "solved" in the film only by pairing her up with a newly self-aware Jim; her sexuality can now be appropriately directed toward marriage and family life. Ultimately, the film restored the patriarchal family by giving it a new, self-reflective emotional structure which serves as a defense against the overpowering tide of affluence, materialism, mass culture, and the organization. Such a family would cease to reproduce mindless groupist punks and social misfits who regress into infantile forms of rebellion and threaten the social order.

If there is any doubt as to how to read *Rebel Without a Cause*, Lindner's *Must You Conform?* explicitly addresses the relationship between conformity, rebellion, and sexuality that is open to debate in the film (which he helped to conceive). As we have already seen, Lindner denounced the conformist as a "mindless integer" and a "psychopath." The juvenile delinquent was one variant of the conformist, and he posed no small threat to the social order, for Lindner believed that the "mutiny of the young" was a seedbed for totalitarianism. The juvenile delinquent, "regressive" and "primitive," represented mass man in the making:

> Youth has abandoned solitude; it has relinquished privacy. Instead, these are days of pack-running, of predatory assembly, of organization into collectivities that bury, if they do not destroy, individuality. And it is into these mindless associations that the young flock like cattle.

More than their privacy, the fee they pay for initiation is abandonment of self and immersion in the herd, with its consequent sacrifice
in personality.[122]

Juvenile delinquency suggested to Lindner the "effeminization of youth."
Like other cold war thinkers, Lindner held the rise of mass culture responsible for the epidemic of groupism, and directly equated mass culture with
emasculation: "culture, the maker of man, can also unmake him. . . . It can,
as it now threatens to do, unman him." Lindner meant this literally. Culture
emasculated men not only because it encouraged behavioral conformity
but because it enforced repressive attitudes toward sex. American society
was a "sex-denying" culture, Lindner insisted. The "rigid sex morality" of
society generated tensions and anxieties that undermined the individual's
psychosexual health and therefore encouraged the individual to seek inappropriate and self-destructive outlets for his or her confused or repressed
sexuality (hence the representation of Judy and her family in *Rebel Without a Cause*).[123]

If Lindner, seeing rigid "sex denial" everywhere, ignored the cultural
changes taking place that provoked so many others to observe that American society was in fact undergoing a sexual revolution, it was because he
was pursuing another line of argumentation. Lindner devoted an entire
chapter in *Must You Conform?* to male homosexuality, a subject that preoccupied him, as his characterization of Plato as a psychopath in *Rebel
Without a Cause* suggests. (Although he spoke of homosexuality in general,
Lindner's discussion and case studies centered on men.) Lindner believed
that the rising incidence of male homosexuality was not, as the psychoanalytic community believed, the result of the decline in traditional patriarchal
orientation in society or the family. Rather, male homosexuality had more
to do with our repressive, "sex-conformist" society. Homosexuality, he insisted, is fundamentally a rebellion against the sex conformity which is transmitted by "sex-distorted elders." Though he was light on specifics, Lindner
seemed to be saying that "rigid sex morality" discourages open and healthy
sexual relations between men and women. Thus, in a sexually conservative
society such as the United States, heterosexual relations become fraught
with tension, and ever more unconsciously undesirable to men, who rebel
against it by becoming "inverts." Lindner implied that wherever sex repression is more pronounced, the incidence of homosexuality will be greater.[124]

Lindner viewed homosexuality as a form of rebellion against rigid social
and sexual norms, yet in one sense his argument looks like a variant of the
"flight from masculinity" phenomenon. Relations with the opposite sex
become so oppressive, anxiety-inducing, traumatizing, or just plain unap-
pealing in a repressed, sex-denying culture that man "escapes" into homo-

sexuality. In certain ways, Lindner's perspective also echoed Wylie's ideas about sex in *Generation of Vipers.* Wylie had denounced the hypocritical sex morality of his time, suggesting that "the restoration of a naturalistic attitude toward sex will do away with much of our insanity and neurosis." Wylie was ambivalent, though; he couldn't decide whether a more "naturalistic" attitude toward sex would break the grip of matriarchy or strengthen it, whether it would enhance heterosexual relations or lead to more bisexuality and degeneration as in ancient Greece.[125]

Having adopted the pose as a rebel against a "sex-denying" society, Lindner might have affirmed the adult homosexual as the quintessential nonconformist who rejects the restrictive norms of sexual behavior that society imposes on him, despite the mighty forces of cultural (and therefore personal) sexual repression. Given the terms in which conformist behavior is discussed here and elsewhere in his work, one might expect Lindner to regard an openly homosexual person as someone who demonstrates an inner strength; rather than taking his directives from the oppressive "sex-denying" culture, the homosexual would seem to act precisely according to what his instincts tell him to do, despite the consequences: offending others, social ostracism, and alienation from society. But Lindner could not bring himself to sanction this kind of nonconformity, either. Homosexuality ("inversion") may constitute an expression of rebellion against conformity, yet it was a "negative" form of rebellion, he insisted. Homosexuality, he wrote, "takes its place with the neuroses, psychoses, and criminoses, all of which . . . are destructive rather than constructive" expressions of rebellion. Why, according to Lindner, was inversion a destructive form of rebellion?

> Presently, homosexuality is the source of immense quantities of unhappiness and frustration to large numbers of individuals and a chronically irritating generator of intrahuman hostility. Its elimination would not only erase much distress but, since it can be eradicated only by a radical alteration in the total sexual condition now obtaining in society, and since this total sexual condition is subversive of human welfare, only good can come out of the process.

Lindner's claim that homosexuality inevitably resulted in profound unhappiness for the individual was the standard rationalization of psychiatrists and mental health professionals in the 1950s who sought to prevent and "cure" homosexuality. Lindner assured his readers that "inversion" derived from cultural and familial dynamics rather than innate biological drives, and thus could be successfully "cured" with psychotherapy.[126]

Lindner's discussion of homosexuality not only speaks to how artificial the revolt against conformity could be. It is also instructive because, in going to such great lengths to sort out the relationship between conformity and homosexuality, it reveals explicitly the anxieties that otherwise lay buried in the wider preoccupation with the passive, self-less conformist male of the fifties. Here, the male homosexual becomes the logical, tragic culmination of the trend toward mass man: loss of self means loss of masculinity; man becomes effeminate, he becomes woman, "regressive," "immature," and finally, for Lindner, an impediment to the progress of mankind:

> Despite the benefits claimed for [homosexuality] as a way of life by its many apologists, e.g., Plato, it appears doubtful whether this "way" assists progress which is, after all, the final measure of value. Certainly, if we define progress in terms of overcoming "the triad of limitations" pointing toward an eventual break-through into another and, presumably, higher order of being, we must reject genuine sexual inversion as a mode of behavior assisting toward such an end.

In *Must You Conform?* the homosexual appears as one more psychopath (as did the latent homosexual puppy-killer Plato in *Rebel Without a Cause*) in a mass society. To the question *Must You Conform?* Lindner's unequivocal answer was *yes.*[127]

What then, was left of the revolt against conformity in American life? Like so many other mental health professionals in the fifties, Lindner endorsed "maturity." He called for "mature" rebellion which would presumably lead to a "higher order of being" for mankind. Short on specific examples of what might constitute a mature, "positive" form of protest, Lindner could only suggest a form of rebellion that no doubt eased the minds of heterosexual middle-class readers, who must have been relieved to discover that being a rebel was as easy as being an old-fashioned liberal individualist in the spirit of the Founding Fathers:

> The productive way toward non-conformity is the way of positive rebellion, of protest that at once affirms the rebellious nature of man *and* the fundamental human values. These values reside in the common treasure of humanity. They form the basic aspirations of all humans everywhere and are expressed most clearly in the great documents and contracts—such as our own Bill of Rights—which men have seen fit to declare from time to time. *Rebellion and protest in their name, and conducted in a fashion that does not in any way violate their spirit, is positive rebellion, authentic rebellion.*[128]

Presumably, homosexuality was a form of rebellion that violated the spirit of our "great" documents as well as our universal values. If there is an obvious contradiction in Lindner's conviction that holding *universal* values ("the basic aspirations of all humans") is the way to "non-conformity," it escaped his notice. In effect, Lindner had turned the liberal centrist into a "positive" rebel against conformity. Years earlier, Schlesinger had done something similar in *The Vital Center*, defining the centrist liberal as the true individualist rebel who courageously fought the emasculating forces of a mass society and the cowardly, groupist politics of the extreme right and left.

For a generation of male intellectuals in the fifties, the image of the softened, conformist male loomed so large in the imagination that rebelling against it—against the group, against the dull, conventional, established way of thinking or acting, against the "conventional wisdom" (a trope that became popular in the fifties)—became something of a "style." For Lindner it was so much a style that he couldn't bear to relinquish his claim to being a rebel even as he revealed, over and over again, his conventional views. No matter; he was a rebel for daring to speak candidly about such matters! Adopting the rebel pose against "overadjusted conformity," Peter Viereck, Pulitzer Prize–winning poet, writer, historian, and "new conservative," even wrote a book in praise of "the unadjusted man" ("a necessary hero because he defends the *inwardness* of the individual against the busybody bustling of external mass progress"). It was in liberal circles, however, that the rebellion against conformity became *de rigueur*, and while the style took numerous cultural and literary forms, it achieved its political expression in the image of the new cold war warrior—the liberal *Übermensch* who rejected the stodgy, timid conformist mentality of Eisenhower and Nixon and joyfully embraced his individuality and power.[129]

To adopt the posture of the rebel against conformity was to recoil from the allegedly placid, complacent mood of the time, to stand for something vaguely unconventional and manly. With every new indictment of the dreary, spiritless 1950s, the rebel style became more exaggerated. By the time Norman Mailer published his essay "The White Negro" in 1957, a more genuine manifestation of the revolt against conformity had already emerged in the work of the Beats—true rebels who actually lived their repudiation of bourgeois life in the 1950s. Male rebellion was now in high style, and it was Mailer's literary task to concoct his own composite of an authentic male rebel and offer it up to the discriminating readers of *Dissent*.[130]

The "white Negro" was Mailer's existentialist vision of a hipster. He was a "psychic outlaw," a rootless urban vagrant who lived in the "present" and had no "intentions" except to take risks in order to enlarge the "arena of the possible." "Childlike" in his "adoration of the present," his only moral code was "to do what one feels whenever and wherever it is possible," which enhanced his own possibilities and worked "reciprocally" to enhance others' as well. He confronted death without undue anxiety and sought pleasure without guilt, and had therefore achieved the all-important "liberation of the self from the Super-Ego of society." Having immersed himself in the vast urban wild, he was capable of discovering "isolated truths" that would otherwise escape him in the square world, where security was the ultimate aim of a man's life and a false, soulless existence the end result.[131]

Mailer's "The White Negro" stands as a defiant, impudent repudiation of books like *The Mature Mind* and all the strictures placed on American men to adjust and mature in the fifties. For Mailer, the choice was to endure "slow death by conformity with every creative and rebellious instinct stifled" or "to live with death as an immediate danger, to divorce oneself from society, to exist without roots, to set out on that uncharted journey into the rebellious imperatives of the self." Alienation and rootlessness, long considered the source of modern man's debilitating anxiety and neurosis, here becomes the source of psychic liberation. "Escaping" from reality, "fleeing" from responsibility, once considered evidence of timidity and fear, here becomes the mark of genuine courage.[132]

The "white Negro" was an admixture of social types: the bohemian hipster, the "Negro," the juvenile delinquent, and the psychopath. Here Mailer collapsed the most marginalized figures in American life into a single composite rebel, one who embodied the very impulses that Lindner denounced in mass man: infantile regression, primitive urges, irrationality, nihilism, and psychopathy. Mailer had obviously read Lindner's work, and borrowing some of its idioms, he turned Lindner's phony war against conformity back upon itself. Mailer's assault on the "empty hypocrisies of mass conformity" took the form of an affirmation, via the hipster, of all things threatening—immoderation, vagrancy, crime, the ghetto, violence, drugs, the search for an "orgasm more apocalyptic than the one which preceded it." His indictment of the "antisexual foundation of every organized power in America" was no less unsettling, expressed in the hipster's appropriation of the "Negro's" supposed raw, unsublimated sensuality. To Lindner, the culture of the psychopath—violent, immoral, nasty, and brutish—was a breeding ground for mass man. To Mailer, the "white Negro's" world was in fact "barbarian," but it was no less barbarian than—and perhaps even preferable to—the "totalitarianism" in American society supported by the "collective violence of the State."[133]

Mailer bemoaned the "conformity and depression" of his time: "A stench of fear has come out of every pore of American life, and we suffer from a collective failure of nerve. The only courage, with rare exceptions, that we have been witness to, has been the isolated courage of isolated people." The courageous Negro was Mailer's archetype for the white hipster because he has lived "on the margin between totalitarianism and democracy for two centuries"; he is an outsider; he knows danger; he lives for "the enormous present"; he lacks "the inhibitions of civilization"; he supplies the "existential synapses"; he is the "source of Hip."[134] Mailer sought a pure and primal kind of male authenticity, one that he associated with the "Negro," one that was obviously meant to shock polite, enlightened readers. The essay had its intended effect. Mailer's many critics rightly assailed him for trafficking in stereotypes among other offenses.

In its essence, the "white Negro" hipster was Mailer's prototype for a new political radical (despite his perfunctory caveats). The old American Communist—repressed, psychically enchained by Stalinist myths, just another conformist trapped in totalitarian "tissues"—was now thoroughly irrelevant. His psyche free from the stifling conformity of Stalin's Russia or Eisenhower's America, the "white Negro" hipster lived on the edge; he absorbed the "courage of isolated people." Courage had to be the basis of a new radicalism, for Mailer assumed that a "partially totalitarian society" required more courage on the part of men than a fully totalitarian one because the "general anxiety is greater" in the former. Schlesinger had used the "the failure of nerve" tropes; he had framed the fundamental questions of mid-century liberalism around the imperatives of courage and willfulness, telling liberals that the choice before them was essentially psychological: one was either a "doer" or a "wailer," a "new radical" or a "Doughface." For Mailer, the choice was also an internal one that set courage against timidity: "One is Hip or one is Square . . . one is a rebel or one conforms, one is a frontiersman in the Wild West of American nightlife, or else a Square cell, trapped in the totalitarian tissues of American society, doomed willy-nilly to conform if one is to succeed."[135]

There is an odd intellectual genealogy that links *The Lonely Crowd* (1950) to "The White Negro" (1957), one that mirrors the vicissitudes of the 1950s as the affluent society began to spawn less temperate critics of conformity, like Mailer's rival Paul Goodman. Where could a man find authenticity in an inauthentic society? How could he avoid being trapped in the "totalitarian tissues" of American life? Where could a man achieve genuine masculine self-realization in a hopelessly feminized, conformist society? That the sober and somewhat romantic liberal individualism of Riesman could give way, by the end of the decade, to the radical individualism of Mailer—to the proposition that one cultivate "the psychopath in oneself"—is not inconceivable. At a time when alienation could be cultivated against the suffocating conformity of the mass, when no one stood for conformity and many staked claims to rebel authenticity; at a time when even the centrist liberal could disingenuously pose as a radical and the old frontiers of manhood were closed off to those seeking masculine reaffirmation—the quest for authenticity led Mailer to the roughest, toughest margins of American life, to places where timid liberal critics would never dare to tread.

For Mailer, it was the Negro, from whom the hipster absorbed his survival instincts, who "must live with danger from his first day." By necessity he was fearless. And the singular attribute that Mailer appreciated in the psycho-pathic killer was his daring act of violence (to commit a murder, "courage of a sort is necessary"). Calculated to unnerve, this was also Mailer's way of charging the liberal establishment with a failure of nerve and will. Consider his contempt for the "professional liberal," full of "committee-ish cant" about racial integration and unable to *understand* the Negro. The liberal is not only dim and overcivilized, Mailer implied, but sexless, which is why he cannot grasp the sexual subtext of the battle over civil rights in the South. ("The orgasm is an anathema to [the liberal] mind because it is the ines-capable existential moment," Mailer later wrote.)[136]

In this sense, Mailer's "white Negro" hipster—autonomous, authentic, fearless, spontaneous, and sexually willful—represented a sort of challenge to establishment liberals and their consensus politics, one that would reap-pear in his subsequent experiments in "New Journalism." In the male anticonformist discourse of the time, Mailer's affirmation of the male rebel was singularly outrageous. But the impulses underlying his celebration of the "white Negro" ultimately speak to the longing for masculine regenera-tion so conspicuous in the 1940s and 1950s, to the search for an alternative to the domesticated, security-seeking American male, doomed forever to Squaresville USA, to "slow death by conformity."

CHAPTER 4

Reinventing the Liberal as Superman

Note the clue that Norman Vincent Peale's *Power of Positive Thinking* was America's most popular nonfiction best-seller during the same years that Eisenhower was America's most popular personality. High-minded evasion of problems, affable relaxation of critical alertness, comfortable religiosity and harmless platitudes, a genuine kindliness blended with pap—there you have the *impression* the decade makes . . .

> —Peter Viereck, *The Unadjusted Man* (1956)

It was a hero America needed, a hero central to his time, a man whose personality might suggest contradictions and mysteries which could reach into the alienated circuits of the underground, because only a hero can capture the secret imagination of the people, and so be good for the vitality of his nation; a hero embodies the fantasy and so allows each private mind the liberty to consider its fantasy and find a way to grow. Each mind can become more conscious of its desire and waste less strength in hiding from itself.

> —Norman Mailer, "Superman Comes to the Supermart" (1960)

When John F. Kennedy accepted the nomination to run for president at the Democratic National Convention in 1960, the "New Frontier" must have seemed a fitting expression of the themes and values he had been stressing in earlier months on the campaign trail—purposefulness, vigor, determination, self-sacrifice. The New Frontier slogan would suggest not a programmatic departure from the past (as with the New Deal), but rather a new national spirit. "The old era is ending. The old ways will not do," Kennedy stressed:

There has also been a change—a slippage—in our intellectual and moral strength. Seven lean years of drought and famine have withered a field of ideas. . . . Too many Americans have lost their way, their will, and their sense of historic purpose. . . . Today some would say that [the] struggles are all over—that all the horizons have been explored—that all the battles have been won—that there is no longer an American frontier. But . . . the problems are not all solved and the battles are not all won—and we stand today on the edge of a New Frontier . . . a frontier of unknown opportunities and perils—a frontier of unfulfilled hopes and threats. . . . Beyond that frontier are the uncharted areas of science and space, unsolved problems of peace and war, unconquered pockets of ignorance and prejudice, unanswered questions of poverty and surplus. It would be easier to shrink back from that frontier, to look to the safe mediocrity of the past, to be lulled by good intentions and high rhetoric. . . . But I believe the times demand new invention, innovation, imagination, decision. I am asking each of you to be pioneers on that New Frontier.[1]

The idea of a New Frontier meshed nicely with the emphasis that Kennedy's advisor, Arthur Schlesinger Jr., placed on the cyclical-historical trends in American politics that now invited what the historian-activist called a "new liberal epoch." In 1959, Schlesinger proposed to Kennedy that this new epoch "would resemble the Progressive period of the turn of the century more than it would the New Deal," since "the Progressive revolt grew out of spiritual rather than economic discontent; and this seemed the situation in 1959." Schlesinger recounted that his historical analysis raised Kennedy's awareness of the need for a demonstrable departure from the "passivity and acquiescence" which had characterized the Eisenhower years. That "vigorous public leadership would be the essence of the next phase— evidently corresponded to things which Kennedy had for some time felt himself," Schlesinger recalled.[2]

The New Frontier trope served the Kennedy campaign well. It functioned as a symbolic response to the exhaustion of the old American frontier, the effects of which had been an implicit theme in the writings of so many postwar social critics concerned that the historic shift from production to consumption, from the Protestant Ethic to the social ethic, had brought about a decline in the tough, striving, purposeful spirit that had once characterized the nation's citizens. If the old frontier was exhausted, heretofore unexplored frontiers would be found and conquered, providing an outlet for national energies which had lain dormant in the previous decade. But the New Frontier was more than a metaphor for potential avenues of American exploration or conquest. It promised to reinvigorate the nation with the spirit of courage, adventure, daring, and self-sacrifice that its would-be leader personified. Its resonance and power, I want to suggest here, lay in a new vision of masculinity, scripted years earlier in *The Vital Center*, nourished by the postwar crisis of self, shaped by the male writers and rebels of the fifties, and come to life in the figure of John F. Kennedy.

Sympathetic, critical, and popular commentary on Kennedy has invariably highlighted what has now become a cliché about the president who presided over Camelot: his youthful vitality and charisma, his confidence and sophistication, and, in a word that reappears in so much of the historical and popular literature on Kennedy, his "coolness," all of which reportedly put him in good stead. With varying degrees of emphasis, Kennedy's slim victory over Nixon appears as the triumph of the new consensus liberal, the "postideological" liberal statesman, who prevailed, despite his Catholicism, his youth, and his unspectacular congressional record, by the force of his style and personality.[3]

The attributes that became assets for Kennedy—intellectuality, cultural refinement, urbanity, eastern wealth, an Ivy League education—had been previously suspect in the political culture of the 1950s; so too was liberalism, to which those attributes were inextricably wedded. Certainly, time had healed old wounds by 1960; the fear of internal subversion and perversion had run its course by the end of the fifties. But a wealthy eastern Democratic candidate with Choate and Harvard pedigrees still had to prove himself more than worthy of occupying the White House. While it is sometimes acknowledged that Kennedy managed to redeem the liberal Democrat and turn those very attributes that had handicapped Adlai Stevenson into the virtues of his persona and his presidency, such a feat has been attributed to something called his "style"—another word that persistently reappears in the historiography on Kennedy and his New Frontiersmen.

By way of an exploration of the political currents and the cultural milieu within which the image of the New Frontier was shaped, I want to pursue the notion that Kennedy and the vital center politics he embodied represented a new liberal *style*. Garry Wills observed that in 1960, "ideology had been replaced by 'style,' yet that style was aggressive, ready to 'bear any burden,' determined the world should not remain 'half free, half slave.'" Other scholars, including Christopher Lasch, David Halberstam, Bruce Miroff, and more recently Robert Dean, have commented on the "tough-minded" style that was institutionalized within the ranks of the "best and the brightest"—the mixture of accomplished Ivy Leaguers, World War II veterans, and former intelligence officers recruited into the Kennedy administration.[4]

The Kennedy style was distinctly and resolutely masculine, and if there was one notable stylistic accomplishment that marked Kennedy's presidency, it was a reconciliation of intellect, education, cultural refinement, and liberalism itself with masculine virility. The disjuncture between American manhood and virility so often observed in the 1950s found its antidote in the New Frontier. If one significant dimension of Kennedy's popular appeal lay in the promise that he could remake the nation, and by extension the nation's men, in his own potent self-image, much of his appeal to his own New Frontiersmen lay in the same promise. Schlesinger's parallel between the mood of the Progressive era and the late 1950s was on the mark; the sense at the turn of the century that the exhaustion of the frontier had closed off avenues for American men to affirm their manhood had reemerged, albeit in altered form, in the fifties. In strategic political terms, Kennedy was a boon for Democrats. Not since Teddy Roosevelt had the nation been roused by a leader who, in name of the reform tradition, promised a restoration of the nation's vitality, and by extension American men's virility, through strenuous—in this case *vigorous*—endeavor.

Perhaps few presidents were ever more historically conscious than John Kennedy; perhaps no other cohort group who came to Washington to work under a newly elected president was more aware of itself as a distinct generation that would make its indelible mark on history. Since childhood, Kennedy had admired the heroic statesmen of the past; although not a professional historian, he published historical monographs and could count among his braintrusters at least two professional historians, Schlesinger and Walt Rostow. Robert Dallek has credited Schlesinger with helping Kennedy "find a distinct liberal outlook." In many ways, Schlesinger did more than that: he was the chief architect of the New Frontier's liberal identity, an identity crafted from the very beginning with an unusually sharp eye on history, toward the past as well as the *future* history that Kennedy and his New Frontiersmen *would* make. Kennedy's speeches, composed by Ted Sorensen, Richard Goodwin, and Schlesinger, placed great emphasis on the historical role of the New Frontier in the context of generational change— logical themes to stress given Kennedy's youth and the need to present his age as an asset rather than a liability. Schlesinger recalled that when his bid for the presidency began, Kennedy felt his "greatest need . . . was to give his campaign identity."[5] Much of the historiography tells us how determinedly and meticulously Kennedy's identity was crafted, with attention to symbols and gestures large and small. From the flaunting of Kennedy's competitive cold warrior qualities in countless campaign and presidential speeches, to his reluctance to play golf during the campaign lest he be caught indulging in the sport of retirees like Eisenhower, to his efforts to micromanage and influence the press and punish offending journalists and publishers, Kennedy and his spokesmen always gave rather compulsive attention to the identity he projected.

Kennedy and his New Frontiersmen did not invent identity politics, and Richard Nixon became well known for his obsessive manipulation of his image. Each candidate, in his own way, embraced and touted his image with a self-consciousness that would have been unfamiliar to statesmen like Truman, Eisenhower, or even Franklin Roosevelt. Yet in comparison to Kennedy, Nixon's image management was typically more defensive, and it often backfired on him. Early on, Nixon had shaped for himself an image as a common man, a "self-made" man, yet he had to worry about so many things that Kennedy didn't: his awkward mannerisms and physical appearance, his frequent intellectual gaffes and blunders, his reputation as a hatchet man and an overzealous red-baiter, his "Checkers" past. In this sense, Nixon's image construction served to mitigate the deficiencies of a sitting vice president who had already been the object of considerable criticism, and whose primary defect, it was often said, was his abject inauthenticity. Kennedy's image, however, was crafted with less defensiveness and a highly attuned attention to "identity" in a stricter sense of the term—to his and his generation's distinct experiences, style, habits of thought, and portending role in the grand sweep of American history. Kennedy and the New Frontiersmen, "tempered by war, disciplined by a hard and bitter peace," full of unbridled vitality, guts, and tough-minded intelligence, would usher in a new historical epoch that would reflect their own very positive self-image, thus making the crucial break from the lethargy and complacency of the Eisenhower era.[6]

The generational break that the Kennedy campaign proclaimed was at once artificial and very real. In ideological terms, Kennedy scarcely departed from the basic tenets of the centrist, consensus politics that had been evolving for more than a decade and came to fruition under Eisenhower. If the generational difference was one of disposition, the men of Eisenhower's generation had experienced the Second World War and had presumably been "tempered" and "disciplined" by it; they too had learned the "hard" lessons of Munich. Eisenhower's generation was older by the time World War II broke out, and this was not their first encounter with world war in any case. For the best and the brightest, younger and much more awed by the historic confrontation with totalitarianism and their own military service, the Second World War more thoroughly shaped their outlook and identity. As Michael Sherry noted, the New Frontiersmen, "proud of their ability to break from their elders . . . were nonetheless more the prisoners of World War II than Eisenhower's generation."[7]

A difference in temperament there was. Of course, to some extent each generation professes to be sobered by historic events, more realistic and toughminded than the last. But the New Frontiersmen elevated the generational break to a matter of such import that the identity they constructed, and the leadership style they cultivated in conscious opposition to that of Eisenhower, had the effect of making them hostages to the virile image and style they had cut out for themselves. Kennedy, to be sure, did not manufacture the cult of toughness out of whole cloth; he inherited it, inflated it, changed its style, built his presidency around it, and bequeathed it to Lyndon Johnson. But in overcompensating for the timidity that had been associated with the liberal establishment for at least a decade, Kennedy and the consensus liberals shaped a heady liberal nationalism based on fantasies of liberal potency.

Affluence and Its Discontents

The first and most obvious tactic that established Kennedy's difference from Eisenhower was the crisis mentality that the former projected in his speeches—a mentality that Eisenhower had always rejected. In his nomination speech at the Democratic National Convention, Kennedy spoke with an urgency that would come to mark his presidential rhetoric, turning the issue of courage into a matter of national survival. "Courage, not complacency, is our need today; leadership, not salesmanship. . . . Can a nation organized and governed such as ours endure? That is the real question. Have we the nerve and the will?" Underlying this notion that the nation's very survival was now in doubt (a point he also stressed in his first State of the Union address) was the disturbing fact that America's enemies had demonstrated a "harder" sense of national purpose. Kennedy placed the imperative for courage, nerve, will, and self-sacrifice in competitive cold war terms: "Are we up to the task? Are we equal to the challenge? Are we willing to match the Russian sacrifice of the present for the future, or must we sacrifice our future in order to enjoy the present? *That is the question of the New Frontier.*"[8] While courage and will in the face of Soviet determination became the dominant theme of the Kennedy campaign, the subtext was always America's decline.

Like Teddy Roosevelt, Kennedy was an astute reader of the political and cultural mood of his time. One social commentator after another in the 1950s had decried the softness of Americans, their lack of self, of character and inner strength. A society of abundance, social critics charged, had created a nation of overindulged, overfed, overentertained Americans grown self-absorbed and apathetic. Like other speeches he delivered, Kennedy's nomination address was laden with references to the spiritless and listless leadership of the fifties, the "eight years of drugged and fitful sleep" the nation had experienced under Eisenhower, the latter's "timid executive leadership," the "safe mediocrity of the past," and a vice president whose youth belied the fact that he was an old man in spirit—his approach "as old as McKinley," his speeches full of "generalities from *Poor Richard's Almanac*." In a 1960 campaign speech entitled "Are We Up to the Task," Kennedy stressed that Americans had "gone soft—physically, mentally, spiritually soft," and lamented the "erosion of our courage." The cyclical dynamics of history itself, Kennedy implied in his campaign speeches, made it practically a *fait accompli* that aged, exhausted leadership would now give way to that of youth, strength, and courage.[9]

In an address to the National Press Club in 1960, Kennedy stressed his vision of a strong, assertive presidency while alluding to Eisenhower's deficiencies, particularly Ike's "restricted concept of the Presidency." Kennedy spoke of the nation's demand for a "vigorous proponent of the national interest," as opposed to a "passive broker for conflicting private interests." Employing the imagery of war, Kennedy promised to place himself on the front lines: "In the decade that lies ahead—in the challenging revolutionary sixties—the American presidency will demand more than ringing manifestos issued from the rear of the battle. It will demand that the president place himself in the very thick of the fight. . . ." The image of Teddy Roosevelt, the "Rough Rider" president whose muscular rhetorical style was emulated by Kennedy throughout his presidency, hovers over Kennedy's ideal of the warrior-president. "In the coming months," Kennedy proclaimed, "we will need a real fighting mood in the White House—a man who will not retreat in the face of pressure from his congressional leaders." He insisted that the White House "must be the center of moral leadership—a 'bully pulpit,' as Theodore Roosevelt described it." The overriding message of the speech was clear: only a leader who would place himself "in the very thick of the fight" could counteract the primary problem of the nation, what Kennedy called a "lost national purpose and a soft national will."[10] Slippage, withering, timid, passive, retreat, soft—these were the words that summed up Eisenhower and Nixon's tenure.

While the growing characterological softness of Americans was linked to the Eisenhower and Nixon interregnum, so too was its corollary, conformity. John Kenneth Galbraith, refusing to celebrate the affluence that was the subject of his famous 1958 book *The Affluent Society*, denounced its by-product: "These are the days," he wrote, "when men of all social disciplines and all political faiths seek the comfortable and the accepted; when the man of controversy is looked upon as a disturbing influence; when originality is taken to be a mark of instability." It was a time when "the bland lead the bland," Galbraith groaned. While he was speaking generally to the intellectual implications of an affluent conformist culture, this oft-quoted phrase came to signify Eisenhower and Nixon's uninspiring personalities. Other critics more directly implicated Eisenhower and Nixon in the insipid conformity that plagued American culture in the 1950s. Liberal journalist Marquis Childs portrayed Eisenhower as a man whose "view of himself was the official view of the Eisenhower personality, the view seen through channels." If Childs's Eisenhower looked suspiciously "other-directed," Schlesinger was less oblique when he described Nixon, in a 1960 Kennedy campaign manifesto, as the "'other-directed' man in politics." Even a "new conservative" like Peter Viereck could sneer at the "overadjusted conformity of the Eisenhower-era prosperity," as if that conformity had arrived with the Republican victory of 1952.[11]

The decision to base a campaign strategy on the idea that the nation was in need of some kind of massive character regeneration rested on the assumption that America's internal problems were primarily psychological, the consequences of an abundant society. Such an assumption, moreover, presupposed the notion—bolstered by one prominent social scientist after another in the 1950s—that the United States had largely overcome its most serious internal economic and social problems. The general tenets of Daniel Bell's "end of ideology" thesis became the accepted wisdom of the postwar intelligentsia: capitalism had successfully delivered the goods; the welfare state provided a safety net for the few Americans who couldn't get the goods; a mixed economy and a pluralist political system ensured the greatest degree of economic opportunity and political freedom possible; and thus ideology was now finished as a consequence of the successes of capitalist democracy. Of course, the problem of combating global Communist expansion remained the singular challenge of American foreign policy, but by and large the nation (and the West in general) seemed to have resolved its most pressing social and economic problems. So confident was the prominent political scientist Seymour Martin Lipset that he declared in 1960: "the fundamental political problems of the industrial revolution have been solved."[12]

That conviction complemented the oft-expressed idea in the 1950s that social classes had become nearly extinct in the United States. Social commentators in the 1950s frequently observed the transformation of American society into a middle-class nation. In a bestselling 1952 book, Frederick L. Allen argued that, despite the persistence of "islands" of poverty, the "big change" in American life that culminated in the 1950s was "the democratization of our economic system." In a more irritable mode, *Atlantic Monthly* writer Herbert Gold, having denounced the mindless materialism infecting nearly all Americans in his time, seemed almost rueful of the fact that "now, there are no workers left in America; we are almost all middle class as to income and expectations." Historian Eric Goldman credited "New Dealism" for turning America into "a nation of the middle-class." While the New Deal could be praised for diminishing poverty among the elderly or facilitating economic gains won by unionized, now "middle-class" workers, it was more often the economic boom of the 1940s and 1950s that was hailed as the great equalizer. So striking was the economic leveling brought on by postwar prosperity that the National Bureau of Economic Research called it "one of the great social revolutions of history."[13]

To the casual observer and not a few social critics, that revolution could be confirmed at a mere glance. Since even blue-collar workers bought television sets, Chevrolets, and packaged foods, class seemed to have disappeared in America; since nearly everyone seemed to be fleeing to the suburbs, poverty seemed to have disappeared also—at least as quickly as the white middle class fled from urban America, rendering urban poverty officially "invisible." There was in fact much validity in the notion that the middle class had grown larger as a result of the postwar boom. By the mid-fifties, ten years of prosperity, punctuated by periodic recessions, had given a lift—albeit an uneven one—to all social classes, permitting many Americans to enter some rung of the middle class and participate in the great celebration of private life in the 1950s. While it is true that no major redistribution of income had taken place in the fifteen years after the war, it is also true that, according to Todd Gitlin, "all segments of the population were improving their positions—not necessarily in relation to one another, but in relation to their pasts and those of their families." The results were remarkable, more so in the eyes of those Americans who now enjoyed a much higher standard of living than their parents or grandparents. But the postwar intelligentsia turned what was indeed an impressive increase in economic mobility into something like a social revolution. Observers often mistook consumer trends as markers of class, just as they presupposed the growth of well-groomed suburbs as proof of a ubiquitous American middle class. The disappearance of the working class, like the disappearance of poverty, was a myth.[14]

Before Michael Harrington's 1962 book *The Other America* exposed the extent of poverty in the nation and thereby exploded the myth of classlessness in the United States, affluence was assumed to be a national condition. The word "affluence" denotes a kind of flowing abundance, and was preferable to the word "rich," as Gitlin observed, "harnessed as that brutal syllable is to its natural counterpart, 'poor,' thus bringing inequality to mind." Liberals in the fifties typically acknowledged that there remained vestiges of poverty and blight in the nation that needed to be addressed, and there was still the problem of racial segregation and inequality in the South, issues that remained on the Democratic Party agenda. But throughout the 1950s, America lacked what most leading politicians and intellectuals on both sides of the partisan fence considered urgent domestic issues.[15]

In the absence of any need for major social or political reform in the 1950s, what, then, was the aim of modern liberalism? When Harvard economist Alvin Hansen stressed to Congress that the achievement of material abundance in the United States necessitated a shift toward new challenges, he asked: "Have we not by now reached in the United States a degree of plenty with respect to the physical necessities which would permit greater attention to education, health, recreation, and the rich, varied range of cultural activities in general?" Here, too, affluence was presumed to be such a universal condition that Hansen's list of "challenges" ranked issues of "health" and "education" on the same level as "recreation" and "cultural activities" and ignored the problems of poverty, urban decay, and racial inequality altogether.[16]

Hansen's comments echoed the kind of "qualitative liberalism" that Schlesinger began calling for in the mid-fifties. In a 1956 article in *The Reporter*, Schlesinger proclaimed the aim of qualitative liberalism was to "better the quality of people's lives and opportunities." Such a qualitative liberalism was fitting for an "economy of abundance" in which the effort to secure the "necessities of living" for Americans was no longer required. "We should be able to count that fight won and move on to the more subtle and complicated problem of fighting for individual dignity, identity, and fulfillment in a mass society." While improvement in education, urban planning, medical care, and minority rights appear on his list of aims, as well as the need for slum clearance, protection of free speech, improvement of mass media, and the elevation of popular culture, none stood out as especially urgent. For Schlesinger, the United States suffered above all from the "miseries" of riches: "As a nation, the richer we grow, the more tense, insecure, and unhappy we seem to become. Yet too much of our liberal thought is still mired in the issues, the attitudes, and the rallying cries of the 1930s." The primary liberal challenge, as he summed it up, was to improve the "quality of civilization to which our nation aspires in an age of ever-increasing abundance and leisure." In early 1960, Schlesinger reiterated the same arguments in an *Esquire* piece, "The New Mood in Politics." Conceding that "there are still pools of poverty which have to be mopped up," he added that doing so would still raise the "central problem" of "fighting for individual dignity, identity, and fulfillment in an affluent, mass society."[17]

Prosperity had in fact cooled economic discontent from below, but postwar intellectuals tended to blur the absence of visible oppositional politics with the absence of problems. When Nathan Glazer and David Riesman assessed the political mood of the nation in 1955, they concluded that the "sources of discontent" which had encouraged reformist movements in the past had "virtually disappeared as a result of fifteen years of prosperity." Those further to the left almost seemed to despair of the affluence that had undercut political and social discontent. Harvard sociologist Barrington Moore Jr. worried in 1958 that "as we reduce economic inequality and privileges, we may also eliminate the sources of contrast and discontent that put drive into genuine political alternatives." No sector of the population (with the exception of Negroes, he added) "has a vested material interest on behalf of freedom." Once the ideals of liberty and equality have been achieved, or come close to being realized, "the driving force of discontent disappears, and a society settles down for a time to a stolid acceptance of things as they are. Something of the sort seems to have happened in the United States."[18]

The absence of problems became something of a problem itself for liberals, and here the "end of ideology" discourse turned back upon itself. Ideology, according to its leading analyst, Daniel Bell, denotes an all-en-compassing world view, "a set of beliefs infused with 'passion,'" the com-mitment to which involved a "yearning for a 'cause,' or the satisfaction of deep moral feelings." Since political passion grew in conditions of inequal-ity and deprivation, intellectuals, it seemed, had nothing much to get pas-sionate about any longer. In Bell's judgment, the workers, "whose grievances were once the driving energy for social change, are more satisfied with the society than the intellectuals"; hence the intellectuals' "search for a 'cause.'" Looking back to the 1950s, Barbara Ehrenreich, in a more caustic appraisal, called it the "problem of problemlessness."[19]

Ideology was a bogey; to be overly passionate about any cause—long the mark of political fanaticism—still raised eyebrows in the late 1950s. But in the absence of passion lay complacency and apathy, the charge liberals leveled against Republican leadership. What was a Democrat to do? Democrats in the late fifties found their cause in denouncing American softness and self-indulgence. Spurred by the shock of Sputnik, a phantom missile gap (pro-moted by Kennedy himself), and a growing sense that America's enemies in the U.S.S.R. were tougher and more purposeful than comfortable Ameri-cans might ever be, a chorus of social commentators in the late fifties con-demned American softness and lack of will. George Kennan echoed many liberals when he complained of the "overwhelming accent of life on per-sonal comfort and amusement" in the United States and the corresponding decline in our sense of "national purpose." By the close of the decade, every-one was talking about the need for a sense of national purpose. Columnist Walter Lippman insisted that something was amiss in paradise, that the "critical weakness" of American society is that "our people do not have great purposes which they are united in wanting to achieve. The public mood of the country is defensive . . . to conserve, not to push forward and to create." Americans, it seemed, had succumbed to utter lethargy: Eric Goldman com-plained that, while the Soviets were busy launching Sputnik, Americans "meander along in a stupor of fat"; Norman Mailer proclaimed that the "energies" of the people had everywhere "slowed down" and minds "atro-phied" from disuse; Schlesinger derided the "politics of fatigue" and "national exhaustion" that characterized the 1950s, "a listless interlude" that will be "quickly forgotten"; journalist Marquis Childs wrote of the "haunted sleep" to which the nation had fallen in the fifties. The subtitle of Bell's famous book, *The End of Ideology*, announced the spirit of the time: "On the Exhaustion of Political Ideas in the Fifties."[20]

The dilemma was that the complacency of the 1950s was the consequence of America's cumulative successes. If political ideas were exhausted and ideology was dead (and here Bell meant leftist ideology), it was in part because socialism had been discredited by the obvious failure of the Soviet experiment, and in large part because the postwar economic miracle had the effect of winning over so many converts to the vital center, which was, by its very nature, complacent. By the mid-fifties, an ideological consensus had evolved, one that would have been unthinkable in the absence of a sustained economic boom. Republicans had accepted New Deal reforms such as social security as permanent fixtures of the political economy, and—absent any attempt to enlarge it radically—the welfare state seemed an insidious manifestation of creeping socialism only in the imagination of a few diehard reactionaries on the far right. For their part, Democrats abandoned calls for a radical social reform agenda and atoned for the sins of the past by enthusiastically endorsing an aggressive anti-Communist foreign policy, one that would never again descend to even the mere appearance of appeasement.

The consensus that evolved in the 1950s cannot even be described as a political trade-off; no painful partisan concessions were officially brokered; no decisive debates led to a newfound partisan rapprochement. Democrats and Republicans gravitated easily toward the center, with both sides accepting what seemed axiomatic: the indisputable superiority of the American system, with its mixed economy and democratic pluralism, and the imperative of halting Communist expansion abroad. Partisan wrangling would continue over methods, policies, and egos, but the fundamentals had been agreed upon. After the initial shockwaves of the cold war, the Korean War and the traumas of McCarthyism in the early fifties, consensus politics was reassuringly soothing and steady, as was "Ike," its standard-bearer in the fifties. And insofar as consensus politics appeared to be entirely centrist, it could function as a defense against the passions that bred ideological extremism. Ideology wasn't dead, to be sure; it had just moved to the center. Although the liberal intelligentsia had taken the American electorate's preference for Eisenhower over Stevenson as a shocking repudiation of intelligence itself—a confirmation that something had gone terribly awry in America, Eisenhower's moderate Republicanism was, in substance if not in style, barely distinguishable from Adlai Stevenson's centrist liberalism.

It was the spectacular success of the postwar economy that made the consensus possible, for it convinced nearly everyone that capitalism "worked"; even more significantly, it had the revolutionary potential to bring economic justice—a comfortable standard of living—to nearly everyone. It was economic growth, the great panacea of the late fifties and early sixties, that fueled these assumptions. And as long as that growth was actively cultivated (the approach to which was the subject of partisan disagreement), there would be no need, almost everyone agreed save for a few Marxist hangovers from the old left, for a redistribution of wealth, since all Americans would continue to share in the ever-enlarging economic pie. Both party platforms in 1960 called for economic growth in a game some dubbed "growthmanship." Even as poverty began to be increasingly acknowledged by Democrats as a problem to be reckoned with, economic growth, managed by experts, seemingly had the potential to extinguish inequality without much of a fuss. In the consensus viewpoint, it appeared as though only some technocratic "fine-tuning" of the economy and minor adjustments in social policy were necessary to eliminate remnants of urban decay, poverty, and social injustice.[21]

As liberals obsessed on affluence and its psychic discontents in the 1950s, the perception of the decade as an era of spiritlessness and conformity made it inevitable that Eisenhower, rather unfairly, would become the symbol of the mindless consumption that seemed to be sapping the nation's energy. The dread of national torpor was not without its political implications: when the U.S.S.R. outran the United States in the satellite race by launching Sputnik in 1957, the Soviets bragged that they had been working hard to build satellites while Americans were preoccupied with building silly tailfins for their cars.

The charge struck a sensitive chord. For years liberals had been heaping scorn on the Eisenhower administration for its lack of a sense of public interestedness. As proof of a dim, luxury-loving Republican leadership, liberals could cite the comments of Eisenhower's chairman of the Council of Economic Advisors, Raymond Saulnier, who defined the "ultimate purpose" of the American economy as follows: "to produce more consumer goods. That is the goal. This is the object of everything we are working at: to produce things for consumers." Liberals scoffed at such pronouncements as evidence of the shallow, self-interested business mentality of the Eisenhower administration, long derided ever since the "what's good for the country is good for General Motors" heresy. Consumption was, after all, the problem, the source of the sluggishness and conformity of the 1950s. Yet, while liberals' critique of the emptiness, materialism, and apathy of postwar America was warranted, even if given excessive political import, they could come up with little to replace GOP exhortations to "consume" and "spend," save for a liberalism whose primary aim was to improve the *quality* of an affluent society that had so degenerated in the Eisenhower years.[22]

Kennedy vs. Nixon

By the 1960 presidential election, Kennedy, who had already made his mark on foreign policy by sparring with Republicans over space and missile gaps, would have to give meaning to his domestic agenda. If public spiritedness was now to be the counterweight to private gratification, and self-sacrifice the alternative to self-indulgence, substantive issues had to be harnessed to the amorphous call for a "national purpose." Galbraith's work had raised the problem of the great disparity between American prosperity and the decaying public sector. Kennedy took up the call for federal investment in the public realm (education, healthcare, and housing); he advocated increased social security benefits and a higher minimum wage; and he also placed more emphasis on the need to combat pockets of poverty in the nation and racial inequality in the South. Yet these "liberal" issues, which Kennedy stressed rhetorically in order to give substance to the theme of national purpose and heroic self-sacrifice in his campaign, were never given the urgency that might have laid the basis for a genuinely vigorous reform program. Such urgency would have clearly distinguished Kennedy's domestic agenda from that of Nixon, a moderate Republican whose position on most domestic issues was to the left of Eisenhower. This did not occur, in part because the idea of universal affluence could never be fully exorcised from the minds of Kennedy and his New Frontiersmen (at least in the early years), and in part because liberal reform legislation would have undoubtedly faced considerable congressional opposition against which Kennedy would not have a broad mandate. But the primary reason was that Kennedy's preoccupations always lay elsewhere, in the all-important competitive struggle with the Soviets, the obsession that underlay all the talk of "national purpose" in the first place.

The problem with consensus politics was that there was little in the way of policy or program to distinguish partisan political positions from each other. Democrats found their solution (as Republicans had in previous years) in inventing differences. Red-baiting one's opponents was no longer acceptable by the late fifties; the threat to the United States, almost everyone agreed, lay not in the State Department, the American Communist Party, or any other internal source but rather in the Kremlin, whose tentacles stretched into a vulnerable and increasingly restless, nationalistic third world. The disingenuous claim of a missile gap between the U.S. and the U.S.S.R., publicly made by Kennedy in 1957, provided him with a much-needed "difference." The accusation that Eisenhower and Nixon had dozed through the decade while the Soviets raced ahead of the U.S. in missile production was a potent charge that allowed a Democrat to assume the high ground of anti-Communist vigilance. By 1959, there was also the problem of Cuba, lost to Communism on Eisenhower's watch, and though the question of "who lost Cuba" never had the gravity of the "who lost China" question, it hovered over the 1960 election. This time Republicans could be blamed for a softness and laxity toward Communist aggression in the world. While Kennedy could promise to bolster national defenses, take action against Castro, and aid anti-Castro rebels, Eisenhower and Nixon could not respond to Kennedy's boasts, a fact that infuriated Nixon during the campaign. The Eisenhower administration's nascent plan, hatched by the Central Intelligence Agency, to use Cuban exiles to topple Castro's regime could not be publicly divulged to demonstrate its determination to do *something* about Cuba; nor could the covert U2 reconnaissance flights over the U.S.S.R., which had proved the missile gap bogus, be revealed publicly.

These issues, Kennedy knew, carried great symbolic resonance, for they turned the tables on Republicans and raised the old accusation of softness. Inseparable from the claim of a missile and space gap—and the attack on Eisenhower's platitudes about peace and his cost-cutting policies that had allowed the gap to grow—was always the question of character, of masculinity. Kennedy implied that Eisenhower was insufficiently hard and competitive; he had been too cautious in the arms race, too content with a comparatively smaller missile aresenal than the U.S.S.R.; he was a sentimentalist in foreign policy and too conciliatory toward Khrushchev during the Soviet leader's 1959 visit. Speaking of that visit in a speech at the University of Rochester, Kennedy stressed that Khrushchev was a "tough-minded, articulate, hard-reasoning" statesman; the implication was that neither Eisenhower nor Nixon were a match for Khrushchev's "hard, tough manner." Eisenhower's approach to Khrushchev was all wrong, Kennedy suggested; the time was not right for "relaxation" but rather "redoubled efforts" on our part. In fact, Kennedy implied that Ike's "good-will mission" had not "deterred in the slightest" Khrushchev's objective to destroy what the Soviet leader called the "senile capitalist system . . . this exhausted, limping, and stumbling . . . horse." Kennedy regretted that "Mr. Khrushchev was shown our nation—our might, our strength, our determination. But he did not tremble." Although Kennedy added that peace was a goal to which we should aspire, throughout the speech he stressed the "hard facts," one of which was that "the real roots of the Soviet-American conflict cannot be easily settled by negotiations." He assumed that effective diplomacy could not occur if Soviet strength were not matched, a priori, against American strength. Presumably, Kennedy could make Khrushchev tremble.[23]

More pointedly, Kennedy attacked Nixon's approach to Khrushchev as falsely tough and just plain embarrassing. Nixon liked to recall the moment in the famous "kitchen debate" when he shook his finger at Khrushchev and said: "You may be ahead of us in rocket thrust but we are ahead of you in color television." Kennedy mocked Nixon's kitchen antics, telling audiences, "I will take my television in black and white. I want to be ahead in rocket thrust. . . . Mr. Nixon may be very experienced in kitchen debates, but so are a great many other married men I know." (It wasn't the last time Nixon would be cast as a married, thoroughly domesticated man.) Here as elsewhere, questions of policy were reduced to issues of style, self-presentation, and masculine character. In a Washington, D.C. address delivered in January 1960, Kennedy, without mentioning Eisenhower or Nixon by name, summed up their shortcomings:

> Attitudes, platitudes, and beatitudes have taken the place of a critical and vigilant intelligence marching in advance of events, and by the measures taken, producing the events we want. We have allowed a soft sentimentalism to form the atmosphere we breathe . . . a diffuse desire to do good has become a substitute for tough-minded plans and operations—a substitute for a strategy.[24]

As Kennedy and Nixon competed in the presidential race over their respective skill and expertise in waging the cold war or fostering economic growth, many observers remained unconvinced that there were real substantive political differences between the candidates. Commentators repeatedly bemoaned the vapid, issueless 1960 election, which appeared to be a contest of competing images more than anything else. "Tweedledee and Tweedledum," editorialists on both sides of the partisan divide sighed. Several writers in *Commentary* complained of the absence of meaningful political issues in the campaign and noted that they could hardly distinguish Nixon's domestic and foreign policy from Kennedy's. Norman Podhoretz noted wryly that in choosing between Nixon and Kennedy, "the voters have an opportunity to express their desire for a new approach without having to decide in which direction it ought to move." The American people, he regretted, preferred the vagueness and mediocrity of Kennedy and Nixon to the stature, firmness, and clarity of a Rockefeller or a Stevenson.[25]

The consensus politics of the time appeared so empty that Dennis Wrong worried that it would produce a reaction in the form of political extremism. In a 1959 *Commentary* article, Wrong argued that due to the trauma of totalitarianism in the twentieth century, voters now preferred a safe, flat, nonideological "moderatism," one that, in Wrong's mind, offered no meaningful debate or healthy political divisiveness. To those who extolled the virtues of political moderation, seeing it as a cushion against the kind of fanaticism that can grow in a mass society, Wrong warned that moderatism itself bred a sense of alienation and powerlessness among voters. When the political parties continually fail to address issues meaningful to Americans, they invite a reactive kind of political extremism.[26] Consensus politics did not produce the kind of totalitarian extremism that Wrong anticipated, but in one sense he was prescient: the complacency that consensus politics bred did later summon the exasperated reaction of young people in the 1960s, who perceived no real differences between the mainstream parties and came to regard radical "extremist" alternatives as the only hope for redressing the grievances of powerless Americans.

If Wrong seemed to long for a revamped party system in which ideology would make a comeback, liberal commentator Eric Sevareid, looking scornfully at the 1960 presidential candidates, pined away for the days when men actually had political passions and convictions (in a word, ideology). In a much discussed *Boston Globe* article, Sevareid recalled the 1930s, when politically committed young people were "sickened" by the massacre of striking steel workers, "got drunk and wept when the Spanish Republic went down . . . cheered Roosevelt and adored the poor." Sevareid complained that there was no evidence that Nixon or Kennedy had ever felt such emotions, or any emotion for that matter, when it came to politics. While the dramatic events of the 1930s were inspiring so many young men, Kennedy and Nixon must have been across campus on "fraternity row," Sevareid complained, "wearing the proper clothes, thinking the proper thoughts, cultivating the proper people." Moreover, there was nothing to distinguish Nixon and Kennedy from each other in terms of policy, vision, or character. Nixon and Kennedy were cut from the same public relations mold; they were both ambitious organization men on the make, "processed" politicians devoid of any authentic values and beliefs. The "'managerial revolution'" has come to politics," Sevareid groused, "and Nixon and Kennedy are its first completely packaged products." Other commentators weighed in on the candidates' cynical ambition, careerism, and lack of principle. Theologian Robert E. Fitch saw in both Kennedy and Nixon "a cool power, organized with all the skill of the calculating intellect, and disciplined by every latest device in public relations and in the manipulation of the emotions of men."[27]

The charge that Nixon and Kennedy were interchangeable men did not sit well with the Kennedy campaign, which apparently perceived any likening of Nixon and Kennedy's characters as something of a grave insult. In direct response to Sevareid and other critics, Schlesinger penned a campaign manifesto, published in book form under the title *Kennedy or Nixon: Does It Make Any Difference?* The manifesto began not with dissimilarities in vision, policies, or beliefs between the two candidates, but rather with differences in "identity." Indeed, the first and the worst thing Schlesinger could say about Nixon was that he was "other-directed." That phrase, signifying softness, conformity, and weakness of self—traits once associated with the psychological deficiencies of the radical revolutionary—was now applied to the 1960 GOP presidential contender. Schlesinger cast Nixon as the classic other-directed lonely man who must always seek to be in "harmony with the crowd" and who lacks "inner ideals." Nixon was a "chameleon"; he used his "sensitive antennae" to detect the national mood and then altered his positions accordingly. Thus Nixon supported McCarthy when it was politically advantageous to do so, and distanced himself from red-baiting when it fell out of fashion. Schlesinger reminded readers that an other-directed man has "no inner ideals to violate."[28]

The problem of identity repeatedly came back to the problem of style, and here Nixon was said to be pitifully handicapped. Nixon was the "invisible man of politics," "disembodied," "hollow"; he lacked an appreciation of reading, a "sense of history"; his rhetoric was "vulgar"; he was positively "corny"; he repeatedly mentioned his wife Pat in political speeches. "The hard fact is that Nixon lacks taste." Taste was far from a "frivolous" or "irrelevant" concern, Schlesinger reminded readers, for "a leader's taste can uplift or debase the level of his country's politics." Most appalling to Schlesinger were Nixon's lame attempts to prove his intellectuality—another sign of Nixon's conformity to the prevailing mood. In preparing his acceptance speech to the Republican National Convention, Nixon claimed to have spent a week "reading philosophy and history and political science." To this Professor Schlesinger could only groan: "no one who had read such works would talk about them this way . . . he would say, 'I read Kant and Burke and Macaulay.'" Perhaps Nixon's worse offense, though, was that "as vice president he showed no interest in the intellectuals of the country."[29]

The key to Nixon's personality, Schlesinger insisted, was his obsession with his own image, an obsession unprecedented in "the history of the Republic." The embarrassing displays of fake sincerity and trite sentimentality were proof that Nixon was an other-directed man who could only see "himself reflected in the eyes of others." Borrowing David Riesman's descriptive language, Schlesinger asserted that "Nixon . . . is an expert practitioner of 'false personalization.'" The evidence for this was that Nixon "imports histrionics into politics. His rhetoric is vulgar. He exhorts, denounces, parades emotional irrelevances, even weeps. Kennedy's political manner, on the other hand, is studiously unemotional, impersonal, antihistrionic." The same opposition between private neuroses and public spiritedness that pervades so much of Schlesinger's scholarship and partisan polemics reappears here: "For Nixon, the presidency seems essentially a source of private gratification. For Kennedy, it is a means of public achievement." The implication is that Nixon's desire to be president is rooted in his personal problems—his insecurities and need for acceptance. Kennedy, on the other hand, is motivated by an entirely healthy sense of public responsibility.[30]

It certainly wasn't the first time Nixon had been accused of stylistic lapses and intellectual blunders, nor were the charges of emptyness and insincerity at all novel; those claims were as old as the "Checkers" speech. But they emerged with renewed vigor in the 1960 presidential race. One journalist, responding to an address Nixon gave in which he spoke of the extensive preparation that went into a spontaneous talk and the imperative of "seeming sincere," suggested that the question was not whether there was a "new" Nixon or an "old" Nixon but whether there was any "real" Nixon at all.[31] Nixon surely deserved reproach for his grossly manipulative displays of false sincerity over the years and his perpetual reinvention of himself. But there was more than a troubling undertone of class-baiting here—the liberal's retribution for the years of abuse heaped on "privileged" eastern establishment liberals "born with silver spoons in their mouths." With all its staggering hubris, *Kennedy or Nixon: Does It Make Any Difference?* could give even a liberal post-Watergate reader a twinge of sympathy for Nixon.

Predictably, Kennedy possessed the qualities that Nixon lacked: he had a firm "identity," a "sense of history"; he was "bookish," "non-corny," "anti-histrionic" (not merely *non*histrionic). Kennedy had a "genuine, rather than a manipulative, interest in issues and ideas" and a "penetrating and persistent concern with the substance of problems." Given that he was "studiously unemotional" and "impersonal," he would presumably never make references to his wife in a political speech or weep on national television ("Can anyone imagine Kennedy giving the Checkers speech?"). "It should be evident that Kennedy is an exceptionally cerebral figure," Schlesinger announced. (Here the more manly word "cerebral" was the preferred substitute for "intellectual," joined as the latter word was to the effete "egghead." The ghost of Stevenson hovered over this affirmation of Kennedy's intellect.) Schlesinger made it clear that Kennedy does not cultivate an abstract, mushy, irrelevant kind of intellectuality; rather, his intelligence is "sharp, analytical, practical, and unfettered." "If elected, he will be the most purely cerebral president we have had since Woodrow Wilson." Naturally, Kennedy has "the normal human quota of sympathy and prejudice." But "compared to most politicians," his "habits of thought . . . are unusually detached, consecutive, and explicit. His mind is a first-class instrument, strong, supple, disciplined."[32]

Kennedy was himself attuned to the psychological traits that separated him from the self-less Nixon. In his memoirs, Galbraith recalled Kennedy pondering those differences: "Nixon must always be thinking about who he is," Kennedy told Galbraith. "That is a strain. I can be myself." Galbraith added that he was impressed by the fact that Kennedy was "one of the few public men who was wholly satisfied with his own personality."[33] Galbraith was not alone among Kennedy partisans in his praise for Kennedy's self-possession. It was Schlesinger, though, whose task was to promote such an image of Kennedy publicly. From the ivory tower, he deployed the psychologizing rhetoric of the 1950s conformity discourse to cast Kennedy as the self-possessed, instrumental, goal-oriented, inner-directed man the nation so desperately needed. Schlesinger essentially harmonized his ideal of the manly vital center liberal with Riesman's ideal of the autonomous male whose identity is fortified by necessary boundaries between self and other.

How valid is the distinction between an other-directed obsession with one's image (Nixon) and the self-conscious construction of an identity (Kennedy)? Both men undoubtedly yearned for recognition and a reputation for greatness; but that yearning signals, on Nixon's side, an emotional disturbance reflected in his penchant for "false personalization," the loneliness of the other-directed man who desperately seeks popularity. On Kennedy's side, the search for an "identity" signifies a noble, well-adjusted sense of self and public interestedness, evidenced by a more tasteful, impersonal style.

Dressed up in the fashionable garb of popular social psychology, all the talk of identity, character, and false personalization was essentially a vehicle for talking about style. And it should not be surprising that style should be elevated to such a level of import, for the chief aim of the qualitative liberalism of the fifties had all along been to uplift "the quality of civilization to which our nation aspires." The sense among liberals that American culture had been debased by mass consumerism, commercialism, and the spread of banal, vulgar middle-class tastes—the sense that culture and intellect had atrophied while the bland led the bland—made it seem as if Eisenhower and Nixon had somehow, by the sheer dimness of their personalities, dumbed down America.

Wills aptly noted the New Frontiersmen's "pursuit of style as if it were substance." Indeed, there is a certain irony in all of this too, for the touting of Kennedy's intellect and cultural refinement reflected nothing so much as the conformist, other-directed culture that the New Frontier claimed, in fact, to be extinguishing. To the Kennedy liberals, the problem was not so much the disturbing realization that, in the age of affluence and consumption, Americans had become sadly other-directed and thus compulsively took their cues from others. Rather, it was the poor taste of the *others* from whom Americans took their cues—the two dullards in the White House—that was so offensive. As a corrective, Kennedy would now set the style that impressionable, pliable American citizens would emulate; classical, aristocratic standards of excellence were the first line of defense against the rising mediocrity and conformity in American life. Citizens would follow the lead of their president and embrace his style and his tastes. Underlying Schlesinger's declaration that "taste goes to the heart of the relationship between the politician and the people" was the conviction that a president's style had the power to set the quality and tone of national life. It was a view, wholly consistent with the exaggerated role that the New Frontiersmen always gave to the executive branch, that attributed enormous cultural power to the president to shape the nation in his own image, to set the standards and expectations to which American citizens would aspire. If Kennedy's "personality was the most potent instrument he had to awaken the national desire for something new and better," he had the power to transform the style, and thus the very character, of Americans. From the summit, Sorensen proclaimed the promise fulfilled: "a wave of intellectual interest and excitement rippled out from the White House. Learning and culture were in style."[34]

In the end, the elevation of a president's style to such a level of gravitas speaks more to the attractive image that Kennedy projected back onto the intellectuals themselves. As Lasch and Wills have suggested, the adulation of Kennedy's style had much more to do with the desires and anxieties of the Kennedy intellectuals than it did with the actual power of the president to shape the aspirations of the people. Stung by the indignities that they had experienced in the previous decade, intellectuals could now see in Kennedy—cultivated aristocrat and war hero, patron of the arts and cold warrior—an appealing mirror-image of themselves as intellectuals, as liberals, as *men*.[35]

But it was not just that Kennedy surrounded himself, in the words of Richard Rovere, with "excellent people" (the "best people our present civilization has to offer"), thereby making "thinking respectable in Washington." Nor was it that he composed a Pulitzer Prize–winning book, socialized with Nobel Prize winners, or brought fine art, wine, and tasteful period furniture into the White House with the help of his tasteful wife. So much of Kennedy's attraction as an intellectual lay in the coolness and detachment he projected, even about things he professed to care deeply about. Schlesinger gushed that Kennedy's "coolness was itself a new frontier . . . it meant freedom from the stereotyped responses of the past." There was something "subversive" about this coolness, Schlesinger thought—an irreverence, a wit, a sense of irony and a casual disregard for the dull conventions of the time that promised to subvert the bland, gregarious, organization man mentality of the 1950s. Journalist Murray Kempton understood well the intellectual's infatuation with Kennedy, recasting Kennedy's "coolness" as the president's special ability to exhibit the appropriate "proportion of indifference."[36]

Kennedy's outward coolness, both Sorensen and Schlesinger cautioned, should not be misunderstood as signifying an absence of feeling or passion. Sorensen pointed to a quotation from Kennedy's favorite book, *Pilgrim's Way*, by James Buchan: "He disliked emotion, not because he felt lightly but because he felt deeply." Schlesinger saw the same emotional complexity, and claimed it as Kennedy's singular existential quality: he was cool and dispassionate not because he "felt too little" but because "he felt too much and had to compose himself for an existence filled with disorder and despair."[37]

There was surely an emotional basis for Kennedy's coolness, rooted, perhaps, in the difficulties, the physical pain, and close calls with death that he confronted as his body continually failed him. Whatever the origins of his emotional detachment, it was clearly a source of his attraction. In 1960, James MacGregor Burns (one of the historians to help out in the assembly-line production of Kennedy's 1955 *Profiles in Courage*), published a biography of Kennedy (reprinted in 1961 with a new post-inauguration forward). Burns's book, which set the standard for professorial adulation of Kennedy early on, praised Kennedy's self-possession, his competitive drive and his cool, pragmatic intelligence. The book carried a dust jacket endorsement from a writer at the *Christian Science Monitor*: "I have reason to know that . . . Kennedy likes the Burns book . . . That [he] likes the book is a tribute to his detachment, and to the coolness of his judgment."[38]

If coolness was Kennedy's irresistible quality, what did *uncoolness* mean? In a culture afflicted, it was so often said in the fifties, by neurosis, anxiety, and bland conformity, to be uncool was to be overwrought, overemotional, to lack ease with oneself, to be nervously and artificially overenthusiastic, excessively eager to please. In one sense, to be uncool was to be Richard Nixon. But coolness also signified something more personally resonant for the intellectuals: "freedom from the stereotyped responses of the past," as Schlesinger put it. What was the source of that response? The bumbling, effusive intellectual or absent-minded professor of previous years. Kennedy not only validated the identity of intellectuals as smooth, cultivated, hardnosed men of action; he imbued that identity with an aura of quasi-subversive nonconformity. The best and the brightest could absorb Kennedy's own "worldly and fast-living air," as Wills observed, and wink at the president's secret White House adventures, thinking them "the proper underside of aristocratic graces." Kennedy had masculinized the liberal intellectual, made him tough, cool, cynical, adventurous, and not a little frisky.[39]

The idea that Kennedy was not truly an intellectual (or a liberal) always lingered. "Clearly he was an intellectual," Sorensen wrote before conceding that it was true that Kennedy's "respect for artistic excellence exceeded his appreciation." Rovere extended the point: in truth Kennedy did not much care for painting, literature, or classical music, but dutifully patronized the arts and proclaimed his "respect for excellence" because "people who he thought were excellent people had told him they were excellent things." In this view, it mattered little whether Kennedy was himself truly an intellectual or a lover of the arts and letters; the mere appearance of intellectuality and cultural sophistication was enough to shake philistine Americans out of their mindless torpor, and ward off the commonplace, folksy style of the previous occupants of the White House.[40]

That a preference for Nixon over Kennedy could be treated as an affront to tastefulness itself suggests the degree to which American political culture had changed by 1960. As the Popular Front radicals and revolutionaries of past years—the Henry Wallaces, the Alger Hisses, all the sentimental fellow-travelers and do-gooders—faded from the scene, intellect and culture could again be made safe for real men. The new liberals had never flirted with the Marxist left or associated with the likes of Earl Browder; nor had they ever stood up for Hiss as character witnesses. They were not the impassioned left-wing intellectuals who got drunk and wept when Franco triumphed, but the junior officers of World War II: sobered and cerebral men who came back from the war impatient to put the "hard" lessons they had learned about power, war, human nature, military strategy, and geopolitics into practice. The journey from the OSS to the MLA was "a rude descent," Wills observed. Kennedy, he noted, gave the professors, as well as the journalists and assorted Ivy Leaguers he recruited into the administration, an escape from the mundane world of classrooms, offices, newsrooms, and typewriters into the "real" masculine world of power and responsibility.[41]

The New Frontier style failed to impress many liberals (among them Eleanor Roosevelt), who received Kennedy with a reciprocated kind of coolness, regarding him as something of a smooth operator, too slick and finely crafted. Having for years despised Kennedy's unscrupulous, wheeler-dealer father Joseph Sr., many liberals maintained an instinctive distrust of Kennedy family ambition. Had Schlesinger explicitly labeled Kennedy as an "inner-directed" man (rather than implied it through contrast), such a designation may have hurt Kennedy. After all, the archetypical inner-directed man had qualities that were less than admirable—obsessiveness, arrogance, opportunism, ruthlessness—and since the source of the inner-directed man's inner "gyroscope" lay in his internalization of paternal authority, labeling Kennedy an inner-directed man raised the troubling image of his father. (David Riesman, the sociologist who invented the inner-directed and other-directed archetypes, found the New Frontier's brash liberal nationalism deeply disconcerting.)[42] On the eve of the 1960 election, many liberals in the Democratic Party remained loyal to Stevenson and deeply wary of Kennedy coolness. To them, it reeked of cynical ambition, even boredom with traditional "sentimental" liberal causes and visions.

Negotiating some sort of balance between a "hard" dispassionate liberal rationality and a "soft" liberal humanism was thus necessary. Lest Kennedy appear too hard, Schlesinger tempered his candidate's "unemotional, impersonal" manner with a dose of Stevensonian high idealism, casting Kennedy as "the heir and the executor of the Stevenson revolution." In the end, though, Stevenson's former advisor tipped the scales heavily toward

Kennedy's hardness, implying what his later book made clear: Kennedy "wore no liberal heart on his sleeve." The difference between Kennedy and Stevenson, the new liberalism and the old liberalism, was clear enough in Schlesinger's campaign manifesto, but it was Joe Alsop who summed up the essential point: John Kennedy, he declared to another journalist, was "a Stevenson with balls."[43]

Though Stevenson's political agenda was aligned with the liberal center, he never embodied the vital center style. Stevenson's liberalism, like that of Eleanor Roosevelt and Chester Bowles, represented an older tradition, one that looked rather quaint to the hardnosed New Frontiersmen, and was often experienced as an irritant. Stevenson had been defeated for president twice in a political culture wracked by charges of twenty years of treason, a culture which had tended to regard the intellectual with contempt, his sophistication and worldliness un-American, his rhetoric and affectations effete— the murky marker of suspicious "foreign" influences, or worse, sexual deviance. Stevenson's defeats, it was often said by critics in the 1950s, showed how alienated the intellectual was from the mainstream of America. Stevenson was never able to escape completely the charge, hovering over him from the beginning, that he was soft and unmanly. Even those whom Schlesinger crowned Stevenson's liberal "heirs" mocked Stevenson's deficient manhood. Kennedy himself privately described the man he appointed as ambassador to the U.N. as "a bitter old man with a little thing," sarcastically wondered aloud among friends whether Adlai was a "switcher," and by all accounts always regarded the icon of American liberalism as hopelessly timid and effete.[44]

The hard/soft dichotomies so apparent in the rhetoric of the New Frontiersmen reappeared in considerably less muted form in Mailer's 1960 *Esquire* article, "Superman Comes to the Supermart." The same kind of fashionable postwar existentialism that infused Schlesinger's rhetoric and helped him reduce all political questions to psychological dualities could now be given free expression. Unconstrained by professorial manners or partisan political decorum, Mailer offered a reading of the political scene that conveyed what the Kennedy campaign hype had all along been about. Kennedy, Mailer avowed, was an "existential hero," a "Superman" who was capable of rescuing the nation's citizenry from the mediocrity and national slumber brought on by Eisenhower and Nixon. Once again, style was transmuted into substance; Mailer's presumption of the president's power to shape the self-image of the nation's citizens made real political issues irrelevant. Kennedy would take the nation, Mailer insisted, in a new "psychic direction."[45]

To Mailer, the age of mass man was symbolized by the somnambulant Eisenhower. Ike was the "antihero," the "regulator" who reflected back unto the nation a mirror image of its lifeless self, and thus doomed America to a period of spectacular underachievement:

> Eisenhower embodied half the needs of the nation, the needs of the timid, the petrified, the sanctimonious, and the sluggish. What was even worse, he did not divide the nation as a hero might (with dramatic dialogue as the result); he merely excluded one part of the nation from the other. The result was an alienation of the best minds and bravest impulses from the faltering history which was made. America's need in those years was to take an existential turn, to walk into the nightmare, to face into that terrible logic of history which demanded that the country and its people must become more extraordinary and more adventurous, or else perish . . .

Like Schlesinger, Mailer assumed that it was the desperate yearning for security in the fifties that brought the soothing, grandfatherly Eisenhower to power. "In periods of dull anxiety," he wrote, "one is more likely to look for security than a dramatic confrontation, and Eisenhower could stand as a hero only for that large number of Americans who were most proud of their lack of imagination." Clearly, for Mailer, the "best minds" had suffered an even worse indignity than being scorned in the Eisenhower years. They had been utterly irrelevant.[46]

Here the affable Eisenhower looked much like the classic conformist male of the 1950s—the end product of the closing of the frontier and the triumph of the organization. Eisenhower may have been a military man, but to Mailer he was just as much a "committee man" as any drone imprisoned by corporate America. Eisenhower was widely known for delegating responsibility and working through bureaucratic channels and committees, a fact Mailer parlayed into the most debilitating of character flaws. In the anticonformity discourse, committees glorified group-think; they encouraged passivity and mediocrity while stifling genius, creativity, and self-initiative. Committee men avoided dissension and conflict (what Mailer called "dramatic confrontation" or "dramatic dialogue") because they craved a sense of belonging. Seeking, above all, to be liked by others (Eisenhower's campaign slogan "I Like Ike" must have been a fitting emblem of his vapid conformity), committee men preferred a state of safety and security over the pursuit of individual aims or bold leadership, the achievement of which might alienate or offend their peers. Mailer's Eisenhower, who embodied "benevolence without leadership," was William Whyte's "organization man" *writ large*.[47]

Mailer, like Schlesinger, extended his attack on the old guard to the realm of style and taste. Committees, Mailer wrote, were the instruments of the plodding and pedestrian "small-town mind." When that small-town mind "attempts to direct history the results are disastrously colorless. . . . Committees do not create, they merely proliferate, and the incredible dullness wreaked upon the American landscape in Eisenhower's eight years has been the triumph of the corporation. A tasteless, sexless, odorless sanctity in architecture, manners, modes, styles has been the result."[48]

Sexlessness was of course no small concern for Mailer; nor were virility and impotence preoccupations with which he was unfamiliar. Consider his contrast between the youthful, energetic Kennedy and the shrinking, impotent Eisenhower, here suggested in metaphors of the city (Kennedy) versus the small town (Eisenhower):

> The city . . . is dynamic, orgiastic, unsettling, explosive, and accelerating to the psyche; the small town is . . . rooted, narrow, cautious, and planted in the life-logic of the family. The need of the city is to accelerate growth; the pride of the small town is to retard it.

Here, Eisenhower embodied more than the retarding zeitgeist of the small town: he represented death, the death of the male libido, and thus the death of the nation itself (we become "more adventurous, or else perish"). To Mailer, when "the fatherly calm of the General began to seem like the uxorious mellifluences of the undertaker," it became clear that the nation's deepest yearnings had been repressed to the point of extinction in that nervous quest for security. The remaining problem, as Mailer saw it, was whether Americans "would be brave enough to hope for an acceleration of Time, for that new life of drama which would come from choosing a son to lead them who was heir apparent to the psychic loins."[49]

Eisenhower was the antihero, the regulator; Kennedy, the inverse, was the hero, the antiregulator. Kennedy would unleash, not regulate; he would accelerate, not retard; he would improvise, not conform; he would rise to the occasion, not shrink. The implication was that true existential leadership would be daring and unrepressed; it would circumvent conventional bureaucratic routines and seek "dramatic confrontation." Kennedy would unloose the government from "benevolence without leadership," and in the process unloose the "psychic loins" of the nation. Whatever his limitations, Kennedy's persona would remind Americans that "violence was locked with creativity, and adventure was the secret of love."[50]

Mailer would later recall that he had done his "best to write a piece which would help [Kennedy] to get elected." He paid the usual homage to Kennedy's war heroism, his "cool grace" and "elusive detachment," his "dry Harvard wit," his aura of mystery, his spontaneity, and his elegant wife. Kennedy, Mailer suggested, offered the nation a flattering image of itself, a "mirror of its unconscious," and if his female campaign workers at the Democratic National Convention were any indication of what the future might hold, then so much the better. While Stevenson's "girls" were "good sorts, slightly horsy-faced," Symington's "mulish, stubborn, good-looking pluggers," and Johnson's "plump, pie-faced, dumb, sexy Southern," the "Kennedy ladies were the handsomest; healthy, attractive, tough, a little spoiled . . . the kinds of girls who had gotten all the dances in high school."[51]

The sum of all of this rhetorical excess was the promise, which it was Mailer's job to make explicit and unforgettable, that the oppressive "life logic of the family" would be extinguished once vital urbanity triumphed over the dull provincialism that Nixon represented. To Mailer, Nixon represented "deadening certainty," "all radium spent," even "ugliness." A vote for Nixon was tantamount to a vote for male impotence; indeed, Americans who opted for "the psychic security of Nixon" would vote "the way a middle-aged man past adventure holds to the stale bread of his marriage."[52]

Mailer conceded that Kennedy's public mind may be too "conventional," but no matter—in the age of the supermart, Kennedy was capable of fulfilling a fantasy, and herein lay his significance. The myth of America—of every American's potential to be extraordinary—and the reality—of its complacent, security-seeking, limp self—had diverged too far, and apparently only "an act of propaganda" (as Mailer later described his piece) could help bring the myth in line with reality. Nixon, trapped in the stifling conventions of the fifties, a young man but so middle-aged, so very married and asexual, represented the exhausted manhood of the past. Electing Kennedy would be an "existential event," Mailer suggested. The "psychic direction" the nation would now take was synonymous with the new ideal of American manhood that it would now internalize—bold, potent, fearless, unrepressed, adventurous.[53]

Despite his candidate's admitted limitations, Mailer professed to be hopeful that Kennedy would somehow grow and truly fulfill the fantasy of existential leadership. He hoped, too, that the piece would make some impression on the Superman himself. Mailer had long positioned himself as a cultural renegade against the ideological conventions of both the right and the old Stalinized Communist left. In what arena did Mailer expect Kennedy's "existential" leadership to be realized? What kind of "dramatic dialogue" or "dramatic confrontation" did Mailer expect Kennedy to summon? Would he take on the segregationists in the South? Corporate America? Would Kennedy psychologically transform an entire society that Mailer regarded as sickeningly "totalitarian"? Kennedy, whose rhetoric from the very beginning seemed to anticipate some kind of massive global conflagration, did, in time, bring dramatic confrontation, but it came in the form of the Bay of Pigs and its by-product, the Cuban Missile crisis. Kennedy circumvented conventional routines and dared to go "outside channels" in the former only to summon the most dramatic of historical confrontations in the latter. After the Bay of Pigs catastrophe, Schlesinger received a sarcastic telegram from some graduate students at Harvard that read "KENNEDY OR NIXON: DOES IT MAKE ANY DIFFERENCE?" while Mailer indulged in a good deal of public self-flagellation. That Kennedy ultimately disappointed him, and had failed to become as hip and radically nonconformist as Mailer dared him to be, was hardly a surprise to anyone on the left, except, apparently, Mailer.[54]

Mailer's endorsement of Kennedy seems incongruous with the radical persona that the novelist had been cultivating for years. His attraction to Kennedy could not lie in JFK's centrist politics, which Mailer claimed to reject; nor could it lie in Kennedy's liberal nationalism—in fact, Kennedy's campaign rhetoric on Cuba had struck Mailer as "ugly." The baffling appeal of Kennedy must come, in large part, from Mailer's distaste for "liberals," that is, those whom he had elsewhere cast as canting, sexless, "committee-ish," professional liberals.[55] Like other intellectuals, Mailer longed for a leader who could reconcile intellect, muscularity, and sexual will.

Unlike *Kennedy or Nixon: Does It Make Any Difference?* "Superman Comes to the Supermart" is both a nation-mocking parody and an undisguised piece of political propaganda. The "supermart" was the presidential race itself, and Mailer deliberately hyped his product as absurdly as any public relations huckster, jeering—for the benefit of more discriminating minds—the spectacle of the image-driven, Hollywood-infused Democratic National Convention, within which Mailer obviously inserted himself happily. Writing this piece, Mailer revealed that he was a good deal more enamored of the mainstream society he professed to detest. "Superman Comes to the Supermart" may not have been inspired by the same kind of adulation of Kennedy that infected the New Frontier intellectuals, elated as they were that superior tastes and a respect for "excellence" would now find its home in the White House. But Mailer's motive for writing the piece ultimately came from the same impulse: the desire of the intellectual to be relevant. If the article's hope was that the "best minds" and "bravest impulses" would no longer be "alienated" from the "history that is made," its conceit lay in the presumed power of a novelist to *get* Kennedy elected.

The Liberal as Playboy

As an endorsement, Mailer's "Superman Comes to the Supermart" was surely idiosyncratic, and its impact on the election's outcome was only Mailer's fantasy. But the real significance of the article is the way it reveals the wider sexual (and commercial) currents that had changed the cultural landscape by the early 1960s. The oppositions that lay beneath Mailer and Schlesinger's imagination of an ideal manhood—rebellion vs. complacency, adventurousness vs. squareness, tastefulness vs. corniness, youthful vitality vs. aging impotence, freedom of spirit vs. imprisonment by convention—had been recurrent themes in the fifties masculinity discourse. If those themes were fleshed out and made "personal" in the imagery of the 1960 election, it was because a new competing ideal of manhood had emerged out of the postwar masculinity crisis. At the top, that ideal found its political expression in the New Frontier's institutionalization of virility as well as its much-touted style.

But it was within the wider expanse of American culture that this new masculine ideal, in its various guises and forms, was shaped for a mass audience. As the "human potential" discourse of pop psychology in the 1960s began to replace the male maturity discourse of the 1950s, as James Bond superseded Mike Hammer as a male cultural icon, and as Hugh Hefner replaced Philip Wylie as the most influential spokesman for men's liberation, the male rebellion against conformity met the sexual revolution head-on. Nowhere was the new spirit more apparent and widely disseminated than in the pages of *Playboy* magazine, first published in 1953. When *Playboy's* founder, Hugh Hefner, opened the first Playboy Club in early 1960, he inaugurated a new decade that would see the magazine's readership skyrocket and the clubs proliferate while the sexual revolution accelerated, driven by market forces as well as the counterculture. Though *Playboy* offered its readers "a diversion from the worries of the Atomic Age," underlying this seemingly playful diversion into fantasy—into centerfolds and big-breasted bunnies—was something culturally resonant and historically significant: a prescription for what ailed the beleaguered American male of the 1950s.[56]

The impetus for *Playboy* was two-fold: the masculinity crisis of the 1950s, which convinced Hefner that American men were not just constrained but sadly oppressed by their prescribed conventional roles, and the publication of the bestselling Kinsey reports, which convinced him that there was a lucrative market for sex in America. To some extent *Playboy* was, like the "rat pack" of the fifties, something of a liberal phenomenon. Strip away some of the self-serving *Playboy* strictures against the state's odious coercive control of sexual conduct and "the hurt and hypocrisy of our Puritan heritage," and Hefner's critique of American society sounds much like that of the postwar liberal intelligentsia. In 1963, reflecting back on the cultural context within which *Playboy* had been conceived ten years earlier, Hefner voiced a familiar refrain (the same one that was often invoked to explain the "mystery" of Eisenhower's appeal): Americans in the 1950s, Hefner said, had become "increasingly concerned with security, the safe and the sure, the certain and the known. . . . It was unwise to voice an unpopular opinion . . . for it could cost a man his job and his good name." Convinced that American men had succumbed to the "conformity, togetherness, anonymity, and slow death" that the older ideal of masculine maturity had dictated, Hefner presented himself as an intrepid rebel who would liberate American men from the stifling conventionality of previous years.[57]

In one sense, *Playboy* was the commercial by-product of the anti-conformist mood of the fifties. The concern with "other-direction" and the "social ethic" in American life had always been keyed to men, and it is not surprising that the impetus to free oneself from the dreaded "other," from the doctrine of togetherness, would be extended to freeing oneself psychologically from the confinements of marriage, kids, the suburban ranch home, the PTA—the "life logic of the family," as Mailer had put it. In the name of masculine liberation from dull convention, *Playboy*, as Barbara Ehrenreich observed, celebrated the man who chafed at those constraints, and it allowed him, thanks to its bunnies and centerfolds, to disavow the cumbersome expectations of the male role without having to suffer the taint of homosexuality. Indeed, the new *Playboy* rebel rejected the conventional ideal of masculinity not because he was secretly "soft" and unable to fulfill the specifications of the older masculine role, but because he was so heterosexually "hard," eager to opt out of the conventional male role precisely in order to realize his manhood fully.[58]

The prototypical *Playboy* male reader, as his persona was shaped in the pages of this upscale magazine, was a highbrow, an urbane man of taste and intellect; he digested the magazine's satire, its short stories and science fiction, its interviews with politicians and celebrities as well as its sexy centerfolds and advice on the art of seduction. *Playboy* imbued the male rebellion with an aura of intellectuality and style that made the normative masculine role of the 1950s seem like a prescription for totalitarian mass man. Always looming over the popular critique of the male conformist of the fifties was the problem of being timid, domesticated, sexless, enslaved to "family togetherness" and its corollary in the professional world, the tedious social ethic that hamstrung masculine willfulness. *Playboy's* new rebel, as he was imagined from the very beginning, appeared as a kind of revolutionary on what Riesman had earlier called the "frontier of sex." He would forsake the suburban home for the bachelor apartment, cultivate a taste for jazz, collect modern art, read Nietzsche and Sartre, skillfully seduce women, and thereby develop an "identity" apart from the chains that had bound men: marriage and family life.

Of course, *Playboy* may have repudiated the role of the male conformist-breadwinner, but it did not reject the materialism, the status-seeking, and the self-indulgence that the conformity critics had often scorned. On the contrary, *Playboy* celebrated male "self-realization" through consumerism and hedonism, and was relentlessly didactic in the way it instructed men to live, from the latest stereo systems, Ivy League clothes, and fine brandy that men were encouraged to consume, to the jazz festivals, chic nightclubs, and foreign films they would attend. Since the would-be playboy needed a hefty income to support such a lifestyle, *Playboy* endorsed status-seeking and conventional success—in a word, conformity—as the necessary vehicle for self-discovery.[59]

Indeed, in the *Playboy* imagination, the oppressive ethos of "togetherness" was symbolized less by "the organization" than by the wife, who could be more easily dispensed with—or at least psychologically disavowed—than the institution that bankrolled the playboy's consumerist, swinging lifestyle. *Playboy*, as Ehrenreich noted, "loved women" and "hated wives." "I don't want my editors marrying anyone and getting a lot of foolish notions in their heads about 'togetherness,' home, family, and all that jazz," Hefner once said, summing up the *Playboy* ethos. In the end, though, it really didn't matter whether the *Playboy* reader was legally enchained by the shackles of marriage; even if he was married, as so many readers and club members were, he could be a playboy in fantasy, a bachelor in spirit.[60]

Playboy may have been one of the most influential forces that paralleled and accelerated a wider sexual revolution in American life. But the *Playboy* phenomenon, as Ehrenreich has argued, was ultimately rooted in the masculinity crisis of the 1950s—in the male quest for escape from conventional male role expectations, and its historical significance lay in the male "flight from commitment" that it encouraged and legitimated. The conventional masculine ideal of the fifties, with its emphasis on responsibility, duty, and maturity as the mark of male normalcy, appeared to *Playboy's* writers as a kind of insidious female invention. After all, it was women who yearned for security and safety, not men. (One writer warned readers in the magazine's first year of publication that "all woman wants is security. And she's perfectly willing to crush man's adventurous, freedom-loving spirit to get it."[61]) *Playboy* called upon men to unloose their innate freedom-seeking spirit, which wives and all would-be wives sought to squash, and thereby enjoy the "good life"—a life which included the pursuit of success, wealth, power, high culture, indoor adventure, and, not least of all, attractive women, who were central to the quest for male "self-realization."

Playboy also helped to summon a new accent on youthful male vitality that poised itself against a tired, dreary, conformist American society. The magazine's celebration of male youthfulness was not just a matter of taste and lifestyle; occasionally it took a political form. In a 1959 *Playboy* article by Ralph Ginzburg, "Cult of the Aged Leader," the author called for an end to worship of the aged male in American life. Reciting statistics demonstrating how many "superannuated" leaders there were in government (Eisenhower stood at the pinnacle), Ginzburg reminded readers that studies indicate "older people show greater apathy and inflexibility, fewer signs of pleasure, weaker signs of love and courage, milder hates and fears." Ginzburg chalked up many of the "world's political blunders" to "older men," citing Stalin's "senile dementia" that brought the world to the brink of nuclear annihilation, and the seventy-one year-old Chamberlain's reduction of Britain to a "sorry state of unpreparedness" that led to the appeasement of Hitler at Munich (the "younger Churchill" thankfully saved the day, he noted). The "sexagenarian Eisenhower," he pointed out, presided over the nation as it fell behind Russia in the technology and space race. Great political, scientific, and intellectual advances have typically come from young men, Ginzburg insisted. In American history, the real "giants" and great presidents were all young men.[62]

"With old men in its top positions, our democracy is in danger of dotage," Ginzburg warned. He quoted an interview with the young mover and shaker, Robert Kennedy, who "vigorously" exposed union corruption and had thus made a name for himself on Capitol Hill. Kennedy said: "We have come to put such tremendous *over*-emphasis upon the need for age and maturity in our leaders that young men nowadays just don't have much chance at all to leap into top jobs, even when they are far more capable than their elders. On the rare occasion when a young man comes into the Senate nowadays, he is expected to keep his mouth shut, to think like an old man, to live like an old man, until he actually becomes an old man." Why did the cult of the aged leader persist? Ginzburg asked rhetorically. In times of peace and plenty, he explained, the aged, fatherly statesman was preferred because he did not present "psychological threats" to the average male voter. Female voters, Ginzburg observed, longed for a safe "daddy" figure that would love and protect them. Both male and female voters ultimately preferred a *grand*-fatherly figure who would "let us bask without trauma in the sun of the beautiful status quo." But the nation paid a price for the complacency that aged leadership brought, Ginzburg implied. The benign, grandfatherly Eisenhower spent too many days sitting at his desk; he had hardly broken a sweat as president. The president's job, the author reminded readers, is a "killer and requires a person of superior stamina." While Ginzburg could not yet comment on John Kennedy's embryonic candidacy (in any case, it was *Playboy*'s policy not to endorse political candidates), his glorification of youthful male vigor alongside his indictment of a doddering American political leadership served as an oblique endorsement.[63]

Playboy's founder was hardly a political man in any traditional sense. Hefner's politics were generally liberal, as were the magazine's, but this misses the point. Hefner and his writers and editors promoted a new model of manhood that merged virility, intellectuality, youth, and "non-conformity" into an alternative masculine style, one that was "liberal" insofar as it defined itself against an older model of manhood—sentimental, square, reliable, predictable, security-seeking, uxorious—the attributes which the young

Nixon and the aged Eisenhower both came to represent. Establishment liberals may not have accepted *Playboy* and its "philosophy," or the self-styled cultural radicalism of Hefner or Mailer. But the adulation of power, style, youth, glamour, adventure, and virility that permeated the New Frontier was bound up with the cultural trends that male dissenters like Mailer and Hefner shaped.

The reputation that Kennedy earned as a womanizer, now so widely documented and discussed, was not unknown in the political milieu of his time. The anglophilic Kennedy, a playboy of the aristocratic variety, scarcely worked hard to conceal his sexual exploits, and after he married, it was well known that he remained a bachelor in spirit. Kennedy's compulsive pursuit of women, including one early dalliance with a Danish woman suspected of being a Nazi spy, did not fail to escape the notice of Hoover's FBI, one reason the Kennedys could never challenge the director. Stories about Kennedy's womanizing abounded in the political culture of fifties and early sixties. The conventions of journalism and political life, which rested on age-old assumptions about male privilege and power, precluded open discussion of politicians' private lives. Rumors and innuendo were the vehicles by which a politician's sexual exploits became public knowledge. In any case, ordinary philandering and adultery were hardly great sins for a male politician at the time, and though such behavior could still embarrass a politically ambitious married man, it rarely came to that.

While Kennedy's sexual liaisons were not reported in the mainstream press in any explicit sense, there were enough clues. Mailer provided more than a hint in his suggestion that Kennedy's sexual willfulness and appeal— one to which men could aspire and women could easily succumb—would unleash the yearnings that had been repressed in the previous sexless decade. It is a testimony to the changing currents of the time that Mailer played up Kennedy's sexual energy while mocking Nixon as a dull, domesticated man. (Of course, he was writing in *Esquire* magazine, a male domain in which the perception of masculine sexual willfulness could easily enhance a politician's reputation.) Other writers and journalists also hinted about Kennedy's womanizing. In an October 1960 *New York Post* column Murray Kempton reported with a mixture of amusement and sarcasm that on the campaign trail, Kennedy "treated southern Ohio yesterday as Don Giovanni used to treat Seville. His progress, as ever, was an epic of the history of the sexual instinct of the American female." Kennedy's mere wave to a pretty girl suggested to her that, if he did not have miles to go on the campaign trial, "he would like to walk with her where the Mad river meets the Still water."[64]

It is impossible to determine whether intimations and rumors about Kennedy's womanizing (in the air in 1960) functioned as liabilities for him in the political imagination of either men or women. But given the ambitious, image-conscious Kennedy's apparent willingness to accrue a rakish reputation, it is likely that he assumed, quite correctly, that his sexual exploits (insofar as they were known or vaguely perceived by the public) either did not hurt him or actually worked to enhance rather than diminish his reputation as a *man's man*.

What is clearer is that the popular image of the liberal intellectual had changed by 1960. Intellect had become associated with style, virility, and glamour. Arthur Miller's 1956 marriage to actress Marilyn Monroe had already suggested what the New Frontier would demonstrate in years ahead: that the liberal intellectual was hardly a tedious egghead alienated from the main currents of American life, that he was, in fact, worldly, uninhibited, powerful, and a little risqué. He had "range," as insiders would recall about Kennedy, who, Sorensen reported, "liked Schlesinger's books as well as Ian Fleming's. . . . He was interested in the worlds of Carl Sandburg and Frank Sinatra. He could enjoy communicating at the level of the Bundy brothers and the Cassini brothers." The much-publicized array of notables who made appearances at Camelot—actress Jean Seberg, writer Andre Malraux, cellist Pablo Casals, actor Frederic March (who read from Hemingway when he visited), and superstar Marilyn Monroe, provided the proof that Harvard and Hollywood, high art and middlebrow popular culture, were all within the range of Kennedy and his New Frontiersmen.[65]

Occupied by a president who could mix easily with Nobel Prize winners and rat-packers, the White House reportedly crackled with a new energy. According to the trickle-down theory of presidential style, this energy would enliven the nation and awaken it from its sedated state. Sorensen recalled the "atmosphere of gaity and verve" in the Kennedy White House, which became "a showplace and a dwelling place for the creative and the cultivated." Throughout Schlesinger's *A Thousand Days*, the imagery makes the point: "energies" are everywhere burgeoning, being "released" and "fulfilled." In his book on Robert Kennedy, Schlesinger recalled the evening Monroe sang a sultry "Happy Birthday" to the president on the occasion of his birthday party. He reported that "Adlai Stevenson wrote a friend about his 'perilous encounters' that evening with Marilyn, 'dressed in what she calls skin and beads. I didn't see the beads! My encounters, however, were only after breaking through the strong defenses established by Robert Kennedy, who was dodging around her like a moth around a flame.' We were all moths around a flame that night." Schlesinger recounted what he wrote in his diary: "I do not think I have seen anyone so beautiful. I was enchanted by her manner and her wit. . . . But one felt a terrible unreality about her. . . . Bobby and I engaged in mock competition for her; she was most agreeable to him and pleasant to me—but then she receded into her own glittering mist." Monroe's presence at Camelot provided the ultimate evidence that the liberal intellectual—now playful, competitive, and sexually attuned—had freed himself from the old liberalism. What, after all, did Stevenson's experience of "perilous" encounters with Monroe suggest but the "conditioned reflexes of the stereotyped liberalism" that Kennedy found so tedious?[66]

Mailer essentially got it right. Despite his posture as an outsider to a world in which he had too much invested to be its meaningful critic, Mailer understood that what the New Frontier offered was a fantasy, a "superheated dream life"—a new frontier, an America in which men could become men again. And so too could professors.

The Cult of Toughness

Kennedy's predilection for sexual conquest and indiscretion, well documented by a small army of Kennedy researchers and biographers, might here be dismissed if it were not for the fact of its intimate relationship to the politics, the political "style," of the New Frontier. The flip-side of the sexual willfulness of the New Frontiersman was always his bold aggressiveness, the "ballsiness" of the liberal cold warrior. When Joe Alsop called Kennedy a "Stevenson with balls," he spoke the idiom of the Kennedy men. Ballsiness was the essential quality of the New Frontiersmen, as Wills has suggested. Faced with crisis, members of the administration were mocked by the president for "grabbing their nuts" in fear; those who cautioned about the administration's use of force or subterfuge in the world were lacking the requisite "balls." "Let's grab our balls and go" was a familiar call to action in the executive wing, and it could also serve as a test of the New Frontiersmen's stamina: when the president declared the need for "vigor," his staff members went off on their fifty-mile hikes. Ballsiness was manifest in the president's personal life, in his unconcealed delight in risk-taking and sexual adventure.[67] In the idiom of the New Frontier, it took "balls" to bring women—especially those under the surveillance of the FBI—into the White House, the same "balls" it took to launch the Bay of Pigs adventure or to out-tough Khrushchev in the Cuban Missile Crisis.

Of course, the "official" term for ballsiness was "courage." Courage had always been an obsession with Kennedy. Heroism fascinated him as a child, guided his scholarly work in college and afterward, and prevailed as a theme in his speeches and public addresses. Its affirmation was expressed in the much-publicized narrative of events that occurred on the legendary *PT 109*, which earned Kennedy deserved acclaim for his heroic efforts to save one man's life and rescue his crew (it also earned him a reputation for recklessness). Kennedy's political career was built upon the theme of courage. His 1955 book, *Profiles in Courage*, which won the Pulitzer Prize in 1957, is the most obvious testimony.[68]

Kennedy's senior thesis at Harvard, "Why England Slept," was obliquely about courage, that is, how social institutions foster or discourage it. The root causes of Britain's lack of military preparedness and thus its paralysis in the face of Hitler were social, institutional, and psychological, Kennedy suggested. Capitalist democracies like Britain are inherently oriented toward peace and complacency; they tend to avoid that which would disrupt the equilibrium of the political economy and arouse the opposition of various interest groups, from pacifists to bankers. Since totalitarian states suffer from no such constraints and are free to mobilize for war whenever they please, they have the edge in modern warfare. Kennedy placed the blame for appeasement not on Britain's defective leaders but on the weaknesses of democracy and, by extension, a shortsighted British public incapable of determining what was in the national interest. The implication here is that courageous leadership would become an even greater imperative in a democracy precisely in order to counteract its inherent institutional and social weaknesses. (Schlesinger had made the point in *The Vital Center*.) Such an assumption was generally consistent with Kennedy's promises not to "shrink from" the responsibilities of statesmanship and his strong admiration of Churchill, who could be credited with rescuing Britain from the inertia that democracy breeds. Historian Bruce Miroff stressed that Kennedy's "chief historical model" was Churchill. Kennedy's speeches, including his 1958 "missile gap" speech to the Senate, "drew parallels between Winston Churchill's attempts in the 1930s to warn a complacent Britain of the Nazi threat and his own efforts to awaken an equally complacent America to the enormity of the Soviet challenge." Kennedy saw the "loss" of American superiority in missile production through the lens of Munich.[69]

Courage as a virtue is a theme as old as mankind, yet it obviously had deep personal meaning to Kennedy. The multiple illnesses from which he suffered since childhood, the humiliating medical tests and treatments he endured as a young man, the considerable physical pain he experienced, by all accounts rather stoically, throughout his life, and the prospect of an imminent death that always hovered over him, gave Kennedy an admirable, extraordinary determination to prevail—to serve in the navy despite his physical maladies, and to succeed as a politician even if he had to campaign on crutches while he experienced great discomfort.[70] Much like Teddy Roosevelt, Kennedy was plagued by physical ailments in childhood which limited his activities and embarrassed him as he matured and confronted his emergent sense of masculinity. Also like Roosevelt, Kennedy sought to overcome his physical limitations and placed uncommon emphasis on physical fitness, vigor, heroism, and virility throughout his political career.

Kennedy echoed the "Rough Rider" president's glorification of the "strenuous life," adapting it to the imperatives of a cold war world. In a

December 1960 *Sports Illustrated* article, "The Soft American," Kennedy portrayed the physically soft, sedentary, luxury-loving American as "a menace to our security," warning that "the magnitude of our dangers makes the physical fitness of our citizens a matter of increasing importance." Kennedy stressed the high numbers of young American men who had proved unfit for military service in the Korean War, and invoked Teddy Roosevelt's call for the "strenuous life." Although there had been a wave of concern in the 1950s about the deteriorating physical state of the nation's citizenry (Eisenhower had established a Council on Youth Fitness and a Citizens' Advisory Committee on the Fitness of American Youth), Kennedy noted that despite such efforts "there has been no noticeable improvement." The nation's cultural decline in the 1950s seemed to mirror the decline of the American body. Marking his departure from his predecessor's approach, Kennedy imbued his physical fitness crusade with an aura of classical sophistication by invoking the example of the ancient Greeks. They saw excellence in body as the complement to excellence in mind and regarded these twin values as the "prime foundations of a vigorous state."[71]

The Greek notion of *arete* denoted the masculine pursuit of excellence and the striving for perfection and superiority over others in competition. It fit perfectly the New Frontier image, and helped to underscore the chief theme of "The Soft American": the necessity for "stamina and strength which the defense of liberty requires." Kennedy warned that if we allow ourselves to "dwindle and grow soft then we will destroy much of our ability to meet the great and vital challenges." Softness, previously a term that suggested one's internal sympathy for Communism, was here keyed to the body. Kennedy placed the importance of hardening the soft American body in cold war terms:

> We face in the Soviet Union a powerful and implacable adversary determined to show the world that only the Communist system possesses the vigor and determination necessary to satisfy awakening aspirations for progress and the elimination of poverty and want. To meet the challenge of this enemy will require determination and will. . . . Only if our citizens are physically fit will they be fully capable of such an effort.

Kennedy's physical fitness crusade was supported by a spate of articles in popular publications on the flaccid state of the national body, including a *Reader's Digest* article by Max Eastman, "Let's Close the Muscle Gap." Eastman worried that "the muscle gap between us and those who would bury us" might be as dangerous as the missile gap.[72]

Physical fitness was one dimension of Kennedy's preoccupation with will, courage, and determination. These concerns, moreover, did not just stem from his own personal circumstances, his physical ailments and limitations.

They were obsessions shared by his generation. As we have seen, the relationship between courage and character formation, individuality and will—the courage to *be*—were recurrent themes in so much of the historiography, social criticism, and psychological discourse of the 1950s.

Kennedy's *Profiles in Courage* began by invoking Ernest Hemingway's definition of courage as "grace under pressure." Yet the book's discussion of courage seems at times more like an application of Riesman's concept of "inner-direction" to the challenges of American statesmanship. The introduction established the dilemma of courageous political leadership with a reworking of the "I" vs. "we," "individual" vs. "other" tension that appeared in so much social criticism in the 1950s. The pressures that discourage courageous acts must be understood, Kennedy began. The "path of the conscientious insurgent" in national politics is a "lonely one." Senators, like all Americans, "want to be liked" and are "anxious to get along with" their peers. Kennedy recalled that when he first entered Congress, he was told that "'the way to get along . . . is to go along.'" These were stock phrases in the anticonformity discourse of the 1950s; critics had worried that the imperative to "get along" with others had replaced the imperative to take bold action, to "get ahead" in pursuit of a goal; the individual's need for psychic security had undermined self-initiative and leadership. Kennedy acknowledged that "going along" did not simply mean "good fellowship"; in the political arena it involved a certain amount of artful compromise, the mastery of which was necessary for any politician who hoped to accomplish something. But in celebrating courageous leadership, *Profiles in Courage* affirmed the statesman's willingness to act in accord with his genuine inner convictions (similar to what Riesman called an "inner gyroscope"), to follow an independent course of conscience at the risk of going against the grain of public opinion and thus losing his popularity with his peers or his constituency. Whether his stances were right or wrong, whether they truly worked to enhance the public interest or not, each of the politicians profiled in the book, Kennedy stressed, had followed his inner conscience, sometimes to the detriment of his reputation, alliances, or re-election prospects. In rejecting compromise on issues important to the public good, and in relinquishing the "rewards" that come with "going along" and yielding to "the crowd," he had taken risks. Such was the essence of courage in the political arena. Politics, Kennedy concluded, was merely "one arena which imposes special tests of courage." In stressing that the "basic choice of courage or compliance faces us all . . . whenever we stand against the flow of opinion on strongly contested issues," Kennedy struck a familiar note of the time.[73]

Although the statesmen profiled in his book who took courageous stands in the name of the national or public interest often did so to the detriment of their own private interest or gain, Kennedy stressed that, in the end, personal advantage can never be divorced from any leader's political stances. Pure selflessness in the pursuit of the public good is a sentimental illusion, he implied. Approvingly quoting John Adams ("It is not true, in fact, that any people ever existed who love the public better than themselves"), Kennedy then asked why the statesmen he profiled in the book acted courageously. "It was not because they 'loved the public better than themselves,'" Kennedy answered:

> On the contrary it was precisely because they did *love themselves*— because each one's need to maintain his own respect for himself was more important to him than his popularity with others—because his desire to win or maintain a reputation for integrity and courage was stronger than his desire to maintain his office—because his conscience . . . was stronger than the pressures of public disapproval.

Thus, the kind of courage it takes to champion the public interest at the expense of one's personal popularity or re-election prospects comes not from a selfless commitment to the public good, but rather from a kind of healthy self-respect and self-love. In the end, the public good is the "indirect beneficiary" of that self-love.[74]

Profiles in Courage did not explicitly argue that courageous leadership was on the wane in contemporary America; to do so would have been too audacious for a young senator undistinguished in his congressional career. But the deficiencies of the affable Eisenhower, whom liberals increasingly disparaged for his dread of conflict and his need to promote social harmony above all else, lurked in the background. Moreover, according to Dallek, while Kennedy had always been interested in courageous leadership, writing the book was also for him "a retrospective coming to terms with his moral lapse on McCarthy." Kennedy had maintained a more than cordial relationship to family friend Joseph McCarthy, had made public comments which seemed to endorse McCarthy's anti-Communist crusade in the early fifties, and had failed to show up for the Senate's 1954 vote on McCarthy's censure, adding fuel to the charge that Senator Kennedy consistently showed "more profile than courage."[75]

Whatever the precise impetus for publishing the book, Kennedy was creating an image of himself as a resolute politician driven by his inner convictions and poised to lead the nation courageously. If it was unwise at this point in his career to lament the absence of courageous leadership in contemporary political life, the chord was struck by other liberals, including Schlesinger (who played a role, as did others in the Kennedy orbit, in the collective production of *Profiles in Courage*). In a 1958 *Saturday Evening Post* article, "The Decline of Greatness," Schlesinger lamented that "ours is an age without heroes." He suggested that the ghosts of dictators like Hitler and Stalin, together with the conformity that mass society breeds, left Americans with a suspicion of bold men and a preference for the safe and the secure ("Great men live dangerously"). Our groupist society with its conformity-inducing institutions and committees prefers bland security, but a free, creative, individualist society, he stressed, cannot do without great men. He was already campaigning for Kennedy, shaping the image of a great president. In a postelection *Encounter* article in December 1960, "On Heroic Leadership and the Dilemma of Strong Men and Weak Peoples," Schlesinger took the point further and, with Kennedy heading for the White House, made a case for the assertive exercise of executive power. Traditional democratic ideology had always been distrustful of power and the potential for corruption it posed, he wrote, returning to the familiar theme of democracy's weaknesses. But classical democratic ideology, in "denying positive leadership a role . . . has tied the hands of democratic societies." What is required, then, is a "reconstruction" of democratic theory which will enable us to "decide which styles of leadership democrats can use and which they must ' fight." Schlesinger had in fact already decided on the fundamental style of leadership that Democrats would adopt. "Only strong presidents," he wrote, "have been able to overcome the tendencies toward inertia inherent in a structure so cunningly composed of checks and balances."[76]

What the discussion of heroic leadership and the weaknesses of democracy (and Democrats) signified was a new mood among liberal centrists eager to discard the old skepticism about assertive executive authority. The preoccupation with courageous statesmanship and the affirmation of presidential power achieved its most influential expression in the work of Richard E. Neustadt, a Columbia University political scientist and special advisor to Kennedy in the transition period of 1960–61. In 1960, Neustadt published his study of leadership styles, *Presidential Power*, a book that made a considerable impression on Kennedy and served as a primer for his leadership style and the organization of his administration. In *Presidential Power*, Neustadt profiled the leadership and decision-making styles of a range of American statesmen, but the most instructive lessons for Kennedy lay in Neustadt's analysis of Eisenhower and Franklin Roosevelt's contrasting styles of governing. *Presidential Power*, as well as Neustadt's presence in the Kennedy circle, inaugurated a new era in which liberal centrists would finally heed the call that Schlesinger had been making at least since *The Vital Center*. Liberals must not just accept but fully embrace the will to power. Here was the imperial presidency that Schlesinger would later, in post-Watergate years, repudiate.[77]

To Neustadt, Eisenhower was the negative object lesson in presidential style. Neustadt's Eisenhower looked much like the antihero upon whom Mailer heaped contempt. With his military chain-of-command mindset,

Neustadt's Eisenhower sought order in his ranks by delegating authority. His was a government by "staff system"; "inter-agency committees" and "paper flows" were his only sources of information. Ike lacked a grasp of details, and when broad objectives vexed him, he threw "the issue to the experts" (successful businessmen whom he respected). Moreover, Eisenhower's administration not only lacked "effective competitions" among staff members that would rouse men, summon pressure, and produce competing ideas and policy choices; his bureaucratic style was intended to "smother" competition, lest quarrels over policy reach the Oval Office. To explain this style, Neustadt put Eisenhower on the couch, theorizing that Ike was profoundly uncomfortable with his own power as president. It was not a stretch; Eisenhower's tenure in office was in fact notable for his multiple failures to exercise leadership, especially on domestic issues, and he had on more than one occasion in his career declared that he simply did not *like* politics. But in Neustadt's judgment, Eisenhower was handicapped by more than just his aversion to the sordid business of politicking and his tendency to place himself, as a military general, above the unseemly partisan fray. Eisenhower's problem was that he did not "enjoy" being president; he had no "taste" for power; he was deeply uneasy with his own self-interest or ambition. Indeed, Eisenhower's "confidence was highest when he could assure himself that *personal* advantage had no place among his aims."[78]

Franklin Roosevelt, in Neustadt's judgment, had no such illusions about himself, nor did he have any hang-ups about power. On the contrary, Roosevelt had a natural "hunger" for power, cultivated its use as an art form, and found fulfillment in the pursuit of "personal power." In fact, Roosevelt had a "love affair with power," an "early romance" with it; he relished the "challenge and the fun of power." To Neustadt, Roosevelt had the proper proportion of self-love and self-interest that allowed him to embrace his power without reservation; his "private satisfactions were enriched by public purposes." Roosevelt "wanted power for its own sake; he also wanted what it could achieve." Moreover, Roosevelt had a firm grasp of details; he was flexible, unconstrained by convention; he balanced contending forces in the ranks of his staff as a true "master" of power. In contrast, Eisenhower was sadly a "Roosevelt in reverse. . . . His love was not for power but for duty— and for status." The presidency wasn't Eisenhower's "sport"; it was "certainly not fun" for him. Neustadt's Eisenhower appears as a captive of procedure and protocol, an "arbiter" who feared power and dreaded conflict. No wonder, Neustadt implied, that Eisenhower sought "national unity" above all else.[79]

The newfound appreciation of executive authority and the notion that Eisenhower's greatest defect was his failure to embrace power had already gained currency in liberal circles by the late fifties. Such a view was articulated by journalist Marquis Childs in his 1958 book, *Eisenhower: The Captive*

Hero. Childs portrayed Eisenhower as profoundly uncomfortable with his own presidential authority. From the start, Eisenhower enjoyed a war hero's mandate, but he was a "timid and hesitant" candidate who agreed to "go on the ride of the tiger but . . . never ceased to look back nervously." Full of goodwill and good intentions, seeking peace and unity at home and abroad, Eisenhower had so internalized the image of himself as a hero—a unifier, a healer, a reconciler—that he became captive to this image, a circumstance which left him a weak and passive president. Worse, under Eisenhower the office of the presidency had suffered a serious "erosion of power." Childs asserted that "whoever follows [Eisenhower] will have to reassert the authority that has been permitted to decline."[80]

Neustadt's *Presidential Power* reinforced what Childs, Schlesinger, Kennedy, and others had been saying about Eisenhower for years. Always looming over the scorn for Eisenhower's "good intentions and pious principles" was an obvious disdain for Ike's conflict-resolution proclivities—his effort as a "reconciler" to pursue negotiation with the Soviets (after allowing the missile gap to grow). But the real lesson in Neustadt's book lay in its view of the politician's emotional relationship to power. An enthusiasm to wield power, Neustadt implied, was not dangerous but rather normal, natural, desirable in a man; it suggested a healthy male psychological disposition. A passion to accrue power "for its own sake" and for the purposes of "public achievement" (á la Roosevelt), and the appropriate proportion of self-interest and self-love, appear here as essential psychological prerequisites for heroic leadership.

James MacGregor Burns, a biographer of both JFK and FDR, expressed similar views in his post-inauguration discussion of Kennedy's presidency. Burns depicted Kennedy as a "professional in the care and nourishment of political power," while obliquely criticizing Eisenhower's institutional style ("a president can never become the prisoner of a tight little staff"). Burns wrote that a president, to be an effective "master broker," must ensure "that lines of influence focus in him and radiate from him." Kennedy, Burns confirmed, will operate through a "network of personal control" and will likely "remind us of Franklin D. Roosevelt" in the way FDR dealt directly with second-level men in his administration and encouraged a healthy competition among staff members. Burns noted that "Roosevelt joyously drove a team of spirited horses kept in harness mainly by his own vigor and élan. The result—a disorderly but productive administration—may be duplicated in [the Kennedy administration in] the days ahead." Here again is the image of the president who wields power joyfully, the charismatic president who expertly uses his personal skills to command, the quick-study president who is not buried beneath mounds of documents but can "hold all the data in his head." Thus far, Burns reported, "top decision-making has been a solo performance in the Kennedy administration." Noting that, "unhappily, consistently strong presidential leadership is precisely what our government is designed to thwart," Burns endorsed the Neustadtian presidency.[81]

The heightened appreciation of presidential activism and power, as well as the elevation of the role of the president in determining the course of history and the character of the American people, were part and parcel of the reinvention of the liberal in the spirit of the new ideal of manhood. Unconstrained, fearless, antibureaucratic, and willful, the new liberal president was prepared not just to exercise power, but to exercise it eagerly and with pleasure. Kennedy could thereby be distinguished not only from the exhausted Eisenhower but from the always hesitant Adlai Stevenson. Kennedy partisans jeered Stevenson's desire to be spared "the cup of power."[82] To them, such a comment was unthinkable—indicative of a deficient masculine self, a "stereotyped" liberalism whose day had thankfully passed.

When viewed within the context of the wider cultural currents of the time, Neustadt's primer on presidential power looks like a scholarly affirmation of the celebrated "unencumbered" male of the fifties. Neustadt's judgments on presidential style and effectiveness, his antibureaucratic proclivities and appreciation of individual will and the psychology involved in exercising it, are rooted in the fundamental assumptions of the discourse on conformity and "other-direction" that was so influential in the fifties. Although Neustadt's discussion of presidential power is less peppered with the kind of sexually charged tropes—"ecstasy," "satisfaction," "fulfillment," "gratification"—that saturate *The Vital Center*, it makes the same essential point. Both professors' appreciation of the willful, power-embracing, joyful president reminds us of Mailer's contrast between the security-seeking Eisenhower and the liberal Superman who, unimpeded by dull committees and institutional constraints, was poised to seek "dramatic confrontation" as a kind of existential—perhaps even "orgiastic"—encounter with reality.

In practice, Kennedy's presidential style bore the mark of the intersecting intellectual fashions of the time, from the critique of "the organization man" to the liberal call for heroic leadership. Both strains were fused together in the New Frontiersmen's self-conscious repudiation of Eisenhower's style, which meant a disavowal of bureaucratic formalism and an unfettered exercise of authority from on high. Although Kennedy did not exactly mimic Neustadt's power-loving FDR, he did augment the power of the presidency as well as the entire executive branch, and cultivated a brotherhood of New Frontiersmen, a small, oligarchic elite that huddled, competed, and brainstormed in an informal, lively atmosphere reminiscent of the Roosevelt administration. At the summit of the Kennedy White House stood the president; all lines of power would come from him and go to him, like "spokes of a wheel," Kennedy said. Sorensen regarded Kennedy's philosophical vision of the role of the presidency as nothing less than a substantial contribution to humanity:

> One of John Kennedy's most important contributions to the human spirit was his concept of the office of the presidency. His philosophy of government was keyed to power, not as a matter of personal ambition but of national obligation: the primacy of the White House within the Executive Branch and of the Executive Branch within the Federal Government, the leadership of the Federal Government within the United States and of the United States within the community of nations.[83]

The first task of a presidency thus "keyed to power" was the neutralization of the bureaucracy. If William Whyte had declared "the committee" the enemy, the emasculating force that had turned the nation's men into impotent, benevolent bureaucrats, the New Frontiersmen would create an operational style to counteract it. Dismantling the many committees and administrative bodies that had served as layers of bureaucratic buffers protecting Eisenhower became a source of pride for the New Frontiersmen. Kennedy would be his own chief of staff, eliminating the administrative filter between the president and his men. Kennedy maintained, á la Neustadt, multiple advisors working at cross-purposes, thereby ensuring the kind of healthy competition of ideas and wills that Whyte so longed for in his critique of the organization's "social ethic," which had turned internal conflict and rivalry into an evil instead of a source of momentum and bold new ideas. As Defense Secretary Robert McNamara, the great management czar of the administration, was streamlining the Defense Department, national security advisor McGeorge Bundy went to work disabling the "ponderous" national security apparatus that Eisenhower had set up to channel information to the Oval Office. Schlesinger reported that Bundy "slaughtered committees right and left" and shaped the new, compact, flexible National Security Council into a "supple instrument" that would meet the president's needs.[84]

Kennedy's reluctance to call meetings is well known. Sorensen reported that "not one staff meeting was ever held, with or without the president. Nor was one ever desirable." Cabinet meetings bored Kennedy, and on the occasions when he had to call one, "no decisions of importance were made . . . and few subjects of importance, particularly in foreign affairs, were ever seriously discussed. The Cabinet as a body was convened largely as a symbol, to be informed, not consulted." The president preferred one-on-one talks or small ad hoc group conferencing. Formal meetings and committees wasted time, and were oriented toward tedious discussion and group-think rather than action. Above all, they hamstrung the president, made him (and his top advisors) beholden to the wills and opinions of others less capable, and made covert actions problematic. According to Sorensen, "[Kennedy] never altered his view that any meeting larger than necessary was less flexible, less secret, and less hard-hitting."[85]

Virtually all biographers agree that Kennedy was preoccupied, above all else, with foreign affairs. As a Democrat, he had always been a committed cold warrior; early in his career he accepted the conservative charge that an ailing and feckless Roosevelt "sold out" American interests at Yalta; he blamed Truman and the State Department for "losing" China; and, by the late fifties, he took the high ground on the issue of cold war vigilance, stressed the problem of Soviet superiority in the arms race, attacked Eisenhower's cuts in military spending, and was an early proponent of intervention in Vietnam and other third-world nations. Intending to be his own Secretary of State, Kennedy chose Dean Rusk to head the State Department, a man who was, in Dallek's words, sufficiently "pliable" and would "serve rather than attempt to lead."[86]

Kennedy had declared in *Profiles in Courage* that "great crises produce great men, and great deeds of courage." If courage was demonstrated in times of crisis, Kennedy did much to manufacture a sense of crisis in his rhetoric, which at times verged on the apocalyptic. While the farewell speech of his predecessor stressed internal threats, namely the growing power of the military-industrial complex, Kennedy's inaugural address emphasized external threats, perilous global conflicts on the horizon which he was singularly prepared to confront: "In the long history of the world, only a few generations have been granted the role of defending freedom in its hour of maximum danger. I do not shrink from this responsibility—I welcome it." The speech was addressed "to friend and foe alike."[87]

Kennedy did not invent but rather inherited the hard-hitting anti-Communist truculence of his predecessors. Yet, in contrast to a cold warrior like John Foster Dulles, who threatened "massive retaliation" and railed against "godless Communism" and the moral corruption of the Soviet Union with the fury of a zealous Christian minister, Kennedy was less moralistic in his rhetoric, though no less pugnacious. Repudiating Dulles's sanctimonious cold war idiom, Kennedy adopted a more competitive confrontational tone, treating the cold war as a supreme global contest, a contest not of the moral superiority of two rival superpowers but of masculine will and strength. Even when Kennedy addressed domestic issues such as the need to bolster education or physical fitness, he invariably placed these imperatives in the context of competition with the Soviets. Kennedy often spoke of the need to avoid situations which would bring the U.S. and the U.S.S.R. to the brink of a nuclear conflict, and he disavowed the Eisenhower-Dulles doctrine of massive retaliation. But his persistent emphasis on an impending crisis—one which would determine whether the free world would survive, let alone prevail—always suggested that he expected and was fully prepared for imminent confrontation. "Each day we draw nearer the hour of maximum danger . . ." he proclaimed ominously in his first State of the Union Address. "Our analyses over the last 10 days make it clear that—in each of the principal areas of crisis—the tide of events has been running out and time has not been our friend."[88]

Kennedy's cultivation of a sense of cold war urgency and crisis, as Bruce Miroff argued, "supplied his presidency with the aura of purpose and passion it otherwise lacked." Kennedy tended to treat conflicts in the world as a test of the nation's (and thus his) courage. "There can be no doubt," Kennedy told the National Association of Broadcasters in May 1961, ". . . that this determined and powerful system [of Communism] will subject us to many tests of nerve and will in the coming years—in Berlin, in Asia, in the Middle East, in this hemisphere." When the crisis in Berlin erupted, he declared the divided city "the great testing place of Western courage and will."[89]

Other members of the administration were likewise prone to project their obsession with toughness onto world politics. Consider Walt Rostow's meditation on the fundamental problem of the cold war, which is reduced to a colossal competition of nerve:

> In a sense, the men of Moscow have had to establish whether the nerve and will of the West matched their own. . . . The Cold War comes down to this test of whether we and the democratic world are fundamentally tougher and more purposeful in the defense of our vital interests than they are in the pursuit of their global ambitions.[90]

The competitive, muscular rhetoric of the New Frontiersmen was also intended to have strategic political functions. Central to Kennedy's view of foreign affairs was always the assumption that the projection of toughness was an absolute imperative in dealing with the Soviets; hence his mocking of Eisenhower's spirit of goodwill in negotiating with Khrushchev. But a convincing projection of toughness to the Soviets required demonstrable *action*. Kennedy once told Schlesinger, "that son of a bitch [Khrushchev] won't pay any attention to words. He has to see you move."[91]

For Kennedy, international affairs was *the* arena in which courage and manhood could be demonstrated. (In the prevailing dualisms of the time, the realm of foreign policy was "hard" and masculine, that of domestic policy "soft" and feminine.) Despite the campaign rhetoric of forging new frontiers in "unconquered pockets of ignorance and prejudice" and exploring "unanswered questions of poverty and surplus," there was scarcely a word in Kennedy's inaugural address about domestic issues. "Let's drop the domestic stuff altogether," Kennedy told Sorensen as the latter labored on the speech. Sorensen later proffered the official explanation: the president considered domestic issues too "divisive" to be raised in the inaugural speech. But divisiveness was not the problem; nor should it have been a problem for a courageous leader. Kennedy was simply not very interested in domestic issues, as many historians have noted. On one occasion he remarked to Nixon that foreign affairs was "the only important issue for a president, isn't it? . . . I mean, who gives a shit if the minimum wage is $1.15 or $1.25, compared to something like Cuba."[92]

Though Kennedy was generally regarded as a "liberal" (as he is being treated here), he was not an especially committed reformer; his congressional and presidential record on reform issues is notably lacking. Representing a blue-collar constituency in Massachusetts, he had endorsed several liberal causes in his congressional career— increases in the minimum wage and unemployment compensation, improved veterans' benefits, federally financed housing—and he generally supported organized labor. But Kennedy demonstrated little leadership on reform issues in his congressional and presidential career, and failed to grasp the moral importance of civil rights, at least until the very end of his life, when the mass movement from below propelled him to act on civil rights as well as the problem of poverty. By 1960, his background and education, his vague reformism and membership in what Nixon called "the party of Schlesinger, Galbraith, and Bowles" wedded him to liberalism in the national imagination. But he was always uncomfortable with liberals in the Americans for Democratic Action, maintained an uneasy relationship to the Stevensonian liberal community (to which he was nonetheless linked by his academic braintrust), and avoided the label "liberal," preferring to call himself a "realist" or a "pragmatic liberal" so as to distinguish himself from sentimental liberal types.[93] By the standards of earlier years, Kennedy was not recognizably liberal, but neither was the dominant liberalism of the time recognizably liberal.

"Kennedy forged his own liberalism out of day-to-day experience rather than abstract dogma," according to Burns.[94] But Kennedy's brand of liberal consensus politics was part of a broader shift; it was born out of the experience of World War II and shaped within the context of competing claims to the liberal tradition. After Franklin Roosevelt's death and the onset of the cold war, leading liberals renounced the "soft" liberalism of Progressives like Henry Wallace and instead championed a nonideological, pragmatic anti-Communist liberalism. Impatient to dissociate themselves from a strain of liberal progressivism now regarded as hopelessly deluded and utopian, postwar liberals proclaimed their commitment to political realism and pragmatism, both of which guarded against ideological thinking, while largely abandoning social reform causes. Kennedy's cool rationality and detachment from social reform issues, while much more pronounced than that of many centrist liberal Democrats, was ultimately rooted not just in his own personal preferences but in the advent of a postwar liberalism that distinguished itself from the "Doughface" left by shedding the humanistic emphasis on social reform and laying claim to a "tough-minded" political realism.

Liberal political realism—and its claim to see and possess the "real"— was not only the preoccupation of liberal cold warriors; it had its manifestations in the academic and intellectual life of the postwar years. The ubiquitous use of the word "sentimental" as a term of criticism or insult in postwar intellectual discourse is a marker of the heightened appreciation of the "real" and the rejection of ideological illusions associated with the left. Literary critics repudiated the sentimental proletarian "social realist" literature of previous years and sought to "to redefine 'reality' so as to wrest it from the Stalinists," in the words of one literary critic. Consensus historians implicitly claimed a historical reality that the ideologically minded Progressive historians had obscured in their repeated sentimentalizing of the great battle between "the people" and "the interests" in American history. Political "scientists" now applied "hard" quantitative and scientific methods to political phenomena to uncover a "real" that had been distorted in a scholarly discipline too long preoccupied with soft, ambiguous political rhetoric. Diplomacy experts endorsed a "realpolitik" against the older "legalistic-moralistic" approach; the latter tended to mask the "reality" of national self-interest that diplomats naturally bring to the bargaining table by instilling diplomatic imperatives with overly moral, sentimental, "almost feminine" functions, to use George Kennan's gendered idiom. Even theologian Reinhold Niebuhr, who repudiated the old sentimental liberal Protestantism of the social gospel movement and reprimanded the left for ignoring the "reality of original sin," called for a more realistic view of the imperfect and corruptible human beings whom God had created.[95]

Everywhere, realism was in vogue and ideology in disgrace. While the quest to possess a transparent view of reality had, in each of these cases, its own complex and unique relationship to the issues at hand (as well as the political currents of the time), the cumulative trend nonetheless speaks to a heightened cold war era distrust of that which would obscure or distort reality, something conceived as "emotional," "irrational," "sentimental," "ideological," or "feminine." In its milder form, the turn toward realism encouraged the postwar intelligentsia's interest in the psychological basis of political behavior. In the foreign policy establishment, that realism gave way to a newfound faith in "hard" data, statistics, technology, intelligence-gathering, and analysis by national security managers. By the early sixties, expertise and authority in foreign affairs had shifted from the diplomats in the State Department to the experts and technocrats in national security agencies and councils. In the new national security milieu, the claim to a superior political realism involved the cultivation of a particular style of operating, communicating, and decision-making, one which effectively worked to stifle the uncontrollable vagaries of emotion or intellect, the "fancies" of the intellectual.

In the spirit of the political realism of the day, Kennedy set the style and standards for the new guard he brought to Washington. Impatient with what he regarded as the dull and plodding "long view," Kennedy proffered (and expected from others) concise, sharp, uncomplicated briefings. He eschewed those who were given to detailed ("long-winded") analyses and always maintained distaste for those who were, in his opinion, "slow." Kennedy's speed-reading capabilities became legendary; he was given to boasting among friends that he could read more books in a single week than Adlai Stevenson could read in a year. The reputation he earned as a quick study may have been, as Richard Reeves put it, "a positive way to describe a short attention span," particularly on issues which he considered less than urgent. "Tell me the ten things I have to know about this goddamned civil rights mess," he told Harris Wofford, special advisor on civil rights, in a car while en route to the Capitol Building.[96] Knowledge was something to be digested rapidly and efficiently, and the ability to do so without great effort or fuss was the mark of a man with quick-draw intellect and an ability to use his mind not as a reflective repository of ideas but as a "supple" instrument of power.

The State Department was the institution against which Kennedy defined his own antibureaucratic, action-oriented political style. Like his father, Kennedy had considerable scorn for professional diplomats; he regarded the State Department as slow in processing information, stodgy and passé, mired in the protocol and empty formalism of the old striped-pants set. Along with the Department of Defense, it bore responsibility for the fall of China as well as the missile gap. Kennedy called the State Department "a bowl of jelly," suggesting that it had no solid consistency, no hardness. Like so many conservatives and cold war liberals, Kennedy accepted the charge that "Foggy Bottom," as the State Department became known, was effeminate and thus ineffectual (though in contrast to Joe McCarthy, Kennedy generously qualified his terms). "I know how they are at the State Department," Kennedy told one congressman in an Oval Office meeting. "They're not queer, but, well, they're sort of like Adlai."[97]

To Kennedy, the CIA, with its hard-hitting expertise, was the mirror opposite of Foggy Bottom's effete dilettantism. Along with the NSC, the CIA had increasingly become an instrument of American foreign policy, and given Kennedy's preference for men of action, he put his faith in the CIA's expert efficiency ("I don't care what it is, but if I need material fast, or an idea fast, CIA is the place I have to go").[98] Above all, perhaps, Kennedy was attracted to its style—its tough, stealthy, covert aura, and its lack of fussiness about ethics. For Kennedy, a James Bond aficionado who always courted a certain amount of intrigue and danger in his own personal life (and for those within his inner circle, which included several former intelligence and OSS officers), the CIA was the institution which best reflected the New Frontier's self-image: fast-acting, adventuresome, impatient with conventions, gutsy, and subversive.

While speed-reading and speed thinking became the stuff of real men in the New Frontier, so too did the mastery of a certain rhetorical style. For many within Kennedy's inner circle whose wartime expertise lay more in intelligence gathering and analysis than in military combat, rhetoric became a fetish. It was the means by which a man proved himself not a just reliable cold warrior (for political reliability was no longer really the issue) but a smart, gutsy one. When they weren't writing satiric verse or speaking in code-like insider wisecracks, the New Frontiersmen communicated in a kind of sophisticated shorthand, an mixture of erudition and national security jargon and slang. The slang was blunt, witty, and fast, for verbosity was evidence of hesitation, idealism. Inasmuch as the dialect spoken by Kennedy's inner circle was alien to outsiders, it had the effect of creating the sense of an exclusive club of initiates. Mastery of the shorthand showed that one understood the code, was a member of the club, was a man (not an "Adlai," in New Frontier slang).[99]

When it came to foreign affairs, the Kennedy national security advisors could speak with swaggering authority of "psywar" and "nucs" and "surgical strikes" and "Chicoms" and "taking out" world leaders they didn't like, at the same time showing a blasé attitude toward subterfuge in foreign nations. In his study of the operational code of national security managers in the Kennedy-Johnson years, Richard Barnet commented on the way in which "toughness"—"the most highly prized virtue" in the national security bureaucracy—was demonstrated by those managers. Barnet called it "bureaucratic machismo." In fact, it was a rhetorical style that actually functioned to subvert the older plodding bureaucratic style.

> There is the style of talking to a subordinate—the driving command masked by a superficial informality—or to a superior—fact-loaded, quantitative, gutsy. The Kennedy operators, particularly, cultivated a machine-gun delivery. The man who could talk fast and loud often proved he was "on top of the job." Speed-reading too became a kind of badge of prowess. To be an operator is to be active in "putting out fires," a free-wheeling generalist who is "in on the action" wherever it might be.[100]

The effect of the "machine gun" rhetorical delivery was to preclude the possibility that equivocation, hesitation, or moralistic concerns would complicate or derail the decision-making process.

Kennedy's liberalism has often been called pragmatic, which in the political parlance of the day meant that one was not beholden to any ideological preconceptions but was rather rational, flexible, and instrumental, concerned with the achievement of results through experimentation and dispassionate analysis. Ideology was the enemy of the pragmatist, for it rested upon ideals and moral principles that could only hamper or preclude effective problem-solving and governance. The pragmatist accepts the extant system and its flaws and seeks to accomplish things from within, using the governmental tools at his disposal and always with an eye toward ends, not fanciful ideals. He is "tough-minded" because he is driven not by an emotional attachment to purist principles but by rather tangible goals achieved through experimentation and rational analysis. Burns tells us that in Kennedy's eyes, "to be emotionally or ideologically committed is to be captive."[101]

Certainly the distinction between what philosopher William James called the "tough-minded" pragmatist and the "tender-minded" idealist was not new. Schlesinger had traded on that gendered imagery for years, reworking (and some would say corrupting) James's dichotomy in order to fashion a new liberal self-image that distinguished the pragmatic liberal "doers" from the tender-minded utopian "wailers" (in James' work, the "tough-minded" and "tender-minded" tropes actually corresponded to the philosophical traditions of empiricism and rationalism respectively). But outside of the discipline of philosophy and under the pressures of the cold war, what political pragmatism came to signify by the early 1960s was not a methodology at all, but rather an eagerness to wield power.

Consider Schlesinger's distillation, in his book on John Kennedy, of the distinguishing feature of the pragmatist, laid bare with the usual dualisms: "The pragmatists accepted the responsibility of power—and thereby risked corruption. The utopians refused complicity with power—and thereby risked irrelevance." Unlike the utopian, the pragmatist is self-assured and bold enough to embrace power in an imperfect world, despite the temptations to corruption it poses (which, presumably, he has the resolve to resist). Here and elsewhere, pragmatism is ultimately reduced to the will to power: the question is not, as it might have been, what is *possible* to achieve, given extant circumstances, conditions, and limitations, but rather, whether one has the confidence and the guts to *act*. In a 1963 article Schlesinger wrote in the *New Statesmen,* "The Administration and the Left," he explicitly invoked the Jamesian dichotomy to highlight "the divergence" in the 1950s "between those intellectuals like Galbraith and Rostow, who worked with Stevenson and Kennedy and the Democratic Advisory Council, and those, like David Riesman and Paul Goodman, who explicitly renounced pragmatism and proclaimed the necessity of utopianism." While Goodman was an easy target for Schlesinger's signature charge of radical dreaminess, Riesman may have earned his utopian credentials less by his notable essay on the subject and more by his objection to the hubris of the Kennedy administration. When the counterinsurgency mania began and men like Walt Rostow, with whom Riesman was acquainted in academic circles, were proclaiming their enthusiasm for testing counterinsurgency strategies in Vietnam, Riesman personally scolded two prominent social scientists who worked in the administration: "You all think you can manage limited wars and that you're dealing with an elite society which is just waiting for your leadership. It's not that way at all . . . it's not an eastern elite society run for Harvard and the Council on Foreign Relations." (If this was the voice of the fuzzy-headed utopian, the pragmatism that dubbed it so was of the most ideological sort.)[102]

The pose of the cold war liberal pragmatist was the pose of the intellectual. It represented his defense against the charge of irrelevance, impotence, femininity. Claiming the mantle of pragmatism may have been artifice, but it was not an innocuous pose. The New Frontiersmen internalized the image of the manly pragmatist. Proud of their intellectual prowess and ability to rattle off statistics and facts in rapid-fire mode, proud of their reputation as realists who harbored no illusions about the world, they were often contemptuous of men who acknowledged the limits of power and stifled their voices. Wofford recalled that within the Kennedy circle, the expression of "preachy" rhetoric or "square" inhibitions was effectively banned.[103] Expressions of idealism—so far as they existed in Kennedy's own rhetoric—were reserved for public political speeches, permissible so long as they were couched in the language of confronting "perils" and not "shrinking" from responsibilities. But preachy moralism or idealism had no place in Kennedy's inner circle, and those who spoke its language got a deadly reputation for effeminacy and were marginalized in the administration.

Democratic Party leader and committed liberal Chester Bowles is the obvious example. Bowles, appointed Undersecretary of State as a reward for being the first Stevensonian liberal to come out in support of Kennedy's candidacy, quickly became the object of the kind of condescension and scorn that Stevenson so often suffered in his dealings with the Kennedys. Bowles tended to speak in "long, quasi-theological terms" about fanciful things like the future of freedom, world opinion, and political morality. Even worse than Bowles's tendency to be moralistic and boring (not an inconsiderable sin in the Kennedy administration, as Halberstam noted) was his cautionary manner. It especially exasperated Robert Kennedy, who once descended to calling Bowles a "gutless bastard" when Bowles seemed hesitant to endorse the deployment of U.S. warships close to the coast of the Dominican Republic. Like U.N. Secretary Stevenson, Bowles was considered too cautious and "feminine" to be consulted about the initial planning of the Bay of Pigs operation. (Gore Vidal once observed that "the worst epithet the Kennedys had for a man was that he's a woman.") Bowles fell out of favor in the administration completely when he let it be known to the press that he opposed the Bay of Pigs operation (when he finally learned of it). Regarded by the president and other New Frontiersmen as an embodiment of the slowness and indecisiveness which had long plagued the State Department, and seen as an impediment to post–Bay of Pigs counterinsurgency operations against Castro, Bowles was fired in the "Thanksgiving Day massacre" of November 1961. Schlesinger proffered the official explanation: the president believed that "Bowles was oriented toward discussion rather than action and therefore only reinforced the vacillating and dilatory habits of the Department." It was another way of saying he didn't speak the Kennedy code; he was a moralizer prone to "discussion," a hangover from an older liberal tradition.[104]

In its most troubling manifestation, "coolness" in the Kennedy administration meant the acceptance of the use of force, violence, and subterfuge as routine. Bowles, like Stevenson, was a casualty of what would later be called the "hairy chest syndrome." The term was coined by former Kennedy-Johnson administrators whom Richard Barnet interviewed for his study of the national security bureaucracy. Barnet paraphrased what they had to say in this way:

> The man who is ready to recommend using violence against foreigners, even where he is overruled, does not damage his reputation for prudence, soundness, or imagination, but the man who recommends putting an issue to the U.N., seeking negotiations, or, horror of horrors, "doing nothing" quickly becomes known as "soft." To be "soft"—i.e., unbelligerent, compassionate, willing to settle for less—or simply to be repelled by mass homicide, is to be "irresponsible." It means walking out of the club.[105]

The collective self-image of the New Frontiersmen—a cadre of gutsy, cerebral, potent men rising above the dull minds and impotent wills of the Washington bureaucracy—engendered a kind of esprit de corps, one that ensured loyalty to the president as well as the public reproduction of the Kennedy mystique. The sense of a radical departure from the routines of the past, the atmosphere of thrill and crisis, the cultivation of cerebral prowess, the code-talk, the fifty-mile hikes, and the impromptu hallway conferences and covert adventures abroad had the effect of creating a kind of brotherhood. The cohesiveness that the Kennedys generated in the ranks of the administration, the evidence of which is suggested by the sustained scramble to protect the Kennedy legacy as well as the extraordinarily generous treatment extended to the Kennedys by their house historians, cannot be understood apart from the rites of machismo that served to tie the men of this administration together.[106]

The Counterinsurgent

Despite the aura of realism and pragmatism, there is a certain manly romanticism about the New Frontiersmen's view of the world and their role within it, one that found its ultimate expression in the counterinsurgency and guerilla warfare fad which swept through the administration. Kennedy repudiated the Eisenhower-Dulles reliance on nuclear deterrence and massive retaliation as ineffective in dealing with troublesome "hot spots" in the third world where the cold war was increasingly being fought. Instead he championed a strategy of "flexible response" to global Communist aggression, which included a substantial build-up of conventional forces as well as the development of foreign aid programs and counterinsurgency operations. Kennedy had long been interested in new and unorthodox tactics for combating Communist insurgency in the developing world. As a senator, he was so impressed by the 1958 novel *The Ugly American*, which did much to bring alternative third world foreign policy strategies and counterinsurgency into vogue, that he and five other prominent Americans took out a full-page advertisement in the *New York Times* declaring that they had sent *The Ugly American* to each member of the Senate. The book sold 5 million copies and remained on the best-seller lists during the 1960 presidential campaign.[107]

The Ugly American, written by Eugene Burdick (a political science professor) and William Lederer (a U.S. Navy captain), helped to inspire a rethinking of American tactics in postcolonial regions of the world where Communists exploited the people's nationalist aspirations while American hegemony was continually frustrated. The book also did much to popularize and romanticize counterinsurgency. Advertised as "fiction based on fact," the novel comprised a series of interconnected vignettes about a fictional Southeast Asian nation called Sarkhan, and was based loosely on the "real" experiences of several men, including Lederer himself and especially Edward Lansdale, brigadier general in the U.S. Air Force. Prior to his stint as the CIA station chief in Saigon in the mid-fifties, Lansdale had conducted successful counterinsurgency operations in the Philippines and had developed a legendary reputation as something of a psywar swashbucker.[108] The mythic Lansdale became the Kennedy administration's principal advisor on counterinsurgency.

The Ugly American made its case for alternative strategies in the third world by advancing a damning indictment of the U.S. Foreign Service, portrayed as full of self-aggrandizing, indolent dilettantes who enjoyed lives of colonial privilege and were ignorant and contemptuous of the native people. The book held feminized, luxury-loving, feckless Foreign Service bureaucrats responsible for tainting the reputation of Americans abroad and, in effect, allowing the more savvy, purposeful Communists to outsmart Americans at every turn and gain the allegiance of native peoples in Southeast Asia.[109] The crude and inept U.S. Ambassador to Sarkhan, Louis Sears, who thinks of the Sarkhanese people as "little monkeys," stands in stark contrast to Soviet ambassador Louis Krupitzyn. A refined man, Krupitzyn is a trained, highly professional diplomat studied in Sarkhanese culture and fluent in the Sarkhanese language (as is his entire staff). While Krupitzyn even becomes an accomplished nose flute player as part of his diplomatic effort to win over the Sarkhanese, Sears bides his time in Sarkhan living large and awaiting greener career pastures, a federal judgeship.

The heroes of *The Ugly American* are the smart, vigorous, dedicated men who, scorned by the Foreign Service bureaucracy, correctly recognize that the war against Communism in Southeast Asia requires bold, unorthodox, creative tactics. Collectively, these men represent the range of possibilities for American foreign policy: Tex Wolchek, a paratrooper who reads Mao and schools himself in the art of guerilla warfare; Homer Atkins, a wealthy field engineer who always wears khakis and carries "the smell of the jungle about him," and whose ingenious water pump device provides the basis for a fledgling small-scale industry for struggling farmers; Father Finian, a Jesuit priest who sensitively instructs and guides Burmese anti-Communist groups in their struggle against the Communist insurgency; Ambassador Gilbert White, an anomaly in the diplomatic corps, a "hard and muscular" Princeton alumnus who also studies Mao, understands the mistakes made by French colonialists, and recognizes that American diplomatic personnel need training in counterinsurgency tactics and expertise in hands-on economic development; and Colonel Hillandale (based on Lansdale), a shrewd and perceptive CIA operative whose habit of fraternizing with the locals (he wins over the Filipinos by playing the harmonica in the village square) permits him to learn the nuances of their culture. In Sarkhan, Hillandale discovers that the "key" to unlocking Sarkhanese culture lay in "astrology and palmistry"—much like the real Lansdale, who believed that the Vietnamese people could be manipulated by the spread of astrological "predictions" of the demise of the Vietminh and the unity of Vietnam.

Armed with real expertise and proficient in the culture and language of the native peoples, such men understood and could therefore manipulate the cultural beliefs and symbols of the native people in order to win allies in the war against Communism. As Robert Dean's study has suggested, *The Ugly American* complemented Kennedy's imperial-aristocratic ideal of heroism and self-sacrifice and provided him with a ready-made critique of Eisenhower era foreign policy in areas of the world where cold war anticolonial conflicts and brushfire wars were increasingly fought. In *The Ugly American*, hearty, willful, clever American "pioneers" on a new third world "frontier," willing to relinquish comfort and security, circumventing the ineffectual bureaucracy in order to win the hearts and minds of native peoples in the battle against Communism, fulfilled the manly ideal of the New Frontier. *The Ugly American* helped to encourage new strategies in foreign policy that would take shape during the Kennedy administration, from various counterinsurgency operations to the Green Berets and the Peace Corps.[110]

Headed by Kennedy's brother-in-law, Sargent Shriver (and endorsed by Eugene Burdick), the Peace Corps was the more visionary, "idealistic" expression of Kennedy's romantic heroism. Young, selfless Peace Corps volunteers, opting not for security and status-seeking at home but rather for self-sacrifice, adventure, and virtuous work in conditions of deprivation abroad, would venture into the underdeveloped world, mix with the native people, learn their languages and customs, teach them skills, doctor their sick, show them how to irrigate their fields, and help them build schools, dams, and bridges. Kennedy's call for self-sacrifice was thus fused with American foreign policy objectives: Peace Corps volunteers would export Yankee know-how and benevolence, in the process making the world stable for democracy to flourish where it otherwise might not.

The Peace Corps volunteer represented the possibility of a new American diplomacy of goodwill, while the Green Beret was its mirror opposite, its foreign policy alter ego. The vision of an expertly trained cadre of "special forces"—set apart from the regular army by their skill, muscle, and intelligence, well versed in geopolitics, history, and foreign languages, proficient in revolutionary ideology in the know-your-enemy school of thinking, and fully prepared for "twilight wars" against revolutionary forces in physically and politically uncongenial places in the world—more accurately reflected the Kennedy ideal. The Green Beret, whose testing ground would be Vietnam, was the embodiment of expectations and fantasies about U.S. power; he personified the hope that American forces could prevail in a guerilla war in the harshest of jungle conditions and against a wily and hardened enemy who enjoyed none of the "advantages" of an affluent, comfortable American lifestyle. The Green Beret was political realism romanticized: a stylistic mixture of the soldier, the CIA operative, and the guerilla-enemy himself.

John and Robert Kennedy believed that American success in the global war against Communism lay in counterinsurgency. To this end the president created "Special Group CI" (for counterinsurgency) to preside over the development of Special Forces. He also ordered the Defense Department to place more emphasis on the development of counterinsurgency tactics, the State Department to instruct the diplomatic corps in counterinsurgency theory and techniques, and war colleges to teach mandatory courses in counterinsurgency. Robert Kennedy, the moving force of Special Group CI who kept a green beret on his desk and whose enthusiasm for counterinsurgency was so excessive that some in the administration called him "Mister CI," avidly read the revolutionary theory of Mao Zedong and Ho Chi Minh and held counterinsurgency training exercises with Special Forces troops at his home on Hickory Hill. The heightened interest in counterinsurgency strategies was also expressed in the growing preoccupation with psychological warfare and covert schemes to destabilize and topple undesirable foreign governments, schemes inherited from Eisenhower's CIA. In all its manifestations, the interest in counterinsurgency tactics and covert operations is indicative of several developments; growing nationalist, anti-American sentiment in Latin America; the crisis in Laos and the rising importance of Vietnam on the foreign policy agenda; the augmented power and prestige of the CIA, still flush with confidence after its successful operations in Iran and Guatemala in the mid-fifties; and Khrushchev's 1961 declaration of support for "wars of liberation or popular uprisings" of "colonial peoples against their oppressors" in underdeveloped nations (as well as his boast of Soviet success in such ventures). Kennedy took Khrushchev's speech as a grave challenge to American aims in the third world.[111]

Whatever else the counterinsurgency mania was, it reflected a new romantic pursuit of masculine self-affirmation, one expressed in the popular myths that grew around men like Lansdale as well as *The Ugly American*'s idealization of manly, heroic, virtuous action in the jungles and villages of Southeast Asia. That a political scientist and a U.S. Navy captain made their case for a rehabilitation of third world foreign policy strategies in a novel, as opposed to a more traditional policy critique, permitted them to shape a new style of cold warrior—to use detail and physical imagery to depict vividly the hearty, willful men who, unlike the self-interested bloated bureaucrats of the foreign service, "smelled of the jungle" and were eager to get their hands dirty and act in daring, inventive ways in the struggle against Communist insurgency. The enthusiasm for counterinsurgency, the origins of which surely stretch back to the days of the OSS, lay not just in its geopolitical and strategic aims but also in the appeal of manly adventure and cool subversion that subterranean conflicts in the mountains and jungles of the third world offered American men.

Indeed, the counterinsurgency fad suggests an infatuation with subversion, perhaps even an envy of the tough, sly, and purposeful enemy himself.

For purely strategic reasons, of course, the counterinsurgent attempts to understand and therefore reproduce the mind-set, the tactics, the "dirty tricks," and (superior) totalitarian techniques of a ruthless enemy in order to ultimately defeat him at his own game. Hence the counterinsurgency enthusiasts' close study of the revolutionary ideology of Ho and Mao, or the CIA's plan to destabilize Cuba and topple Castro through a myriad of covert plots, including totalitarian propaganda maneuvers, economic subterfuge, assassination plots, and even one proposed scheme to unman Castro furtively by making his beard fall off (his beard regarded as the symbol of his manly potency and therefore a source of his charismatic appeal to the Cuban masses). The war against Communism required underhanded, extralegal tactics to match a crafty Communist enemy in the third world who took his cues from the Kremlin and did not operate under democratic, ethical, or institutional constraints. While the counterinsurgent's appropriation of the enemy's style serves tactical purposes, it also involves, as Michael Rogin suggested in a slightly different context, "forbidden desires for identity" with the enemy, even a buried attraction to the real or imagined qualities and the extraordinary powers of the enemy subversive.[112]

In this sense, Castro's beard may have been less the "key" to unlocking the source of his irresistible power to mesmerize the Cuban masses and more a symbol of what the counterinsurgent imagination was itself drawn to: the revolutionary leader's raw, undiluted proletarian machismo, which the conventions of the American establishment forbade. From the mountains of Cuba, Castro had, after all, orchestrated a magnificent guerrilla war against the Batista regime and proceeded to create a new revolutionary order founded (it was always assumed) on his own personal charisma. Castro's masculine allure was bound up with his impressive mastery of power, his unapologetic "love affair" with power, to use Neustadt's idiom. The obsession with Castro, especially pronounced in Bobby Kennedy, involved more than the strategic risk the Cuban leader's regime posed to U.S. national security. For American men who experienced an affluent, conformist, bureaucratic culture as dull and emasculating but could never be free from its conventions—men who experienced institutional restraints and democratic ethics as boring, encumbering, and ill-conducive to heroism but who could never repudiate what they were officially conscripted to defend—Castro fulfilled the image of a genuine existential hero. (It's easy to forget Castro's popularity in the United States in the late 1950s, and the many young Americans who were drawn to Castro and actually sought to get into Cuba and fight alongside his fatigue-clad, gun-toting rebel guerrillas.) In a sense, the bearded, cigar-smoking Fidel Castro, so raw and rugged, so fearless and coolly subversive, was to the Kennedy counterinsurgents what the "White

Negro" was to Mailer: authentically masculine, the antithesis of the square, self-relinquishing, gray-flannel suit man of the fifties.[113]

As an impressive and formidable foe, however, Castro needed to be "taken out," even unmanned (Schlesinger dubbed the Bay of Pigs plan "Operation Castration"). Here was the ultimate test of the new administration's ballsiness. Sympathetic historians have stressed that Kennedy inherited the ill-fated Bay of Pigs plan to overthrow Castro from Eisenhower's CIA and, moreover, that Kennedy was (whatever his mistakes in judgment or strategy) a "prisoner of events" or a casualty of "bureaucratic momentum." Yet Kennedy had long been promising to be tough on Castro, tougher than Eisenhower, and the atmosphere of competition and imminent crisis Kennedy created in his own ranks made the decision to invade Cuba seem almost compulsory. If Kennedy was a prisoner to anything, it was to his own public and private rhetoric, to expectations (especially within his inner circle) that he would never recoil from confrontation. Sorensen said as much when he wrote that Kennedy felt that "disapproval of the [Bay of Pigs] plan would be a show of weakness inconsistent with his general stance."[114]

As Wills has argued persuasively, Kennedy's decision to launch the Bay of Pigs operation was motivated not by an imperative to fulfill the plan he inherited from Eisenhower, but by a desire to establish his difference from his predecessor. Kennedy escalated the plan far beyond what the "General" had considered, and executed it in the spirit of bucking the old bureaucratic routines. Being ballsy meant bypassing conventional avenues; it meant that Eisenhower would not be consulted on matters of planning and strategy; nor would those in the defense and military establishments—who might have provided "pragmatic" guidance and assistance—have a consistent role in all stages of planning and execution of the operation; instead, they commented from the sidelines, and were privy only to short briefings and snapshots of a CIA plan under perpetual revision. General Maxwell Taylor, who wrote the post–Bay of Pigs report assessing the operation, concluded that it was precisely the absence of bureaucratic procedure and proper vetting that doomed the plan.[115] The Bay of Pigs operation was intended to be the brainchild of the CIA; its success would represent the triumph not of the military establishment but of the New Frontier counterinsurgent.

Objections to the operation were quashed either by secrecy or by the fear of being labeled less than manly. Sorensen, one of those initially kept in the dark about the plan to invade Cuba, recalled that when he eventually discussed the scheme with the president, Kennedy used an "earthy expression that too many advisors seemed frightened by the prospects of a fight, and stressed somewhat uncomfortably that he had no alternative." (Wofford revealed Kennedy's "earthy expression": "I know everybody is grabbing their nuts on this.") The exclusion of those deemed too "soft" to be consulted in the decision-making process, including Bowles and Stevenson, meant that their objections would never be heard at the roundtable. Although Rusk expressed privately to the president his doubts about the operation and his belief that it would not succeed, he never spoke up against the plan at the meetings in which the operation was touted and outlined by the CIA's Deputy Director of Operations Richard Bissell (a man whose dazzling intellect "transfixed" and "fascinated" those who listened to his briefings, according to Schlesinger, himself rather bewitched by Bissell). Sorensen recalled that "among those privy to the plan in both the State Department and the White House, doubts were entertained but never pressed, partly out of a fear of being labeled 'soft' or undaring in the eyes of their colleagues."[116]

Like Rusk, Schlesinger opposed the Cuban adventure but remained silent at the Cabinet Room meetings. He sent several memos to Kennedy that cautioned the president about the invasion primarily on the grounds that the operation could sully the international reputation of the U.S. and its new "image of intelligence, reasonableness, and honest firmness." In *A Thousand Days*, he elaborated on the point he had made to the president in the memos: failure in the Bay of Pigs operation "might recklessly expend one of our greatest national assets—John Kennedy himself." What Schlesinger failed to say here was that in a second memo entitled "Protection of the President," he proposed to Kennedy several damage control schemes to protect the President: "when lies must be told," Schlesinger wrote, "they should be told by subordinate officials." One of his suggestions was that someone else's "head" be put on the "block" should things go "terribly wrong." Schlesinger also proposed the idea that rogue CIA agents—"errant idealists and soldiers-of-fortune working on their own"—be blamed for the audacious invasion. (In *A Thousand Days*, Schlesinger labeled "curious" Rusk's idea that "someone else be sacrificed if things went wrong.")[117]

Schlesinger explained his failure to raise anything but "a few timid questions," at meetings in which the operation was discussed, by stressing the "circumstances of the discussion," namely, what he called the "rhetorical advantage" that advocates of the plan had:

> They could strike virile poses and talk of tangible things—fire power, air strikes, landing craft, and so on. To oppose the plan, one had to invoke intangibles—the moral position of the United States, the reputation of the President, the response of the United Nations, "world public opinion," and other such odious concepts. . . . But, just as the members of the White House staff who sat in the Cabinet Room failed in their job of protecting the President, so the representatives of the

State Department failed in defending the diplomatic interests of the nation. I could not help feeling that the desire to prove to the CIA and the Joint Chiefs that they were not soft-headed idealists but were really tough guys, too, influenced State's representatives at the cabinet table.[118]

In this discussion of the rhetorical advantage proponents of the adventure had, there is a certain irony in the suggestion that some of the blame for the disaster could be placed on Rusk and his subordinates at State who felt compelled to prove themselves "tough guys." The State Department had long been scorned by cold war liberals precisely for its caution and indecision, its lack of toughness. What Schlesinger could not admit in this apology for the president is that rhetoric has a way of encouraging and necessitating action. Moreover, those men who shaped the *style* of the New Frontier bear a degree of responsibility for what it yielded both in the short and the long term, from Operation Castration to Johnson's Operation Rolling Thunder. When masculine toughness is reified, when it is valued as a thing in and of itself, when virility becomes a virtue to be proven for its own sake independent of other considerations (pragmatic, moral, or otherwise), it proceeds with its own inexorable momentum to produce the circumstances by which it will affirm itself. If a president's persona is experienced by those around him as his most "potent instrument," the result is a cult of personality (or, in this case, a "cult of toughness") which effectively discourages dissent from the leader's mandates and desires, however much they are privately doubted.[119]

After the Bay of Pigs invasion, Kennedy sought to show that America's resolve to combat Communism remained stronger than ever. Addressing the American Society of Newspaper Editors on April 20, 1961, Kennedy spoke of the struggle in Cuba as one between Cuban patriots and the Cuban dictator, stressing that "any unilateral American intervention [in Cuba], in the absence of an external attack upon ourselves or an ally, would have been contrary to our traditions and to our international obligations. *But let the record show that our restraint is not inexhaustible.*" In the battle against Communism, he suggested, we cannot overlook the "advantages" that a police state has over a free nation. He stressed the need to match our enemy in strength: "If the self-discipline of the free cannot match the iron discipline of the mailed fist—in economic, political, scientific, and all the other kinds of struggles as well as the military—then the peril to freedom will continue to rise." His tone was unapologetic and chilling: "The evidence is clear—and the hour is late. We and our Latin friends . . . cannot postpone any longer the real issue of the survival of freedom in this hemisphere itself." He spoke of the "relentless struggle in every corner of the globe that goes far beyond the clash of armies or even nuclear armaments . . . [which] serve primarily as the shield behind which subversion, infiltration, and a host of other tactics steadily advance, picking off vulnerable areas one by one in situations which do not permit our own armed intervention." The implication was that in such a world, the U.S. had no choice but to engage the enemy at his own game and employ equally stealthy tactics of "subversion" and "infiltration." The overriding message was that if the United States always played by the conventional rules—if it remained "soft" (as democracies tended to be)—it would very soon be relegated to the dustbin of history:

> The message of Cuba, of Laos, of the rising din of Communist voices in Asia and Latin America—these messages are all the same. The complacent, the self-indulgent, the soft societies are about to be swept away with the debris of history. Only the strong, only the industrious, only the determined, only the courageous, only the visionary who determine the real nature of our struggle can possibly survive.[120]

Here was the masculine idiom of Teddy Roosevelt ("if we seek merely swollen, slothful ease . . . if we shrink from the hard contests . . . then the bolder and stronger peoples will pass us by, and will win for themselves the domination of the world") fitted to a cold war world. It was also an idiom that tacitly served to justify subsequent covert U.S. operations to counter "subversion" and "infiltration" in situations that "do not permit our armed intervention" and that hinted at future actions ("our restraint is not inexhaustible"). Truculent and portending, the speech could also respond to the certain gloating of Castro and his comrades at the botched Bay of Pigs invasion. When Richard Goodwin later met Che Guevara at a conference in Montevideo in the summer of 1961, Guevara told Goodwin that he "wanted to thank us very much for the invasion—that it had been a great political victory for them . . . [it had] transformed them from an aggrieved little country to an equal.[121]

Much has been made of the lessons Kennedy learned from the failed Bay of Pigs operation. But those lessons, if they existed at all, lay in the realm of strategy and decision-making processes, not in the prudence of covert attempts to overthrow foreign leaders who enjoyed popular support. If the Cuban people would not rise up en masse to welcome the invading forces, the "courageous" and "visionary" men who "determine the real nature of our struggle" would take out Castro themselves *and* transform the will of the Cuban masses. The CIA had been hatching plots to subvert and assassinate Castro since the last months of the Eisenhower administration, but after the Bay of Pigs humiliation, the objective of removing Castro from power gained new urgency.

In order to neutralize bureaucratic resistance to covert counterinsurgency operations, Kennedy authorized "Special Group Augmented" (SGA) in

November 1961, a special high-level arm of the broader CI group, to plan counterinsurgent activities in Cuba. Bobby Kennedy, the SGA's guiding light, noted that "my idea is to stir things up on the island with espionage, sabotage, general disorder, run and operated by Cubans themselves. . . ." Members of SGA group included General Maxwell Taylor, CIA Director John McCone, Deputy Secretary of Defense Roswell Gilpatric, head of Joint Chiefs Lyman Limnitzer, Undersecretary of State U. Alexis Johnson, and national security advisor McGeorge Bundy; others, including Rusk, McNamara, and Edward R. Murrow (head of the United States Information Agency), also attended SGA meetings. Lansdale was named executive officer and chief of operations of the SGA's "Operation MONGOOSE," which would work in conjunction with the CIA's Task Force W to plan and implement propagandistic subversion, industrial and economic sabotage, paramilitary operations, and assassination plots to topple Castro's regime. Lansdale promised the Kennedys he would bring Castro down within a year. Operation MONGOOSE, which encouraged the Soviets to increase their commitment to Castro's regime (a fact that the administration could hardly admit publicly) was disbanded after the Cuban Missile Crisis. But the plots to assassinate Castro, some by Mafia hit men, remained on the CIA's table until they were rescinded by Lyndon Johnson, who groaned that the Kennedys were running "a damn Murder Incorporated in the Caribbean."[122]

The notion of the cleverest minds at the top, bypassing the conventional routines of the timid bureaucracy and taking gutsy, furtive action to protect the free world, fulfilled the fantasies of men who sought to transmute their intellect into international muscle. Not surprisingly, the romance with psywar spawned wild overestimations of the power of the counterinsurgents to alter the course of history. Not only did they assume, for example, that they could remove Castro from power, but they also believed they could psychologically woo the Cuban people away from their leader, lest he become a fallen martyr. Image manipulation was central to this strategy. Lansdale, an architect of the "strategic hamlet" program and the "hearts and minds" strategy in Vietnam, had worked as an ad man in San Francisco before he joined the OSS and began his career as a psywarrior. One of Lansdale's especially audacious "psyop" proposals involved saturating Cuba with rumors to convince the Catholic masses that Castro was the Antichrist. After a suitable dose of indoctrination was administered, insurgents would then spark a "heavenly" uprising that would be staged, with a barrage of phosphorous starshells lighting up the night sky of Havana, to look something like the second coming of Jesus. "Elimination by illumination," one of Lansdale's colleagues called it. This particularly creative scheme of subterfuge never got past the discussion phase.[123] But image manipulation—the effort to subvert the minds and wills of the pliable, superstitious masses—

was the fundamental strategy upon which plenty of other CIA and MON-GOOSE schemes were based.

The Bay of Pigs misadventure may have damaged Kennedy's reputation; yet it also brought forth the circumstances for the supreme confrontation with the U.S.S.R. which would help to redeem Kennedy's manhood—and bring the world closer to nuclear devastation than at any other time during a half century of cold war tensions. In sympathetic accounts, Kennedy was a model statesman during the 1962 missile crisis. He was praised for remaining calm, sensible, and stern, and for his wise decision to launch a blockade of Soviet vessels, against the advice of those in his circle who counseled air strikes and an invasion of Cuba. In critical accounts of the missile crisis, on the other hand, Kennedy's rejection of negotiation with the Soviets, and his "reckless" issuance of an ultimatum to Khrushchev that backed the Soviet leader into a corner, only escalated the missile crisis and brought the world closer to the brink of nuclear war.[124]

A form of image manipulation was also at work in the representation of events surrounding the missile crisis. Kennedy let it be known to his friends in the press, Charlie Bartlett and Joe Alsop, that he would not accept what Stevenson wanted—"a Munich." (To the disgust of Kennedy and others, Stevenson had proposed that the U.S. offer up front a deal to Khrushchev involving a withdrawal of U.S. missiles in Turkey or a ceding of Guantanamo in exchange for the removal of Soviet missiles in Cuba.) The resulting *Saturday Evening Post* article, which quoted an unnamed "high official" on Stevenson's "Munich" proposal, contrasted Kennedy's tough-mindedness with Stevenson's readiness to make concessions to the Soviets. Such an image of Stevenson recalled the old McCarthyite epithet "Adlai the appeaser." However, it was revealed in the 1980s by former members of the administration that the Kennedys had, in the end, brokered a secret agreement with the Soviets to remove (largely useless) U.S. missiles in Turkey, so long as the deal was not publicly revealed.[125] For a time, it seems Kennedy was willing to risk nuclear conflagration rather than admit publicly to an agreement to remove some obsolete Jupiter missiles from Turkey which he had in fact already decided to dismantle prior to the missile crisis, lest his reputation be tainted by what he derided as a "Munich."

Sympathetic historians and commentators suggest that the Bay of Pigs failure tempered Kennedy's youthful impatience. He had matured by the time of the missile crisis in 1962. Thus was he able, after the humiliations of the Vienna summit and the Bay of Pigs disaster, to "finally win his manhood from the Russians," in the words of journalist Joseph Kraft."[126]

The notion of Kennedy's maturation or "growth" is often invoked in the argument that Kennedy was planning to disengage the United States from the conflict in Vietnam. In one variant of this view, Kennedy's triumph in the missile crisis meant that he could subsequently relax, that he personally had "less to prove" and thus had freed himself up to seek peace and even an end to the cold war, as his famous American University speech, with its "détente" themes, seems to suggest. Moreover, historians such as Dallek have stressed that Kennedy had begun to have less faith in his hawkish advisors, who had previously failed him in the Cuban adventure, and was in fact preparing to withdraw from Vietnam after his election to a second term. The underlying implication of the Kennedy-as-peacemaker argument, in all its varied permutations, is that, had Kennedy not been assassinated, he could have prevented the Vietnam War and the painful turmoil and divisiveness which fractured American society by the late sixties.[127]

The notion of the slain hero-father saving the nation from the catastrophe of Vietnam and the domestic disorder of the 1960s (popularized in Oliver Stone's preposterous assassination-conspiracy film *JFK*) is emotionally powerful and appealing, made more so by the tragedy of the assassination itself.[128] But the argument that Kennedy would have "quit" Vietnam often relies upon and thus reproduces the Kennedy mythology. It elides his deeply internalized ideals of courageous leadership borne out by the lessons of World War II: the dangers of letting one's guard down, of disarmament in the face of aggression, of yielding to an enemy. In so many instances throughout his career, Kennedy read events through the lens of Munich, applying (or misapplying) the analogy in a way that privileged bold, unwavering action in the face of enemy aggression over what he disdained as "appeasement." Kennedy may have privately expressed desires to phase out American involvement in Vietnam, as any president would have in light of the enormous military commitment it entailed. But the discussions Kennedy reportedly had with associates about his "withdrawal plan" (the main source of "evidence" that Kennedy intended to withdraw from Vietnam in 1965), if true at all, are difficult to accept as proof of what Kennedy's intentions *would have been* in the future. In any case, U.S. disengagement, according to the anecdotes about Kennedy's withdrawal plan, was predicated on the hope of *progress* in Vietnam—that is, continuing success on the part of the South Vietnamese in maintaining the Saigon government and managing the war for themselves. Of course, that progress did not occur. Given the rhetoric Kennedy had repeated for years about the willingness of Americans to "pay any price, bear any burden" to protect the free world, the very idea that he had *retreated*, where another leader might have stayed the course in Vietnam and prevailed, would have been, at the very least, extremely difficult for Kennedy to bear personally.[129]

A president's metamorphosis is not impossible, of course, and Kennedy's long-touted image as a cold warrior need not have left him forever immutable. A deeply competitive man, Kennedy perhaps loathed the prospect of losing battles as much as he dreaded the appearance of softness or appease-ment. But against anecdotal evidence for Kennedy's intention to quit Viet-nam stands a president who had engaged in a massive build-up of the nation's military capabilities and nuclear arsenal, who had created and nourished Special Forces precisely for guerilla warfare and counterinsurgency in Viet-nam, and who was surrounded by a set of advisors whose confidence in U.S. military and technological superiority was so inflated that it led Johnson right into the front lines of the war. If Kennedy did harbor an increasing skepticism about the advice coming from his national security managers, the fact remains that for Kennedy, a man who had previously ruled out actions that were "inconsistent with the general stance," relinquishing the American commitment to South Vietnam would have required a renuncia-tion of *everything* for which he had stood, from the years of his campaign for president down to the final months before his death. As late as Septem-ber 1963, Kennedy told Walter Cronkite in a television interview that the war belonged to the Vietnamese ("it is their war to win or lose"), but added, "I don't agree with those who say we should withdraw. That would be a mistake." It was a point he would have reinforced in his Dallas address: our involvement in Southeast Asia might be "painful, risky, and costly . . . but we dare not weary of the task."[130]

Either Kennedy lied to the American public (determined to wait until after the 1964 election to pull out of Vietnam safely, so goes the rather un-flattering Kennedy-as-peaceseeker argument) or he changed his mind some-time very shortly before his death. In early November 1963, Kennedy chose not to rescind U.S. approval of a coup against the Saigon regime's leader Ngo Diem by South Vietnamese generals, which resulted in Diem's assassi-nation. The unpopular, repressive Diem had become an impediment to the U.S. effort to maintain a Saigon government that it had spent years invent-ing, nourishing, and aiding with American dollars and military personnel. When considered alongside Kennedy's public statements about the impera-tive of toughing it out in Vietnam, the *de facto* approval of the coup (unless it was to precede a rather undignified U.S. withdrawal and abandonment of a new Saigon regime) seems an act that hardly befit a president who planned to disengage from Vietnam. At best, it could be argued, as Bobby Kennedy indicated, that Kennedy had simply not yet made up his mind about what to do in Vietnam. At worst, it could be said that the cumulative pressures—personal and institutional—make it likely that Kennedy would have stayed the course in Vietnam, lest he be required to confess to the fecklessness of his entire flexible response policy. It is worth recalling that, until the 1968 Tet offensive demonstrated that an American victory was not forthcoming, the majority of Americans supported the war in Vietnam. Moreover, prior to Tet, no one in John Kennedy's orbit, including his brother or the Kennedy house historians, had ever claimed that Kennedy had any intention of quitting Vietnam.[131]

The question of which course of action Kennedy would have pursued in Vietnam will likely never be answered definitively, but what is more significant is that the cult of toughness outlived the slain-hero president and had consequences for the future of the Vietnam War. Lyndon Johnson had always personally felt the sting of the New Frontiersmen's scorn, and he would eventually find himself struggling under the burden of Kennedy's legacy and under the weight of Kennedy's advisors to prove himself a worthy successor. Even more so, Johnson would find himself a prisoner to years of "vital center" tough talk, the implicit promise of which was always that liberals would not lose another China. Johnson confessed to his biographer that he felt himself such a captive:

> Everything I knew about history told me that if I got out of Vietnam and let Ho Chi Minh run through the streets of Saigon, then I'd be doing exactly what Chamberlain did in World War II. . . . I knew that Harry Truman and Dean Acheson had lost their effectiveness from the day that the Communists took over China. I believed that the loss of China had played a large role in the rise of Joe McCarthy. And I knew that, all these problems, taken together, were chickenshit compared with what might happen if we lost Vietnam. For this time there would be Robert Kennedy out in front leading the fight against me, telling everyone that I had betrayed John Kennedy's commitment to South Vietnam . . . that I was a coward. An unmanly man. A man without a spine.[132]

The elements that contributed to Johnson's sense that he had no choice but to send combat troops to Vietnam—the ghosts of Munich and the fall of China, the McCarthyite onslaught and the dread of right-wing recriminations, the Kennedy contempt for cowardice and Johnson's hypersensitivity to it—compress into a single narrative the events and anxieties that shaped cold war liberalism. Nowhere, perhaps, is there more powerful testimony to the historical significance of the cult of toughness in cold war American politics than here. Notwithstanding his need to summon pathos by casting himself as a victim of circumstances as well as the malevolent Kennedys, Johnson's confession reveals a deep psychological investment in masculine self-image, one that is singularly liberal in its hyperdefensiveness and excessive sensitivity to charges of softness, one that has the power to subvert circumspection, logic, prudence, morality, and even national self-interest in matters of national decision-making, and create the illusion that there are no alternatives. Recall that when Sorensen asked the president, before the Bay of Pigs operation was underway, about the plan, Kennedy "stressed somewhat uncomfortably that he had no alternative [other than to carry out the operation]."[133]

The truth is that Kennedy, like Johnson, always had options, and that neither man could perceive them is testimony to how much they were both encumbered by an institutionalized masculine ideal, one that upheld the model of the assertive, power-wielding liberal president who did not shrink from conflict. Ironically, the Neustadtian model of presidential power, which in one sense was meant to free a president from the bureaucratic, institutional, and psychological chains that would otherwise bind him, ultimately constrained Kennedy and, by extension, Johnson. Eisenhower, that slave to "duty," was perhaps much freer than his successors ever were. Of course, a Republican president (let alone onr who was a general and war hero) had less to prove in matters of foreign policy. But Eisenhower was hardly a "captive hero." Wills stressed that Kennedy's teachers on the nature of power "thought that any recognition of limits [on power] signaled a failure of nerve. For them, the question was not *can* you do everything but *will* you do everything? The American resources were limitless—brains, science, talent, tricks, technology, money, virtuosity. The only thing to decide was whether one had the courage to use all that might."[134]

It was not only Kennedy's teachers who framed questions of foreign policy around tests of courage and nerve. Consider the pressure placed on Kennedy and his political heirs by hawkish members of the press, particularly Joe Alsop, one of the most influential columnists of the time. Alsop, who blamed State Department dilly-dallying for the loss of China and was a tireless promoter of the domino theory, saw almost every cold war conflict, and especially Vietnam, as a great test of American manhood. He nearly dared Kennedy in October 1961 to display the balls for which the journalist had once praised the president: "Is there any real foundation for all the talk about the Kennedy administration 'lack of firmness'?" Alsop wrote provocatively. "The talk disturbs the president so much that he came to within an ace of making his recent North Carolina speech a major answer to his critics. But is there anything to it but political hot air? On the way to troubled South Vietnam where the administration's firmness is once again being tested, the foregoing question looms very large indeed. This reporter's 'yes, but' answer begins oddly enough with a typical specimen of modern American academic politics."[135]

Certainly a set of complex political and geopolitical interests converged to shape state foreign policy making in these years. But inasmuch as individual and institutional self-image, and a new and unequaled self-consciousness about leadership style, played a role in that decision-making process, the cult of toughness should not be underestimated. It helped to foreclose the possibility of more meaningful, searching, open debate and decision-making within the White House and the national security bureaucracy and made the demonstration of liberal muscle from Cuba to Vietnam a seeming masculine imperative.

In later years, when the Vietnam War was ripping the nation apart and a younger, angry generation cast its eyes on Washington, it was McNamara who more than anyone else became the loathed symbol of the New Frontier's steely, cool, unsentimental political realism. McNamara, erstwhile president of Ford Motor Company and Defense Secretary under both Kennedy and Johnson, appeared to the New Left as the perfect specimen of what they scornfully called "corporate liberalism." He seemed to be living proof of the degree to which the New Frontier's "liberalism," with its disdain for "preachy" concerns and moralizing "Adlais," had transmuted itself into a cold bureaucratic rationalism, one that seemed to be prosecuting the Vietnam War as if it was an exercise in mathematics and technocratic efficiency. When McNamara once found himself surrounded by Harvard students angrily protesting the war, he stood on his car's hood and lost his characteristic cool. "I was tougher than you are then [in World War II] and I'm tougher than you now," he shouted. McNamara continued to understand issues of war and peace in terms of who was essentially tougher. As Richard Barnet observed, it did not occur to McNamara that the students "doubted his humanity, not his *machismo*."[136] In the dualistic view of the world which limited national security managers like McNamara, to be repulsed by accumulating "kills," "surgical strikes," and "body counts" could only be understood as succumbing to some sort of feminine weakness from within. McNamara's instinctive response to the students—perhaps the worst insult he could think of—was to call into question their toughness.

The mistake of "tough-minded" liberal pragmatists in the years after the Second World War was not their rejection of illusions about the Soviet Union promoted by the likes of Henry Wallace, although the crude caricature of the sentimental "bleeding heart" deeply impoverished liberalism and deprived it of a moral compass. The costliest mistake of the cold war liberal pragmatists lay in the assumption that they were themselves free of ideology and the sins they attributed to it: distortions of reality, wishful ("utopian") thinking, a naive faith in progress and rationality, and romantic notions of rescuing the oppressed peoples of the world from the forces that deprived them of freedom.

What the pragmatic liberalism of the time ultimately demonstrates is that by calling ideology "political realism" and gendering it masculine, cold war liberals built myths considerably more powerful than those they claimed to repudiate. The most fanciful myth centered on the assumption that people around the world would, if not eagerly embrace the American stirring within themselves, at least succumb to the United States by the sheer force of its technological prowess, its intellectual and cultural superiority, and its military might. That exceptional confidence was inextricably bound up with the virile image that the New Frontiersmen shaped for themselves and internalized. The cold war liberalism of the early 1960s—with its adulation of power, glamour, adventure, and virility, its fixation on appearances, "identity," and the psychology of image manipulation, its romantic emulation of the enemy's hard, stealthy, subversive style—yielded not to reality but to fantasies of a restored American potency. A favorite Green Beret axiom speaks to those fantasies: "If you have them by the balls, their minds and hearts will follow."[137]

Afterword

The loss of sex polarity is part and parcel of the larger disintegration, the reflex of the soul's death, and coincident with the disappearance of great men, great deeds, great causes, great wars. . . .
— Henry Miller (1939)

[S]ociety must be a good master, a garrulous old nurse to her children. She must take care of them; teach them what to do; lead them by the swaddling bands; coax them into feeble and well-regulated activity. . . . The state must strengthen her apparatus, improve her machinery. She must put her subjects down . . . teach them to be tame and tractable; to go at her will . . . to wake at her bidding, to be humble and meek. All this with the belief that men so subordinated and put down can be, should be, great and happy.
— John Clark Ridpath (1890)

The cold war cult of masculine toughness was diffused by the crises of authority that brought Johnson and then Nixon down. It was delegitimized by the catastrophe of Vietnam, which called into question the morality of America's assertion of will and power in Southeast Asia. From another angle, it was disgraced by the fall of Saigon, which demonstrated the fecklessness of U.S. military power and intelligence strategies, laid bare the false foundations upon which America's claim to global prowess rested, and in the end left the United States defeated and humiliated by what Lyndon Johnson once called a "raggedy-ass fourth-rate country." It was discredited, too, by Watergate, which exposed the extent to which the power of the executive branch had run dangerously amok, and raised questions about the imperial presidency that had corrupted not only Nixon but, as it became clearer,

237

lesser presidential offenders. The cold war cult of toughness was also discredited by feminism and the counterculture whose values, insofar as they were absorbed by the mainstream and endorsed in therapeutic culture, repudiated the traits upon which masculinity has historically been based (aggression, competition, ego, dominance) and named them a source of immense mischief in the world. Masculine posturing and the privileging of manly attributes and values, always present in the political arena especially during wartime, did not of course completely vanish from American political life. But the exaggerated cult of toughness so conspicuous in the early cold war years lost its credibility, and its excesses came to an end.

The fixation on masculine virility, courage, will, and individuality that surfaced in cold war culture was in one sense unique to mid-century America, and we should be cautious about making easy comparisons to other eras, past or present. The preoccupation with masculine regeneration and toughness, nourished during World War II and culminating, in its various permutations, in the 1950s, was the product of a singular historical moment in which a complex of shock-waves and circumstances—global tensions and militarization, unparalleled affluence, commercialization and corporatization, the dread of collectivism and conformity, and deep undercurrents of change in sex and gender roles and relations (including, as I have stressed, a sharp awareness of male homosexuality)—converged to summon the sense of a beleaguered manhood in need of rehabilitation. Barbara Ehrenreich suggested that "Communism kept masculine toughness in style long after it became obsolete in the corporate world and the consumer marketplace."[1] The anxious assertion of a crisis in masculinity in the 1940s and 1950s was born of a collision between two conflicting trends: the imperatives of a newly proclaimed superpower determined to protect national security and lead the free world, and the waning of older sources of masculine identity and the erosion of patriarchal ideals in the family and beyond.

In another sense, however, the mid-twentieth century crisis in masculinity was the product of a much longer trend: almost a century of apprehensions and effusions about the feminization of American society, punctuated by surges of masculine self-affirmation meant to restore an older, mythic manhood and neutralize the emasculating culprits (modernity, reformism, mass culture, and women). When Henry James's protagonist in *The Bostonians*, Basil Ransom, declared his generation sadly "womanized," and merged liberal reformism, do-goodism, and feminism into a single ominous force responsible for the "coddled sensibilities" of his time, he gave voice to an impulse that was particularly pronounced in the 1950s, and remains manifest in American political culture to this day: the association of liberalism with feminine and feminizing values.

While the kind of excessive masculine posturing and politicking that characterized the early cold war years (and the Gilded Age) has been largely diffused in mainstream political life, the gendered dualities that separated liberal reformers from their critics in late nineteenth-century partisan politics remains a powerful, partly subterranean dynamic in American political life. This dualism is still very much a part of the conscious and unconscious life of American political culture: liberalism embodies feminine, maternal values (emotion, nurturance, sentimentality, tolerance, communitarianism, permissiveness, cooperation, conflict resolution, and pacifism) while conservatism embodies masculine, paternal values (rationality, tough-mindedness, individualism, realism, instrumentality, self-assertion, and self-reliance). These associations are encouraged by a two-party system that yields easily to a feminine/masculine dichotomy: the Democratic Party, with its traditional emphasis on "maternal" issues (health care, social welfare, education, social inclusion, labor issues, and social harmony), versus the Republican Party, with its emphasis on "paternal" issues (individual responsibility, government austerity, law and order and national defense, and global security). Like Basil Ransom, contemporary critics of liberalism have not regarded these female values as benign. The second wave of feminism, whose ethos became linked to the Democratic Party, accelerated the sense among conservative critics that liberal, "feminine" values would be imposed upon America by "hard," determined feminists. The line between soft and hard has always been an unstable one; if the overbearing, "destroying" mothers were once held responsible for emasculating the nation, their feminist progeny now bear the onus of that sin.

Cognitive scientist and linguist George Lakoff has argued that underlying the discourse of American politics is a conceptual system of meaning through which individuals process political phenomena. People reason and formulate their political worldviews within a framework of metaphors. According to Lakoff, the chief metaphor is the family. Thus the liberalism of the Democratic Party suggests a "nurturant parent ethic" of caring, empathy, cooperation, and growth, while the Republican Party's conservatism promotes a strict "fatherly morality" that seeks to protect and secure the family and punishes transgressive acts with firm authority. In the liberal "nurturant parent ethic," the individual, like the child, is understood as essentially good, and through understanding, nurturing, and education is capable of becoming much better. In the conservative "fatherly" ethic, the world is divided between good and bad people; the bad people, like the bad child, must be constrained and disciplined. In the former, the individual, like the child, must be encouraged and emotionally supported to become a moral member of the community of citizens; in the latter, the individual, like the child, must internalize the values of self-reliance and self-responsibility to avoid becoming weak and dependent.[2]

As Lakoff's work suggests, Americans consciously and unconsciously process partisan politics and their corresponding ideologies through the lens of family (and more generally gender, I would stress). Moreover, as we have seen in the early cold war years, the personalities attached to partisan ideologies are mediated by the sexually charged dynamics of image and style. Those dynamics have played themselves out in a variety of ways in post-Vietnam and post–cold war political life: honest and gentle Jimmy Carter, the antidote to the lies and hubris of the previous era until his feminine gentility and fecklessness were perceived as an international liability; the courtly paternalism of Ronald Reagan, who revived the idiom of cold war toughness and promised a restoration of old-fashioned values of family, self-reliance, and patriotism that would morally strengthen America as the global bulwark against an "evil empire"; George H. W. Bush, bearer of a kinder, gentler conservatism intended to mitigate the accusation of right-wing callousness, and briefly, the carrier of an alleged "wimp factor" who waged war in the Persian Gulf, but whose failure of nerve left Saddam Hussein in power; centrist Democrat Bill Clinton, the soulful, empathetic seducer ("I feel your pain") and easygoing adulterer whose compulsive sexual exploits, unlike Kennedy's, did not enhance his reputation as a man's man but rendered him, in the polemics of critics, the symbol of a baby-boomer liberalism grown self-indulgent and decadent; Al Gore, the wooden, inauthentic vice president and presidential candidate whose projection of a sensitive façade so feminized him that he appeared to be practically "lactating" in his campaign, as Maureen Dowd saw it; and George W. Bush ("Dubya"), whose rugged cowboy image and corresponding appurtenances (ranch, belt, and boots), unilateralist foreign policy, and showdown with Saddam Hussein in the "we must always react forcefully to evil men no matter what" school of thought, mark him in some quarters as a macho President of the immature sort. Indeed, to the insurgents in Iraq, Bush retorted with a swagger that some thought reckless: "Bring 'em on."

The assertion of masculine toughness is still very much present in political life, an inevitable by-product of wartime politics. But as Al Gore's attempt to nourish the "feminine within" demonstrates, the dynamics of image and gender have changed in complicated ways which resist neat generalization or comparison to the early cold war political culture, which had yet to experience the second wave of feminism, the rise of the civil rights and gay liberation movements, and other democratizing trends. Despite much analysis of the gender gap, the jury is still out on whether the projection of a masculine or feminine demeanor works more to help or hurt a candidate these days. Much depends on the mood of the electorate, the circumstances of the moment, the perceived failures of the political opposition, and the skill with which a candidate can negotiate a gendered self-image without going too far in either direction and alienating a majority of voters. Gore's lack of an alpha-male persona, when viewed alongside his relative success in 2000—he won 54% of the female vote next to Bush's 43% and scored a victory in the popular election—tells us that the projection of "sensitivity" is certainly not the liability it once was, at least in peacetime, and is probably an asset in some quarters of the electorate. Moreover, the persona that a politician projects must be distinguished from the politician's agenda, which can itself become gender-coded. It is one thing for a candidate to project a masculine or feminine persona that appeals to voters in the personal "likeability" area (increasingly the gendered imagery is skillfully mixed—consider the way George W. Bush's "compassionate conservatism" is balanced against the rugged cowboy image). But more serious issues arise when a candidate advances a political agenda that corresponds to the conceptual framework that Lakoff discusses. The candidate who would call for, say, a vast enlargement of the welfare state and a reduction in military spending will, in some quarters, always be seen as "soft" in the sense that his or her political policies are perceived as weakening the nation to internal or external dangers. The circumstances of the moment (economic depression, war) certainly affect the way in which such an agenda would be received by Americans. But in a political culture that has historically privileged the masculine ideals of individualism, self-reliance, and a kind of toughness of character born of the frontier experience, the candidate who advocates a left-wing agenda, especially one perceived as "dovish" in foreign policy, is inevitably vulnerable to the stigma of femininity that has historically disadvantaged left-liberal politicians in American political life.[3]

The career of Barney Frank offers another case in point that distinguishes twenty-first century political culture from that of the recent or distant past. Though the openly gay congressman from Massachusetts has endured slurs and innuendoes about his homosexuality, the fact of his presence in political life is testimony to the way in which American political culture has grown, outwardly at least, more tolerant. To be sure, in the mainstream political arena conventions of politeness and civility—what some would derisively call political correctness—now make open expressions of homophobia, racism or sexism, and even machismo unacceptable, at least for ambitious politicians. And surely one openly gay politician's stature in national political life and popularity in a liberal state does not necessarily signal widespread acceptance of the man, his sexual orientation, or his politics. But beneath the seemingly elusive currents of political correctness lie political forces that—despite an overestimation of their power by the right wing—represent a very real constituency that is open to, or even applauds, the diversification of the mainstream political arena.

There are conservatives, especially those unencumbered by institutional proprieties or the demands of getting elected and thus freer to speak their frustrations and hatreds, who attack liberalism in ways that are reminiscent of the early cold war years. While the Communist threat is now absent in American life, the anxieties that underlie current right-wing grievances and fulminations against liberals (and leftists in general) bear some resemblance to the fears of moral disorder that accompanied attacks on liberals in the 1940s and 1950s. Whether they now emanate from religious fundamentalists or right-wing talk radio participants, the charge that liberals have weakened America, leaving it vulnerable to internal decay and external threats, is voiced in ways that hold feminine (and feminist) values responsible for the degeneration of American society. Often expressed in an idiom that excoriates "bleeding hearts" and "sniveling" liberals, these recriminations suggest a historical continuum in American political culture: a sense that our "coddled sensibilities" and feminine sensitivities to the plight of the victimized and oppressed (not to mention trees and spotted owls) have enfeebled Americans and extinguished older ideals of self-reliance, frontier toughness, and individual responsibility. To critics, those sensitivities, along with the relinquishment of moral, legal, and cultural restraints on individuals (easier divorce laws, women in military combat, gay sit-coms) have ushered in an "anything goes" kind of moral anarchy that has undermined American society. Liberalism, now inextricably associated with feminism, multiculturalism, gay and lesbian liberation, civil rights, secularism, welfare statism, affirmative action, corporate regulation, environmentalism, immigrant rights, and multilateralism or dovishness in foreign policy, is thus held in contempt by conservatives for weakening and—yes, it is sometimes said—emasculating America. Right-wing disgust at what is seen as the "demonization" of white males makes for a potent brew; the emasculation of the nation is both metaphorical and literal. Here, the feminine and feminizing forces responsible for such a state of affairs take the shape of a wicked, monstrous tyranny imposed on the nation by those who can only be adjudged as "femi-Nazis." Seeking deliverance from such a hideous totalitarianism—the manipulation of Americans by the liberal press, the media, and academia raising the specter of totalitarian brainwashing of citizens—conservatives promise to restore an older America in which the values of freedom, individualism, self-responsibility, and traditional "fatherly morality" will prevail.

This is not to say that conservative opposition to liberal politics rests primarily upon issues and grievances related to sex and gender; nor does a conservative position necessarily suggest a preference for some sort of older patriarchal order. But given the obsessions and sexually charged invective expressed in crankier right-wing quarters (of which there are many), it is hard to escape the conclusion that the bitter recriminations expressed against liberals are often deeply and inextricably bound up with issues of gender. If one listens to conservative talk radio, it is Hillary Clinton, more than any other figure in American political life, who inspires a contempt that suggests comparisons to the right-wing attacks on eastern establishment liberals, and particularly Eleanor Roosevelt, in the 1940s and 1950s. One need not be a Clinton partisan to see that she evokes spectacular, indeed obsessive loathing on the part of the right-wing—hatred often tinged with bitter class, status, and gender-laced acrimonies. Like Roosevelt, Clinton has been a casualty of the animus that exists for her husband in right-wing circles (despite her successful carpetbagging bid for the Senate seat in New York), and is castigated for presuming herself fit to become a major political player. Like Roosevelt, Clinton appears in the right-wing imagination as an elite, eastern-educated, leftist, feminist career woman, and has become a despised symbol of liberalism. (And like Roosevelt, she appears as the aggrieved wife of an adulterer who pursues her career with a determination that suggests her "feminist" ambition to wield influence and power overrides all else, or somehow sadly compensates for a deeply troubled "modern" marriage). Unlike Roosevelt, however, Clinton, who leans toward the center on many issues despite her reputation as a leftist, has entered politics in an age when it is not unthinkable that a woman would make a presidential bid, a fact that makes Clinton's ambition all the more troubling to her enemies.

"What conservatives know and liberals don't," Lakoff argues, is that politics is essentially about family values. In the unconscious system of concepts operative in American political discourse, conservatives have had the edge, he claims, for they have grasped this fundamental point and successfully use the metaphorical language of family and morality to appeal to voters. Whether, as Lakoff argues, the key for liberals is to shed the dry, rational language of the Enlightenment and instead develop a rhetorical strategy keyed to morals and family values remains open to question.

But it is likely that, rhetorical strategies aside, the gender imaginary through which Americans process the political world will remain a significant factor in partisan politics, if only because political issues and stances themselves are inherently gendered, and perhaps always will be. A conservative who supports an aggressive, punishing policy toward rogue nations that sponsor state terrorism will be seen as a stern father figure, while a liberal who supports international cooperation and negotiation through the United Nations will be perceived as maternal and conflict resolution–oriented, regardless of the language and imagery expressing such views. The same is true for domestic issues that lend themselves to the paternal/maternal, masculine/feminine dichotomy: social welfare, capital punishment, gun control, or crime. Rhetoric and imagery certainly play a considerable role in shaping political ideas and the political unconscious of voters. But the advantage that Lakoff sees in conservative political discourse may lie less in the great skill with which conservatives deploy the metaphorical language of family and morality, and more in a simple fact of prime importance: the deeply embedded, age-old authority of the *father*, inherent in the political positions that conservatives tend to take. If it is true that conservatives are more successful than liberals in working the "unconscious system of concepts" to their advantage, as Lakoff suggests, it is primarily because they possess, by virtue of their very political convictions, the voice of the authoritative father which, absent error, excess, or failure, carries enormous power in the political imagination. Liberals may heed Lakoff's advice and adopt newfangled rhetorical strategies that will appeal to—and exalt—the ideal of the healthy, nurturing, cooperative, equalitarian family as a political model for the nation-state. But the playing field upon which these family models rest is not equal. In this world, still, the paternal is privileged over the maternal, the masculine over the feminine, and there is nothing much liberals can do about that.

Of course, liberals reinvented themselves during the cold war and adopted an ultramasculine anti-Communist posture suited to the mood of the times. But cold war liberalism, having overreached and then discredited itself, was laid to rest by Vietnam, and the arrogant U.S. nationalism associated with that war came to be regarded by liberal Democrats themselves as the underlying problem of American foreign policy in the fifties and sixties. The end of the cold war and the arrival of new global challenges threw the old dichotomies between hawks and doves, hards and softs, and doers and wailers into a state of confusion. As the question of American foreign policy in the 1990s hinged upon what the international role of United States should be given the absence of the Soviet empire, liberal interventionists were the ones to call for an assertive use of American military force in conflicts around the world—Somalia, the Balkans, Rwanda—in the name of a humanitarian foreign policy determined to halt tribal wars and genocide in the world. At the same time, conservatives tended to uphold a kind of "America-first" foreign policy stance that supported U.S. intervention around the world only in cases involving American national self-interest. When former U.N. ambassador Madeleine Albright made her case for an American role in the crisis-ridden Balkans and asked Colin Powell, "What are you saving this superb military for if we can't use it?" she could present herself (as she did in her memoirs) as a tough-minded proponent of the use of American military power—a "hawk" against a reluctant and even timid military establishment.[4] Of course, Albright's revisionism did not amount, in the end, to a reconstitution of foreign policy signifiers. Indeed, an activist, interventionist foreign policy in pursuit of "idealist" humanitarian aims could be denounced by critics as hopelessly sentimental and feminine, the utopian fancies of those who would place the United States in the position of selflessly saving the world from itself while squandering its resources and energies and naively dragging the nation into Mogadishu-style disasters or "quagmires" from which it could not easily extricate itself.

If the foreign policy dilemmas and debates of the 1990s did for a time make it seem as if the older cold war divisions between hawks and doves, hards and softs, no longer corresponded to the realities of a post-cold war world, September 11, 2001 brought those divisions back into partisan politics, at least symbolically. In the shadow of a war on terrorism not likely to go away any time soon, and in a climate of anxiety and frustration about historically new types of threats to American national security, the dualisms that separated the hards from the softs in the cold war political arena have reemerged (in altered form) in partisan politics, and remain obstacles for Democrats to overcome. James Traub, writing in the *New York Times Magazine*, noted that while all the Democratic candidates in the 2004 presidential election could be considered nationalist liberals of some sort or another, the war in Iraq has nonetheless become the "manhood test" for Democrats who must now recoil from their party's association with a soft, post-Vietnam antiwar legacy if they hope to prevail in the age of terrorism.[5] How well Democrats will negotiate the politics of gender, image, and policy in an age when national security is once again a priority on federal agenda remains to be seen.

There is currently no meaningful ideological division that separates the hawks from the doves as in the Vietnam era; indeed, every major political player adopts a tough-minded posture in the war against international terrorism, and the debate is largely about means, not ends. But the war in Iraq has in fact summoned a reconstitution of the old images: "hard" unilateralists bravely willing to go it alone in the world, regardless of what others—European allies, the United Nations, and the rest of the world—think, launching a preemptive strike against Iraq that could be justified on the grounds that a show of American force, in and of itself, is a deterrent to global terrorism. The Munich analogy has been deployed again and again as a justification for preemptive war in Iraq. Richard Perle, chairman of the Pentagon's Defense Policy Board, made the case for war in Iraq in the London *Daily Telegraph*, stressing that "a preemptive strike against Hitler at the time of Munich would have meant an immediate war as opposed to the one that came later. Later was much worse."[6] Hardnosed unilateralists are pitted against those seen as "soft" multilateralists—nervous nellies who worry too much about our allies and world opinion, and favor group-think and collective action via the UN or NATO. The link between collectivism, groupism, and femininity lives on.

Like the cold war liberals of a previous era, ambitious Democrats are highly keyed to the problem of image, and often tend to speak in an idiom that suggests a tough, unapologetic, and self-interested American nationalism. As Traub points out, "they forswear 'mushy multilateralism,' in John Kerry's phrase, for what Joe Lieberman calls 'muscular multilateralism'— multilateralism not as an instrument of legitimacy but as an instrument to advance our own interests." Democrats who endorse multilateralism, or question the wisdom of going to war, must do so always wearing their muscularity proudly. Americans feel more vulnerable now than they have since the worst days of the cold war, a fact reflected in the support for a war in Iraq that was touted, with the ghosts of Munich hovering, as the necessary "tough-minded" response to terrorism, despite the dubious benefits (and perhaps greater perils) it promised, from the very beginning, for American national security and the global war against terrorism. In times when Americans feel vulnerable, Bill Clinton once remarked, they tend to prefer a message that is "strong and wrong" over one that is "weak and right."[7] Whether the "hard" unilateralist foreign policy of the Bush administration has so overreached itself that it becomes just as discredited in the eyes of American electoral majority as it is in the eyes of the rest of the world remains to be seen.

Notes

Notes to Prologue

1. Daniel Bell, "Interpretations of American Politics," in *The Radical Right*, Daniel Bell, ed. (1955; New York: Anchor Books, 1964), 67–70.
2. Arthur M. Schlesinger Jr., *The Vital Center: The Politics of Freedom* (1949; New Brunswick, NJ: Transaction Press, 1998); Garry Wills, *Nixon Agonistes: The Crisis of the Self-Made Man* (New York: Signet, 1971), 521.
3. Robert Dean, in *Imperial Brotherhood: Gender and the Making of Cold War Foreign Policy* (Amherst: University of Massachusetts Press, 2001), has illuminated with impressive new research the relationships between the elite eastern institutions that cultivated ideals of imperial manhood, the politics of cold war foreign policy, and the inner workings of the national security state. With differing objects of focus and degrees of analysis, other scholars have linked national security, cold war politics and sexual anxieties: John D'Emilio, *Sexual Politics, Sexual Communities: The Making of a Homosexual Minority in the United States, 1940–1970* (Chicago: University of Chicago Press, 1983); Elaine Tyler May, *Homeward Bound: American Families in the Cold War Era* (New York: Basic Books, 1988); Geoffrey S. Smith, "National Security and Personal Isolation: Sex, Gender and Disease in the Cold War United States," *International History Review* 14 (May 1992): 307–337; Emily S. Rosenberg, "'Foreign Affairs' After World War II: Connecting Sexual and International Politics," *Diplomatic History* 18 (Winter 1994): 59–70; Joanne Meyerowitz, "Gender, Sex, and the Cold War Language of Reform," and Jane Sherron De Hart, "Containment at Home: Gender, Sexuality and National Identity in Cold War America," in *Rethinking Cold War Culture*, Peter J. Kuznick and James Gilbert, eds. (Washington: Smithsonian Press, 2001).
4. On McCarthy, see David M. Oshinsky, *A Conspiracy So Immense: The World of Joe McCarthy* (New York: Free Press, 1983); Thomas C. Reeves, *The Life and Times of Joe McCarthy: A Biography* (New York: Stein & Day, 1982); Richard H. Rovere, *Senator Joe McCarthy* (1959; New York: Harper & Row, 1973); Allen J. Matusow, ed., *Joseph R. McCarthy* (Englewood Cliffs, NJ: Prentice Hall, 1970). For more general treatments of anti-Communist politics, see Ellen Schrecker, *Many Are the Crimes: McCarthyism in America* (Boston: Little Brown, 1998); Richard M. Fried, *Nightmare in Red: The McCarthy Era in Perspective* (New York: Oxford University Press, 1990); David Caute, *The Great Fear: The Anti-Communist Purge under Truman and Eisenhower* (New York: Simon & Schuster, 1978); Stephen J. Whitfield, *The Culture of the Cold War* (Baltimore: Johns Hopkins University Press, 1991); Lawrence S. Wittner, *Cold War America: From Hiroshima to Watergate* (New York: Praeger, 1974).
5. On postwar liberalism, see Richard Pells, *The Liberal Mind in a Conservative Age: American Intellectuals in the 1940s and 1950s* (Middletown, CT.: Wesleyan University Press, 1985);

Alonzo Hamby, *Liberalism and Its Challengers* (New York: Oxford University Press, 1985); Hamby, *Beyond the New Deal: Harry S. Truman and American Liberalism* (New York: Columbia University Press, 1973); Mary McAullife, *Crisis on the Left: Cold War Politics and American Liberals, 1947–1954* (Amherst: University of Massachusetts Press, 1978); Steven M. Gillon, *Politics and Vision: the ADA and American Liberalism* (New York: Oxford University Press, 1987); John Patrick Diggins, *The Proud Decades: America in War and Peace, 1941–1960* (New York: W. W. Norton, 1988).

6. On the roots of anti-Communism in American life, see M. J. Heale, *American Anti-Communism: Combating the Enemy Within, 1830–1970* (Baltimore: Johns Hopkins University Press, 1990). For a sample of anti-Communist excess, see Fried, *Nightmare in Red*, 29–36. On the New York State Supreme Court Justice's opinions on Communism and motherhood, see "Communism and Children," *Newsweek*, August 9, 1948, 21.

7. Mickey Spillane, *One Lonely Night* (New York: E. P. Dutton, 1951), 171, 129; Whitfield, *Culture of the Cold War*, 34–37.

8. Spillane, *One Lonely Night*, 99; Kenneth C. Davis, *Two-Bit Culture: The Paperbacking of America* (Boston: Houghton Mifflin, 1984), 182.

9. Bricker is quoted in Paul Boyer, et. al., *The Enduring Vision: A History of the American People* (Lexington, MA: D. C. Heath, 1996), 924.

10. Real breaches in American national security did occur; the debate continues about just how many spies there were in the U.S. government, who they were, and the level of damage they did. The evidence is extremely compelling but not conclusive beyond a doubt that Alger Hiss was a Soviet agent, as was Julius Rosenberg. On the case for more extensive espionage than previously thought, see Allen Weinstein and Alexander Vassiliev, *The Haunted Wood* (New York: Modern Library, 1999) and John Earl Haynes and Harvey Klehr, *Venona: Decoding Soviet Espionage in America* (New Haven: Yale University Press, 1999). The limited incidences of espionage, however, do not redeem McCarthy's reckless and politically opportunistic crusade, which never uncovered a single Communist agent; they neither legitimize the extent of the federal government's purge of "suspect" individuals from its ranks (including those who were deemed "security risks" for dubious reasons such as their sexual orientation), nor do they make acceptable the suspensions of constitutional rights and the attempts to expose and purge Communists (real or imagined, former or current) from all walks of American life (universities, the entertainment industry, labor unions, etc.). I refer here to the wildly inflated estimations of the danger posed by the depleted American Communist Party and the absurd belief that Communists and their fellow-travelers, having infiltrated so many areas of American life, had the influence and power to seduce Americans, corrupt their values, and subvert the nation from within.

11. James T. Patterson, in *Grand Expectations: The United States, 1945–1974* (New York: Oxford University Press, 1996), provides perhaps the best general synthesis of this period, highlighting the transformations (and heightened expectations) that characterized postwar American society. Also see Michael S. Sherry, *In the Shadow of War: The United States Since the 1930s* (New Haven: Yale University Press, 1995); William H. Chafe, *The Unfinished Journey: America Since World War II* (1986; New York: Oxford University Press, 1995), 108; Godfrey Hodgson, *America in Our Time* (New York: Random House, 1976); Paul Boyer, *The Bomb's Early Light: American Thought and Culture at the Dawn of the Atomic Age* (New York: Pantheon 1985); Tom Engelhardt, *The End of Victory Culture: Cold War America and the Disillusioning of a Generation* (New York: Basic Books, 1995).

12. On wartime and postwar currents of social change, see, in addition to the above, William Graebner, *The Age of Doubt: American Thought and Culture in the 1940s* (Boston: Twayne Publishers, 1991); Lewis A. Erenberg and Susan E. Hirsch, eds., *The War in American Culture: Society and Consciousness During World War II* (Chicago: University of Chicago Press, 1996); Morton Blum, *V Was for Victory: Politics and American Culture During World War II* (New York: Harcourt Brace, 1976); John Costello, *Virtue Under Fire: How World War II Changed Our Social and Sexual Attitudes* (Boston: Little Brown, 1985).

13. Neil A. Wynn, *The Afro-American and the Second World War* (New York: Holmes and Meier, 1976); Richard M. Dalfiume, *Desegregation of U.S. Armed Forces: Fighting on Two Fronts, 1939–1953* (Columbia, MO: University of Missouri Press, 1969).

14. The literature on American women in the 1940s and 1950s is immense; see May, *Homeward Bound*; Susan Hartmann, *The Homefront and Beyond: American Women in the 1940s*

(New York: Twayne, 1995); William H. Chafe, *The American Woman: Her Changing Social, Economic and Political Roles, 1920–1970* (London: Oxford University Press, 1972); Sherna Gluck, *Rosie the Riveter Revisited: Women, the War and Social Change* (Boston: Twayne, 1987); Joanne Meyerowitz, ed., *Not June Cleaver: Women and Gender in Postwar America, 1945–1960* (Philadelphia: Temple University Press, 1994); Daniel Horowitz, *Betty Friedan and the Making of the Feminine Mystique: The American Left, the Cold War and Modern Feminism* (Amherst: University of Massachusetts Press, 1998). Men's perceptions of female self-assertiveness are discussed later in this book.

15. On postwar American culture, in addition to Patterson, *Grand Expectations*; Pells, *The Liberal Mind in a Conservative Age*; Diggins, *The Proud Decades*; Whitfield, *The Culture of the Cold War*; Engelhart, *The End of Victory Culture*, see Lary May, ed., *Recasting America: Culture and Politics in the Age of Cold War* (Chicago: University of Chicago Press, 1989); Morris Dickstein, *Leopards in the Temple: The Transformation of American Fiction, 1945–1970* (Cambridge: Harvard University Press, 2002); Thomas Hill Schaub, *American Fiction in the Cold War* (Madison: University of Wisconsin Press, 1991); David Halberstam, *The Fifties* (New York: Villard, 1993); William E. Leuchtenburg, *A Troubled Feast: American Society Since 1945* (1973; Boston: Little Brown, 1979); Todd Gitlin, *The Sixties: Years of Hope, Days of Rage* (New York: Bantam, 1987), 1–77; Christian G. Appy, ed., *Cold War Constructions: The Political Culture of United States Imperialism, 1945–1966* (Amherst: University of Massachusetts Press, 2000); Joel Foreman, ed., *The Other Fifties: Interrogating Midcentury American Icons* (Urbana: University of Illinois Press, 1997); Margot A. Henriksen, *Dr. Strangelove's America: Society and Culture in the Atomic Age* (Berkeley: University of California Press, 1997).

16. On modernism in art and other anti-Communist targets, see Fried, *Nightmare in Red*, 29–36. On Senator Eastland, see Patterson, *Grand Expectations*, 392. The American Medical Association's denunciation of national health care is mentioned in Whitfield, *The Culture of the Cold War*, 23. On parenting, see Ethel Kawin, *Parenthood in a Free Nation, Volume I: Basic Concepts for Parents* (1954; New York: Macmillan, 1963; italics mine). The parent education project headed by Dr. Benjamin Spock, "Parenthood in a Free Nation," is also discussed in Barbara Ehrenreich and Deirdre English, *For Her Own Good: 150 Years of the Experts' Advice to Women* (New York: Doubleday, 1978), 255. Issues concerning anti-Communism, religion, the family, and sexual deviance are discussed later in this book.

17. Norman Mailer, *The Presidential Papers of Norman Mailer* (1960; New York: Bantam Books, 1964), 40.

18. May, *Homeward Bound*.

Notes to Chapter 1

1. Arthur M. Schlesinger Jr., *The Vital Center: The Politics of Freedom* (1949; New Brunswick, NJ: Transaction Press, 1998), xxi–xxii, 144–145.

2. Ibid., 163, 147.

3. On postwar liberalism see Richard Pells, *The Liberal Mind in a Conservative Age: American Intellectuals in the 1940s and 1950s* (Middletown, CT.: Wesleyan University Press, 1985); Alonzo Hamby, *Beyond the New Deal: Harry S. Truman and American Liberalism* (New York: Columbia University Press, 1973), especially his chapter on "The Vital Center"; Hamby, *Liberalism and its Challengers* (New York: Oxford University Press, 1985); Mary McAuliffe, *Crisis on the Left: Cold War Politics and American Liberals, 1947–1954* (Amherst: University of Massachusetts Press, 1978); Steven M. Gillon, *Politics and Vision: the ADA and American Liberalism, 1947–1985* (New York: Oxford University Press, 1987); John Patrick Diggins, *The Proud Decades: America in War and Peace, 1941–1960* (New York: W. W. Norton, 1988).

4. On the "strut and swagger" of liberals, see Garry Wills, *Nixon Agonistes: The Crisis of the Self-Made Man* (New York: Signet, 1971), 523.

5. On the New York intellectuals, see Terry A. Cooney, *The Rise of the New York Intellectuals: Partisan Review and Its Circle, 1934–1945* (Madison: University of Wisconsin Press, 1986); Alexander Bloom, *Prodigal Sons: The New York Intellectuals and Their World* (New York: Oxford University Press, 1986); Alan M. Wald, *The New York Intellectuals: The Rise and Decline of the Anti-Stalinist Left from the 1930s to the 1980s* (Chapel Hill: University of

North Carolina Press, 1987); John Patrick Diggins, *Up From Communism: Conservative Odysseys in American Intellectual History* (New York: Harper & Row, 1975).

6. For biographical information on Schlesinger, see Marcus Cunliffe and Robin Weeks, eds., *Pastmasters: Some Essays on American Historians* (New York: Harper & Row, 1969) and John Patrick Diggins, ed., *The Liberal Persuasion: Arthur Schlesinger Jr. and the Challenge of the American Past* (Princeton: Princeton University Press, 1997). Also see the first volume of Schlesinger's autobiography, *A Life in the Twentieth Century: Innocent Beginnings, 1917–1950* (Boston: Houghton Mifflin, 2000).

7. Schlesinger, *The Vital Center*, xx–xxi.

8. Thomas Hill Schaub, *American Fiction in the Cold War* (Madison: University of Wisconsin Press, 1991), 5–13; Schlesinger, *The Vital Center*, 146, xxi. Suggesting the appeal of Niebuhr's thought to postwar liberals, Daniel Bell remarked that "Niebuhr's explanations became much more congenial to us" because they were premised upon "a kind of tough-minded attitude about human nature, a complex view of society, a complex view of human motivation and a willingness to talk about politics." Quoted in Bloom, *Prodigal Sons*, 188–189.

9. Schlesinger, *The Vital Center*, 1–6.

10. Ibid., 1-10, 52–58, 106.

11. Wilhelm Reich, *The Mass Psychology of Fascism* (New York: Simon & Schuster, 1933); Erich Fromm, *Escape from Freedom* (1941; New York: Avon Books, 1965); Schlesinger, *The Vital Center*, 52–53.

12. Schlesinger, *The Vital Center*, 243–248.

13. Ibid., 57–58, 244–246, 256.

14. Ibid., 53, 7, 28, 46. Eliot is quoted in Andreas Huyssen, "Mass Culture as Woman: Modernism's Other," in *After the Great Divide: Modernism, Mass Culture, Postmodernism* (Bloomington: University of Indiana Press, 1986), 58.

15. Schlesinger, *The Vital Center*, 188; Robert M. Lindner, *Prescription for Rebellion* (New York: Grove Press, 1952), 291. Lindner's work is discussed more fully in chapter 3 of this book.

16. On trends in postwar fiction, see Schaub, *American Fiction in the Cold War* (especially 1–17, 137–162); Morris Dickstein, *Leopards in the Temple: The Transformation of American Fiction, 1945–1970* (1999; Boston: Harvard University Press, 2002) esp. 17–20. Mailer is discussed in chapters 3 and 4 of this book. On the psychological underpinnings of fascism, see Reich, *The Mass Psychology of Fascism*; Theodor W. Adorno, et al., *The Authoritarian Personality* (New York: Harper & Row, 1950).

17. Schaub, *American Fiction in the Cold War*, 154–155.

18. Arthur M. Schlesinger Jr., "The Crisis of American Masculinity," *Esquire* (November 1958, 63–65); reprinted in *The Politics of Hope* (Boston: Houghton Mifflin, 1962), 237–246.

19. On American manhood, see E. Anthony Rotundo, *American Manhood: Transformations in Masculinity from the Revolution to the Modern Era* (New York; Basic Books, 1993); Michael Kimmel, *Manhood in America: A Cultural History* (New York: Free Press, 1996); Gail Bederman, *Manliness and Civilization: A Cultural History of Gender and Race in the United States, 1880–1917* (Chicago: University of Chicago Press, 1995); Robert L. Griswold, *Fatherhood in America: A History* (New York: Basic Books, 1993); Mark C. Carnes and Clyde Griffen, eds., *Meanings for Manhood: Constructions of Masculinity in Victorian America* (Chicago: University of Chicago Press, 1990); Elizabeth H. Pleck and Joseph H. Pleck, eds., *The American Man* (Englewood Cliffs, NJ: Prentice Hall, 1980); Peter G. Filene, *Him/Her/Self: Sex Roles in Modern America* (Baltimore: Johns Hopkins University Press, 1986); Joe L. Dubbert, *A Man's Place: Masculinity in Transition* (Englewood Cliffs, NJ: Prentice Hall, 1979).

20. On the intersection of antimodernist quests with the desire for masculine regeneration, see T. J. Jackson Lears, *No Place of Grace: Antimodernism and the Transformation of American Culture, 1880–1920* (New York: Pantheon, 1981), 98–139. On women, Protestantism, and mass culture, see Ann Douglas, *The Feminization of American Culture* (1977; New York: Doubleday, 1988). On gender, reform, and partisan politics, see Rebecca Edwards, *Angels in the Machinery: Gender and American Party Politics from the Civil War to the Progressive Era* (New York: Oxford University Press, 1997); Paula Baker, "The Domestication of Politics: Women and American Political Society, 1780–1920," *American Historical Review* 89 (June 1984): 620–647; Richard Hofstadter, *Anti-Intellectualism in American Life* (New York: Vintage, 1962), 189–190.

21. Henry James, *The Bostonians* (1886; New York: Modern Library, 1956), 343. Arthur M. Schlesinger Jr., *A Pilgrim's Progress: Orestes A. Brownson* (1939; Boston: Little Brown, 1966).

22. Bederman, *Manliness and Civilization*, 18–19.

23. On the Boy Scouts and other efforts to shore up masucline fiber, and the muscular Christianity of the time, see Rotundo, *American Manhood*, 222–283; Kimmel, *Manhood in America*, 177–188. The turn-of-the-century enthusiasm for militarism, the martial arts, the medieval warrior ideal, and competitive athletics is discussed in Lears, *No Place of Grace*, 98–139. On G. Stanley Hall, see Bederman, *Manliness and Civilization*, 77–120.

24. Sarah Watts, *Rough Rider in the White House: Theodore Roosevelt and the Politics of Desire* (Chicago: University of Chicago Press, 2003); Joe L. Dubbert, "Progressivism and the Masculinity Crisis," in Pleck and Pleck, eds., *The American Man*, 303–320; Arnaldo Testi, "The Gender of Reform Politics: Theodore Roosevelt and the Culture of Masculinity," *Journal of American History* 81 (March 1995): 1509–1533; Kristin L. Hoganson, *Fighting for American Manhood: How Gender Politics Provoked the Spanish-American and Philippine-American Wars* (New Haven: Yale University Press, 1998).

25. Roy Helton, "The Inner Threat: Our Own Softness," *Harper's Magazine* 181, September, 1940: 337–343.

26. David M. Levy, *Maternal Overprotection* (New York: Columbia University Press, 1943); Edward Strecker, *Their Mothers' Sons: The Psychiatrist Examines an American Problem* (Philadelphia: Lippincott, 1946); Geoffrey Gorer, *The American People: A Study in National Character* (New York: W. W. Norton, 1948); Philip Wylie, *Generation of Vipers* (New York: Farrar and Rinehart, 1942).

27. Bederman, *Manliness and Civilization*, 11. Bederman continues: "[Men] might not have been entirely certain *how* these three factors were related, but few seem to have lost confidence *that* they were related."

28. Schlesinger, "The Crisis of American Masculinity," 237–238.

29. Ibid., 240–244.

30. Ibid., 242–244.

31. Ibid., 244–246 (Schlesinger's italics). See also Ferdinand Lundberg and Marynia F. Farnham, *Modern Woman: The Lost Sex* (New York: Harper & Brothers, 1947).

32. Schlesinger, *The Vital Center*, 12–15.

33. Ibid., 13–15.

34. The titles of Schlesinger's essays in *The Politics of Hope* convey a sense of these themes and preoccupations: "The Decline of Greatness," "The Causes of the Civil War: A Note on Historical Sentimentalism," "The Crisis in American Masculinity," "The Politics of Nostalgia," and "On Heroic Leadership: The Dilemma of Strong Men and Weak Peoples." In the last, Schlesinger discussed the problems of underdeveloped countries in characteristic terms: "The real division in these countries is not between left and right; it is between hard and soft—between leadership that has the will to do what must be done to lay the foundations for economic growth and leadership which falters before the vested interests of traditional society and the preemptory challenges of rising social groups" (*The Politics of Hope*, 14). On Kennedy's interest in courage and statesmanship, see John F. Kennedy, *Why England Slept* (New York: W. Funk, 1961) and *Profiles in Courage* (1956; New York: Harper & Row, 1964).

35. Schlesinger, *The Vital Center*, 15–16.

36. Ibid., 16–31.

37. On imperial manhood, see Robert D. Dean, *Imperial Brotherhood: Gender and the Making of Cold War Foreign Policy* (Amherst: University of Massachusetts Press, 2001). For another interpretation of Ivy League masculinity, see Kim Townsend, *Manhood at Harvard: William James and Others* (New York: W. W. Norton, 1996).

38. Schlesinger, *The Vital Center*, 18–34.

39. The rhetoric of Gilded Age politicians is quoted and discussed in Hofstadter, *Anti-Intellectualism in American Life*, 184–191.

40. For a classic analysis of the gendered connotations of republican virtue, see Ruth H. Bloch, "The Gendered Meanings of Virtue in Revolutionary America," *Signs* 13 (1987): 37–59. An outstanding discussion of manhood and the shifting language of nineteenth-century politics can be found in Rotundo, *American Manhood*, 270–274. On fears of the "woman within" as well as changing scholarly conceptions of sexual inversion and male

homosexuality in the late nineteenth century, see ibid., 274–279. Like many scholars, Rotundo emphasizes the shifting focus among medical authorities "from homosexual acts to the people who engaged in them." He notes that "instead of identifying the event ('unnatural act,' 'crime against nature,' 'sodomy') as the core of same-sex eroticism, the descriptive language turned its emphasis to the individual"; hence the rise of new labels—homosexual, invert, pervert, fairy—that marked a individual's personal identity as homosexual (*American Manhood*, 275). Since male homosexuality was so deeply equated with womanhood, the accusation of effeminacy could imply that an individual man was a homosexual. Also see John D'Emilio and Estelle B. Freedman, *Intimate Matters: A History of Sexuality in America* (New York: Harper & Row, 1988), 224–227.

41. In 1886, when Senator Ingalls of Kansas denounced the reformers as "the third sex," he added that they were "effeminate without being either masculine or feminine, unable either to beget or bear; possessing neither fecundity or virility; endowed with the contempt of men and the derision of women, and doomed to sterility, isolation and extinction." See Hofstadter, *Anti-Intellectualism in American Life*, 188.

42. Theodore Roosevelt, *Theodore Roosevelt: An Autobiography* (1913; New York: Da Capo Press, 1985), 88; Watts, *Rough Rider in the White House*; Kimmel, *Manhood in America*, 181–183.

43. Schlesinger, *The Vital Center*, 21.

44. Ibid., 35–50. The term "doughface" goes back to the Civil War. According to Schlesinger, doughfaces were the northerners in antebellum America who supported slavery—"northern men with southern principles." Hence his analogy: Progressives are "'democratic men with totalitarian principles'" (*The Vital Center*, 37–38).

45. Ibid., 36–37, 46.

46. Ibid., 36–42. In an otherwise favorable review of *The Vital Center*, Gerald W. Johnson pointed out that Schlesinger "mops up the earth with Wallace and his third party, oblivious to the fact that he is flogging a horse that has been dead since November 2, 1948" ("In Defense of Liberalism," *New York Times*, September 11, 1949, 6).

47. Schlesinger, *The Vital Center*, 41–46, 170.

48. Ibid., 46; Christopher Lasch, *The New Radicalism in America: The Intellectual as a Social Type* (New York: Vintage Books, 1965), 286–349, exp. 289.

49. Schlesinger, *The Vital Center*, 41–43, 159–160, 170.

50. Ibid., 37, 40, 115, 118.

51. Ibid., 104, 54 (Schlesinger's italics).

52. Ibid., 6, 40, 51–54, 65, 83–85, 88, 126, 151, 245–246.

53. Ibid., 127.

54. Wherry is quoted in Max Lerner, *The Unfinished Country: A Book of American Symbols* (New York: Simon & Schuster, 1959), 313.

55. Schlesinger, *The Vital Center*, 56.

56. Ibid., 159–172.

57. Ibid., 159; Garry Wills, *The Kennedy Imprisonment: A Meditation on Power* (New York: Simon & Schuster, 1981), 183–185.

58. Schlesinger, *The Vital Center*, 255–256.

59. Ibid., 160, 156, 147, 171.

60. Ibid., 54, 247–248; Reinhold Niebuhr, *The Irony of American History* (New York: Scribner's Sons, 1952), 4. See also Niebuhr's discussion of right and left politics in *The Children of Light and the Children of Darkness: A Vindication of Democracy and a Critique of Its Traditional Defense* (New York: Scribners, 1942).

61. Schlesinger, *The Vital Center*, 256.

62. Lasch, *The New Radicalism in America*, 289, 306.

63. Schlesinger, *The Vital Center*, 190.

64. For Bertrand Zadig's illustration, see Arthur M. Schlesinger Jr., "Not Left, Not Right, But a Vital Center," *New York Times Magazine*, April 4, 1948, 7. On Ernest Hemingway, see Malcolm Cowley, "A Portrait of Mister Papa," *Life*, January 10, 1949, 93–94.

65. In Hamby's *Beyond The New Deal* (277-281), he suggests that the vital center was "a new liberal self-image," and later stresses that it "was not a new liberal *program*; it was essentially a new *mood*" (Hamby's italics). Reviews of *The Vital Center* mentioned here include Johnson, "In Defense of Liberalism"; Jonathan Daniels, "Ready to Be Radical," *Saturday*

Review of Literature 32, September 10, 1949, 11; Henry Steele Commager, *The New York Herald Tribune Weekly Book Review*, September 11, 1949, 1; S. R. Davis, *The Christian Science Monitor*, September 15, 1949, 15; Robert Bendiner, "Politics and People," *The Nation*, September 17, 1949, 267–269; Donald Derby, *The Springfield Republican*, September 25, 1949, 4. The *Cleveland News* and *Washington Star* are quoted in "Cross-Section," *The New York Times*, October 23, 1949, 8.

Notes to Chapter 2

1. William G. McLoughlin, *Billy Graham: Revivalist in a Secular Age* (New York: Ronald Press, 1960), 111–112; Marshall Frady, *Billy Graham: A Parable of American Righteousness* (Boston: Little Brown, 1979), 238–239; Stephen J. Whitfield, *The Culture of the Cold War* (Baltimore: Johns Hopkins University Press, 1991), 80.
2. McLoughlin, *Billy Graham*, 94–122.
3. On the McCarthyites' status anxieties, see the essays in Daniel Bell, ed., *The Radical Right* (1955; New York: Anchor Books, 1964); see also Richard Hofstadter, *The Paranoid Style in American Politics and Other Essays* (1952; New York: Knopf, 1965), 52. These scholars suggested that the irrational politics of the McCarthyite radical right be understood within the context of the fluidity and mobility of American society, in which issues of status take on a special intensity. Fueling McCarthyism were the "status anxieties" of upwardly mobile immigrant groups, especially German and Irish Americans, who desired status and resented the privileges of the eastern establishment, and of old-stock white Americans who were anxious about losing their status.
4. David Riesman and Nathan Glazer, "The Intellectuals and the Discontented Classes," *The Radical Right*, 118–119.
5. Alistair Cooke, *A Generation on Trial: USA v. Alger Hiss* (Westport, CT: Greenwood Press, 1982); Allen Weinstein, *Perjury: The Hiss-Chambers Case* (New York: Knopf, 1978).
6. Eds., "The Hards and the Softs," *The New Leader* 32 (May 20, 1950): 30–31.
7. Sam Tanenhaus, *Whittaker Chambers: A Biography* (New York: Random House, 1997), 344–345; Weinstein, *Perjury*, 399–400.
8. Tanenhaus, *Whittaker Chambers*, 285, 342–345; 360–364; Weinstein, *Perjury*, 182–184, 377–384; 492–493. On Alsop's role in helping the Hiss defense, see also Tony Hiss, *Laughing Last* (Boston: Houghton Mifflin, 1977), 133–136. Alsop's double life is discussed in Robert W. Merry, *Taking on the World: Joseph and Stuart Alsop, Guardians of the American Century* (New York: Viking, 1996), 360–362.
9. Tanenhaus, *Whittaker Chambers*, 360–362; Weinstein, *Perjury*, 377–384; 492–493. On the FBI's role in intimidating Hobson and Hiss, see Kurt Gentry, *J. Edgar Hoover: The Man and the Secrets* (New York: W. W. Norton, 1991), 363. Hiss's refusal to put Hobson on the witness stand was explained by Hiss partisan William Reuben (interview with the author, May 21, 1991).
10. Weinstein, *Perjury: The Hiss-Chambers Case*, 383–384.
11. Whittaker Chambers, *Witness* (New York: Random House, 1952); Arthur M. Schlesinger Jr., "Whittaker Chambers and His *Witness,*" *Saturday Review*, May 24, 1952, reprinted in Schlesinger, *The Politics of Hope* (Boston: Houghton Mifflin, 1962), 183–195. See also Sidney Blumenthal, "The Cold War and the Closet: The True Legacy of Whittaker Chambers," *New Yorker*, March 17, 1997, 112–115.
12. Quoted in William H. Chafe, *The Unfinished Journey: America Since World War II* (1986; New York: Oxford University Press, 1995), 108. For other surveys of the postwar era, see James T. Patterson, *Grand Expectations: The United States, 1945–1974* (New York: Oxford University Press, 1996) and Godfrey Hodgson, *America in Our Time* (New York: Random House, 1976).
13. For Nixon's rhetoric, see Whitfield, *The Culture of the Cold War*, 28–29; for Butler's, see Patterson, *Grand Expectations*, 200–201.
14. Garry Wills, *Nixon Agonistes: The Crisis of the Self-Made Man* (1969; New York: Signet, 1971), 88–89; Whitfield, *The Culture of the Cold War*, 19.
15. Allen Matusow, ed., *Joseph R. McCarthy* (Englewood Cliffs, NJ: Prentice Hall, 1970), 19–26; Eric Goldman, *The Crucial Decade—and after: America, 1945–1960* (New York: Vintage, 1960), 142.

16. Quotations taken from Richard H. Rovere, *Senator Joe McCarthy* (1959; New York: Harper & Row, 1973), 49; Lawrence S. Wittner, *Cold War America: From Hiroshima to Watergate* (New York: Praeger, 1974), 95–99; Thomas C. Reeves, *The Life and Times of Joe McCarthy: A Biography* (New York: Stein & Day, 1982), 299; David Halberstam, *The Fifties* (New York: Villard, 1993), 54.

17. Richard M. Weaver, "The Roots of Liberal Complacency," *The National Review* (June 8, 1957), reprinted in A. G. Heinsohn, *Anthology of Conservative Writing in the United States* (Chicago: Henry Regnery Company, 1962), 54–58.

18. Ibid. For a conservative interpretation of the liberal "guilt complexes" and dangerously naïve "social service mentality" of do-gooders like Eleanor Roosevelt, see James Burnham, *Suicide of the West: The Meaning and Destiny of American Liberalism* (New York; John Day Company, 1964).

19. Louis Bromfield, "The Triumph of the Egghead," *Freeman*, December 1, 1952, 155-158. The term "egghead" was coined by journalist Stuart Alsop, who applied it not in a pejorative sense but rather to denote the intelligentsia, that is, Stevenson's likely basis of popular support in the 1952 presidential race. "Egghead" became an epithet used by conservatives to ridicule Stevenson and his supporters, whose points of view were supposedly "out of touch" with the sentiments of most ordinary Americans. For another caustic view of the egghead, see A. G. Heinsohn, "Eggheads Adrift," in Heinsohn, *Anthology of Conservative Writing*, 28–30.

20. E. Merrill Root, "The Quicksands of the Mind," reprinted in Heinsohn, *Anthology of Conservative Writing*, 283–290.

21. John D'Emilio, *Sexual Politics, Sexual Communities: The Making of a Homosexual Minority in the United States, 1940–1970* (Chicago: University of Chicago Press, 1983), 40–53; D'Emilio, "The Homosexual Menace: The Politics of Sexuality in Cold War America," in D'Emilio, ed., *Making Trouble: Essays on Gay History, Politics and the University* (New York: Routledge, 1992), 57–73. For a more recent discussion, see Robert D. Dean, *Imperial Brotherhood: Gender and the Making of Cold War Foreign Policy* (Amherst: University of Massachusetts Press, 2001), 76–96.

22. D'Emilio, *Sexual Politics, Sexual Communities*, 41–42; "Inquiry by Senate on Perverts Asked," *New York Times*, May 20, 1950, 8; "Senators Find Homos a Peril, Ask Full Probe," *New York Daily News*, May 20, 1950, 2. Wherry is quoted in Max Lerner, "'Scandal' in the State Dept. XI: Sex and Politics," *New York Post*, July 21, 1950, 2. On the dubious mathematical calculations that led Blick to estimate the number of "sex perverts" in Washington, see Lerner, "'Scandal' in the State Dept. VIII: Blick of the Vice Squad," *New York Post*, July 18, 1950, 2.

23. Bridges's speech is quoted in John O'Donnell, "Capital Stuff," *New York Daily News*, March 30, 1950, 6. Robert Davies, former ambassador to the Soviet Union, portrayed the USSR in a favorable light and seemed to rationalize Stalin's crimes in *Mission to Moscow* (New York: Simon & Schuster, 1941).

24. Reeves, *The Life and Times of Joe McCarthy*, 240, 257. Dean (*Imperial Brotherhood*, 104–105) has provided the fullest account of the purge of homosexuals from the federal government to date; he identifies Carmel Offie as the CIA official whom McCarthy "outed."

25. See John O'Donnell's columns, "Capitol Stuff," *New York Daily News*, March 27, 1950, 4; March 30, 1950, 5; May 1, 1950, 6; May 5, 1950, 6; May 7, 1950, 4; Lerner, "'Scandal' in the State Dept. XI: Sex and Politics," 2. Lillian M. Oliveros, letter to the editor, *New York Daily News*, March 29, 1950, 4.

26. U.S. Congress, Senate, Committee on Expenditures in the Executive Departments, *Employment of Homosexuals and Other Sex Perverts in Government*, 81st Cong., 2nd sess., November 27, 1950 (Washington, DC: U.S. Government Printing Office, 1950) 2–5, 19.

27. Ibid., 2–4.

28. Ibid., 3–5; D'Emilio, *Sexual Politics, Sexual Communities*, 43.

29. For the full text of Miller's speech, see *Congressional Record* (U.S. Congress, *Appendix to the Congressional Record—House*, 81st Cong., 2nd sess., May 15, 1950, A3660-A3662). Miller is also quoted in Jack Lait and Lee Mortimer, *Washington Confidential* (New York: Crown Books, 1951), 91–96.

30. Ibid. On Wherry, see Lerner, "'Scandal in the State Dept., IV: Kinsey in Washington," *New York Post*, July 13, 1950, 2, 26. See also "Senators Find Homos a Peril, Ask Full Probe," 2.

31. On Dewey, see "TRUMAN 'FARO DEAL' DERIDED BY DEWEY," *New York Times*, May 5, 1950, 1, 15; O'Donnell, "Capitol Stuff," *New York Daily News*, March 27, 1950, 4. The quotation from the *Brooklyn Tablet* (June 10, 1950) is taken from Donald F. Crosby, *God, Church and Flag: Senator Joseph R. McCarthy and the Catholic Church* (Chapel Hill: University of North Carolina Press, 1978), 3.

32. On the Welles episode, see Gentry, *J. Edgar Hoover*, 308–310; Irwin Gellman, *Secret Affairs: Franklin Roosevelt, Cordell Hull and Sumner Welles* (Baltimore: Johns Hopkins University Press, 1995).

33. Dean, *Imperial Brotherhood*, 97–145, esp. 121. On the randy atmosphere of the Moscow mission and George Kennan's sexually charged rhetoric describing it, see Frank Costigliola, "'Unceasing Pressure for Penetration': Gender, Pathology, and Emotion in George Kennan's Formation of the Cold War," *Journal of American History* 83 (March 1997): 1309–1339.

34. Max Lerner, "The Washington Sex Story I: Panic on the Potomac," *New York Post*, July 10, 1950, 4; Lerner, "'Scandal' in the State Dept. XII: What Can Be Done About It?" *New York Post*, July 22, 1950, 4, 20; Lerner, "'Scandal' in the State Dept. IX: They Never Appeal," *New York Post*, July 19, 1950, 4, 38.

35. Lerner, "The Washington Sex Story I: Panic on the Potomac," 4; Lerner, "'Scandal' in the State Dept. IV: Kinsey in Washington," 2; Lerner, "'Scandal' in the State Dept. XII: What Can Be Done About It?" 4 (Lerner's italics).

36. Lerner, "'Scandal' in the State Dept. VII: Wherry's Crusade," *New York Post*, July 17, 1950, 2, 20; Lerner, "'Scandal' in the State Dept. V: The Problem of Blackmail," *New York Post*, July 14, 1950, 2, 24; Lerner, "'Scandal' in the State Dept. VI: Are Homosexuals Security Risks?" *New York Post*, July 16, 1950, 2, 7.

37. Lerner, "'Scandal' in the State Dept. VI: Are Homosexuals Security Risks?" 2, 7.

38. Lerner, "Washington Sex Story I: Panic on the Potomac," 4, 24; Lerner, "'Scandal' in the State Dept. II: the Scientists Speak," *New York Post*, July 11, 1950, 2; Lerner, "'Scandal' in the State Dept. XII: What Can Be Done About It?", 4, 20.

39. Lerner, "'Scandal' in the State Dept. XI: Sex and Politics," 2.

40. Joseph and Stuart Alsop, "Why Has Washington Gone Crazy?" *Saturday Evening Post*, July 29, 1950, 20–21; Edwin R. Bayley, *Joe McCarthy and the Press* (Madison: University of Wisconsin, 1981), 161–162; Dean, *Imperial Brotherhood*, 93.

41. Merry, *Taking on the World*, 215–216; Bayley, *Joe McCarthy and the Press*, 161–162; Edwin M. Yoder, *Joe Alsop's Cold War: A Study of Journalistic Influence and Intrigue* (Chapel Hill: University of North Carolina Press, 1995), 156. The full text of McCarthy's letter appears in the *Congressional Record—Senate*, 81st Cong., 2nd sess., August 8, 1950, 1278.

42. Leslie Gelb, "The Ultimate Insider," *New York Times Book Review* (April 2, 1995), 6. O'Donnell ("Capitol Stuff," *New York Daily News*, March 27, 1950, 4) notes that, prior to the sex scandal, Washington correspondents had long used "polite euphemisms" ("cookie pushers," "striped-pants boys," "precious dilettantes") to denote homosexuals in the diplomatic corps. On the Alsops' subsequent relationship to the *Saturday Evening Post*, see Merry, *Taking on the World*, 217.

43. On Robert Kennedy, see Peter Collier and David Horowitz, *The Kennedys: An American Drama* (New York: Summit Books, 1984), 248. On Roy Cohn, see Nicholas von Hoffman, *Citizen Cohn: The Life and Times of Roy Cohn* (New York: Doubleday, 1988).

44. Joseph McCarthy, *McCarthyism: The Fight for America* (New York: Devin-Adair, 1952), 14–15, 23–24.

45. Arthur M. Schlesinger Jr., *The Vital Center: The Politics of Freedom* (1949; New Brunswick, NJ: Transaction, 1998), 166; Demaree Bess, "Why Americans Hate the State Department," *Saturday Evening Post*, August 19, 1950, 22; Lait and Mortimer, *Washington Confidential*, 9–11, 90-97. Alan Dunn's cartoon appeared in *The New Yorker*, June 17, 1950, 21.

46. Dean, *Imperial Brotherhood*, 119–145; Gentry, *J. Edgar Hoover*, 436; David M. Oshinsky, *A Conspiracy So Immense: The World of Joe McCarthy* (New York: Free Press, 1983), 287–293.

47. Dean, *Imperial Brotherhood*, 63–167, esp. 96. See also Charles E. Bohlen, *Witness to History, 1929–1969* (New York: W. W. Norton, 1973).

48. Dean, *Imperial Brotherhood*, 97–145.

49. D'Emilio, *Sexual Politics, Sexual Communities*, 44–46; Dean, *Imperial Brotherhood*, 66.

50. On the tale of the Austrian officer, see Dean, *Imperial Brotherhood*, 86. On the Prince Eulenburg affair, see R. G. Waldeck, "The Homosexual International," *Human Events*, April 16, 1952, 1; Waldeck's article appears in the *Appendix to the Congressional Record*—House, 82nd Cong., 2nd Sess., May 1, 1952, A2652–2654. Waldeck's article is also excerpted, with a brief introduction by Martin B. Duberman, in "The International Homosexual Conspiracy," *The New York Native*, September 21, 1981, 12. See also James D. Steakley, "Iconography of a Scandal: Political Cartoons and the Eulenburg Affair in Wilhelmin Germany," in Martin B. Duberman, Martha Vicinus, and George Chauncey Jr., eds., *Hidden from History: Reclaiming the Gay and Lesbian Past* (New York: Meridian, 1989), 233–257.

51. Merry, *Taking on the World*, 360-363; Yoder, *Joe Alsop's Cold War*, 153–158.

52. Richard Hofstadter, *Anti-Intellectualism in American Life* (New York: Vintage, 1963), 41–42.

53. On the "drift toward sex anarchy," see Pitirim A. Sorokin, *The American Sex Revolution* (Boston: Porter Sargent, 1956), 66, 137.

54. Waldeck, "The Homosexual International," *Appendix to the Congressional Record*—House, 82nd Cong., 2nd sess., May 1, 1952, A2652-2654.

55. Ibid.

56. Sorokin, *The American Sex Revolution*, 114–111; see also D'Emilio, *Sexual Politics, Sexual Communities*, 59. For Koestler's opinion, see Arthur Koestler, et. al., *The God that Failed: Six Studies in Communism* (London: Hamish Hamilton, 1950), 55–56.

57. On national security and secret "cells" of homosexuals, see Dean, *Imperial Brotherhood*, 97–113. Waldeck, "The Homosexual International," *Appendix to Congressional Record*, A2652–2654.

58. Riesman and Glazer, "The Intellectuals and the Discontented Classes," *Radical Right*, 118–119.

59. Michael Rogin, *Ronald Reagan, the Movie: And Other Episodes in Political Demonology* (Berkeley: University of California Press, 1987), xiii, 236-237.

60. This sexual inquisition coincided with what George Chauncey Jr., in "The Postwar Sex Crime Panic," in *True Stories from the American Past*, William Graebner, ed. (New York: McGraw Hill, 1993), 160–178, has called the "postwar sex crime panic," which peaked in 1949–1950 and had the effect of heightening homophobia in American life. Though the most serious of sex crimes involving rape, pedophilia, gruesome violence, and murder were no more statistically prevalent in the late forties and fifties than they were in years past, sensational stories proliferated, featuring psychopathic homosexuals as murderous perverts and pedophiles menacing the nation. As the *New York Daily News* ran stories about the "homo scandal" in the State Department in mid-1950, it also ran a special feature headlined "Are Sex Criminals on a Rampage?" (May 14, 1950, 6) that called attention to a seeming national epidemic in sex crimes. Also see "The Abnormal," *Time*, April 17, 1950, 86.

61. Riesman and Glazer, "The Intellectuals and the Discontented Classes," *The Radical Right*, 118–119. In the 1950s, many scholars, medical professionals and social critics assumed male homosexuality was on the rise. See for example, Abram Kardiner, *Sex and Morality* (New York: Bobbs-Merrill, 1954), 160–164; Ralph H. Major, "New to Our Youth," *Coronet*, September 1950, 101–108. The phrase "epidemic" was used, for example, by Frank S. Caprio, *The Sexually Adequate Male* (Greenwich, CT: Fawcett, 1952), 173. For an analysis of "experts'" perspectives on sexual deviance, see Estelle B. Freedman, "'Uncontrolled Desires': The Response to the Sexual Psychopath, 1920–1960," *Journal of American History* 74 (June 1987): 83–106.

62. John D'Emilio and Estelle B. Freedman, *Intimate Matters: A History of Sexuality in America* (New York: Harper & Row, 1988), 288–291; D'Emilio, *Sexual Politics, Sexual Communities*; Alan Berube, *Coming Out under Fire: The History of Gay Men and Women in World War Two* (New York: Free Press, 1990).

63. D'Emilio, *Sexual Politics, Sexual Communities*, 76, 124. According to D'Emilio, the Daughters of Bilitis, the lesbian counterpart to the Mattachine Society formed in 1953, was also subject to FBI surveillance and infiltration in the 1950s.

64. Richard Gid Powers, *Secrecy and Power: The Life of J. Edgar Hoover* (New York: Free Press, 1987), 288–289 and J. Edgar Hoover, *Masters of Deceit: The Story of Communism in America and How to Fight It* (New York: Henry Holt, 1958), 103–105.

65. In addition to Gentry, see Athan Theoharis, *J. Edgar Hoover, Sex and Crime: An Historical Antidote* (New York: Ivan Dee, 1995). For allegations that Hoover was gay, and Hoover's

anger at the Mattachine Society (which put all head of federal agencies on its mailing list), see Anthony Summers, *Official and Confidential: The Secret Life of J. Edgar Hoover* (New York: G.P. Putnam's Sons, 1993), 84, 93.

66. On the FBI surveillance of Roosevelt and Hoover's perception that she had protected Welles due to his "softness" toward the Communist party, see Gentry, *J. Edgar Hoover*, 299–306, 310, 390–391. For Hoover's comment about why he never married, see Summers, *Official and Confidential*, 142–150.

67. Lait and Mortimer, *Washington Confidential*, 90–98, 144–154.

68. Ibid., 9–11, 90–106. According to one legend, Georgetown had acquired such an unsavory reputation as the home of "effete" left-wing bohemianism (a reputation no doubt encouraged by *Washington Confidential*) that when Republicans came to Washington after Eisenhower's election, they shied away from the disreputable Georgetown neighborhood. The new President himself reportedly "warned his top officials to stay away from the trendy enclave." Merry, *Taking on the World*, 242.

69. Mortimer and Lait, *Washington Confidential*, 92, 100–103.

70. For an interesting look at the scandal magazines of the era that exploited cold war anxieties and presented lurid images of Communists, homosexuals, criminals, perverts and spies, see Barbara Epstein, "Anti-Communism, Homophobia, and the Construction of Masculinity in the Postwar U.S.," *Critical Sociology* 20, no. 3 (1994): 21–44.

71. John McPartland, "Portrait of an American Communist," *Life*, January 5, 1948, 75, 77.

72. John Kosa, *Two Generations of Soviet Man: A Study in the Psychology of Communism* (Chapel Hill: University of North Carolina, 1962), 155. Herbert E. Krugman's "The Interplay of Social and Psychological Factors in Political Deviance" (PhD dissertation, University of Michigan, Ann Arbor, 1952), 99–102, made more direct correlations between Communism, neurosis, and sexual perversity. Krugman, researcher and collaborator with a noted scholar of Communism, Gabriel Almond, compiled "psychoanalytic data" on Communist party members which purported to show that the typical Communist showed signs of passivity, emotionalism, neurosis, and "sexual deviance." The data he compiled included statistics showing the incidence of latent and manifest homosexuality among party members and the corresponding presence of weak fathers and overbearing mothers in the families of Communists. He concluded that "'homosexual' weakness" and the complex of neuroses that underlay it was one source of the party member's "hostility to society" and thus a source of the psychological appeal of Communism. Murray Kempton, in *Part of Our Time: Some Ruins and Monuments of the Thirties* (New York: Simon & Schuster, 1955), 200, cited Krugman's study to explain the emotional problems of "red spy queen"–turned-informant Elizabeth Bentley. On Bentley and the stereotype she came to represent, see Kathryn S. Olmsted, *Red Spy Queen: A Biography of Elizabeth Bentley* (Chapel Hill: University of North Carolina Press, 2002), 135.

73. Elizabeth Janeway, "Why They Become Communists," *New York Times Magazine*, June 14, 1953, 13. On the neurosis of Communists, see Robert M. Lindner, *Must You Conform?* (New York: Holt, Rinehart and Winston, 1956), 86–88; Gabriel A. Almond, with Herbert E. Krugman, Elsbeth Lewin, and Howard Wriggins, *The Appeals of Communism* (Princeton: Princeton University Press, 1954). For an example of government-issue archetypes of Communist recruits, see the journal published by the Office of Armed Forces Information and Education, Department of Defense, *Know Your Communist Enemy* (Washington, DC: Government Printing Office, February 23, 1955), 7–8. On the explanation of Communist psychology offered by the fictional Mike Hammer, see Mickey Spillane, *One Lonely Night*, (New York: E. P. Dutton, 1951), 171–172.

74. Morris L. Ernst and David Loth, *Report on the American Communist* (New York: Henry Holt, 1952), 7, 127, 162–163.

75. Ibid., 162–165, 180. On Bentley's view of Raissa Browder and the report on the Rosenbergs, see Ellen Schrecker, *Many Are the Crimes: McCarthyism in America* (Boston: Little Brown, 1988), 147. Gentry, noting that the same suspicions of female dominance and malevolence were held about Priscilla Hiss, suggested that Hoover assumed that "behind every bad man . . . was an even worse woman" (*J. Edgar Hoover*, 366).

76. Julie Whitney, "Women: Russia's Second Class Citizens," *Look*, November 30, 1954, 114; Gertrude Samuels, "Why Russian Women Work Like Men," *New York Times Magazine*, November 2, 1958, 23; Elaine Tyler May, *Homeward Bound: American Families in the Cold War Era* (New York: Basic Books, 1988), 19.

77. Jack Lait and Lee Mortimer, *USA Confidential* (New York: Crown, 1952), 2, 46–53; Rogin, "Kiss Me Deadly," in *Ronald Reagan, the Movie*, 236–271.

78. Richard Condon, *The Manchurian Candidate* (1959; New York: Jove Books, 1988); *The Manchurian Candidate*, dir. John Frankenheimer, prod. George Axelrod and John Frankenheimer (United Artists, 1962).

79. Rogin, "Kiss Me Deadly," 252–253. The Kennedy administration's interest in "psywar" and counterinsurgency is discussed in chapter 4 of this book. While Kennedy wanted to "breathe new life into the cold war," as Rogin suggests (253), he and his New Frontiersmen were interested in battling Communist expansion *outside* of the U.S., seeking popular support by emphasizing the perils of a world in which nuclear annihilation loomed in our "hour of maximum danger." Domestic anti-Communist infiltration was no longer an issue.

80. Fredric Wertham, *Seduction of the Innocent* (New York: Rinehart, 1954); Vance Packard, *The Hidden Persuaders* (New York: D. McKay, 1969). On the "brainwashed" Korean War POWS, see Adam J. Zweiback, "The '21 Turncoat GIs': Nonrepatriations and the Political Culture of the Korean War," *Historian* 60 (Winter 1998): 345–363; "Korea: The Sorriest Bunch," *Newsweek*, February 8, 1954, 40. Journalist and former OSS officer Edward Hunter coined the term "brainwashing" in *Brain-washing in Red China: The Calculated Destruction of Men's Minds* (New York: Vanguard, 1951). See also Michael S. Sherry, *In the Shadow of War: The United States Since the 1930s* (New Haven: Yale University Press, 1995), 186.

81. McLoughlin, *Billy Graham*, 5, 54, 85, 90, 139–140; Whitfield, *The Culture of the Cold War*, 78.

82. McLoughlin, *Billy Graham*, 80–86.

83. Ibid.

84. Alfred C. Kinsey et al., *Sexual Behavior in the Human Male* (Philadelphia: W. B. Saunders, 1948), 550–555, 585, 597, 650–651.

85. For Lionel Trilling's critique of the Kinsey Report, see Trilling, *The Liberal Imagination* (New York: Doubleday, 1953), 216–235. For the *Reader's Digest* symposium involving Norman Vincent Peale, see "Must We Change Our Standards?" *Reader's Digest*, June 1948, 1–6. For further commentary, see Erdman Palmore, "Kinsey Received," in *The American Sexual Dilemma*, William L. O'Neill, ed. (New York: Holt, Rinehart and Winston, 1972), 63–71; Morris L. Ernst and David Loth, *American Sexual Behavior and the Kinsey Report* (New York: Greystone, 1948); Wardell B. Pomeroy, *Dr. Kinsey and the Institute for Sex Research* (New Haven: Yale University Press, 1982). For a summary of responses to Kinsey's work, including Reinhold Niebuhr's critique and the *Catholic Mind* editorial, see James H. Jones, *Alfred C. Kinsey: A Public/Private Life* (New York: W. W. Norton, 1997), 576–578, 632, 720–721.

86. Jones, *Alfred C. Kinsey*, 712, 720; Alfred C. Kinsey, et al., *Sexual Behavior in the Human Female* (1953; Philadelphia: W. B. Saunders, 1965), 233, 286, 416, 474–475, 499.

87. Jones, *Alfred C. Kinsey*, 712–713; Halberstam, *The Fifties*, 280.

88. Jones, *Alfred C. Kinsey*, 723–724; Whitfield, *The Culture of the Cold War*, 185–186.

89. Billy Graham, "The Sin of Tolerance," Concerned Clergy and Laity of the Episcopal Church, Online Publications, June 2004. http://www.episcopalian.org/cclec/publications. htm.

90. Jones, *Alfred C. Kinsey*, 701–737.

91. Patterson, *Grand Expectations*, 358–360.

92. Bell, "Interpretations of American Politics," *The Radical Right*, 64.

93. Patterson, *Grand Expectations*, 252–255; Halberstam, *The Fifties*, 219–233; Whitfield, *The Culture of the Cold War*, 44; Oshinsky, *A Conspiracy So Immense*, 242.

94. The *New York Daily News* is quoted in Hofstadter, *Anti-Intellectualism in American Life*, 227.

95. Wittner, *Cold War America*, 108; Rovere, *Senator Joe McCarthy*, 49.

96. Wittner, *Cold War America*, 108; Oshinsky, *A Conspiracy So Immense*, 242; "Ike Charges Treason in Coddling of Reds," *New York Daily News*, October 4, 1952, 3; "Khaki in White House Better'n Pink," *New York Daily News*, October 10, 1952, 3.

97. Stevenson is quoted in Goldman, *The Crucial Decade*, 222; Hofstadter, *Anti-Intellectualism in American Life*, 224; Alonzo Hamby, *Beyond the New Deal: Harry S. Truman and American Liberalism* (New York: Columbia University Press, 1973), 503.

98. Rudolph Field, *Ike: Man of the Hour* (New York: Universal, 1952), 28–29.

99. Quotes are found in Hofstadter, *Anti-Intellectualism in American Life*, 226–227; Patterson, *Grand Expectations*, 255.

100. On Alsop's reaction, see Merry, *Taking on the World*, 234. The speech was derided by the pro-McCarthy *New York Daily News*, which noted that "when a man takes to likening himself to the savior, it is logical to assume that he at least has delusions of grandeur, and may be a religious fanatic who could prove dangerous in high public office." This excerpt from Stevenson's speech and the *Daily News* response is quoted in Herbert J. Muller, *Adlai Stevenson: A Study in Values* (New York: Harper & Row, 1967), 88–89.

101. Marquis Childs, *Witness to Power* (New York: McGraw Hill, 1975), 66–69; Gentry, *J. Edgar Hoover*, 402–403. In Gentry's account, McCarthy was prevented from using "gutter language" against Stevenson on that occasion because the Democrats had ammunition of their own—a copy of a letter written by General George Marshall to Eisenhower, which made reference to Eisenhower's plans to divorce his wife Mamie and marry his WAC driver—which they threatened to make public.

102. Gentry, *J. Edgar Hoover*, 402–403. Gentry also notes that the FBI sought out and investigated Stevenson's evidently emotionally distraught ex-wife, who was known to tell people that her former husband was a homosexual, had numerous affairs with women, and had once murdered someone.

103. Athan Theoharis, "'Operation Adlai/Adeline': How the FBI Gaybaited Stevenson," *The Nation*, May 7, 1990, 1; Summers, *Official and Confidential*, 181–182. According to Theoharis and Gentry, Hoover also spread the rumor that Stevenson was a "notorious homosexual" to members of the Kennedy administration, and forwarded Stevenson's FBI file to the Kennedy White House.

104. Hofstadter, *Anti-Intellectualism in American Life*, 227.

105. Ibid., 4; Bromfield, "The Triumph of the Egghead," 155–158; Muller, *Adlai Stevenson*, 191–193.

106. Arthur M. Schlesinger Jr., "The Highbrow in American Politics," *Partisan Review* 20 (March–April 1953): 162–165, reprinted in Schlesinger, *The Politics of Hope*, 219–229.

107. Oliver Pilat and William V. Shannon, "Smear, Inc.: The One-Man Mob of Joe McCarthy," *New York Post*, September 4, 1951, 3; Oshinsky, *A Conspiracy So Immense*, 310–311.

108. Hank Greenspun, "Where I Stand," *Las Vegas Sun*, October 25, 1952; Oshinsky, *A Conspiracy So Immense*, 310–311, Gentry, *J. Edgar Hoover*, 432–434. In Gentry's account, Greenspun's grudge against McCarthy stemmed from the senator's comments on a Las Vegas radio show in which the McCarthy called Greenspun an "ex-Communist." Greenspun took great offense, insisting he was no ex-Communist—only an ex-convict, having been convicted for smuggling arms to Israel. McCarthy later retracted the comment, claiming that he meant to say Greenspun was an "ex-convict."

109. Joseph and Stewart Alsop, "McCarthy-Cohn-Schine Tale Was Half Told," *Washington Post*, March 15, 1954. Hellman, herself a victim of HUAC, is quoted in Hoffman, *Citizen Cohn*, 185.

110. Oshinsky, *A Conspiracy So Immense*, 427, 451. During the hearings, the subject was raised of a doctored photograph, presumably cropped by McCarthy's staff, showing Schine with a smiling Army Secretary Robert Stevens—at a time when the latter was claiming he had in fact been angry with the McCarthy staff because of its demands for privileged treatment of Schine. Army counsel Joseph Welch asked sarcastically if a "pixie" (which he defined as a "close relative to a fairy") was responsible for the mysterious change in the original photo; to this sly innuendo about Cohn and Schine, McCarthy responded to Welch, "I think you might be an authority on what a pixie is."

111. The innuendoes still followed Stevenson in the 1956 election. Walter Winchell announced to his Mutual Radio audience that "a vote for Adlai Stevenson is a vote for Christine Jorgensen," the first well-known recipient of a sex-change operation. Winchell's remark left sponsors uneasy, and actually cost him his first television show (Gentry, *J. Edgar Hoover*, 445).

Notes to Chapter 3

1. For the classic analysis American conformity in the age of affluence, see David Riesman with Nathan Glazer and Reuel Denney, *The Lonely Crowd: A Study of the Changing American Character* (1950; New Haven: Yale University Press, 1965).

2. For an explication and critique of the concept of mass society, see Daniel Bell, "America as a Mass Society: A Critique," in *The End of Ideology: On the Exhaustion of Political Ideas in the Fifties* (1960; Cambridge: Harvard University Press, 1988), 21–38.

3. Wilhelm Reich, *The Mass Psychology of Fascism* (New York: Simon & Schuster, 1933); Theodor W. Adorno, et. al., *The Authoritarian Personality* (New York: Harper & Row, 1950).

4. Theodor W. Adorno, *The Culture Industry* (New York: Routledge, 2001).

5. Erich Fromm, *Escape from Freedom* (1941; New York: Avon Books, 1965); Fromm, *Man for Himself: An Inquiry into the Psychology of Ethics* (New York: Rinehart and Company, 1947).

6. Fromm, *Escape From Freedom*, 19–20, 155; John Dewey, *Freedom and Culture* (New York: Putnam, 1939), 49.

7. When Reich asked why Europeans turned toward fascism rather than socialism, he noted that Marxism had no real understanding of mass psychology. Reich, *The Mass Psychology of Fascism*, 5, xxiv.

8. Paul Tillich, *The Courage to Be* (New Haven: Yale University Press, 1952), 35.

9. Tillich, *The Courage to Be*, 49, 62.

10. Rollo May, *Man's Search for Himself* (New York: W. W. Norton, 1953), 223–224. Also see May, *The Meaning of Anxiety* (1950; New York, W. W. Norton, 1977).

11. W. H. Auden, *The Age of Anxiety: A Baroque Eclogue* (New York: Random House, 1947); Dale Carnegie, *How to Stop Worrying and Start Living* (New York: Simon & Schuster, 1948). The other self-help books are listed in Richard H. Pells, *The Liberal Mind in a Conservative Age: American Intellectuals in the 1940s and 1950s* (Middletown: Wesleyan University Press, 1985), 190. On Americans, mental health and tranquilizers, see William E. Leuchtenburg, *A Troubled Feast: American Society Since 1945* (Boston: Little Brown, 1979), 104. On the survey assessing Americans' "anxiety neurosis," see Samuel A. Stouffer, *Communism, Conformity and Civil Liberties: A Cross-Section of the Nation Speaks Its Mind* (1955; New Brunswick, NJ: Transaction, 1992), 58–88.

12. Herbert Gold's essay "The Age of Happy Problems" first appeared in *The Atlantic Monthly* (March 1957) 58–61, and is reprinted in *The Age of Happy Problems* (New York: Dial Press, 1962), 3-13.

13. Josselyn is quoted in *Look* eds., *The Decline of the American Male* (New York: Random House, 1958), 24.

14. Riesman, *The Lonely Crowd*, 3–35, 21.

15. Ibid., 3-83, esp. 16, 26, 49.

16. Ibid.

17. Ibid., 79; Erich Fromm, *Man for Himself*, 77–78.

18. Riesman, *The Lonely Crowd*, 71; William H. Whyte, *The Organization Man* (1956; New York: Anchor Books, 1957).

19. Whyte, *The Organization Man*, 7, 3-15.

20. Ibid., 44, 440.

21. Ibid., 13, 166–169.

22. Ibid., 14, 34–35.

23. Riesman, *The Lonely Crowd*, 18–19 (Riesman's italics).

24. Pells, *The Liberal Mind in a Conservative Age*, 248.

25. Arthur Koestler, et. al., *The God that Failed: Six Studies in Communism* (London: Hamish Hamilton, 1950), 25–26, 39.

26. Murray Kempton, *Part of Our Time: Some Ruins and Monuments of the Thirties* (New York: Simon & Schuster, 1955), 220, 319–334 (Kempton's italics). Herbert E. Krugman, in "The Interplay of Social and Psychological Factors in Political Deviance" (PhD dissertation, University of Michigan, 1952), 99–102, suggested that among the many maladjusted people attracted to the Communist party were romantically needy women.

27. Kempton, *Part of Our Time*, 319–334.

28. Ibid.

29. Ibid; Harold Rosenberg, "Couch Liberalism and the Guilty Past," *Dissent* (Autumn 1955): 317–328.

30. Pells, *The Liberal Mind in a Conservative Age*, 273–275. Fiedler "Hiss, Chambers and the Age of Innocence," reprinted in *An End to Innocence: Essays on Culture and Politics* (1955; Boston: Beacon Press, 1957), 3-24.

31. Fiedler, *An End to Innocence*, 3-24.
32. Fiedler, "Afterthoughts on the Rosenbergs," reprinted in Fiedler, *An End of Innocence*, 25–45.
33. Robert Warshow, "The 'Idealism' of Julius and Ethel Rosenberg: 'The Kind of People We Are,'" *Commentary* (November 1953): 413–418; Julius and Ethel Rosenberg, *Death House Letters* (New York: Jero Publishing, 1953).
34. Andrew Ross, *No Respect: Intellectuals and Popular Culture* (New York: Routledge, 1989), 15–41; Morris Dickstein, *The Gates of Eden: American Culture in the Sixties* (New York: Basic Books, 1977), 41–45; Pells, *The Liberal Mind in a Conservative Age*, 278–279. On public perceptions of Ethel Rosenberg, see Ilene Philipson, *Ethel Rosenberg: Beyond the Myths* (New York: Franklin Watts, 1988), 4; Ellen Schrecker, *Many Are the Crimes: McCarthyism in America* (Boston: Little Brown, 1998), 147.
35. Rosenberg, "Couch Liberalism and the Guilty Past," 327 (Rosenberg's italics).
36. Robert M. Lindner, *Must You Conform?* (New York: Grove Press, 1956), 22–23, 80–101.
37. Ibid., 23, 100–101, 177; Robert M. Lindner, *Prescription for Rebellion* (New York: Grove Press, 1952), 193.
38. Also see Robert M. Lindner, *Rebel without a Cause: The Story of a Criminal Psychopath* (New York: Grove Press, 1944); Lindner, *The Fifty Minute Hour: A Collection of True Pscyhoanalytic Tales* (New York: Bantam, 1958).
39. Tillich, *The Courage to Be*, 86–112, esp. 104, 112 (Italics mine).
40. Ibid., 112.
41. Pells, *The Liberal Mind in a Conservative Age*, 247.
42. Bell, *The End of Ideology*, 16–17.
43. David Riesman, *Individualism Reconsidered and Other Essays* (New York: Free Press, 1954), 27.
44. Barbara Ehrenreich, *The Hearts of Men: American Dreams and the Flight from Commitment* (New York: Doubleday, 1983), 32–35.
45. Ibid (Ehrenreich's italics).
46. Riesman, *Individualism Reconsidered,* 35, 118; Whyte, *The Organization Man*, 12–14.
47. Whyte, *The Organization Man*, 14–17; Riesman, *The Lonely Crowd*, 18, 115–116, 131.
48. Riesman, *The Lonely Crowd,* 38–55; Riesman, *Individualism Reconsidered*, 27. Riesman's "boys can be boys" comment is quoted in a 1958 article by J. Robert Moskin, "The American Male: Why Do Women Dominate Him?" reprinted in *Look* eds., *The Decline of the American Male*, 4.
49. Riesman, *The Lonely Crowd*, 154–156.
50. Ibid.
51. Adlai E. Stevenson, Smith College Commencement Address, June 6, 1955. Class of 1955. Commencement Speaker, AES, Box 2199, Smith College Archives.
52. Ibid.
53. Ibid.
54. Ibid.
55. Ibid.
56. George B. Leonard Jr., "Why is He Afraid to Be Different?," in *Look* eds., *The Decline of the American Male*, 25–48.
57. Ibid.
58. Moskin, "Why Do Women Dominate Him?" 3–24.
59. Ibid.
60. Ibid.
61. Ibid.
62. Claude C. Bowman, "Are Husbands Slaves to Women?" *Coronet*, April 1950, 111–114; William Attwood, "Why Does He Work So Hard?" in *Look* eds., *The Decline of the American Male*, 49–66. On the heightened concern in the 1950s and 1960s about male stress and resulting heart attacks and other maladies, see Ehrenreich, *Hearts of Men*, 68–87.
63. Philip Wylie, *Generation of Vipers* (New York: Farrar and Rinehart, 1942), 48–51, 184–204. On Wylie's life, see Truman Frederick Keefer's biography, *Philip Wylie* (Boston: Twayne Publishers, 1977). For Wylie's assessment of the historical consequences of decades of momism, see Wylie, *Sons and Daughters of Mom* (New York: Doubleday, 1971).
64. Wylie, *Generation of Vipers*, 50, 184–204.

65. Geoffrey Gorer, *The American People: A Study in National Character* (New York: W. W. Norton, 1948), 50–69, 85–86, 94.

66. Wylie, *Generation of Vipers*, 190–191.

67. Philip Wylie, "The Abdicating Male . . . and How The Gray Flannel Mind Exploits Him Through His Women," *Playboy*, November 1956, 29. Also see Wylie, "The Womanization of America," *Playboy*, September 1958, 52.

68. On the paternity suit against Wylie, see Keefer, *Philip Wylie*, 33.

69. David M. Levy, *Maternal Overprotection* (New York: Columbia University Press, 1943); Edward Strecker, *Their Mothers' Sons: The Psychiatrist Examines an American Problem* (Philadelphia: Lippincott, 1946).

70. Strecker, *Their Mothers' Sons*, 30–31, 212–220.

71. Ralph Wentworth-Rohr, "Momism," in J. E. Fairchild, ed., *Women, Sex and Society* (1956; New York: Sheridan House, 1962), 101–110. Articles in this book were originally delivered as lectures at the Cooper Union Forum in New York City.

72. Max Lerner, *America as a Civilization: Life and Thought in the United States Today* (New York: Simon & Schuster, 1957), 556–557.

73. Erikson is quoted in Barbara Ehrenreich and Deirdre English, *For Her Own Good: 150 Years of the Experts' Advice to Women* (1963; New York: Doubleday, 1978), 237; Betty Friedan, *The Feminine Mystique* (New York: Doubleday, 1984), 273–276, 285–287.

74. William H. Chafe, *The American Woman: Her Changing Social, Economic and Political Roles, 1920–1970* (London: Oxford University Press, 1972), 214–215.

75. Michael Rogin, "Kiss Me Deadly," in *Ronald Reagan, the Movie: And Other Episodes in Political Demonology* (Berkeley: University of California Press, 1987), 236–271.

76. Ibid., 242.

77. On the experts who worried about mother-smothered boys in the twentieth century, see Robert L. Griswold, *Fatherhood in America: A History* (New York: Basic Books, 1993), 208–209.

78. Arthur M. Schlesinger Jr., "The Crisis of American Masculinity," *Esquire* (November 1958), 63–65; reprinted in *The Politics of Hope* (Boston: Houghton Mifflin, 1962), 241, 244.

79. Ibid., 243.

80. Vance Packard, *The Hidden Persuaders* (1957; New York: McKay, 1969).

81. Sloan Wilson, *The Man in the Gray Flannel Suit* (New York: Simon & Schuster, 1955); Richard Yates, *Revolutionary Road* (1961; New York: Dell, 1983); Alan Harrington, *Life in the Crystal Palace* (New York: Knopf, 1959); Arthur Miller, *Death of a Salesman: A Play in Two Acts* (1949; New York: Dramatists Play Service, 1976); John Cheever, "The Country Husband," in *The Stories of John Cheever* (New York: Knopf, 1978), 325–346.

82. *Rebel without a Cause*, dir. Nicholas Ray, prod. David Weisbart (Warner Brothers, 1955). For an example of Wylie's obsessions, see his science fiction novel, *Tomorrow* (1956; New York: Popular Library, 1957). On *Playboy* as the "bible of the beleaguered male," see Myron Brenton, *The American Male* (New York: Fawcett, 1966), 73. Examples of Mailer's preoccupations may be found in "The White Negro," *Dissent* (Summer 1957), 276–293, reprinted in *Advertisements for Myself* (1959; New York: New American Library, 1960), 302–322, and "Superman Comes to the Supermart," *Esquire* (November 1960), 123–130, reprinted in *The Presidential Papers of Norman Mailer* (New York: Bantam Books, 1964), 25–61. Also see Mailer, *An American Dream* (New York: Dell, 1966).

83. On the history of American manhood, see Griswold, *Fatherhood in America*; E. Anthony Rotundo, *American Manhood: Transformations in Masculinity from the Revolution to the Modern Era* (New York: Basic Books, 1993); Michael Kimmel, *Manhood in America: A Cultural History* (New York: Free Press, 1996); Gail Bederman, *Manliness and Civilization: A Cultural History of Gender and Race in the United States, 1880–1917* (Chicago: University of Chicago Press, 1995); Elizabeth H. Pleck and Joseph H. Pleck, eds., *The American Man* (Englewood Cliffs: Prentice Hall, 1980); Peter Filene, *Him/Her/Self: Sex Roles in Modern America* (Baltimore: Johns Hopkins University Press, 1986); Joe L. Dubbert, *A Man's Place: Masculinity in Transition* (Englewood Cliffs, NJ: Prentice Hall, 1979).

84. Henry James, *The Bostonians* (1886; New York: Random House, 1956), 343.

85. On gender and imperialism at the turn of the century, see Kristin L. Hoganson, *Fighting for American Manhood: How Gender Politics Provoked the Spanish-American and Philippine American Wars* (New Haven: Yale University Press, 1998). On World War II and the

militarization of the U.S., see Michael S. Sherry, *In The Shadow of War: The United States Since the 1930s* (New Haven: Yale University Press, 1995).

86. On the Korean War, see Sherry, *In the Shadow of War*, 186; Hanson W. Baldwin, "Our Fighting Men Have Gone Soft," *Saturday Evening Post,* August 8, 1959, 82.

87. H. A. Overstreet, *The Mature Mind* (New York: W. W. Norton, 1949), 52.

88. Philip Roth, *My Life as a Man* (1970; New York: Vintage, 1993), 170. On the rise of therapeutic culture, see Eva S. Moskowitz, *In Therapy We Trust: America's Obsession with Self-Fulfillment* (Baltimore; Johns Hopkins University Press, 2001). Heightened expectations in postwar American life is a major theme in James T. Patterson's survey of postwar American history, *Grand Expectations: The United States, 1945–1974* (New York: Oxford University Press, 1996).

89. Elaine Tyler May, *Homeward Bound: American Families in the Cold War Era* (New York: Basic Books, 1988).

90. On revisionist historians' challenge to the assumption of a pervasive feminine mystique in postwar American culture, see Joanne Meyerowitz, "Beyond the Feminine Mystique: A Reassessment of Postwar Mass Culture, 1946–1958," *Journal of American History* 79 (March 1993): 1455–1482; Meyerowitz, ed., *Not June Cleaver: Women and Gender in Postwar America, 1945–1960* (Philadelphia: Temple University Press, 1994); Daniel Horowitz, *Betty Friedan and the Making of the Feminine Mystique: The American Left, the Cold War and Modern Feminism* (Amherst: University of Massachusetts Press, 1998); also see Chafe, *The American Woman*, 219.

91. Abram Kardiner, *Sex and Morality* (Indianapolis: Bobbs-Merrill, 1954), 233.

92. For the *Life* magazine quote, see Steven Mintz and Susan Kellogg, *Domestic Revolutions: A Social History of American Family Life* (New York: Free Press, 1988), 195; John A. Schindler, *Woman's Guide to Better Living 52 Weeks a Year* (Englewood Cliffs, NJ: Prentice Hall, 1957), quoted in *Look* eds., *The Decline of the American Male*, 24; Schlesinger, "The Crisis in Masculinity," 240.

93. Griswold, *Fatherhood in America*, 185–218. On the companionate marriage ideals of the postwar era, see Mintz and Kellogg, *Domestic Revolutions*, 186.

94. Ferdinand Lundberg and Marynia F. Farnham, *Modern Woman: The Lost Sex* (New York: Harper & Brothers, 1947), 140–241.

95. Ibid., 236–237, 241, 275.

96. Other observers noted that the disquiet and uneasiness of American women in the late 1940s and early 1950s. A spate of articles appeared highlighting what *Life* magazine in 1949 called an "eerie restlessness" on the part of women, which came on for "no plain reason." On the articles noting women's restless state, see Leila Rupp, "The Survival of American Feminism: The Women's Movement in the Postwar Period," in *Reshaping America: Society and Institutions, 1945–1960,* eds. Robert H. Bremner and Gary W. Reichard (Columbus, OH: Ohio State University Press, 1982), 38. Meyerowitz, *Not June Cleaver*, 247.

97. Lena Levine, "Women's Changing Role in Marriage," in Fairchild, *Women, Sex and Society*, 83; John McPartland, *Sex in Our Changing World* (New York: Rinehart and Company, 1947), 262; Ehrenreich and English, *For Her Own Good*, 243 (Ehrenreich and English's italics).

98. Ehrenreich and English, *For Her Own Good*, 245.

99. Moskin, "Why Do Women Dominate Him?" *The Decline of the American Male*, 3–24, esp. 8–12.

100. Ibid., 8–12, 19–22. Milton R. Sapirstein, with Alis De Sola, *Paradoxes of Everyday Life: A Psychoanalyst's Interpretation* (New York: Random House, 1955), 3–36.

101. Moskin, "Why Do Women Dominate Him?" 8–12, 19–22.

102. Kinsey's work did not support the idea that homosexuality was statistically on the rise in American life; however, the assumption that the incidence of homosexuality *was* increasing was voiced by many of the writers, social critics, and experts discussed here (Wylie, Friedan, Lindner, Wentworth-Rohr, Kardiner, McPartland, Lundberg and Farnham). Whether male homosexuality was actually increasing is, for obvious reasons, difficult to determine with any precision; but as Donald Webster Cory stressed in his study, *The Homosexual in America* (1951; New York; Greenberg Publisher, 1963), 93, "the conclusion seems indisputable that people are today more aware of the existence of homosexuality

because of a growing revolt against the oppressive taboos and against the conspiracy of silence. There is every reason to believe, based on a study of history, that in former times the impulse toward, and, in all likelihood, the gratification of homosexual love were as prevalent as today. This conclusion is verified by the findings of Kinsey to the effect that the frequencies of homosexual gratification of twenty years ago were not unlike those of our day." For Lerner's comments, see *America as a Civilization*, 683.

103. On World War II as a watershed in gay and lesbian history, see John D'Emilio, *Sexual Politics, Sexual Communities: The Making of a Homosexual Minority in the United States, 1940–1970* (Chicago: University of Chicago Press, 1983), 23–39; John D'Emilio and Estelle B. Freedman, *Intimate Matters: A History of Sexuality in America* (New York: Harper & Row, 1988), 288–291. Also see John Costello, *Virtue Under Fire: How World War II Changed Our Social and Sexual Attitudes* (Boston: Little Brown, 1985); Jonathan Katz, *Gay American History: Lesbian and Gay Men in the USA, A Documentary* (New York: Avon, 1978); Allan Berube, *Coming Out under Fire: The History of Gay Men and Women in World War Two* (New York: Plume, 1990).

104. Ehrenreich, *Hearts of Men*, 14–28.

105. Kardiner, *Sex and Morality*, 160–192, esp. 175.

106. Ibid., 170–179.

107. Ibid., 164–192.

108. Hendrik M. Ruitenbeek, *The Problem of Homosexuality in Modern Society* (New York: E. P. Dutton, 1963), 84–86, 91.

109. Lionel Ovesey, "The Homosexual Conflict: An Adaptational Analysis," *Psychiatry* 17 (August 1954): 243–250 (Ovesey's italics).

110. *Tea and Sympathy*, dir. Vincente Minnelli, prod. Pandro S. Berman (MGM Studios, 1956); *Look Back in Anger*, dir. Tony Richardson, prod. Harry Saltzman (MGM Studios, 1959). For a fascinating analysis of the film adaptation of *Tea and Sympathy* from a Broadway play and the controversy surrounding its homosexual theme, see George F. Custen, "Strange Brew: Hollywood and the Fabrication of Homosexuality in *Tea and Sympathy*," in *Queer Representations*, Martin B. Duberman, ed. (New York: New York University Press, 1997), 113–134. On the representation of gay men in film, literature and theater, and gay men's resistance to dominant cultural norms, see Robert J. Corber, *Homosexuality in Cold War America: Resistance and the Crisis of Masculinity* (Durham: Duke University Press, 1997); also see David Savran, *Communists, Cowboys and Queers: The Politics of Masculinity in the Work of Arthur Miller and Tennessee Williams* (Minneapolis: University of Minnesota Press, 1992).

111. McPartland, *Sex in Our Changing World*, 152–155.

112. Alfred C. Kinsey, et al., *Sexual Behavior in the Human Male* (Philadelphia: W. B. Saunders, 1948), 650–651.

113. For discussions of psychiatric and psychoanalytic views of male homosexuality in the 1940s and 1950s, see D'Emilio, *Sexual Politics and Sexual Communities*, 16–17; Henry L. Minton, *Departing from Deviance: A History of Homosexual Rights and Emancipatory Science in America* (Chicago: University of Chicago Press, 2002).

114. Frank S. Caprio, *The Sexually Adequate Male* (Greenwich, CT: Fawcett, 1952), 159–160, 173.

115. Quoted in May, *Homeward Bound*, 147.

116. *Parents* magazine is quoted in Filene, *Him/Her/Self*, 172–173; other experts are discussed and quoted in Griswold, *Fatherhood in America*, 206–207.

117. Griswold, *Fatherhood in America*, 201–202.

118. Lerner, *America as a Civilization*, 559; Lindner, *Rebel without a Cause: The Story of a Criminal Psychopath*.

119. On Talcott Parsons and the discourse on juvenile delinquency, see Kimmel, *Manhood in America*, 244–245.

120. Leonard, "Why is He Afraid to Be Different?" *Decline of the American Male*, 40–41; Lindner, *Rebel Without a Cause*, 2.

121. Peter Biskind, *Seeing is Believing: How Hollywood Taught Us to Stop Worrying and Love the Fifties* (New York: Pantheon, 1983), 202.

122. Lindner, *Must You Conform?* 11.

123. Ibid., 40–41, 75. On the association of mass culture with femininity, see Andreas Huyssen, "Mass Culture as Woman: Modernism's Other," in *After the Great Divide: Modernism,*

Mass Culture, Postmodernism (Bloomington: University of Indiana Press, 1986), 44–62.

124. Lindner, *Must You Conform?*, 31–44, 58.
125. Wylie, *Generation of Vipers*, 60.
126. Lindner, *Must You Conform?* 41–42.
127. Ibid., 43.
128. Ibid., 177–178 (Lindner's italics).
129. Peter Viereck, *The Unadjusted Man: A New Hero for Americans* (New York: Capricorn Books, 1956), 259, 312 (Viereck's italics).
130. Norman Mailer, "The White Negro," *Dissent* (Summer 1957), 276–293, reprinted in *Advertisements for Myself*, 302–322.
131. Mailer, *Advertisements for Myself*, 302–22, esp. 304, 318–319.
132. Ibid., 304.
133. Ibid., 309–310, 312, 319–320.
134. Ibid., 304–306.
135. Ibid., 304–305, 321.
136. Ibid., 312, 321; Mailer's comment about the liberal mind is in Mailer, *The Presidential Papers*, 199.

Notes to Chapter 4

1. John F. Kennedy, "Address Accepting the Democratic Party Nomination for the Presidency," July 15, 1960, *Selected Speeches: John F. Kennedy*, John F. Kennedy Library and Museum, July 13, 2003. http://www.cs.jfklibrary.org.
2. Arthur M. Schlesinger Jr., *A Thousand Days: John F. Kennedy in the White House* (Boston: Houghton Mifflin, 1965), 17–18. The cyclical theory of history was pioneered by Schlesinger's father, historian Arthur M. Schlesinger Sr.
3. The literature on Kennedy, his administration, and his family is immense. For insider accounts, see Schlesinger, *A Thousand Days*, and Theodore C. Sorensen, *Kennedy* (New York: Harper & Row, 1965). For a highly sympathetic biography (written in 1959), see James MacGregor Burns, *John Kennedy: A Political Profile* (New York: Harcourt, Brace and World, 1961). For other notable works, see Robert Dallek, *An Unfinished Life: John F. Kennedy, 1917–1963* (Boston: Little Brown, 2003); Theodore White, *The Making of the President 1960* (New York: Atheneum House, 1961); Garry Wills, *The Kennedy Imprisonment: A Meditation on Power* (New York: Simon & Schuster, 1981); Richard Reeves, *President Kennedy: Profile of Power* (New York: Simon & Schuster, 1993); Bruce Miroff, *Pragmatic Illusions: The Presidential Politics of John F. Kennedy* (New York: McKay, 1976); Henry Fairlie, *The Kennedy Promise: The Politics of Expectation* (Garden City, NY: Doubleday, 1973); Herbert S. Parmet, *JFK: The Presidency of John K. Kennedy* (New York: Dial Press, 1983); Parmet, *Jack: The Struggles of John F. Kennedy* (New York: Dial Press, 1980); Seymour M. Hersh, *The Dark Side of Camelot* (Boston: Little Brown, 1997). On the Kennedy administration, see David Halberstam, *The Best and the Brightest* (New York: Random House, 1972). On the Kennedy dynasty, see Peter Collier and David Horowitz, *The Kennedys: An American Drama* (New York: Summit Books, 1984). For a collection of early essays and previously published articles on JFK, see Aida DiPace Donald, ed., *John F. Kennedy and the New Frontier* (New York: Hill and Wang, 1966).
4. Garry Wills, *Nixon Agonistes: The Crisis of the Self-Made Man* (New York: Signet, 1971), 523; see also Wills, *The Kennedy Imprisonment*, in which he explores the relationship between the liberal "style" and the machismo of the Kennedy administration. I rely heavily on Wills's work here, building on some of his insights and relating them to the cultural context within which the Kennedy style was born. More recently, Robert D. Dean, in *Imperial Brotherhood: Gender and the Making of Cold War Foreign Policy* (Amherst: University of Massachusetts Press, 2001), 169–199, has published the most exhaustive examination of Kennedy's masculine ideals and their relationship to foreign policy. For another commentary on the "toughminded" liberalism of the era, see Christopher Lasch, "The Anti-Intellectualism of the Intellectuals," in *The New Radicalism in America 1889–1963: The Intellectual as a Social Type* (New York: Knopf, 1965), 286–349.
5. On Kennedy's historical awareness, see Miroff, *Pragmatic Illusions*, 11–15; Dallek, *An Unfinished Life*, 238; Schlesinger, *A Thousand Days*, 17.

6. Nixon was only a few years older than Kennedy, but he didn't claim to represent his generation; in any case, he was too wedded to the "aged" Eisenhower to make the claims to youthful generational change that Kennedy could. On Kennedy's image, see Thomas Brown, *JFK: History of an Image* (Bloomington: Indiana University Press, 1988); John Hellmann, *The Kennedy Obsession: The American Myth of JFK* (New York: Columbia University Press, 1997); Wills, *The Kennedy Imprisonment*, 144–165. Nixon's image manipulation is discussed in David Greenberg, *Nixon's Shadow: The History of an Image* (New York: W. W. Norton, 2003) and Wills, *Nixon Agonistes*.

7. Michael S. Sherry, *In the Shadow of War: The United States Since the 1930s* (New Haven: Yale University Press, 1995), 233.

8. Kennedy, "Address Accepting the Democratic Party Nomination for President," July 15, 1960, *Selected Speeches* (italics mine).

9. Ibid. John F. Kennedy, "Are We Up to the Task?" January 1, 1960, reprinted in *The Strategy of Peace* (New York: Harper & Row, 1960), 199–202.

10. John F. Kennedy, "The Presidency in 1960," January 14, 1960, *Selected Speeches*.

11. John Kenneth Galbraith, *The Affluent Society* (1958; Boston: Houghton Mifflin, 1984), 4–5; Arthur M. Schlesinger Jr., *Kennedy or Nixon: Does it Make Any Difference?* (New York: Macmillan, 1960), 4; Marquis Childs, *Eisenhower: Captive Hero, A Critical Study of the General and the President* (New York: Harcourt Brace, 1958), 117; Peter Viereck, *The Unadjusted Man: A New Hero for Modern America* (New York: Capricorn, 1956), 12, 312.

12. Daniel Bell, *The End of Ideology: On the Exhaustion of Political Ideas in the Fifties* (New York: Free Press, 1962); Seymour Martin Lipset, *Political Man* (Garden City, NY: Doubleday, 1963), 442.

13. The National Bureau of Economic Research is quoted in Frederick Lewis Allen, *The Big Change: The United States, 1900–1950* (1952; New Brunswick, NJ: Transaction Publishers, 1993), xiii, 209. Herbert Gold, "The Age of Happy Problems," *Atlantic Monthly* (March 1957), 58–62, reprinted in *The Age of Happy Problems* (New York: Dial Press, 1962), 10. Goldman is quoted in Godfrey Hodgson, *America in Our Time* (New York: Random House, 1976), 82. On the myth of classlessness, see Hodgson, *America in Our Time*, 83–85; Barbara Ehrenreich, *Fear of Falling: The Inner Life of the Middle Class* (New York: Pantheon, 1989), 22–29.

14. Hodgson, *America in Our Time*, 83–85; Todd Gitlin, *The Sixties: Years of Hope, Days of Rage* (New York: Bantam, 1987), 13. While estimates vary, James T. Patterson, in *Grand Expectations: The United States, 1945–1974* (New York: Oxford University Press, 1996), 32, puts the minimum percentage of Americans who remained "poor" in the mid-fifties at 25 percent.

15. Gitlin, *The Sixties*, 12; Michael Harrington, *The Other America: Poverty in the United States* (New York: Macmillan, 1962); Ehrenreich, *Fear of Falling*, 19–29.

16. Hansen is quoted in Vance Packard, *The Waste Makers* (New York: David McKay, 1960), 295.

17. Arthur M. Schlesinger Jr., "The Future of Liberalism: The Challenge of Abundance," *The Reporter* 14 (May 3, 1956): 8–11; "The New Mood in Politics" *Esquire* (January 1960), 58–60, reprinted in *The Politics of Hope* (Boston: Houghton Mifflin, 1962), 81–93. Although the article didn't mention Kennedy, it was a barely disguised Kennedy campaign piece.

18. Nathan Glazer and David Riesman, "The Intellectuals and the Discontented Classes," in Daniel Bell, ed., *The Radical Right* (New York: Doubleday, 1964), 105–159; Barrington Moore, Jr., *Political Power and Social Theory* (Cambridge: Harvard University Press, 1958), 183.

19. Bell, *The End of Ideology*, 399–404; Ehrenreich, *Fear of Falling*, 19–20.

20. On the calls for a "national purpose," see Eric Goldman, *The Crucial Decade—and After: America, 1945–1960* (1956; New York: Vintage, 1960), 342–343; William E. Leuchtenburg, *A Troubled Feast: American Society Since 1945* (Boston: Little Brown, 1983), 110. Also see Norman Mailer, "Superman Comes to the Supermart," *Esquire* (November 1960), 123–130, reprinted in *The Presidential Papers of Norman Mailer* (New York: Bantam Books, 1964), 25–61; Schlesinger, "The New Mood in Politics," 84–85, 93; Childs, *Eisenhower: Captive Hero*, 273.

21. The issue of economic growth in the context of consensus politics is discussed in Hodgson, *America in Our Time*, 79–81.

22. Saulnier's comments are quoted in Packard, *The Waste Makers*, 294–295. Also see Schlesinger, "The New Mood in Politics," 83; Goldman, *The Crucial Decade*, 343–345.
23. Kennedy's speech, "The Khrushchev-Eisenhower Visits," October 1, 1959, Rochester, New York, is reprinted in Kennedy, *Strategy of Peace*, 8–11.
24. On Kennedy's comments on the kitchen debate, see Sorensen, *Kennedy*, 182–183; Kennedy's speech, "The Global Challenge," January 1, 1960, Washington, D.C., is reprinted in Kennedy, *Strategy of Peace*, 3–8.
25. Norman Podhoretz, "The Issue: September 1960," *Commentary* 30 (September 1960): a; Dennis H. Wrong, "Rockefeller as Liberal Hero," *Commentary* 30 (September 1960): 201–205; Dwight MacDonald, "The Candidates and I," *Commentary* 29 (April 1960): 287–294.
26. Dennis H. Wrong, "The Perils of Political Moderation," *Commentary* 27 (January 1959): 1–8.
27. Sevareid and Fitch are quoted in Schlesinger, *Kennedy or Nixon*, 1–2. See also Eric Sevareid, *Candidates 1960: Behind the Headlines in the Presidential Race* (New York: Basic Books, 1960).
28. Schlesinger, *Kennedy or Nixon*, 1–18. On Kennedy's reaction to the Sevareid piece and the decision to write the campaign manifesto, see Schlesinger, *A Thousand Days*, 65.
29. Schlesinger, *Kennedy or Nixon*, 9–17, 23.
30. Ibid., 15, 27, 34.
31. Patterson, *Grand Expectations*, 434–435; Leuchtenburg, *Troubled Feast*, 115.
32. Ibid., 23–34.
33. John Kenneth Galbraith, *A Life in Our Times: Memoirs* (New York: Ballantine, 1982), 287–288.
34. Wills, *The Kennedy Imprisonment*, 144–155, esp. 152; Sorensen, *Kennedy*, 384.
35. Lasch, "The Anti-Intellectualism of the Intellectuals," 311–315.
36. Richard H. Rovere, "Letter from Washington," *The New Yorker*, November 30, 1963, 53, reprinted in DiPace Donald, *John F. Kennedy and the New Frontier*, 247–254; Schlesinger, *A Thousand Days*, 115; Murray Kempton, "The 'Chic' Complex," *Spectator*, February 7, 1964, 168–169.
37. Sorensen, *Kennedy*, 14; Schlesinger, *A Thousand Days*, 115.
38. Burns, *John Kennedy: A Political Profile*. The 1961 Harcourt, Brace and World edition has this dust jacket endorsement as well as "Inauguration 1961—A New Foreword," which also appeared in slightly altered form in the *New York Times Magazine*, January 15, 1961.
39. Wills, *The Kennedy Imprisonment*, 147, 151–152.
40. Sorensen, *Kennedy*, 386–387; Rovere, "Letter from Washington," 250.
41. Wills, *The Kennedy Imprisonment*, 154.
42. On Riesman's differences with the New Frontiersmen, see Halberstam, *The Best and the Brightest*, 54–55.
43. Schlesinger, *Kennedy or Nixon*, 34; Schlesinger, *A Thousand Days*, 14, 115. Alsop is quoted in Halberstam, *The Best and the Brightest*, 34.
44. On Kennedy's disdain for Stevenson, see Reeves, *President Kennedy*, 16; Collier and Horowitz, *The Kennedys*, 290; Wills, *The Kennedy Imprisonment*, 184, 244. According to Curt Gentry, Hoover had forwarded his files on Stevenson (with the allegations of sexual deviance) to the Kennedys, should they wish to use the information to keep Stevenson from being appointed UN ambassador. Curt Gentry, *J. Edgar Hoover: The Man and the Secrets* (New York: W. W. Norton, 1991), 403.
45. Mailer, "Superman Comes to the Supermart"; the article is retitled "Superman Comes to the Supermarket" in *The Presidential Papers*.
46. Ibid., 43.
47. Ibid., 40–43.
48. Ibid., 43.
49. Ibid., 43, 41, 59.
50. Ibid., 40, 43.
51. Ibid., 27, 45, 51.
52. Ibid., 59–60.
53. Ibid., 39, 49, 60.
54. For Mailer's thoughts about Kennedy and the Bay of Pigs, see *The Presidential Papers*, 63–69. On the telegram to Schlesinger, see *A Thousand Days*, 285.
55. On Mailer's scorn for the "professional liberal," see Mailer, "The White Negro," reprinted in *Advertisements for Myself* (New York: New American Library, 1960), 302–322.

56. *Playboy* and its promise of "diversion" is discussed in James R. Petersen, *The Century of Sex: Playboy's History of the Sexual Revolution, 1900–1999* (New York: Grove Press, 1999), 264–270. Also see Barbara Ehrenreich, *The Hearts of Men: American Dreams and the Flight from Commitment* (New York: Doubleday, 1983), 42–51; Thomas Weyr, *Reaching for Paradise: The Playboy Vision of America* (New York: Time Books, 1978); David Halberstam, *The Fifties* (New York: Random House, 1993) 571–576; Gay Talese, *Thy Neighbor's Wife* (1975; New York: Doubleday, 1980), 71–92. Mailer described the Playboy Club atmosphere in *The Presidential Papers*, 236–238.

57. On Hefner's complaints about Puritanical hypocrisy and state coercion, see Petersen, *The Century of Sex*, 268; Hefner's 1963 recollections are quoted in Ehrenreich, *Hearts of Men*, 44.

58. Ehrenreich, *Hearts of Men*, 50–51.

59. Ibid. See also Weyr, *Reaching for Paradise*, 55–87.

60. Ehrenreich, *Hearts of Men*, 42.

61. Ibid., 47.

62. Ralph Ginzburg, "Cult of the Aged Leader," *Playboy* (August 1959), 59–60, 96–98.

63. Ibid.

64. Dallek, *An Unfinished Life*, 281–282; Murray Kempton, "Mommy May I," reprinted in *America Comes of Middle Age: Columns, 1950–1962* (New York: Viking Press, 1972), 284–286. JFK's appeal to women was noted early on in his career; see Paul E. Healy, "The Senate's Gay Young Bachelor," *Saturday Evening Post*, June 13, 1953, 26–27, 123–124, 126–127, 129.

65. Sorensen, *Kennedy*, 388.

66. Sorensen, *Kennedy*, 384. For Schlesinger's recollections of the evening with Monroe, see Schlesinger, *Robert F. Kennedy and His Times* (Boston: Houghton Mifflin, 1978), 590–591. On the "stereotyped" liberalism, see Schlesinger, *A Thousand Days*, 14, 115.

67. Wills, *The Kennedy Imprisonment*, 26–37, 148, 244.

68. Kennedy's interest in heroism and courage is discussed in Miroff, *Pragmatic Illusions*, 11–17; Hellmann, *The Kennedy Obsession*, throughout.

69. John F. Kennedy, *Why England Slept* (New York: W. Funk, 1961); Miroff, *Pragmatic Illusions*, 14.

70. For the most recent and exhaustive treatment of Kennedy's physical ailments (primarily colitis, back trouble, and Addison's disease) see Dallek, *An Unfinished Life*.

71. John F. Kennedy, "The Soft American," *Sports Illustrated*, December 26, 1960, 15–19. For an excellent examination of the cold war physical fitness crusade, see Robert L. Griswold, "The 'Flabby American,' the Body and the Cold War," in *A Shared Experience: Men, Women, and the History of Gender*, Laura McCall and Donald Yacovone, eds. (New York: New York University Press, 1998), 323–347. For samples of the physical fitness discourse of the 1950s, see Jean Mayer, "Muscular State of the Union," *New York Times Magazine*, November 6, 1955, 17; John B. Kelly, "Are We Becoming a Nation of Weaklings?" *American Magazine* 161 (March 1956), 28–29, 104–107; National Affairs Special Report, "Are We Becoming 'Soft'?: Why the President is Worried about our Fitness," *Newsweek*, September 26, 1955, 35–36.

72. Kennedy, "The Soft American," 16; he also published "The Vigor We Need," *Sports Illustrated*, July 16, 1962, 12–15. See also Max Eastman, "Let's Close the Muscle Gap," *Readers' Digest* (November 1961), 124; Charles Bud Wilkinson, "In a Dangerous World, Is American Youth Too Soft?" *U.S. News and World Report*, August 21, 1961, 75–76; R. M. Marshall, "Toughening Our Soft Generation," *Saturday Evening Post*, June 23, 1962, 13.

73. John F. Kennedy, *Profiles in Courage* (1955; New York: Harper & Row, 1964), 21–28, 258–266. The longstanding question as to the authorship of this Pulitzer Prize–winning book has essentially been settled; Kennedy wrote, at best, a small part of it. Numerous people were involved in its preparation, including Dean Landis, Alan Nevins, and professors Arthur M. Schlesinger Jr., James MacGregor Burns, and Jules Davids, providing ideas, suggestions for the personalities to be included, and commentary. Davids wrote sketches for the first four chapters; Sorensen did most of the actual writing. For discussions of the book's authorship, see Parmet, *Jack: The Struggles of John F. Kennedy*, 330–333; Wills, *The Kennedy Imprisonment*, 140–143. While Dallek confirms the book's collective authorship (*An Unfinished Life*, 198–199), he claims the book was essentially Kennedy's. In his argument, he notes that "Sorensen and Professor Jules Davids of Georgetown University, with whom

Jackie had taken courses, gathered materials for the book and *drafted* chapters, but the final product was essentially Jack's. He *edited* what Sorensen and Davids gave him and then dictated final chapter drafts for a secretary to type." Dallek cites the audio tapes of Kennedy's dictations as "conclusive evidence of Jack's *involvement*" and that "the *final product was essentially Jack's*" (all italics mine). Nonetheless, Dallek admits that the book was "more the work of a 'committee' than of any one person." Given the preponderance of evidence for collective authorship noted here, I have treated *Profiles in Courage*'s ideas as indicative of the general New Frontier mindset.

74. Kennedy, *Profiles in Courage*, 257–259 (Kennedy's italics).
75. On Kennedy and McCarthy, see Dallek, *An Unfinished Life*, 162–163, 189–192, 197. In 1950, Kennedy publicly declared that McCarthy, then on his crusade to purge the federal government of alleged Communist spies, "may have something." Kennedy also said that he was pleased when Nixon beat Democrat Helen Gahagan Douglas in the 1950 Senate race in California, because she would have been "hard to work with." See Collier and Horowitz, *The Kennedys*, 209.
76. Schlesinger, "The Decline of Greatness" reprinted in *The Politics of Hope*, 23–33; "On Heroic Leadership and the Dilemma of Strong Men and Weak Peoples" appeared in *Encounter* (December 1960), 3–11, and is reprinted in *The Politics of Hope*, 3–22.
77. Richard E. Neustadt, *Presidential Power: The Politics of Leadership* (1960; New York: John Wiley, 1962).
78. Neustadt, *Presidential Power*, 161–171 (Neustadt's italics).
79. Ibid.
80. Childs, *Eisenhower: Captive Hero*, 4, 291, 300.
81. Burns, *John Kennedy: A Political Profile*, viii–x.
82. Wills, *The Kennedy Imprisonment*, 184. In his private diary, Schlesinger confessed reservations about Stevenson: "S is a much richer, more thoughtful, more creative person; but he has been away from power too long; he gives me an odd sense of unreality . . . a certain frivolity, distractedness, over interest in words and phrases? I don't know; but in contrast K gives a sense of cool, measured intelligent concern with action and power. I feel that his administration would be less encumbered than S's with commitments to past ideals or sentimentalities." *Robert F. Kennedy and His Times*, 203.
83. Reeves, *President Kennedy*, 52; Sorensen, *Kennedy*, 389.
84. On Kennedy's administrative style, see Richard H. Rovere, "Letter from Washington," *The New Yorker*, December 17, 1960, 52. On the reorganization of the NSC, see Schlesinger, *A Thousand Days*, 209–210; Reeves, *President Kennedy*, 46, 52; Sorensen, *Kennedy*, 281.
85. Sorensen, *Kennedy*, 262, 281–283; see also Reeves, *President Kennedy*, 52–53.
86. On Rusk, see Dallek, *An Unfinished Life*, 315–316.
87. Kennedy, *Profiles in Courage*, 75; John F. Kennedy, "Inaugural Address," January 20, 1961, *Selected Speeches*.
88. Miroff, *Pragmatic Illusions*, 13, 43, 65–109.
89. Ibid., 16–18, 65.
90. Ibid., 18, 65–109. Walt Rostow, *View from the Seventh Floor* (New York: Harper & Row, 1964), 43.
91. Wills, *The Kennedy Imprisonment*, 274.
92. Sorensen, *Kennedy*, 242. Kennedy's comment on the minimum wage is quoted in Michael R. Beschloss, *The Crisis Years: Kennedy and Khrushchev, 1960–1963* (New York: Edward Burlingame Books, 1991), 48.
93. For critical assessments of Kennedy's record on civil rights, see Miroff, *Pragmatic Illusions*, 223–270; Victor S. Navasky, *Kennedy Justice* (New York: Atheneum, 1971); Taylor Branch, *Parting the Waters: America in the King Years, 1954–1963* (New York: Simon & Schuster, 1988). On Kennedy's reluctance to label himself a liberal, see Healy, "The Senate's Gay Young Bachelor," 126; Collier and Horowitz, *The Kennedys*, 291; Fairlie, *The Kennedy Promise*, 78–79.
94. Burns, *John Kennedy: A Political Profile*, 280.
95. The literary criticism of the time is discussed in Mark Krupnick, *Lionel Trilling and the Fate of Cultural Criticism* (Evanston, IL: Northwestern University Press, 1985). The behaviorist trend in cold war era political science is discussed in Frederick M. Dolan, *Allegories of America: Narratives, Metaphysics, Politics* (Ithaca: Cornell University Press, 1994),

60–113. On Kennan's realism, see George Kennan, *American Diplomacy, 1900–1950* (New York: Mentor Books, 1951), 50. On Niebuhr's Christian realism, see Reinhold Niebuhr, *An Interpretation of Christian Ethics* (New York: Meridian Books, 1956); Niebuhr, *The Children of Light and the Children of Darkness: A Vindication of Democracy and a Critique of Its Trditional Defense* (New York: Scribner's Sons, 1972). On consensus history as well as Niebuhr's realism, see Richard H. Pells, *The Liberal Mind in a Conservative Age: American Intellectuals in the 1940s and 1950s* (Middletown, CT: Wesleyan University Press, 1985), 136–137, 156–162. See also Lasch's critique of Niebuhr in *The New Radicalism in America,* 300–306.

96. Reeves, *President Kennedy,* 53, 280; Collier and Horowitz, *The Kennedys,* 290.

97. On Kennedy's view of the State Department, see Halberstam, *The Best and the Brightest,* 11; Wills, *The Kennedy Imprisonment,* 176; Collier and Horowitz, *The Kennedys,* 330. According to Reeves, *President Kennedy,* 72, Kennedy made a similar comment about the State Department to his friend, journalist Charlie Barnet.

98. Reeves, *President Kennedy,* 72.

99. Several authors make mention of the Kennedy administration's rhetorical style. See for example Halberstam, *The Best and the Brightest,* 29; Wills, *The Kennedy Imprisonment,* passim; Richard Barnet, *Roots of War: The Men and the Institutions Behind U.S. Foreign Policy* (New York: Penguin Books, 1971), 109–111.

100. Barnet, *Roots of War,* 109.

101. Burns, *John Kennedy: A Political Profile,* 264.

102. Schlesinger, *A Thousand Days,* 741; Schlesinger, "The Administration and the Left," *New Statesman* 65 (February 8, 1963): 185. On Riesman's view of the administration, see Halberstam, *The Best and the Brightest,* 54. The two "distinguished social scientists" chided by Riesman are unnamed by Halberstam.

103. Wofford is quoted in Wills, *The Kennedy Imprisonment,* 152; Halberstam, *The Best and the Brightest,* 30.

104. On Bowles's problems within the administration, see Halberstam, *The Best and the Brightest,* 29–30, 46–47; Wills, *The Kennedy Imprisonment,* 244; Dallek, *An Unfinished Life,* 436–437; Schlesinger, *A Thousand Days,* 439, 437–442. For Robert Kennedy's comment to Bowles, see Reeves, *President Kennedy,* 152. Vidal's remarks are found in Jon Wiener, "The Scholar Squirrels of the National Security State: An Interview with Gore Vidal," *Radical History Review* (April 1989): 109–137. Sorensen denied that Bowles was given his marching orders because he was too "soft" (*Kennedy,* 288–289). Bowles's perspective is discussed in Parmet, *JFK: The Presidency of John F. Kennedy,* 203–205.

105. Barnet, *The Roots of War,* 109.

106. On "honorary Kennedys," see Wills, *The Kennedy Imprisonment,* 86–101.

107. William J. Lederer and Eugene Burdick, *The Ugly American* (New York: Fawcett, 1958); Reeves, *President Kennedy,* 46–47; Dean, *Imperial Brotherhood,* 172–179.

108. On Lansdale, see Cecil B. Currey, *Edward Lansdale: The Unquiet American* (Boston: Houghton Mifflin, 1988).

109. Dean, *Imperial Brotherhood,* 172–179.

110. On the institutionalization of *The Ugly American,* see Reeves, *President Kennedy,* 69.

111. On Kennedy and counterinsurgency, see Dallek, *An Unfinished Life,* 350, 436–440; Fairlie, *The Kennedy Promise,* 179–208; Halberstam, *The Best and the Brightest,* 152–156; Reeves, *President Kennedy,* 46–50, 69–87, 335–337; Dean, *Imperial Brotherhood,* 169–199; Wills, *The Kennedy Imprisonment,* 257–263; Loren Baritz, *Backfire* (New York: Ballantine, 1985), 91–100. On Robert Kennedy's obsession with counterinsurgency, see Collier and Horowitz, *The Kennedys,* 365–377.

112. Michael Rogin, in *Ronald Reagan, the Movie: And Other Episodes in Political Demonology* (Berkeley: University of California Press, 1987), xiii, 237, passim, wrote of the "countersubversive" imagination in American history, which has shown a tendency to demonize enemies of the United States and turn them into monsters—"the Indian cannibal, the black rapist, the papal whore of Babylon, the monster-hydra United States Bank, the demon rum, the bomb-throwing anarchist, the many-tentacled Communist conspiracy, the agents of international terrorism." A "counterinsurgent" such as a Green Beret or CIA agent is a rather different animal than the "countersubversive" Rogin discusses, but his point is, in my view, applicable here.

113. On the Americans who saw Castro as a romantic hero, see Van Gosse, "We Are All Highly Adventurous": Fidel Castro and the Romance of the White Guerrilla, 1957–1958," in *Cold War Constructions: The Political Culture of United States Imperialism, 1945–1966*, Christian G. Appy, ed. (Amherst: University of Massachusetts Press, 2000), 238–256.

114. On the phrase "Operation Castration," see Dean, *Imperial Brotherhood*, 184. For Schlesinger's representation of Kennedy as a "prisoner of events," see *A Thousand Days*, 256, 233–26; also see Sorensen, *Kennedy*, 297.

115. On Kennedy's dismantling of Eisenhower's National Security Council apparatus which might have discovered the plan's errors in judgement and tactics, see Wills, *The Kennedy Imprisonment*, 239, 242–243; 251–252.

116. Sorensen, *Kennedy*, 295, 306; Wills, *The Kennedy Imprisonment*, 244, 230–239; Reeves, *President Kennedy*, 80; Schlesinger, *A Thousand Days*, 241.

117. Schlesinger recalled that it was "depressing" to watch at these meetings (in which the Bay of Pigs operation was discussed) the "collection of officials, some of them holdovers from the previous administration, contentedly prepare to sacrifice the world's growing faith in the new American president in order to defend interests and pursue objectives of their own"—as if the most pressing problem raised by the plan to overthrow a foreign government secretly was preserving Kennedy's image (*A Thousand Days*, 252–259). On Schlesinger's memos to Kennedy, see Reeves, *President Kennedy*, 85.

118. Schlesinger, *A Thousand Days*, 255–259.

119. On Kennedy's cult of personality and the establishment of "honorary Kennedys," see Wills, *The Kennedy Imprisonment*, 86–101, 147–148.

120. John F. Kennedy, "Address to the American Association of Newspaper Editors," April 20, 1961, *Selected Speeches* (my italics).

121. Roosevelt is quoted in Arthur Schlesinger, Jr., *The Vital Center: The Politics of Freedom* (New Brunswick, NJ: Transaction Press, 1998), 21. Dallek, *An Unfinished Life*, 438.

122. Reeves, *President Kennedy*, 335–337; Robert Kennedy is quoted in Dallek, *An Unfinished Life*, 439–440; Parmet, *JFK: The Presidency of John F. Kennedy*, 214–215; Currey, *Edward Lansdale*, 239–258; Hersh, *The Dark Side of Camelot*, 268–293. On Lyndon Johnson's response to the secret war against Castro, see Wills, *The Kennedy Imprisonment*, 261.

123. Currey, *Edward Lansdale*, 243–244; Hersh, *The Dark Side of Camelot*, 283. Lansdale later denied he had proposed this specific plan, but acknowledged that it could have been submitted by someone else and discussed.

124. For examples of sympathetic accounts, see Dallek, *An Unfinished Life*, 535–574; Schlesinger, *A Thousand Days*, 794–841. For critical accounts, see, for example, Hersh, *The Dark Side of Camelot*, 341–371; Wills, *The Kennedy Imprisonment*, 274–284.

125. On Kennedy's comments to the press, see Reeves, *Presidential Power*, 389; Halberstam, *The Best and the Brightest*, 39. On the secret missile deal and the Stevenson controversy, see Wills, *The Kennedy Imprisonment*, 277–281; Dallek, *An Unfinished Life*, 569, 576–77.

126. Kraft's comment is quoted in Collier and Horowitz, *The Kennedys*, 378.

127. Dallek, *An Unfinished Life*, 664–686, makes the argument that Kennedy was planning to pull out of Vietnam in his second term. Central to this argument is JFK's May 1963 plan to withdraw 1000 U.S. military advisors from Vietnam by the end of 1963 as part of a larger goal of complete withdrawal by 1965. Such a plan was allegedly intended to place pressure on the Diem government to shape up and fight more effectively. For an overview of the debate about what Kennedy would have done in Vietnam, see Ronald Steel, "Would Kennedy Have Quit Vietnam?" *New York Times*, May 25, 2003, 5.

128. For a symposium on Kennedy's assassination, legacy, and representation in the media and in particular Oliver Stone's film *JFK*, see *American Historical Review* 97 (April 1992): 487–511, including contributions by Marcus Raskin, "*JFK* and the Culture of Violence"; Michael Rogin, "*JFK*: The Movie"; and Robert A. Rosenstone, "*JFK*: Historical Fact/Historical Film."

129. If Kennedy aide Kenneth O'Donnell's recollections are credible, it appears that, even when Kennedy did speak of the possibility of withdrawing from Vietnam by 1965, he spoke of it in terms of "appeasement," telling O'Donnell he was sure he'd "be damned everywhere as a Communist appeaser" if he disengaged from Vietnam. According to O'Donnell, Kennedy added, "But I don't care. If I tried to pull out completely now, we would have another Joe McCarthy red scare on our hands, but I can do it after I'm reelected." Quoted in Brown, *JFK: History of an Image*, 40.

130. Kennedy's comments to Cronkite are quoted in Steel, "Would Kennedy Have Quit Vietnam?" 5. On JFK's Dallas speech, see Stanley Karnow, "JFK," in Mark C. Carnes, *History According to the Movies* (New York: Henry Holt, 1995), 270–273. On Kennedy and Vietnam, also see Frederik Longevall, *Choosing War* (Berkeley: University of California Press, 1999); Lawrence Freedman, *Kennedy's Wars* (New York: Oxford University Press, 2000).

131. Revisionism by Kennedy's New Frontiersmen, largely based on weak conjectures and anecdotes, emerged only *after* Tet. There is nary a word of Kennedy's withdrawal plan in Schlesinger's long, blow-by-blow account of the administration in *A Thousand Days* (the 1963 withdrawal idea merits one sentence and appears only within the context of a discussion about McNamara). Nor does Sorensen's 1965 book on Kennedy even remotely suggest that JFK planned to quit Vietnam; on the contrary, he states that Kennedy intended to "weather it out" in Vietnam (*Kennedy*, 661). After Tet, however, both men changed their tune; the "withdrawal" plan achieved a new significance which is not attributed to any new evidence or information. In Sorensen's post-Tet *The Kennedy Legacy* (New York: Macmillan, 1969), 154–162, the author was now "convinced" that Kennedy would have pursued diplomatic courses of action in Vietnam, citing the withdrawal plan that would result in complete disengagement by 1965. In *Robert F. Kennedy and His Times* (1978), Schlesinger devoted an entire chapter to JFK's withdrawal plans, and here shaped a new history and Kennedy legacy on Vietnam. In 1970, a post-Tet anecdote emerged from Kennedy aide Kenneth O'Donnell, who reported that in the spring of 1963 Kennedy told Senator Mike Mansfield that he agreed that a complete withdrawal from Vietnam was necessary and he would do so after the 1964 election; this story is repeated in Kenneth P. O'Donnell and David F. Powers with Joe McCarthy, *"Johnny We Hardly Knew Ye": Memories of John Fitzgerald Kennedy* (Boston: Little Brown, 1972). For an overview of the revisionism, see Brown, *JFK: The History of an Image*, 34–41; as Brown notes, if the O'Donnell story is true, Kennedy may very well have been telling Mansfield what the senator wanted to hear.

132. Quoted in Doris Kearns Goodwin, *Lyndon Johnson and the American Dream* (New York: Harper & Row, 1976), 264. On Johnson and the Vietnam War, also see Halberstam, *The Best and the Brightest*, and Baritz, *Backfire*.

133. Sorensen, *Kennedy*, 295. The source of Kennedy's sense that he had no choice but to proceed with the Bay of Pigs plan may have been the "disposal problem"; once the Cuban exile forces had been augmented and trained by the CIA, calling off the invasion would create the problem of "disposing" of a secret (and now disbanded and presumably disgruntled) Cuban exile army. Whatever the institutional momentum at work here, the point remains that Kennedy did in fact have an "alternative."

134. Wills, *The Kennedy Imprisonment*, 288.

135. Alsop is quoted in Halberstam, *The Best and the Brightest*, 204.

136. Barnet, *The Roots of War*, 115.

137. Wills, *The Kennedy Imprisonment*, 296.

Notes to Afterword

1. Barbara Ehrenreich, *The Hearts of Men: American Dreams and the Flight from Commitment* (New York: Doubleday, 1983), 103.

2. George Lakoff, *Moral Politics: What Conservatives Know that Liberals Don't* (Chicago: University of Chicago Press, 1996).

3. Franklin D. Roosevelt would seem to be the great exception, if one considers him a left-liberal. But circumstances are key: the Depression had undermined Herbert Hoover and the Republicans, and it had so discredited free market capitalism that FDR had a unique mandate to institute liberal reform. In a time of crisis, he offered a reassuring *paternal* authority to Americans. Allegations of weakness in foreign affairs ("softness" toward Stalin, the naïve selling-out of America at Yalta) came at the end of his life.

4. Albright is quoted in James Traub, "Can Any Democrat Win on National Security?" *New York Times Magazine*, January 4, 2004, 32.

5. Traub, "Can Any Democrat Win on National Security?", 28–5; also see Paul Waldman, "The Stud Factor," *Washington Post*, July 13, 2003, BO5.

6. Richard Perle, "Why the West Must Strike First Against Saddam Hussein," *Daily Telegraph*, September 8, 2002, 22.

7. Quotations in this paragraph are in Traub, "Can Any Democrat Win on National Security?", 28–53.

Index